COMPOSITION AND TRADITION IN THE
BOOK OF HOSEA

SOCIETY
OF BIBLICAL
LITERATURE

DISSERTATION SERIES
J.J.M. Roberts, Old Testament Editor
Charles Talbert, New Testament Editor

Number 102
COMPOSITION AND TRADITION IN THE BOOK OF HOSEA
A Redaction Critical Investigation
by
Gale A. Yee

Gale A. Yee

COMPOSITION AND TRADITION IN THE BOOK OF HOSEA

A Redaction Critical Investigation

Scholars Press
Atlanta, Georgia

COMPOSITION AND TRADITION IN THE BOOK OF HOSEA
A Redaction Critical Investigation

Gale A. Yee

Ph.D., 1985
The University of St. Michael's College
Toronto

Advisor:
Anthony R. Ceresko, O.S.F.S.

©1987
Society of Biblical Literature

Library of Congress Cataloging in Publication Data

Yee, Gale A.
    Composition and tradition in the book of Hosea.

    (Dissertation series / Society of Biblical Literature ;
no. 102)
    Bibliography; p.
    Includes indexes.
    1. Bible. O.T. Hosea--Criticism, Redaction.
I. Title. II. Series: Dissertation series (Society of
Biblical Literature) ; no. 102.
BS1565.2.Y44 1987   224'.6066   87-9715
ISBN 1-55540-090-6 (alk. paper)
ISBN 1-55540-091-4 (pbk. : alk. paper)

Printed in the United States of America
on acid-free paper

To Mom and Dad, Phil, Karen, Therese, David, Joan,
Rita, Steven, Donna, Willy, Danny and Eddy

TABLE OF CONTENTS

Page

PREFACE . . . . xi-xii

CHAPTER ONE - Theories of Hosean Composition.
A Forschungsbericht 1-25

CHAPTER TWO - Presuppositions in
Hosean Scholarship: An Argument
for Methodological Clarity. 27-50

   I. Presupposition One: The "Original"
    is the Most Valuable 28

  II. Presupposition Two: The Oral or
    Preliterary Stage is the Proper Focus
    of Research forUnderstanding the
    Prophetic Message 32

 III. Presupposition Three: There is No Qualitative
    Difference between the Oral and
    Written Stages 35

 IV. The Radical Peculiarities of the Oral and
    Written Stages 36

  V. The Redactional Selection of Traditional
    Material for the Larger
    Literary Framework 41

 VI. Summary 44

VII. The Methodological Task: A Redaction Critical
    Examination 46

CHAPTER THREE - The Composition of Hos 1-3:
Final Redacted State   51-95

I. Introduction to the Macrostructure:
Hos 1-3, 4-11, and 12-14   51

II. Theories Regarding Hos 1-3:
The Story of Hosea's Marriage   52

III. The Final Redacted State of Hos 1-3   54

IV. Summary of the Final Redacted State
of Hos 1-3   90

CHAPTER FOUR - The Composition of Hos 1-3:
The Earlier Stages of the Tradition.   97-125

I. Hos 1* and Hos 2*: Reconstructed Text   97

II. Possibility 1: Hos 1* and 2* as Two
Independently Authored Texts
Joined Later   102

III. Possibility 2: Hos 1* as a Secondary
Introduction to Hos 2*   103

IV. The Collector (C) of the Saying Attributed
to Hosea   112

V. The First Redactor (R1) of the Collection. . . .   115

VI. The First Redactor (R1) and the Final
Redactor (R2)   120

VII. The Saying Attributed to the Prophet
Hosea (H)   122

CHAPTER FIVE - The Redactional History of
    Hos 1-3: A Summary 127-130

CHAPTER SIX - The Composition of Hos 4-11, 12-14:
    Final Redacted State 131-259

    I. Hos 14:2-10 - The Redactional
       Conclusion 131

    II. The Macrostructure of Hos 4-11 142

    III. The Final Redaction of Hos 4 158

    IV. The Final Redaction of Hos 5 170

    V. The Final Redaction of Hos 6 174

    VI. The Final Redaction of Hos 7 179

    VII. The Final Redaction of Hos 8 189

    VIII. The Final Redaction of Hos 9 198

    IX. The Final Redaction of Hos 10 207

    X. The Final Redaction of Hos 11 214

    XI. The Final Redaction of Hos 12 229

    XII. The Final Redaction of Hos 13 248

CHAPTER SEVEN - The Composition of Hos 4-10;
    12-13: Earlier Stages of the Tradition 261-304

I. The Earlier Stages of Hos 4* 262

II. The Earlier Stages of Hos 5* 272

III. The Earlier Stages of Hos 6* 278

IV. The Earlier Stages of Hos 7* 282

V. The Earlier Stages of Hos 8* 286

VI. The Earlier Stages of Hos 9* 289

VII. The Earlier Stages of Hos 10* 294

VIII. The Hosean Tradition in Hos 12* and 13* . . . 298

CHAPTER EIGHT - Conclusion 305-313

APPENDIX: The Redactional History of the
    Book of Hosea. 315-317

ABBREVIATIONS 319-322

NOTES 323-418

BIBLIOGRAPHY. 373-418

INDEX OF AUTHORS. 419-420

INDEX OF BIBLICAL REFERENCES. 421-428

PREFACE

This work is a revision of a doctoral dissertation presented to the Faculty of Theology of the University of St. Michael's College, Toronto in 1985.

We all have, I think, our favorite passages in the Book of Hosea. They might be Hos 1-3 which describe the marriages of Hosea and YHWH, or Hos 11, to which the evangelist, Matthew, took a fancy (Mt 2:15), or Hos 13:14, which Paul cites (I Cor 15:55) and Handel immortalized in song. My concern, however, was how these diverse passages inter-related as a *book*; how these passages fit within the whole literary thrust of the Book of Hosea. I saw the need to do justice to the work as a whole, and, at the same time, reckon with the text's literary history which past scholarship highlighted.

My first chapter is a *Forschungsbericht* where I outline the various theories of composition on how the Book of Hosea came to be as a book.

In my second chapter, I offer a critique of the different methodological approaches. I argue for a method which does justice not only to the text's literary history, but also to its final literary state. I argue for a redaction critical investigation which *begins* with the final redacted state of the text and *then* proceeds to discuss its earlier stages of tradition.

In Chapter Three, I apply this method to the final redacted state of Hos 1-3, the story of Hosea's marriage. I try to demonstrate the structure and theological orientation of these chapters which the final redactor imposed upon his tradition.

Having determined the literary contribution of the final redactor, I turn to the earlier stages of the Hos 1-3 tradition in my fourth chapter and summarize my results on the literary history of Hos 1-3 in my fifth.

On the basis of my findings for Hos 1-3, the first major division of the book, I deal in Chapter Six with the final redacted state of Hos 4-14, the second division of the book. As with Hos 1-3, I try to discern the final redactor's structure and religio-political thrust.

In Chapter Seven I investigate the earlier literary stages of Hos 4-14, and make my final summary of the book's literary composition in Chapter Eight.

I wish to acknowledge several for their support in the completion of this work. I thank the College of St. Thomas for its generous financial help in the book's word processing. In this respect, I owe a lot to Sue Carlson for her care, patience, and good humor in the formatting. I also express my deep thanks to Kay Ruhland and especially Ginny Lyons for proofreading and helping with the indexing.

I would like to thank Professors Roderick MacKenzie, S.J. and Leo Laberge, O.M.I. who served as examiners of the thesis for their perceptive criticism and suggestions.

I thank Professor William H. Irwin, C.S.B., the chair of my doctoral committee, for introducing me to the beauty of the Hebrew Bible. I deeply appreciate his support in my studies and, in particular, his encouragement in my thesis work.

A very special word of thanks goes to my thesis director, Professor Anthony Ceresko. I am indebted to him for his patient and insightful critique of my work. I will always be grateful for his willingness to supervise me in this endeavor.

I dedicate this work to my family with deep love and appreciation.

CHAPTER ONE

Theories of Hosean Composition:
A Forschungsbericht

Any theory of composition regarding the Book of Hosea must be able to explain the difficult Hebrew text, particularly in Hos 4-14. This section of the book "competes with Job for the distinction of containing more unintelligible passages than any other book of the Hebrew Bible."[1] Abrupt changes from direct address to third person and continual shifts in theme and mood give the appearance that Hosea's words have been "set down in chaotic confusion."[2] The variety of possible and even contradictory solutions proposed by scholars gives witness to the textual difficulties of the Book of Hosea.

The following report of the literature will proceed for the most part chronologically. The reader will notice in the course of the discussion that, in the chronological development of particular methods, scholarly debate alternates between those methods which partition the text into sources, forms, etc., and those which try to maintain the text's unity. Moreover, we shall see that the various methods arose to counteract what they saw as the limitations of their predecessors.

I. The 19th Century Discussion

In the nineteenth century, Graetz suggested that the dissimilarity between the two major sections of the book, Hos 1-3 and Hos 4-14, could be explained by two different Hoseas living fifty years apart from each o ther.[3] Ewald, on the other hand, argued for just one prophet who labored during two different times and conditions in the northern kingdom.[4] The whole book, for Ewald, had an artistic and systematic organization, which led him to conclude "that it was published finally by the prophet as a whole in the form before us" (p. 222). Only Hos 1:1 could not have come from the prophet himself (p. 230). Although maintaining the artistic composition of Hos 4-14, Ewald was aware of the difficulties of the written text. However, he explained them as a reflection of the prophet's inner grief:

> To his painfully agitated heart, foreseeing calamity, it is impossible to unfold his thoughts in calm sentences, and arrange his words in firm and strong order. The thought is too full, the sentence rapid and abrupt, the whole discourse often breaking itself up into sobs (p. 218).

In contrast to Ewald, Cheyne found no clear evidence of logical connections of thought in Hos 4-14.[5] He criticized Ewald's proposal for the strophic arrangement for the difficult Hos 4-14 as too artificial (p. 33). He was one of the first to be aware of the problematic relationship between what we had in the written text and what could have been its oral form. For Cheyne, Hosea could not have delivered any part of this "book" in its present form. The Book of Hosea could only have been a reproduction by the prophet himself of the main points of his discourse. It was based partly on free composition and partly on prepared notes (pp. 21-22). Moreover, in a later work Cheyne saw in the Book of Hosea marks of later editing in the transmission process. He believed, however, that these later insertions misrepresented the original Hosea and must be omitted.[6]

The 19th century discussion represented on a smaller scale two major camps which would distinguish the 20th century debate. On one side, this debate would involve those who, like Ewald, supported the unity and artistic coherence of the text. On the other side would be those who, following Cheyne and Graetz, detect different hands in the work. The literary critical methods representative of the latter group dominated the beginning of the 20th century.

II. 1900-1935: The Literary Critical Discussion

During the first three decades of the twentieth century, studies on the Book of Hosea focused primarily on the extent and type of secondary material in the text. These discussions were consistent with the general understanding at the time regarding the origin and transmission of the prophetic books.[7]

Since they judged the origins of the book to be literary in character, they tried to resolve inherent problems through literary critical means.

Arguing against the customary two-part division of the Book (Hos 1-3; 4-14), Marti in 1904 observed that Hos 2 could not be separated from Hos 4-14. In both form and content Hos 2 had much more in common with Hos 4-14 than with either Hos 1 or 3. He preferred to treat the work as a whole rather than separate it into two main sections. Hos 1 introduced the collections of Hosea's speeches, Hos 2-12. Hos 13:1--14:1 formed the conclusion to the collection. If one regarded Hos 1-3 in some way connected to Hos 4-14 (and not disjoined from it), numerous sections of various sizes could then be detached as *later additions* to a *basic layer* of the book. For instance, he argued that Hos 3:1-5 was inserted much later by an editor. In its present position, 3:1-5 separated Hos 2 from Hos 4-14, to which it was once originally attached.

Marti devoted much of his study to a precise separation of original and secondary units.[8] In addition to certain minor accretions, all passages mentioning Judah[9] and all the oracles of salvation[10] were eliminated as non-Hosean. The former indicated a later editing when the oracles circulated in Judah after the fall of the northern kingdom. The latter, being inconsistent with the contents of the original Hosea, bespoke an exilic redaction.

In regard to the origin of the book and its transmission, Marti thought that the prophet himself assembled his own sayings and supplied them with a narrative introduction, Hos 1. During the course of time, this basic material was augmented by exilic or post-exilic Judaistic redaction, as well as editing reflecting the needs of the post-exilic community. The final redaction occurred during the Hellenistic period, since 14:10, one of the latest additions in the book, had its best parallel in the Psalms and Proverbs.[11]

Marti's judgment that Hos 1-3 should not be separated from 4-14, while noted in 1905 by W. R. Harper, was not adopted by him. Instead, Harper maintained the traditional Hos 1-3 and 4-14 division. However, with some modifications, he basically agreed with Marti on the extent of secondary material, as well as the nature of the origin and transmission of the book.[12]

Like Marti, Harper discerned 1) a later Judaistic editor,[13] 2) exilic messianic passages which were inconsistent with Hosea's point of view and which interrupted the logical development of thought in particular passages, and 3) a group of miscellaneous glosses and interpolations. Harper enlarged Marti's list of secondary additions by others of a technical, archeological or historical character. These were inserted by way of expansion and explanation.[14]

Both Marti and Harper isolated a group of passages which reflected the concerns of the exilic community. On the basis of these exilic passages, E. Day in 1901 concluded that the whole Book of Hosea was an exilic pseudepigraphic work and not the work of the prophet at all.[15]

Peiser, however, took up the question of the original Hosean text and its redaction again in 1914. He thought that the inquiry into the textual history of individual writings, from their origin or redaction until their fixation by the Masoretes, had not been handled methodically.[16] Peiser's own procedure was, first, to free the text as much as possible of all secondary material. For Peiser, the number of accretions amounted to a considerable part of the text. He found the remaining text, the reconstructed "original," to be metrically and strophically regular (pp. 2-59). After analyzing this hypothetical text, he then gave a detailed classification and dating for all the secondary additions (pp. 78-83). While he may be faulted for overestimating the metrical and strophic regularity of the original,[17] the strength of his work at the time was his recognition that the whole history of the text, from its origin to its final Masoretic state, must be taken into consideration.

In 1922, K. Budde presented a theory of redaction, not just of Hosea, but of the whole corpus of the twelve minor prophets. For Hos 1-3, Budde understood Chapters 1 and 3 as the original consecutive narrative about Hosea's marriage. Chapter 2, a later supplement, intruded between the two accounts and highlighted the relationship between YHWH and the people. The aim of the redactor in inserting this and similar passages into the corpus of the minor prophets was a theological one: to permit nothing other than the word of YHWH to be read in the book. This would be achieved at the expense of everything that was human. Budde would date this redaction around the time of the book's adoption into the canon, i.e. in the third, or perhaps even fourth, century BCE. Its purpose in removing all that would detract from the sovereignty of YHWH would be to make from the collection of prophetic books *one holy book* in which opponents to the canonization of the prophets would find nothing unsound. The redactor himself would be an advocate of the book's canonization. Moreover, Budde would associate the preoccupations of this redactor with the preoccupations of the writer of the P source.[18]

Not all may agree on all of Budde's points, particularly his opinion that Hos 2 was a later addition and that canonization was the motivating factor for the redaction. Nevertheless, Budde's work was an important one for understanding Hosean redaction. First, it placed the redaction of the Book of Hosea within the larger context of the collection of minor prophets. Second, it was the first to characterize the overall religio-political intent of the later editorial activity as well as the person and function of the redactor himself. Finally, it was the first to suggest a possible relationship between this redactor and authors of other known sources of the biblical tradition.

1935 marked a turning point in studies regarding Hosean composition. Two works appeared which put forth opposing positions regarding the text. The first was R. E. Wolfe's article, "The Editing of the Book of the Twelve."[19] The second was H. S. Nyberg's *Studien zum Hoseabuch.*[20]

Using Budde's study as a springboard, Wolfe examined the later editing of the minor prophets, according to a method which he described as "the strata hypothesis" (p. 1). Instead of one extensive redaction of the Twelve, as Budde proposed, Wolfe thought that the corpus underwent successive editings by thirteen different redactors: 1) the Judaistic editor of Hosea, 2) the anti-high place editor, 3) the late exilic editor, 4) the anti-neighbor editor, 5) the messianist, 6) the nationalistic school of editors, 7) the day of YHWH editor, 8) the eschatologists, 9) the doxologists, 10) the anti-idol polemicists, 11) the psalm editor, 12) the early scribal schools, 13) the later scribal schools (pp. 91-122).

Even though Wolfe thought that the secondary material was not on par with the original prophecy, he still judged it important for understanding the historical times during which it was produced. The redactors, for Wolfe, functioned somewhat like commentators on the oracles, inserting their interpretations at various points in the text. At times, the amount of literary commentary exceeded that of the original (p. 90). Moreover, Wolfe thought that the secondary writers perhaps exerted a greater influence on later ages than did the primary prophets (p. 127).

The main objection to Wolfe's analysis, which he himself admitted, was the excessive and improbable number of editors. Wolfe tried to answer this objection by pointing out that, when one considered the whole long process of the book's formation, the average number of editors would only be a little more than two per century (p. 126). However, Wolfe did not consider the possibility that characteristics in his stratified list of editors could overlap. For example, the late exilic editor, the messianist and the eschatologist could have been just one editor. In other words, Wolfe's strata hypothesis isolated various motifs, but did not discuss the possible relationship of these motifs within a larger religio-political scheme of editing.

Nevertheless, Wolfe still contributed to our understanding of the redaction of the minor prophets, in general, and of Hosea in particular. He made more precise the criteria for discerning later editing. Furthermore, he had noted that the internal commentary of a particular work was more extensive and probably more influential than the original prophecy. Finally, his list was helpful in sorting out the peculiar religious and political concerns of redactional stages.

III. 1935: Nyberg and the Tradition-History Discussion

Alongside Wolfe's investigation, H. S. Nyberg's seminal *Studien zum Hoseabuch* also appeared in 1935. According to some scholars, it had launched the so-called "Scandinavian School."[21] Backlash against the literary-critical atomizing of the text into primary and secondary sources appeared here in the development of a completely different theory of composition.[22]

For Nyberg, the composition and transmission of a particular work in the Ancient Near East in general, and the Old Testament in particular, were predominantly *oral*, not written. The written Old Testament was the creation of the post-exilic Jewish community, which at a late date fixed the traditions that had hitherto circulated orally (pp. 7-9).

Given the preponderance of oral composition and transmission, Nyberg would hesitate to consider the prophets and poets as writers. One must now reckon with circles of tradents which preserved their material and passed it on. This material was not circulated without some modification. This modification, however, was a living transformation of tradition and not a written corruption of texts. All unevenness in the material most probably occurred at the oral stage. Nyberg thought that, even amid the changes of the material in the long transmission process, the primitive remembrances were more reliable than if they had been fixed early in written form (pp. 8-9).

Moreover, given the nature of oral composition and transmission, Nyberg was skeptical that the *ipsissima verba* of the prophet could be recovered. The biblical scholar should not attempt to separate primary and secondary material. Rather, one must be content with what the traditions said about the prophet, since this was all that one had (p. 9).

Regarding the composition of the Book of Hosea specifically, Nyberg thought that the tradition that lay beneath Hos 1-3 could be traced to Hosea's circle. This material was greatly transformed in Jerusalem and had taken on a new eschatological meaning. This Jerusalemite revision was also noticeable in Hos 4-14, particularly in 6:11 and the frequent insertions of Judah in passages where "Israel" was the original. Taking his cues from Mowinckel, Nyberg found that Hos 4-14 was basically a collection of individual poems interconnected according to catchword composition. Hosea himself did not arrange Chapters 4-14. It was a collector who organized it according to his own particular point of view (p. 18).

While acknowledging his debt to his former teacher, H. Birkeland in 1938 pointed out that Nyberg had not dealt with the ramifications of his opinions for understanding the OT texts themselves.[23]   He contributed to Nyberg's theory by making more precise the method involved in the study of the prophetic books (pp. 5-25). According to Birkeland, the customary explanation for the disheveled nature of prophetic compositions rested upon a theory of the predominantly written character of Hebrew tradition. The prophet had left behind a written set of notes, diaries, etc. These were preserved in the prophet's circles and often confused with other literary products. In the course of time, the texts suffered one or more redactions which rearranged the material and made new insertions. Thus, the task of literary-critical study hitherto had been to reconstruct the original text, to restore the original sequence, and to remove the non-authentic material.

However, Birkeland, following Nyberg, cautioned that the character of prophetic preaching and transmission was largely oral (p. 6). The written tradition as we have it in the OT functioned to preserve the oral word from being lost. Furthermore, under normal circumstances there was no antithesis between the written text and its oral recitation. In other words, the written text was a reliable representation of a tradition already fixed at the oral stage. It was the oral tradition, however, which had preserved, carried and formed the tradition (p. 13; cf. p. 20).

Given the primacy of oral modes of composition and transmission in the Ancient Near East, one may not, according to Birkeland, reckon with the literary *Haupt-grundlagen* of the tradition first. Rather, one must deal first with the oral *Traditionsgrundlage* which was fixed in written form in the OT (p. 13). Thus, for Birkeland, the tradition-historical investigation had a methodological priority over the literary critical one.

Furthermore, Birkeland maintained that we have only a *selection* of the tradition. The prophets obviously spoke more than what was preserved in the written text. What had somehow caught the attention of the collector, what had shown itself to be applicable and relevant for the future, was transmitted and reinterpreted up until its late literary fixing. The material stemming from the prophet and from the circles of tradition, therefore, can never be determined with certainty (p. 18). Because of this, Birkeland cautioned against what he called a false optimism in the literary-critical enterprise to recover the authentic sayings. One will never be free from the work of the circles.

> For the product which has been preserved has passed through the smelting-oven of the community. In most cases, it would be exceedingly difficult for us to go back to the product of the great geniuses themselves. Mostly, we see only their effect (pp. 23-24).

Birkeland then applied his tradition-historical theory to the prophetic books. With respect to Hosea he, like Nyberg, understood the composition as a gradual collection of independent poems into larger complexes and collections at the oral stage by the tradents. The organization of Hos 4-14 seemed to be determined by loose thematic associations among the poems (p. 59). If one took into account that the book as a whole was the product of a long process in the transmitting circles, the question whether or not the oracles of salvation were authentic played no decisive role in this composition. For example, in the eyes of the tradents, 14:2-9 served as the conclusion of the whole book. The question of authenticity was without particular interest to them (pp. 59-60).

Hos 4-14 already formed a whole before its conjunction with Hos 1-3. Moreover, Hos 1-3 itself had undergone a special development before it was placed at the beginning of the book. Against Eissfeldt, Birkeland maintained that the problem of Hos 1-3 was related to the tradition history

occurring at the oral stage and not to the literary history at
the written stage. For Birkeland, Hos 3 was attached later to
an earlier complex of tradition which we have in Hos 1-2.
With the inclusion of Hos 3, where Hosea was commanded to
take a harlot for a wife, a gradual change took place in the Hos
1-2 unit. The wife in Hos 1 became a wife of harlotry and the
children became children of harlotry. The earlier tradition of
Hos 1-2 did not speak of a whoring wife. Moreover, only the
"children of Israel" in Hos 2 were represented as a harlot's
children. Thus, the later inclusion of Hos 3 transformed the
tradition even before the literary stage was reached (p. 61).

With the works of Nyberg and Birkeland, studies on
Hosean composition proceeded in a new direction.[24] A new
theory regarding the development of the text emerged which
reacted to the current literary-critical treatments of Hosea.
The latter tended to reduce the textual material to the original
plus the successive editings which ostensibly misrepresented
this original. The new approach, on the other hand, regarded
the text not as a literary distortion whose true meaning must
be recovered, but as a product of a living process of collection,
transmission and transformation. This transformation had its
own logic which could be ascertained by examining its
tradition history. Besides the works of Nyberg and Birkeland,
later studies on Hosea, particularly by Good,[25] adopted the
position of the new approach which focused on oral tradition
and transmission, on the late written fixation of this tradition,
on the work of circles in selecting and forming the tradition,
and on the skepticism in recovering the *ipsissima verba* of the
prophet.

IV. 1950-1965: H.W. Wolff and the Form-Critical Discussion

Hosean studies proceeded in a new direction with the
tradition-historical approach parting company with literary
criticism. At this juncture, we see the literary-critical
approach also developing in a distinct direction. The
outgrowth of literary criticism, viz. form criticism, centered
upon the formal units in the text. One of the most important
and influential commentaries on Hosea, that of H. W. Wolff,

began to appear during the 1950's.[26] Wolff's theory of Hosean composition was consistent with the results of past literary-critical scholarship. However, he introduced a different slant by his systematic application of the form-critical method to the Book of Hosea.

According to Wolff, not everything in the book belonged to the *ipsissima verba* of the prophet. For the most part, however, the oracles were Hosean (p. xxiii). Wolff's position on the authenticity of the sayings preserved in the Book of Hosea was consonant with his optimism in correlating these sayings with actual historical events during Hosea's time (p. xxi). He thought that Hosea's sayings circulated in three large complexes of tradition: Hos 1-3, 4-11, 12-14. These complexes had achieved written, but not final, form during the prophet's lifetime. From a form-critical viewpoint, they were self-contained. They paralleled each other to the extent that all three moved from accusation to threat, and then to proclamation of salvation (p. xxxi). Moreover, all three had their own literary prehistory.

With regard to Hos 1-3, Wolff thought that Hosea himself probably had a hand in this written collection, since the first person style of the *memorabile* was to be traced back to him. This *memorabile*, according to Wolff, probably had its beginning in 2:4-17. On the other hand, the third person style of the *memorabile* in 1:2-6, 8f. indicated a different composer than the prophet. For Wolff, a disciple had reinterpreted the old Hosean text (2:4-17 and 3:1-5) with his own version of the *memorabile* (1:2-6, 8f) and probably expanded the old Hosean unit with later sayings of Hosea (2:18-25 and 2:1-3).

In his treatment of Hos 4-14, Wolff suggested a form-critical classification, "kerygmatic units," for the divisions of Hos 4-11 and 12-14. The precise form-critical nature and determination of these units, however, seemed to be unclear even for Wolff.[27] Some of these units, Wolff thought, had clear beginnings signified by a change from divine to prophetic speech or a change in person. Moreover, the various sayings were joined together by means of initial copulas, pronominal suffixes or the repetition of the former theme. Wolff concluded from this "that the sayings within a series combined in this manner were proclaimed by the prophet on one and the same occasion. They thus form a 'kerygmatic unit'" (p. xxx). The curious manner in which the sayings were linked was, for Wolff, explicable only if these kerygmatic units presented sketches of scenes which were written down soon after the prophet delivered his message (p. xxx. Cf. pp. 75-76). Wolff suggested that the poor condition of the text may have been the result of this transcription of Hosea's sayings under difficult conditions. Hosea's followers "were quite probably responsible for these sketches" (p. xxx).

In addition to the proclamation of Hosea and its initial writing down by the disciples, the three separate transmission complexes underwent stages of redaction covering two hundred years. This redaction consisted only in interpretive or supplementary glosses. Wolff detected four types of these glosses: a Deuteronomic redaction by an ideological cousin of Hosea's followers; an early Judean redaction; a later Judean redaction; and a final redaction. He thought that the three complexes were joined together in their present form during the final redaction, which for him took place some time in the sixth century (p. xxxii).

Wolff's understanding of the composition of the Book of Hosea was decidedly in keeping with literary-critical presuppositions concerning the text: that the preaching of the prophet was written down and collected soon after it was proclaimed; that during the transmission process, particularly that which involved their migration to Judah, the documents suffered textual corruption and augmentation by a series of redactions. Nevertheless, Wolff was more conservative than earlier scholars in estimating the extent of redaction in the book. For instance, he thought that the hopeful sections of the book were authentic.

The form-critical method which influenced his understanding of Hosean composition did, however, present him with difficulties. This was particularly evident in his discussion of Hos 4-14. In contrast to Hos 1-3, the rhetorical devices that define and link formal units were largely absent here. While Wolff admitted this fact, he still tried to grapple with the heterogeneity of the text by using form criticism (p.xxx). The resulting theory of literary composition thus had its weaknesses. For example, while Wolff explained the collection of small sayings units by postulating "kerygmatic units," he failed to define the exact character and meaning of these kerygmatic units.

Moreover, in spite of Wolff's conservatism regarding the redactional activity in this book, his form-critical approach still tended to reduce the text, not to its primary and secondary elements, but to its smallest formal units. The method was inadequate in demonstrating the function of these units within the overall compositional structure of the book. Despite these shortcomings, Wolff's theory of composition was adopted by later studies.[28]

V. 1957: Hellmuth Frey

After a brief survey of the German literary-critical studies on Hosean composition, including Wolff's fascicle on Hos 1-3, H. Frey found that the numerous different suggestions for divisions of the same book revealed the uncertainty in scholarship concerning the *original* elements in the work. This scholarly "groping in the dark" gave him cause to seek after an objective basis for the demarcation of the original units.[29] He thought that his "objective basis" would be founded on the structural uniformity of the original material. Again we see a swing away from the atomizing of the text towards an emphasis on the text's unity. We have already seen such an emphasis characterizing the tradition-critical reaction against literary criticism.

In his examination of the text, Frey concluded that the prophet himself, and not his interpreters, was responsible for structurally regular units. The prophet generally spoke and wrote in large collections of sayings and sayings sequences (p. 51). The regularity in this original production showed itself in the similar number of strophes and lines, in a symmetrical juxtaposition of thoughts, images and catchwords, as well as in a consistency in formal structures (p. 10). Frey's analysis was reminiscent of Peiser's work[30] in that it discovered a structural orderliness in the original version. Frey, however, retained most of the text as authentic, whereas Peiser eliminated a major portion of it as secondary.

In these large symmetrically constructed poems, the prophet made his position clear regarding the problems in Israel. According to Frey, Hosea organized his pastoral and theological concerns chronologically. This was reflected, for the most part, in the arrangement of Hosea's sayings in the book as we now have it. The sequence began with the time of Jeroboam II, when Hosea preached in sign-acts with his marriage and the naming of his children (Hos 1:2-9). It ended after the fall of Samaria in 722, when the prophet performed his last sign in retaking his wife (3:1-5), in prophesying the glory of the renewed community and day of YHWH (2:1-3), and in prompting the shattered community with a teaching of repentance, confession and prayer in 14:2-10 (pp. 102-103).

These sayings, Frey thought, were joined in two parallel collections (Hos 1-3 and 4-14). Both collections presupposed the fall of Samaria and were possibly attributable to Hosea's circle of disciples. The two collections were then united at a later stage in Judah and provided with a superscript, Hos 1:1. Certain smaller collections or pamphlets contained within this framework, such as 5:8--9:9; 9:10--11:11 and 12:1-14, did not, however, presuppose the end of Samaria, but anticipated it. They were joined during the time of the prophet and were attributable to Hosea himself (p. 103; cf. pp. 51-52).

In view of the uniform style and arrangement of Hosea's speeches, Frey readily distinguished the activity of the redactor which interrupted this unity. In his concern to clarify the relationship between Hosea and his interpreters, Frey made some suggestions, not only with regard to the theological thought world of the redactors, but also with regard to the type and manner of the redactors' insertions into the text.

In the first place, the redactor filled in the larger units of sayings already assembled by the prophet with detached material from the sayings of the master. Second, he was not reluctant in this activity to disrupt the poetic form and outer construction of a poem. Third, he did not, however, perform this work arbitrarily. Rather, he intended a particular point of view. The theological connections were for him more important than formal, aesthetic or historical connections. Finally, the redactor acted like a sensitive interpreter who commented on the sayings of the master in their proper arrangement. He interpreted by utilizing other words of his teacher rather than with his own commentary. If necessary, however, he did insert foreign material (pp. 10, 50-51).

Discernible in Frey's work was a reaction against previous treatments of the Book of Hosea that had split the text apart into its primary and secondary components and smallest units.[31] As such, it shared the same motivations that prompted the Scandinavians to develop a more agreeable holistic theory of composition. The correspondence between Frey and the Scandinavians ended here, however. In contrast to their theory of oral tradition, Frey considered the origins of the book to be the prophet himself and not the tradition circles. The literary text was not a late written fixation. Rather, the prophet who spoke had written down his proclamations. These poems were noticeable in their compositional regularity. Moreover, the prophet himself arranged most of his material. The thematic and ideological catchword connections, as well as the overall symmetry of the work, were due to his own literary activity. Later editing of the material was done by his disciples in complete fidelity to the sayings of their master. It consisted primarily in interpreting the larger text with additional separate sayings of the prophet. The concept of a tradition history which figured so prominently in the Scandinavian debate was therefore practically nonexistent in Frey.

We see, then, that Frey's theory of composition tried to preserve the wholeness of the book, while still taking into consideration the editorial activity that was obvious in the text. It did this by maintaining the authenticity of the written material, the uniformity of its composition, and the coherence of the redaction with the larger body of the original.

To a certain extent, we shall encounter this position again in the most recent commentary on Hosea by Andersen and Freedman.

VI. 1969: M. Buss and the Morphological Discussion

The next major study dealing with the composition and transmission of the Book of Hosea was M. Buss's revised doctoral dissertation published in 1969.[32] Buss described his method as a "morphological" investigation. It was a modified form-critical approach which did not limit itself to analysis of genres, but dealt freely with "any form of verbal patterns and also with stylistic tendencies which may not be absolutely rigorous or may cut across other aspects of classification" (p. 1). He reacted against Wolff's narrow form-critical concern to isolate units, since such a task had proven to be difficult in Hosea. Instead, he approached the problem of the size of the units with two working assumptions: 1) "that the individual oracles began in a full manner, i.e. mentioning Israel by name rather than opening with an expressed or unexpressed 'they' without antecedent," 2) that catchword associations were made by a collector to aid memory, or were deliberate repetitions of the prophet in the internal development of his thought (pp. 28-31).

On the basis of these two working hypotheses, Buss divided the book into three main collections: Hos 1-3, 4-11, and 12-14. He then subdivided these collections into cycles of oracles and oracle units according to his working criteria. From this literary examination, he concluded that most of the oracles revealed "a remarkable internal unity despite their jagged style" (p. 36).

Buss's theory of composition lay midway between the speculations of literary criticism, on the one hand, and tradition criticism, on the other. The collection, Hos 1-3, consisted of three complexes, each having a complicated and apparently long period of oral history. These complexes had developed independently and were united as a whole at different stages. Also present were at least two Judean additions, 1:7 and 2:1-3 (pp. 33-34).

Regarding Hos 4-14, Buss thought that the collections and cycles of oracles were similarly compiled at the oral stage, either by the prophet or by a collector. However, in contrast to Hos 1-3, these seemed to have been reduced to writing fairly early (p. 34). According to Buss, this early written stage would account for the jagged style in the sections and the relative lack of secondary growth (pp. 34, 36).

On the question of the origins of the book, Buss seemed to be neutral:

> So far it has been taken for granted that a single author stands behind most of the traditions in the book; should this be a false assumption, one must speak of a tradition originating within related circles in the Northern Kingdom and continuing in varying ways in Judah (p. 34).

Consistent with the suppositions of literary criticism, he assumed, on one hand, composition by Hosea himself. On the other hand, he was open to the possibility of tradent circles creating and circulating the material--a conviction of the tradition-history school.

Buss's description of the composition and transmission process tried to mediate between different streams of thought regarding the origin and circulation of the book. The openendedness of his conclusions, however, only succeeded in leaving the precise nature of this process ambiguous. Both the prophet and the circles could have created and transmitted the tradition. This tradition, furthermore, could have had both an oral and a written history. In view of the inconclusiveness of his opinions, Buss could not apply a theory of composition to the text to determine the extent and nature of prophetic speech and later additions. Thus, he could not comment on the relationship of the two in composing the whole book, even in view of his insistence on the unity of the oracles.

Moreover, like most form critics, he examined the text primarily in smaller sections. Although his criteria for determining units were more loosely defined than past form critical studies, he still described the book in terms of certain isolated phenomena, such as types of narrative, accusations, threats and *rîb* forms (pp. 37-80), or in terms of themes or images found in the book, such as "day of YHWH," *hesed* and *šûb* (pp. 81-115). All these, however, were not situated and related in context. He failed to present an overall picture of the book's composition and literary thrust.

VII. 1971: I. Willi-Plein and the Redaction-Critical Discussion

An important work appeared in 1971 which signalled a major change in attitude towards the study of the text. This work was I. Willi-Plein's doctoral dissertation on the prophets, Amos, Hosea and Micah.[33] Reacting against the negative bias which regarded later additions as "inauthentic" and thus of lesser importance, Willi-Plein tried to understand the principles by which these additions came to be in the text. Rather than simply dismiss secondary insertions as "inauthentic," she maintained that the glossators certainly did not consider their work as "superfluous" or "unjustified," but *necessary* (p. 4). Thus, in her more positive position towards glosses and expansions, she took a big step forward in understanding the composition of the Book of Hosea. She did not view the book simply as a mine to prospect for the gold nuggets of authentic prophetic sayings. Instead, she tried to give the text as a whole its due weight. Her study was novel in the importance she had placed on the redactors. She allowed for the compositional development of the book in terms of an original *text* and subsequent interpretive *commentary* by these redactors.

Unfortunately, Willi-Plein's undertaking labored heavily under certain methodological assumptions that had adversely influenced previous scholarship on the book's composition. In the first place, while ostensibly a redactional study, Willi-Plein viewed the material form critically. She regarded the book as collections of small individual sayings and sayings units upon which subsequent redaction was built. Her form-critical concern was particularly evident in her reconstruction of Hosea's original sayings. This reconstruction can be found in an appendix to her book (pp. 274-277). Out of 197 verses approximately 67 individual sayings represented the core tradition. Willi-Plein's results were consistent with R. E. Wolfe's observations that the redaction of the book outweighed the original.[34] However, as they are presented in this reconstruction, these sayings were merely isolated statements with little or no relationship to one another. They seemed to have no real context or development.

While grasping the fact that an original text and subsequent commentary composed the Book of Hosea, she had misconstrued this interpretive development by allowing a form-critical point of view to dictate her method. Thus, her resultant theory of composition basically proceeded from her form-critical suppositions rather than a study of the redaction. She suggested the following eight groups of sayings and their chronological sequence. While not as extreme as R. E. Wolfe's theory of thirteen redactional strata in the book's formation,[35] it was still rather complicated:

1.	5:8--6:6	small composition(s?) of sayings units during the ministry of the prophet
2.	1:2--3:4	a biographical memoir on the life and message of Hosea, written by an intimate circle of disciples soon after 722
3.	4:1--9:9	an oral collection of the prophet's sayings according to mnemonic norms, begun before 722 BCE but apparently completed later in Judah
4.	9:10-11:9	a collection regarding the history and sayings tradition of Israel without reference to the southern kingdom
5.	12:1--14:9	a collection actualizing the threats and reproaches of Hosea as a warning for the southern kingdom after 722, probably at the time of Manasseh, perhaps to be conceived in connection with the rise of Deuteronomy
6.		a final collection and assemblage of the Book of Hosea with the super-scription 1:1, after 586
7.		a post-exilic expansion and new arrangement of the book in the framework of its recitation or

		liturgical use in the post-exilic community
8.	14:10	a postscript by a teacher after the end of the prophetic tradition (p.244)

It was especially in steps 1 to 6 that Willi-Plein's form-critical understanding of the material was most pronounced. "Redaction" was seen mainly in terms of the "collection" of oracles.

Her second presupposition was directly related to her form-critical position on the book. Given her assumption that the work was an aggregate of smaller forms, she thought that the *present structure* of the book, Hos 1-3 and 4-14, was due simply to the joining of separate complexes of tradition (cf. steps #1-6 above). And yet, she demonstrated that the redaction of the book was more extensive than simply glosses. Moreover, she had even shown that subsequent redactions had imposed a secondary organization on parts of the book (pp. 248-50). However, her form-critical supposition that the book was an aggregate precluded her recognizing that a redactor may have deliberately shaped the original material into its final structure. In other words, the present structure of the book, which scholars took for granted as Hos 1-3 and 4-14, could perhaps be an artificial structure resulting from a redactor commenting on a received text. Marti had already pointed out the redactional creation of the Hos 1-3 and 4-14 division.[36] The final structure, then, would not be just the compilation of the tradition but a deliberate framework for the tradition constructed by the final redactor.

Finally, Willi-Plein suggested that the nature and function of secondary additions could be illuminated by the methods of rabbinic exegesis. She used the exegetical principles of Rabbis Hillel, Ishmael and Eliezer as models for certain glosses in Hosea (pp. 4-9; 263-66). While a concrete step in describing the character of the text's transmission, this suggestion had its problems. Rabbinic exegesis presupposed institutions, theological developments (including strong notions of canon) and methods not known to be in existence during Hosea's time. Willi-Plein thus risked the danger of anachronism, i.e., of imposing later principles of interpretation on earlier material. Even with these difficulties, however, Willi-Plein still offered an investigation of major worth. It threw into relief the need to study the book as an integrated literary whole. It stressed the importance of later interpretive development and had built upon the results of other scholars, like Peiser, in classifying and dating this later activity (pp. 254-68). As Budde and Wolfe had done, it had placed the redaction of the Book of Hosea within the context of other prophetic books.[37] However, in contrast to Budde and Wolfe's studies, Willi-Plein's was a more systematic and complete treatment of the redactional tendencies. Furthermore, even though it has some drawbacks, Willi-Plein's correlation between later interpretations and rabbinic principles of exegesis has merit. It had placed the redaction of the text within a typological scheme of Hebraic interpretation, rather than impose alien criteria to determine the nature of the additions.

VIII. 1980: F. I. Andersen and D. N. Freedman and the Rhetorical Critical Discussion

In 1980, F. I. Andersen and D. N. Freedman published the most recent commentary on the Book of Hosea.[38] It is an important work because it represents the state of Hosean scholarship at present. The overall method of these authors was rhetorical criticism, which analyzed the text according to Hebrew rhetorical conventions. According to Andersen and Freedman, many textual difficulties could be eliminated, not by considering them as later redaction or by emending them, but by taking into account certain grammatical features hitherto unrecognized such as broken construct chains, and double-duty prepositions, suffixes and conjunctions (p. 67). On the basis of these rhetorical devices, the authors were convinced, "not only that there was a high level of coherence in the composition, but that it is the deliberate result of an artistry far more sophisticated than anything previously suspected" (p. 70).

With regard to the composition of the Book of Hosea, Andersen and Freedman did not present anything substantially new. Hos 1-3 was the original composition of a disciple or follower of Hosea, whose primary purpose was to portray the mission of the prophet as an expression of his personal experience in marriage and parenthood (p. 58).

Hos 4-14, on the other hand, was largely the production of the prophet himself. In trying to explain the heterogeneity of this section, Andersen and Freedman suggested that the Book of Hosea did not present Hosea's oracles in a polished state which were ready for delivery:

> Rather it offers material from an earlier stage in the process, from the actual deliberations of Yahweh in the divine council. In fact, since Yahweh does not consult the council, these talks seem to be his preliminary reflections or soliloquies (p. 45).

According to Andersen and Freedman, this hypothesis would account for the incongruities of the text, such as shifts in person, number and theme. They also maintain that such soliloquies would not have reached the stage at which form-critical analysis would be profitable (p. 45).

A disciple or a group of followers was probably responsible for "collecting, preserving, organizing and editing the surviving materials" (pp. 52, 60). The sayings of the prophet were preserved in these circles because of their relevance for later religio-political situations. The initial compilation was probably assembled during the time of Manasseh, during the first half of the seventh century. This written record of Hosea was then reactualized during the subsequent periods of Josiah's reform and the Babylonian Captivity (pp. 54-56). It was during the Exile that the Book of Hosea achieved its final form (pp. 56-67). Hos 1-3 and 4-14 possibly circulated independently for a while before they were joined. Andersen and Freedman, however, insisted that during these periods, there were no major changes in the material and that "Hosea remained essentially untouched," although editorial activity was apparent in the book (pp. 52, 57, 59).

Certain questions arise concerning Andersen and Freedman's discussion of the composition of the Book of Hosea.

In the first place, their rhetorical-critical method precluded any appreciable examination of the process of the book's composition. Questions regarding the evolution of the text would be subordinate to the examination of its final literary organization.[39] The authors thus presupposed one author and one text (p. 59). These assumptions confirm the literary artistry which they see in this final state. Like Frey, the authors believe that the finely crafted rhetorical structure of the book is attributable to the prophet. However, that literary artistry is a hallmark of authenticity is in itself a gratuitous assumption. Nevertheless, the authors implicitly modify their position on unity and authorship by admitting that a disciple composed Hos 1-3, that redaction was recognizable in Hos 4-14, and that the texts were reinterpreted for new historical situations. Yet, in spite of these qualifications, they are adamant that the bulk of Hosea's oracles was undisturbed throughout these developments.

Secondly, Andersen and Freedman's speculation, that the difficulties of the text could be explained by the fact that they were the soliloquies of God, actually creates more problems than it solves. Presumably, the authors mean that the text reflects Hosea's perception of YHWH's psychological state.[40] Thus, on one hand, the text represents Hosea's unrefined notes regarding the deliberations of God. On the other hand, however, Andersen and Freedman contend that the texts were "sophisticated compositions employing a variety of literary devices and reflecting the creative genius of the prophet himself" (p. 59). Consequently, the Book of Hosea, according to the authors, was both a rough draft and a carefully crafted literary product. The incompatibility of these two notions is obvious.

Moreover, the literary sophistication that purportedly characterizes the Book of Hosea for Andersen and Freedman may not even have been consciously planned or intrinsic to the texts:

> We do not insist that our approach is inherent in the material. Rather, we are trying to describe the material as we have it and consciously avoiding the apparently unattainable goals of critics who concern themselves with origins and

developments in a way we find impossible. We assume in
general the fewer hands the better, though that point is
immaterial to our premises about observing unities of form
and composition. Ours is an approach, not a provable
conclusion. It is essentially a statement that most biblical
criticism has not proved successful and that more can be
gained by looking to other, more truly literary approaches to
texts (p. 316).

Like the works of Frey and those involved in the
Scandinavian debate, we see in the work of Andersen and
Freedman a concern to preserve the wholeness of the book and
still deal with textual difficulties. Weary of "the impasse and
frustration of inconclusive form-critical studies" and other
methods that partitioned the text (p. 45), these scholars offer
an alternative. However, they must also admit that the
artistry they perceive in the work may be alien to the work
itself. In trying to find a literary and structural coherence,
they may also marginalize a tension in the text that is
deliberate, which could only be explained as later
interpretation.

Finally, and related to the above limitations of the
method, Andersen and Freedman's manner of dealing with the
question of later redaction and composition is, from the first,
to avoid it:

> As we turn to the question of the literary character of the
> work, we must consider two anterior issues: the unity of the
> work, and the integrity of the text. In both cases, our premises
> and point of departure are conservative, that the book is
> essentially the work of a single person, and that the text is
> basically sound. These are hardly ringing affirmations; *they
> are more like defensive desperation.* If the opposite were true,
> if many hands and voices could be found in the book, then we
> would have the thankless and ultimately fruitless task of
> apportioning the work among a variety of people whose
> existence is hypothetical, and whose only distinguishing
> mark is some obscurity or inconsistency in the text (p. 59.
> Italics mine).

Thus, Andersen and Freedman turn a blind eye to the
conclusions of past scholarship on the composition of Hosea.
They refuse to deal with issues that this scholarship

spotlighted in its investigations, viz. the extent of editorial activity and the relationship between authentic and secondary material.

This discussion of Andersen and Freedman's commentary brings to an end our survey of the literature. These authors articulate the most recent attempt to explain the difficult problem of Hosean composition. They do this essentially by offering a new method. The strength of this method is its sensitivity to the literary characteristics of the text's present state. Its weaknesses, however, are its indifference to the historical development of the work, i.e., its stages of composition, and the tendency to marginalize a tension in the text which should be explained as a later redaction.[41]

CHAPTER TWO

Presuppositions in Hosean Scholarship:
An Argument for Methodological Clarity

A brief observation can be made regarding the history of Hosean studies to date. Scholarly discussion on the Book of Hosea swings back and forth between studies which disassemble the text and those which try to maintain its unity. In certain respects, the various methods arose as correctives to previous scholarship. For example, in reaction to the literary-critical approach, the tradition-history discussion emerged. Likewise, rhetorical criticism sought to remedy what it saw as the inconclusiveness of form-critical studies. Both sides upheld the merits of their own methodological stances, while at the same time pointing out the deficiencies of their predecessors.

From our review of the literature, however, we detect three presuppositions which inform these studies. How these presuppositions influence the understanding of the book's literary formation dictates the specific elements of the method involved. In this chapter, we will discuss these assumptions. We formulate Presupposition One as, "The 'original' is the most valuable." By "original" we mean either the original words of the prophet or the original *Sitz-im-Leben*.

Presupposition Two reads: "The oral or preliterary stage is the proper focus of research for understanding the prophet's message." This preliterary stage would include the *ipsissima verba* concerns of some exegetes. Investigations into the preliterary stages of the tradition are, therefore, given a methodological priority over the analysis of the written literary stage of the tradition.

Finally, a corollary of Presupposition Two is Presupposition Three: "There is no qualitative difference between the oral stage and the written stage." The written stage is regarded more or less as a reliable "recording" of the oral stage. The written stage is thus valuable only insofar as it provides access to the oral stage.

We will then evaluate the cogency of these presuppositions in view of investigations into oral and written genres which are significant for research in the Book of Hosea. On the basis of these studies, we will show how scholarship on the Book of Hosea has been adversely hampered by these presuppositions. We will then be prepared to suggest directions which an investigation into the Book of Hosea should take.

I. Presupposition One: The "original" is the most valuable.

A. Literary Criticism and the Recovery of the Original Saying

As we have seen, the assumption that the recovery of the "original" is the goal of biblical investigation is one that is most characteristic of the literary-critical school. According to its literary theory, the text is here viewed from the outset as a literary distortion. Indeed, the literary critic comes to the text "with, so to say, a dissecting knife in his hand."[1] Through the systematic divestment of the text of secondary accretions,[2] this type of criticism hopes to arrive at the *ipsissima verba* of the prophet.

Related to this presupposition regarding the "authentic" sayings is the judgment that what is "secondary" is less significant. The hypothetical reconstruction of the "original" is vested with an authority that supersedes all later material and even the text as a whole.[3] This secondary material is either dismissed outright as the tendentious work of redactors (Cheyne, Wolff),[4] or subordinated to the "original" (Marti, Peiser, Harper, Wolfe).

The preoccupation with the recovery of the "original" seems to rest on a belief that the "original" in some way brings us closer to what is "historical."[5] This concern for history is certainly legitimate. However, as practiced by the late 19th and early 20th century exegetes, literary criticism placed a premium on authenticity and historicity to the exclusion of the final form of the text. In this regard, Mays makes the following remarks:

> But because exegesis had set a preeminent value on the 'historical,' and did not see how to apply the term to the present form of texts, it has been too much content with the resulting fragmentation, has lingered among literary fragments and sources, archeological ruins, etymological roots, religious phenomenology - and not found the way back.[6]

Moreover, the overemphasis on the original appears at times to be motivated by certain unconscious or even conscious theological agenda, such as theories of inspiration and *Heilsgeschichte*.[7] Thus, if one can uncover the true words of the prophet, one encounters the word of God itself. Or similarly, if one can detect amid the accretions the true event, one can see God at work in the history of humankind. Secondary material was therefore overlooked or regarded with suspicion because of its distance from the actual word of the prophet and the actual historical event.[8]

B. Form Criticism and the Recovery of the Original Form and Sitz-im-Leben

Because of its stress on the oral circulation of units in a particular *Sitz-im-Leben*, some scholars would consider form criticism as a corrective to literary criticism.[9] However, form criticism likewise reveals its partiality towards the "original" in its weighted concern for the preliterary stage of the material.[10] Here, the search for the original *Sitz-im-Leben* seems "more theoretical than practical, stemming more from philosophical notions than from experience of living societies."[11] Thus, on the basis of its own theory of the literature, the form-critical approach as well is culpable of reducing the text, not to its sources but to its smallest formal units.

With respect to the Book of Hosea, the study of Wolff is particularly significant as an example of this concern with the prophetic *ipsissima verba*.[12] It is an investigation whose theory of transmission and composition is consistent with that of literary criticism. However, it enlarges the scope of literary criticism by the conclusions of form criticism.

Adopting the classical form-critical observation that the basic unit of prophetic speech is the short independent saying,[13] Wolff finds that the main portion of Hosea's oracles are authentic. The kerygmatic units which he postulates from the collections of small sayings not only have a *Sitz-im-Leben* in the community, but also an historical referent in the life of the prophet himself. For Wolff, the kerygmatic units indicate "scenes" of the debates between the prophet and his audience. Jeremias has recently stated that, if Wolff's theory is correct, "we would be in the unusually fortunate situation with Hosea, in comparison with other prophetic books, of possessing almost direct access to the oral preaching of the prophet."[14] Confident that his form-critical analysis can recover these scenes, Wolff is optimistic in correlating the sayings with actual historical events of Hosea's time.[15] We have already noted the problems of Wolff's literary theory of Hosean composition.[16] These problems are based in part on an assumption that the "original" is the most valuable, viz. the "original" words of the prophet spoken on a definite historical occasion, and which were transmitted in different life settings.

This scholarly bias in favor of the "original" and the methods that issued from it were not without reaction. Our discussion focuses upon two of these responses: Willi-Plein's redaction criticism and rhetorical criticism.

C. Redaction Criticism as the Final Analytical Step

The emphasis on the recovery of the "original words of the prophet" found a strong opponent in the redaction-critical investigation of Willi-Plein. Her work insisted that the secondary material not only should but must be given its due in the examination of the text. Only in such an examination will one properly understand how the book was composed.

However, one could fault Willi-Plein also for allowing the assumption that the "original" is the most valuable to influence her understanding of the book's formation. One can see this supposition influencing her application of the form-critical method. She first presumes the results of form criticism that there is a core tradition of "original" short

sayings units. Later redaction is seen in terms of collections
and amplifications of these small units. In other words, the
material is approached with a certain form-critical notion of
what constitutes prophetic oracles, viz. short sayings units
believed to be the "original" word of the prophet. These
sayings are regarded as the earliest material which
underwent later editorial activity. Although the focal point of
Willi-Plein's analysis is the later redaction, her point of
departure is not the final redacted state. Her starting point,
rather, is the smaller form-critical unit of the text upon which
this redaction was built.

Willi-Plein's application of the redaction-critical method
is not surprising. It is consistent with the methodological
procedures of most of scholarly exegesis. Here, redaction
criticism is considered the *final stage* in the analysis of the
text. One undertakes a redaction-critical investigation only
after the literary, form, genre and tradition-historical analysis
is completed.[17] We will argue, however, that the proper
approach to the text is to begin with the redaction-critical
investigation.[18]

D. Rhetorical Criticism and the Style of the Original Prophetic Composition

Rhetorical criticism arose to break through the limitations
of the form-critical method.[19] As applied to the Book of Hosea
by Andersen and Freedman, it investigated the text as a
literary whole. It tried to resolve the problems of the text by
relating them to Hebrew rhetorical conventions.

The presupposition that the "original" is the most
valuable, however, can be observed in the application of this
method to the Book of Hosea. Andersen and Freedman were
quite clear about their assumptions. The first is single
authorship: that the oracles are, for the most part, authentic.
Therefore, it is not a question in this method of recovering the
"original" words of the prophet. They are presumed to be
"original" from the beginning! The value of the "original" now
lies in the literary artistry which the prophet gives to his
work.

Furthermore, Andersen and Freedman assume the unity of the text. This assumption justifies the authenticity of the work and vice-versa. It thus bypasses any discussion of the formation of the book. We therefore have an ironic state of affairs evolving from this particular presupposition regarding the value of the "original." Literary- and form-critical studies overlook the present state of the text in their pursuit of the "original word" or "original form." Rhetorical criticism, on the other hand, assumes the authenticity of the present text and neglects its literary history.

II. Presupposition Two: *The oral or preliterary stage is the proper focus of research for understanding the prophetic message.*

The second presupposition maintains that the oral or preliterary stage is the locus for a more authentic understanding of the prophetic message. This presupposition is informed by other assumptions regarding the prophets, e.g., the prophets were speakers of the word, rather than writers; prophetic experience, such as ecstasy or trance, dictated that the spoken word was the short independent saying, rather than long literary compositions; the oral nature of the message is reflected in the different speech forms which the prophets adopted; it was at the oral stage that the prophetic tradition was transmitted and transformed.

We do not deny the accuracy of these ancilliary presuppositions. However, we hope to show that the weight given to these presuppositions places a strong value on the oral or preliterary stage of the text. The resulting fragmentation of the text into smaller forms and sayings becomes problematic for understanding the whole work. Furthermore, the oral stage becomes idealized as the creative stage of the material. This idealization overlooks the fact that the only avenue to this stage is the written text, a problem which we will address in our discussion of Presupposition Three.[20]

A. *Literary criticism*

Although literary criticism understood the origins of the book to be literary in character, the oral stage still played some sort of role in the formation of the book. This role was seen mainly at the earlier stages of the text. At the beginning were the prophet's oral pronouncements themselves, his oracles. Influenced by certain theories of what constituted prophetic experience, e.g., ecstasy and trance, scholars did not consider these oracles to be long rhetorical speeches but short, separate sayings uttered on a particular occasion.[21] These brief sayings were either published by the prophet himself[22] or transmitted orally by his hearers. They were gathered later into small collections and written down, either during the lifetime of the prophet or after his death.

B. *Tradition Criticism*

Among the Scandinavian critics, a skepticism prevails regarding any reconstruction of the authentic words.[23] The tradents who preserved and transmitted the tradition in a particular community at the oral stage now receive the emphasis. The scholars felt that it was impossible to separate the work of the tradents from that of the prophets themselves.[24] This approach thus elevates the status of secondary material and places it in the context of the living transformation of the tradition by the tradents.

Despite this reaction to literary- and form-criticism and the laudable concern to keep the unity of the text intact, one could fault the tradition-critical approach for shifting the focus of importance from a hypothetical reconstruction of the "original" prophetic word to the equally hypothetical activity of the "oral stage." Instead of the notion that the "original" word of the prophet is the most valuable, now the assumption is that the "oral stage" and its tradition history becomes the proper focus of research.[25]

Problematic is the fact that the oral stage is idealized as the "creative" stage. What is asserted is that the prophets were men of the spoken word, not writers.[26] Their words "lived" in the tradent circles where they were orally preserved, transmitted and transformed. Here, the tradition developed organically in the community, not mechanically at the hands of scribes.[27] The written stage is regarded disparagingly. The oral stage, on the other hand, is infused with the vitality, originality and power of the believing community. Thus, if one can penetrate the written text and uncover the tradition at this stage, one can encounter the dynamism of the community. In commenting on the tradition-historical method, Knight states:

> Internal to the literature, below the surface level, there are indications which point to the formation of that literature, and by retracing its development and determining the forces which affected it we can perceive its intense, vital, dynamic relation to life.[28]

C. Form Criticism

The oral stage plays a major part in the form-critical method. "The first basic principle of form criticism is that most of the literature of the Old Testament had a long and often complicated oral prehistory."[29] Like the literary critics, the first oral stage of the material for the form critics was the oral delivery of the prophet on a particular historical occasion. The basic form-critical unit of prophetic speech was the short independent saying. These brief oracles in their fragmentary and enigmatic style reflected the ecstatic condition of prophetic revelation.

The second stage of oral history, according to the form critics, is the circulation of these sayings in a particular setting in the life of the folk community, their *Sitz-im-Leben*.[30] The life situation of particular genres can change in the process of oral transmission. Thus, one can speak of *Sitze-im-Leben* at the oral stage. Throughout this process, the forms exhibit a certain stability. At the same time, however, they also display a flexibility to adapt to the particular demands of the community. The material circulating at this stage is composed of both oral and written forms. However, the latter had a long process of oral transmission before they actually came to be written down.[31]

III. Presupposition Three: *There is no qualitative difference between the oral and written stages.*

The particular emphases on the oral stage of the tradition in the above methods imply two conclusions regarding the written stage. The first is that the written stage reflects the oral stage with little or no alteration. For the literary critics, the prophet's actual sayings, the "authentic" material in the text, were either published in written form by the prophet himself or faithfully recorded soon after their proclamation by his disciples.

For the tradition-history critics, a theory of oral tradition which highlighted the preliterary stage naturally affected the understanding of the book's formation at the literary or written stage. Significant is the fact that the theory of the development of the written text is not based on the written text itself. Rather, it is based on a theory regarding the formation of the work at the oral stage. In other words, the tradition-history critics use the theory of how the written text came to be primarily to support a theory of oral tradition and only secondarily to explain the written text itself.[32] Thus, they regard the text as a late written fixation of the oral tradition.[33] Although the transmission of the material involved a living transformation of the tradition, "still in all essentials the tradition remained fixed and reliable."[34] Therefore, the late written text simply reflects the oral stage with little or no difference. Engnell makes the following comment:

> What we have before us are living, oral traditions, committed indeed to writing, but firmly formed and fixed already in the oral stage so that even *the written form signifies in itself nothing absolutely new and revolutionary.*[35]

For the form and redaction critics, the written stage becomes the literary fixation of the oral transmission of forms in particular life situations. The editing of forms at the final stage of the tradition is commonly referred to as its redaction history.[36] The process that governs the tradition at the oral stage is the same for the final stages of written composition: the redactor collects, edits, modifies and reassembles the formal units, *operations which had already begun at the oral stage*. Thus, for the form critics, the written stage of the tradition is in organic connection with the history of the material at the oral stage. Nothing essentially new, therefore, is created with the final work of the redactors.[37] They are not considered "authors" who composed an original piece. Rather, they are anonymous collectors of the traditions of the people.[38] At most, they give the material its final direction and thrust. At the very least, they simply end the process which was begun at the oral stage.

Concomitant with the oral/written stage equation, however, is a depreciation of the written stage. At worst, the written stage robbed the oral stage of its power and vitality.[39]

At best, "this writing down gives us simply the mechanical preservation of an already completed structure."[40] It functioned only to provide access to the oral stage, believed to be the fertile soil for the tradition. It occurred mainly as a support for memory (Nyberg) or because "the culture itself is felt to be threatened - from within by syncretism and from without by political events,"[41] and thus needed to preserve its ancient traditions in written form. The remarks of Koch are typical:

> The material which (the redactor) put into writing had taken shape long ago. He *merely* took it out of the linguistic flow of oral tradition, and by writing it down *he froze it into fixed form. He banished it to a piece of papyrus.*[42]

IV. *The Radical Peculiarities of the Oral and Written Stages*

At this point, we need to focus on two issues that deal directly with the depreciation of the written stage in favor of the oral stage as the above methods understand it. In this section we will discuss the first issue, viz. the radical peculiarities of the oral and written stages. In the following section, we will look at a second issue, the redactional selection of traditional material for the larger literary framework.

A. *The Nature of the Tradition at the Oral Stage*

Recent field studies have found that the recovery of the original *Sitz-im-Leben* of a particular oral form is quite difficult.[43] Moreover, the problem of dealing with oral tradition is compounded by the fact that "oral literature exists only in the act of performance."[44] A. B. Lord has concluded from empirical studies of oral Yugoslavian narrative poetry that, while certain formulas, rhetorical devices and thematic groupings are traditionally standard for each oral piece, the compositional organization of the oral "text" is dependent upon the actual performance itself.[45] The dynamics of performance are such that they involve the complex interaction of three variables: the performer, the audience and the occasion.[46] Each of these variables is affected by a number of sociological and cultural concerns, to the extent that each performance involves a *re-creation* of the material.[47]

Lord's findings have certain ramifications for the form and tradition-critical understanding of the transmission of the tradition. On account of the mutability in each act of performance, there is no normative text to which subsequent orally transmitted material is to be compared. The composition of oral tradition is contingent upon the circumstances of its performance. According to Lord:

> It follows, then, that we cannot correctly speak of a 'variant' since there is no 'original' to be varied! Yet songs are related to one another in varying degrees; not, however, in the relationship of variant to the original, in spite of the recourse so often made to an erroneous concept of 'oral transmission'; for 'oral transmission,' 'oral composition,' 'oral creation,' and 'oral performance' are all one and the same thing. Our greatest error is to attempt to make 'scientifically' rigid a phenomenon that is fluid.[48]

The problem arising in form criticism is that it has imposed a literary model of the transmission of written material onto the oral process of the transmission of tradition.

It has taken the distinguishing feature of the written stage, i.e. a fixed text,[49] and applied it to a fluid one. In other words, it has used the concept of an *Urtext*, a typical form which reflects a typical life situation, to describe a phenomenon that is all but typical.

The difficulty in tradition criticism regarding transmission is similar. The insistence of Nyberg, Birkeland and Engnell on the reliability of the oral transmission process for faithfully preserving the tradition down through the centuries has been modified by Mowinckel, Culley, Knight and others.[50] The tendency now, however, is to perceive "phases" in the oral tradition process, in which one distinguishes an oral stage of formation and composition, on one hand, and an oral period of transmitting traditions already fixed, on the other.[51] Such a distinction does not fully reckon with the performance factor in any oral operation.[52] Every act of performance recreates the tradition. This tradition is continually variable.

The performance component intrinsic to the oral stage also raises another problem for both form and tradition criticism. Because by definition oral tradition cannot be examined in isolation from its performance, the question must be asked whether conclusions regarding oral tradition can be made on the basis of written texts. For ancient Semitic cultures all we have are written texts. The premise of scholars, hitherto, has been that there is no formal or functional difference between the oral and written stages. However, without its performance a study of oral tradition is exceedingly difficult simply on written evidence. Indeed, Knight states that:

> The obvious consequence of Lord's thesis is that traditio-historical research becomes basically invalid. How can one reconstruct the history of a tradition if the recording stage itself becomes an impenetrable barrier?[53]

Scholarship which has focused primarily on the preliterary stage of the tradition is replete with ambiguous vocabulary which misrepresents the relationship between the oral and written material. We are asked to get "behind" the text,[54] to seek "below the surface level"[55] to encounter this stage of the material. The oral and written stages of the tradition, however, are two completely different phenomena. Each operates according to its own peculiar laws of composition. Thus, Kelber states:

> The circumstances of performance, the composition, and the transmission of oral versus written materials are sufficiently distinct so as to postulate separate hermeneutics.[56]

With respect to the Book of Hosea, it becomes crucial, therefore, to understand properly the dynamics of the written text, since this is the only evidence for Hosean traditions. We do not mean to deny the existence of an oral stage of the material. Nevertheless, we think that access to the oral stage is highly problematic. It is mediated by a literary text which must be appreciated first for its own sake and according to its own principles of composition. We shall now examine the written literary stage more thoroughly.

B. The Nature of the Tradition at the Written Stage

Roger Lapointe has described the transition from the oral to the written stage as "a passage probably as important as the passage through the Sea of Reeds."[57]   As we have seen, however, the separation between these two has been blurred in most scholarship on Hosea.

The radical difference between the oral and written stages has been demonstrated empirically by Lord. Lord observed that when a singer was asked to repeat the words of a song in order that it could be transcribed, the singer found this experience very trying. Factors, such as the actual singing itself, the interaction with the audience and the particular live situation, were not present as in his previous performances. The singer could relate only to his scribe in such an artificial situation. He had to stop continuously for his scribe in this process of dictation. The usual dynamics of creating and delivering his oral work for a particular occasion were thus interrupted.[58]

Moreover, the written text which was produced under these conditions never exactly reproduced the oral text. Lord found that during the dictation process, the singer frequently reverted from poetry into prose. Breaks in the rhythmic structure of an oral text occurred when the usual tempo of the production is slowed down and the singer becomes disoriented by the transcription proceedings.[59]

Once a song was finally put into writing, however laboriously, a *fixed* text was unintentionally established. In the literate world this text became "the song" to which all other oral editions of the same song were compared. This fixation of the material, this stability, "was to become the difference between the oral way of thought and the written way."[60]

Like the oral stage, the written stage has its own idiosyncrasies. Studies in linguistics have determined that the written stage is radically distinct from the oral on all structural levels, viz. phonology, morphology, syntax, vocabulary, and style.[61] In its intrinsically fixed and portable nature, the written makes information more easily and widely circulated. The broader audience addressed, i.e. the reader, now assumes an entirely different relationship to literary media than a speaker/hearer relationship. In an oral situation, the dynamics are such that a dialogue can occur between the speaker and hearer instantaneously. A particular point may be debated, clarified, reinterpreted or modified during the course of the performance itself.

However, this immediate dialogical process does not happen at the written level. The original author may even have been dead for some time and the text socially and culturally removed from its provenance by the time the reader encounters it. Thus, the text can assume both a spatial and temporal existence apart from its originator. A reader can now pause over a particular passage, refer to previous statements and check the cogency of the argument. S/he can read the material at her/his own pace, not bounded by the constrictions of performance.

V. *The Redactional Selection of Traditional Material for the Larger Literary Framework*

We have tried to show in the foregoing that one cannot simply assume that the written text exactly reproduces the oral stage. Moreover, we questioned whether the precise nature of the oral stage can be inferred from the present stage of the text. We can now turn our attention to the second issue regarding the denigration of the written for the oral: the selection of traditional material by the redactor for insertion into the larger literary framework.

While Lord's work is based on data which is temporally, thematically, and geographically removed from our material, his conclusions still qualify by analogy any investigation into oral and written texts.[62] Lord offers empirical evidence that the transition from the oral to the written involves a qualitative leap. The written biblical material cannot now be regarded simply as a recording of the oral stage. Because the biblical traditions exist in their present state as *literary* texts, the journey back to a *preliterary* state is accomplished only by means of a hypothetical reconstruction. These texts were written in the remote past. Since there are no tape recordings of the ANE oral stage, it would follow, then, that any theory of the preliterary stage on the basis of these texts, whether it be of the prophetic experience under which the oracles were uttered, their historical referent or their later oral transmission, would be empirically unproveable. This is not to say that investigations into these areas are illegitimate. It is to say, however, that because theories of the preliterary stage would be empirically unproveable, they should not dictate method in the exegesis of *written* texts.[63] Since the written text in its completed form is the one immediately before us, it should constitute the point of departure for any analysis.

If we must now speak of a written literary text, we should attend to it according to the laws of *written* composition. We should now speak in terms of *authors*. A literary work in its completed form is not the sedimentation of the oral stage of tradition. Rather, it is the systematic effort of a particular individual. In learned biblical parlance, this individual is designated the "redactor." However, the particular role of this anonymous person was considered to be relatively minor. He was regarded simply as a gatherer and arranger of already fixed traditions. He was not an author with all the creativity which that word implies. In his joining of the material, he created nothing essentially new.[64]

From a literary perspective, however, much more weight should be given to this final redactor as both an artist and an author. In the first place, any form or tradition in the text is contingent upon the manner in which the final redactor understood and chose this material. This material is not simply a collection of traditions. Rather, it belongs to the work as *selected* traditions.[65] Something would not even appear in the book unless the redactor thought it important enough to be retained. Certain religio-political motivations had prompted the author in his choice of a tradition. Each selection had some particular relevance for the overall design of his work. In some way, the tradition supported (or contradicted), harmonized with (or opposed) the theological intent of the final redactor. For that reason, he considered it necessary to include it in his publication. The redactor was not neutral towards his sources; he was not indifferent. Whatever he picked was a deliberate choice. One should presume intentionality on his part.

In the second place, the final redactor is responsible for the governing structure of the work, its framework. This framework gives the material its unity. Into this unifying structure, the redactor inserts and arranges his selected material. He has divorced it from its former setting and given it a totally new context, a literary context. Whatever *Sitz-im-Leben* a tradition may have had at the preliterary stage, it is once, twice, or even three times removed from it. It now has a fundamentally new setting in the literary work. According to Güttgemanns:

> From a purely superficial standpoint, it may appear that hardly anything has been changed in a pericope, e.g. stylistically and with respect to a reasonable consistency of words. However, because of the bare fact of its "framework,"

of its insertion from a "preliterary level" to a larger "literary connection" with its own laws, it is subject to a change in structural and functional respects. In certain circumstances, this change can lead to a radical reinterpretation of its original meaning...*The "framework" of the earlier pericopes necessitates a structural and functional alteration.* Insofar as the *history* of the form is concerned, this framework has consequences which cannot be overlooked.[66]

This means, then, that any traditional material should be examined first for its intentional function within the larger literary framework. This framework becomes the hermeneutical principle for the interpretation of any tradition in the book.[67] Any unit perceived in the text should now be scrutinized according to its positioning with other units of tradition, the redactional commentary on it, and its contribution to the meaning of the whole. A unit derives its primary sense, not from its prior status at the preliterary stage, but in its standing in the book.

Finally, a redactor is an author in his own right. He uses traditional material to create his own literary achievement. One perceives this immediately in the structure of the work itself. In this respect, Güttgemanns' discussion of the *gestalt theory* is excellent.[68] Most simply put, the gestalt theory holds that an object is more than a development from or even the sum of its parts. The collection and juxtaposition of particular elements create a unified complex that is independent in form and function from the nature of its parts. So, for example, a table is not simply a collection of wood and nails but an entirely new object with specific functions. A different juxtaposition of the same wood and nails can become a chair with an equally distinct form and function. Despite the heterogeneity of the composite elements, the total effect of the interrelated parts constitutes a *gestaltist unity.*

> This unit ... is the opposite of a summation, since, as a whole, precisely as a 'gestalt', it causes the individual 'components' or 'traits' to appear in *a correlation that alters the 'components' qualitatively.* (Güttgemanns, *Offene Fragen*, 185. Italics his. Translation mine.)

In gestaltist terms, then, a redactor's selection, insertion and expansion of the material - his moulding of the tradition - would be guided by the particular literary "gestalt" which he ultimately intends to create. A literary work, therefore, is not just an aggregate of smaller units of tradition. Nor can the meaning of the total work be dependent on the meaning of its isolated units. The meaning of a literary piece is derived from the dialectic interaction among the complexes of tradition and redactional commentary: *its gestaltist unity*. In the end, the redactor creates a new tradition out of the old. He thus is an author to be reckoned with.

VI. *Summary*

We would now like to summarize the results of our discussion of the three presuppositions involved in past scholarship on Hosean composition. We have specified the first assumption, "the *original* is the most valuable." The term, "original", has a different meaning for each of the particular methods involved. It refers to the particular locus of inquiry which is given preeminence over the final written, redacted state of the text. In the case of literary criticism, the "original" consists in the *ipsissima verba* of the prophet. It is the gold nugget which must be mined in the text, the kernel which must be separated from its husk. In form criticism, the "original" is applied to the "original form" or "original *Sitz-im-Leben*" of this form. In Willi-Plein's redaction-critical study, the final stages of the composition are ostensibly the focus of attention. However, as we have seen, form-critical assumptions that the book is composed of original sayings units that were later redacted underlie her treatment of the book.

In the case of rhetorical criticism as is represented by Andersen and Freedman, this presupposition is given a different slant. These scholars presume the final literary text as the authentic literary composition of the prophet himself. Questions of literary history are of little concern to these scholars. To the detriment of the text's literary history, they implicitly presume the present state as "original" whose value now lies in its allegedly sophisticated literary artistry. They sometimes propose a stylistic/artistic explanation for tensions in the text which could be better explained by redactional reasons.

In all these methods, an investigation of the literary composition of the book becomes skewed on account of this presupposition. Either the methodological focal point is concentrated on the stages that lie behind the final text (literary and form), informed by these notions (redaction), or concentrated on the final stage with little or no regard to the text's literary pre-history (rhetorical).

The second presupposition regarded the oral or preliterary stage as the proper focus of research for interpreting the prophetic literature. Literary, form, redaction and tradition criticism all presume an oral stage of the tradition. The oral stage for literary criticism was principally the time of the oral pronouncements themselves. These pronouncements, transcribed by the prophet himself or by his disciples, ostensibly reflected the prophet's ecstatic state. As such, they were considered brief, independent statements addressed on a particular occasion.

The initial oral stage of prophetic pronouncements was also assumed by form criticism. However, form criticism supposed a longer stage of oral history as the pronouncements circulated in various *Sitze-im-Leben*. In this process of oral transmission, the pronouncements attained a certain formal stability as well as an adaptability to the particular life situations. The final stages of the tradition were considered to be its redaction history. During this time, the fixed oral traditions were joined together and put into written form. This written stage was, in the opinion of the form and redaction critics, a crystallization of the oral.

Tradition criticism's understanding of the oral stage was similar to the form-critical understanding, but with some modifications. Like form criticism, tradition criticism presumed a long, creative period of oral history which ended in the fixation of the tradition in writing. However, for the tradition critics the *ipsissima verba* of the prophet, the actual oral pronouncements themselves, were indistinguishable from

the oral transmission of the tradents of the tradition.
Moreover, the concern here was a growing stability and
adaptability of *tradition* rather than of *form*.

Presupposition Three was a corollary of Presupposition
Two. According to Presupposition Three, there was no
qualitative difference between the oral stage and the written
stage. In reaction to the equation of the oral and written
stages (with the implicit subordination of the latter to the
former), we argued that the two stages of composition were
radically different in form and function. The distinguishing
feature of the oral stage was its performance factor. The most
significant trait of the written stage was its fixity. The
diametrically opposed idiosyncrasies, fluidity and fixity,
characterizing the respective stages should now be fully
reckoned with. On this account, we maintained that
retrieving an oral stage of the tradition was fraught with
difficulties.

Furthermore, we argued that, since the tradition is only
available in written texts, we should treat the work according
to the laws of written composition. To that extent we should
now deal with an authorial personality. In his unique
collection, arrangement and commentary on the tradition, he
has *composed* a literary work. The particular
interconnections among the redactionally created complexes
of tradition and redactional commentary embody a *gestaltist
unity*. In this unity the work becomes a totally new tradition.
Any earlier tradition in the book would be seen, as it were,
through the final redactor's eyes.

VII.   *The Methodological Task: A Redaction-Critical
        Examination*

In view of the above discussion, it is apparent to us that
the question of the composition of the Book of Hosea is still an
open one. As we have seen, the traditional methods have
skewed their analyses of the book's composition by focusing on
the preliterary levels of the text. Because of the literary
nature of the material, any reconstructions of this level were
necessarily hypothetical. Moreover, they themselves were

built upon questionable presuppositions. The results of these investigations were thus quite frail with respect to the actual composition of the work. A new approach to the composition of the work is needed which takes seriously the "literary" nature of the text as we presently have it.

We offer such an approach in this study. The method which informs our analysis is redaction criticism. However, it is not a redaction criticism as has been traditionally practiced, i.e. the *final* stage of the exegetical endeavor. On the basis of the foregoing discussion, we maintain that with the Book of Hosea it should be the *first analytical step* in understanding the book's formation. Only in this way would one obtain a more holistic grasp of the book and still deal with its obvious literary history.

Although most scholars consider redaction criticism as the last investigation of the book's composition, there are differences in scholarly descriptions of the book's redaction.[69] For example, the tradition history critics, in general, and scholars, such as Buss and Willi-Plein on Hosea in particular, perceive the redaction involved in the book's formation as *collection.* The redactors functioned primarily as collectors of sources and traditions. They joined the material by various techniques, such as catchwords, chronological or thematic arrangements, etc. While observing that the redactor's main task was collecting and joining, these scholars differ on the extent to which the redactor expanded and reworked the tradition. For instance, Willi-Plein allows for more extensive editorial activity in the composition of the book.

Another approach is to view the redaction of the book with respect to the historical situation of the particular redactor.[70] This approach is evident in H.W. Wolff and those who adopt his literary theory. These scholars would identify the various redactional insertions according to their early Judean, later Judean, or exilic stages. Such redaction would be limited to certain interpretive and supplementary glosses which would indicate a particular time and place in history.

Related to this second approach but much broader in scope is that typical of most of the literary critics (cf. Marti, Harper, Peiser, Budde, Wolfe). Here redactional strata are identified, not only by history, but also by certain theological concerns of the redactor. Thus, not only are there Judean and exilic editors but also those characterized by messianistic, eschatological and cultic concerns. Larger blocks of material, such as the oracles of salvation, would be attributed to this later editorial activity.

All of these approaches to the redactional formation of the book have merit in pointing out that the text as we have it is a product of a literary development. However, as we have also demonstrated, these approaches have been skewed by allowing theories of the formative *preliterary* stage to dictate methodological procedures regarding a *literary* text. Redaction criticism, as we perceive it, should begin with the final redacted state. As such, our investigation will treat the literary composition of the final redactor first. Whereas previous studies view the book's formation as an aggregate of smaller units with layers of redactional accretions, we choose to see the final redacted state as the work of an author, the final redactor who used literary traditions attributed to Hosea.

Because of this focus on the composition of the final redactor, redaction criticism could quite conceivably be called "composition criticism."[71] As we have shown, the redactor's selection of the tradition, arrangement and reinterpretation of older material in a new literary framework had resulted in a new literary work.[72] However, we have elected to call our investigation of the text a *redaction-critical* analysis. It would refer to a wider spectrum of editorial activity observable in the text, from interpretative glosses to actual new compositions.[73]

Our method, then, reverses the usual practices which concentrate on the earliest form of the material and then move to the latest. It opts, rather, to investigate the latest and then proceed to what would be earlier. When one has determined the literary gestalt of the final composer and the structure which he has imposed upon the work, when one has ascertained his religio-political thrust in the selection and arrangement of his material, one then has a more secure foundation to deal with the question of older traditions in the text. In his remarks on methods dealing with the prophets, Schottroff makes this comment:

> Only when the redactional contribution to a given text-complex has been clarified, may one ask about the individual traditions which are assimilated into it and their origin. Such a reversal of the current procedure of methods would accommodate itself to the real state of affairs: that the prophetic traditions are, indeed, not accessible to us as individual words guaranteed in their authenticity, but are mediated by redaction, which assimilates the traditions, in the prophetic books which lie before us. These are formed in a definite way redactionally.[74]

We have two main criteria for determining the extent of the final redaction. The first is the presence of *aporiae* or difficulties in the text. Such difficulties may include sudden changes in person and number, repetitions, expansions, or inconsistencies in thought. Other problems are observable in the juxtaposition of contradictory themes, such as oracles of hope next to judgments and condemnations. Furthermore, the presence of later theological ideas or perspectives, such as those that presuppose the exile, can indicate a redactional hand.

Although the mere presence of isolated *aporiae* would not automatically prove extensive later editing, we will see that these *aporiae* tend to group themselves in recurring patterns. For example, some *aporiae* take the form of later mitigations or reversals of condemnations. Others feature a systematic commentary based on certain themes, such as a condemnation of idolatry, exhortation to repentance, or hope for restoration in the land. We will note each of these difficulties contextually: Do they interrupt the present flow of the passage? Are they repetitious? Do they conflict stylistically or theologically with the surrounding verses? The cumulative patterns in which these *aporiae* cluster suggest that the Book of Hosea as we presently have it is the product of a development involving more than one literary stage.

Scholars have explained these disparities in the text variously, e.g. emotional upheavals in the prophet's domestic life,[75] or to the fact that the book is a type of rough draft,[76] or more commonly, as textual corruption in the transmission of the text from its migration to Judah from the North after its fall to the Assyrians. Although we do not rule out such explanations, we think that a more promising explanation of the tensions in the book's composition is that they reflect redactional commentary on the tradition. The text, as we shall see, is composed of *alternating tradition* and *redactional commentary*.

Because we would regard many of the problems in the text as resulting from later commentary on earlier tradition, we have assumed for the sake of argument the reliability of the Masoretic text. We are aware of text-critical analyses that try to solve some of the apparent problems of the text of Hosea, such as Nyberg's *Studien zum Hoseabuch*.[77] However, since our work offers possible solutions for these difficulties from a redaction-critical point of view, we have kept textual emendations based on other ancient versions to a minimum.

The second criterion for determining the extent of the final redaction is the analysis of its *structure*. We have already discussed the strategic importance of the final literary structure above. This structure, as we will see shortly in our investigation of the final redacted state of Hos 1-3, gives its own clues to the internal thrust of the final redaction. It is within this overarching framework that the final redactor articulates the literary purpose of the work. Early tradition is refracted through the literary prism which is the final structure of the redactor's commentary.

Our redaction-critical method has its limits. We are concerned principally with the final redaction of the book: how the final redactor shaped the tradition for his own intents and purposes. Hence, most of our discussion focuses on the work of this redactor. We have, however, given our suggestions as to the literary and theological thrust of the earlier stages of the tradition. We attempt to show in each case how the later stages transformed the earlier stage with their own editorical commentary. We try to demonstrate how the tradition was reactualized through its successive editions until it reaches its final edition in the last redactor's hands.

CHAPTER THREE

The Composition of Hos 1-3: Final Redacted State

I. Introduction to the Macrostructure: Hos 1-3, 4-11, 12-14

While scholars differ in their understanding of the book's smaller structural units, they agree almost unanimously that its macrostructure is divided between Hos 1-3 and 4-14. Wolff would modify this structure by his divisions of the book into Hos 1-3, 4-11, and 12-14.[1] The only exception to the Hos 1-3 and 4-14 partition is Ewald who divides the book into Hos 1-2 and 3-14. For Ewald, these two sections are each composed of a narrative sign (Hos 1 and Hos 3) followed by discourse (Hos 2 and Hos 4-14).[2]

Anticipating our results, we find a three part structure in the Book of Hosea, which follows Wolff's divisions: Hos 1-3, 4-11, 12-14. This tripartite structure results from the work of the final redactor of the tradition; it is the literary gestalt which he imposes upon his tradition. The final redactor creates this structure by inserting his own blocks of composition which concludes each of the three sections: Hos 3, Hos 11 and Hos 14. Each division of the book is characterized by a particular motif which represents for the final redactor the covenantal relationship between God and Israel. In Hos 1-3, the final redactor focuses upon the marriage motif that describes this relationship. In Hos 4-11, the youth/Israel metaphor is at the forefront. Finally, in Hos 12-14 the final redactor returns to the marriage motif to portray the covenant between God and Israel.

For the sake of organization and manageability, we will begin our examination by treating the shorter but very significant section of the book, Hos 1-3. In this chapter, we will deal with the final redaction of Hos 1-3. We will demonstrate that the final redactor is responsible for the first section of the book. Having determined the nature and thrust of the final redaction, we will treat the earlier stages of the Hos 1-3 tradition in Chapter Four. In Chapter Five we will summarize our results of the literary history and composition of Hos 1-3.

On the basis of these results, we will investigate in Chapter Six how the final redactor creates the Hos 4-11 and 12-14 structure. We will then explore the compositional relationship of Hos 1-3 to the Hos 4-11 and 12-14 structure to determine the final redactor's literary gestalt.

II. Theories Regarding Hos 1-3: The Story of Hosea's Marriage

A. The Disparity between Hos 1-3 and 4-14

At first glance, the most striking features of Hos 1-3 vis-à-vis Hos 4-14 are its contents and organization. Chapters 1 and 3 depict accounts of Hosea's marriage to an unfaithful wife. These two chapters frame a similar conjugal portrayal of the relationship between YHWH and Israel in Hos 2. On the basis of contents and a perceptible logical coherence, scholars have questioned whether the unit, Hos 1-3, belongs to Hos 4-14 where this marital imagery and a recognizable principle of organization are not so obviously present.

To explain the conspicuous differences between Hos 1-3 and 4-14, several suggestions have been offered. The disparity can be explained by attributing the sections to two different authors. Kaufmann, for example, by analogy to the composition of Isaiah, has designated the two authors, First Hosea and Second Hosea.[3] The differences, however, can just as well be accounted for by positing just one author. He could, as Kraeling suggests, have composed his work at two different times.[4] Or, as G. L. Robinson maintains, the prophet had different purposes for each of the two divisions. Hos 1-3 focuses on the messenger; it is Hosea's own spiritual autobiography. Hos 4-14 relates his message. It is a series of the prophet's homilies of warning and promise. It has no systematic regularity because, according to Robinson, Hosea's theology is of the heart rather than of the head.[5]

B. The Disparity within Hos 1-3 Itself

Exegetes have pointed out four disparities within Hos 1-3 itself which give rise to different theories of its composition.

There are, first of all, formal dissimilarities. Hos 1 and 3 are both narratives, whereas Hos 2 is a poetic oracle of YHWH.[6] Moreover, these chapters are thematically different. Hos 1 and 3 deal with Hosea's marriage with Gomer. Hos 2, on the other hand, portrays YHWH's marriage with Israel.

Related to the thematic disparity, a third difference in all three chapters is a rhetorical one. Threats of punishment (Hos 1:2-9; 2:4-15) are juxtaposed with promises of salvation (2:1-3, 16-25). The full force of the threat is therefore mitigated by passages of hope. For some scholars, it is quite inconceivable that Hosea would have preached two different messages on the same occasion and so blunt the impact of his own words.[7]

The fourth disparity is the historical incongruities in the accounts of Hosea's marriage (Hos 1 and 3). Do they form a consecutive narrative of Hosea's domestic problems? Or, are they simply parallel accounts? Was Gomer really a prostitute--temple, conventional, or otherwise? Was she simply an unfaithful wife? Is she the same woman in Hos 3 or was Hosea bidden to take another wife? Was Hosea's own bitter marital tragedy the basis for his insight into the covenantal relationship between God and the people? Much of the secondary literature on Hos 1-3 is devoted to the historical difficulties which these chapters present.[8]

The four difficulties within Hos 1-3 have resulted in six theories which attempt to solve them.

1. The differences are due to composition during different periods of Hosea's life. The hope passages were written at a later stage of the prophet's marital experience when hope and reconciliation were possible.[9]

2. The difficulties are due to scribal error or scribal reinterpretation.[10]

3. For some scholars, the disparities are the result of a long process of oral transmission.[11]

4. Other scholars think that the inconsistencies in Hos 1-3 can be explained by distinguishing between the work of

Hosea and that of one of his disciples. The autobiographical first person narrative, Hos 3, indicates the work of Hosea himself. On the other hand, its biographical third person counterpart, Hos 1, is to be attributed to one of his disciples who knew the intimate details of his marital life. The compilation of Hosean oracles, Hos 2, is also the work of this disciple.[12]

5. A large number of scholars, however, view certain passages in Hos 1-3, such as 2:1-3, 3:1-5, 2:16-25, as much later than either Hosea or a disciple. They consider these units as secondary insertions by exilic or even post-exilic redactors.[13] Opinions regarding the actual shaping of these chapters by later redactors vary. T. H. Robinson, for example, thinks that the redactor had two finished collections of sayings at hand, Hos 2 and Hos 4-14.[14] Budde, on the other hand, holds the view that Hos 2 was a post-exilic insertion between a consecutive narrative found in Hos 1 and 3.[15]

6. Finally, the most recent commentators on Hos 1-3 concentrate on the structural unity or coherence in these chapters rather than their disparities. They prefer a synchronic rather than a diachronic approach to this material. While Hos 2 has been the chief focus of the synchronic investigations,[16] Vogels has recently attempted such an analysis on all three chapters.[17]

III. The Final Redacted State of Hos 1-3

The synchronic analyses of Hos 1-3, described in #6 above, have demonstrated that these chapters form a structurally self-contained and artistically constructed unit. Past studies, however, have highlighted the text's unmistakable internal contradictions and dissonances. In light of this unity and diversity, a unilateral investigation of one or the other does not do justice to the composition. Exegesis of these chapters must reckon with the homogeneity as well as the heterogeneity within this story of Hosea's marriage.[18]

We have argued in the previous chapter that the final redactor is the one responsible for the work's overall unity. We will now discuss the redactional framework of Hos 1-3 in order to discern the final thrust of the material. After examining the final redaction, we will then treat the redactor's received material which gives evidence of the contrapuntal voices in the text. In order to facilitate our discussion, we present in the following chart our understanding of the editorial history of Hos 1-3. In this chapter, we will concentrate on the verses in the far right column, which we attribute to the final redactor, R2. In Chapter Four, we will discuss the earlier stages: Hosea (H), the collector (C), and the first redactor (R1).

H	C	R1	R2
			1:1
	1:2-4		1:5
	1:6abA		1:6bB-7
	1:8-9		2:1-3
2:4aA	2:4aB		
2:4b-5	2:6-7a		
2:7b			2:8-9
		2:10a	2:10b
		2:11	
2:12		2:13-15a	2:15b-18aA
	2:18aBb		2:19-20
	2:21-22a		2:22b-25
			3:1-5

A. Hos 1:1 - The Redactional Beginning of the Unit

The story of Hosea's marriage, and indeed the whole book itself, begins with the statement:

> "The word of the Lord that came to Hosea ben Beeri in the days of Uzziah, Jotham, Ahaz, and Hezekiah, kings of Judah, and in the days of Jeroboam the son of Joash, king of Israel" (Hos 1:1).

This opening in its immediate context is problematic. In the first place, Hos 1:1-2 repeats three times the names of the addresser, YHWH, and the addressee, Hosea:

1:1aA   *děbar-yhwh 'ăšer hāyâ 'el-hôšēaʿ ben-bĕʾērî*
         "The word of YHWH which came to Hosea ben Beeri"

1:2a   *tĕḥillat dibber-yhwh bĕhôšēaʿ*
         "The beginning of YHWH's speaking through Hosea"

1:2b   *wayyōʾmer yhwh 'el-hôšēaʿ*
         "And YHWH said to Hosea"

In the second place, the order of Hos 1:1 gives priority to the southern kings. Scholars argue that if Hosea were a northern prophet, it would not be likely that he would have dated his work by the reigns of the Judean rulers.[19] Moreover, the reigns of the Southern kings together exceed the reign of the northern monarch, Jeroboam II. Why is Jeroboam II the only king mentioned from the North? Or, to put it another way, why are the other Israelite kings, viz. Zechariah, Shallum, Menahem, Pekahiah, Pekah and Hoshea who were all contemporaries of the Judean kings listed in 1:1, overlooked?

Because of these problems, the majority of scholars have assigned Hos 1:1 to later redaction.[20] The two introductions, 1:aA and 1:2a contain a description of the nature of the revelation, *dbr*.[21] *Dbr*, however, is pointed differently in each case. It appears in 1:1aA as a noun as in other prophetic superscriptions (Mic 1:1, Jl 1:1, Zeph 1:1). This fact, coupled with the repetition of the addresser and addressee, seems to indicate a secondary character. The final redactor had prefixed his own heading to the material which he had received. This material was already entitled: *tĕḥillat dibber-yhwh bĕhôšēaʿ*.[22] Following this title, the oracle begins with 1:2b. The final redactor had made his own editorial comment without seemingly changing a word of the tradition itself.

The nature of this redaction can also be more precisely defined. The emphasis on the Judean kings points to a Judean provenance. Phraseology and formal structure in common with other prophetic superscriptions, as well as their similar grammatical detachment from what follows, indicate that Hos 1:1 was part of a joint redaction of the prophetic books.[23] The *terminus a quo* would be determined by information from the superscriptions of the later prophets which are part of this corpus. Hence, this editing probably occurred during the exilic or post-exilic period.[24] Commentators, moreover, have related the phraseology and chronology of these super-scriptions to the concerns of the deuteronomistic editors.[25] We will see other marks of a *deuteronomistic* redaction in Hos 1-3 shortly.

B. Hos 3:1-5 - The Redactional Conclusion to the Unit

The secondary character of Hos 3:1-5 has been a topic of much dispute. Some scholars argue that the first person style indicates an autobiographical composition by the prophet himself.[26] Others, while maintaining the integrity of the whole unit, would regard 3:5[27] or the phrases, "David their king" and "in the latter days" in 3:5 as later redaction.[28] Still others would attribute a larger portion of 3:1-5 to later redaction. Buss, for instance, considers 3:4-5 as secondary.[29] Peiser regards as secondary 3:1aA (to *'ôd*), 3:1b, most of 3:2-3 and 3:4-5.[30] In Schreiner's recent discussion 3:1b, 3b, and 5 are believed to be later.[31] Finally, a large number of scholars consider the whole unit, 3:1-5, an exilic or post-exilic interpretation of Hosea's marriage.[32]

Against those who consider only certain portions of 3:1-5 as secondary, Stinespring makes the astute observation: "Many have failed to see that all five verses of this so-called chapter belong to the same fabric and must stand or fall together."[33] In itself, Hos 3:1-5 is a complete unit. The question is whether this unit is totally original or totally secondary.

First of all the argument that 3:1-5 must be an autobiography or a *memorabile* (Wolff) because of the "I" style has weaknesses. It overlooks the fact that the use of the first person can be a literary/rhetorical device. If we were to take all first person narrations at face value, we would be in a difficult position in maintaining the authenticity of the "I am" sayings in John's gospel and the Isis aretalogies, as well as the animal discourses in Aesop's fables! We will soon see that one of the indicators of our final redactor is a seemingly deliberate change of person from the received material.

Secondly, commentators have already noted that 3:1-5 contains ideas which presume the exile and imminent return.[34] Although Israel must live expatriated, without leadership or cult, she will eventually return to the land (3:4-5). Moreover, 3:1-5 contains deuteronomic terms[35] which argue for a later dating. These include the reunion with Judah under Davidic dominion,[36] the notion of God's love (*'hb*) for his people,[37] the "turning to other gods" and the "latter days."[38]

The secondary character of 3:1-5 can also be made on literary grounds. The unit in its present position presupposes the content of Hos 1-2. In the first place, the *'ôd* "again" in 3:1 implies the previous narrative of YHWH's command to Hosea in Hos 1. There are verbal and structural similarities between the two renditions of Hosea's marriage which suggest that the later rendition (Hos 3) had used the earlier narrative (Hos 1) as a springboard:

1. *wayyō'mer yhwh 'el-hôšēaʿ* (1:2bA)
   wayyō'mer yhwh 'ēlay (3:1aA)
2. *lēk* (1:2bA and 3:aA)
3. *'iššâ* (1:2bA in cs. and 3:1aA)   ⎱ COMMAND
4. *yhwh* (in the subordinate clauses
         1:2bB and 3:1bA)
5. *mē'aḥărê* (1:2bB)
   'ăḥērîm (3:1bC)

Moreover, this divine *command* is followed by an immediate *response* from Hosea in both narratives (Hos 1:3, "he took"; Hos 3:2, "I bought"). While it is true that literary agreements between two units can be probative for a common source or common authorship as well as literary dependence, when one considers the historical and terminological evidence for later dating, the literary agreements between Hos 1 and Hos 3 argue strongly for a secondary dependence of the latter on the former.

In addition, the implied return of the faithless wife to Hosea (3:3)[39] is not found in the Hos 1 account of the marriage. It is, however, foreshadowed in the predicted return of Israel, represented as YHWH's wife, to her first husband (2:8-9). Within the context of Hos 1-2 the marital narrative of Hos 3 is thus more complete.

Other terminological and thematic contacts between Hos 3 and Hos 1-2 are also present. These are found mainly in 1:5, 7, 2:1-3 and 2:16-25, which have long since been considered secondary additions. It will be argued below that these additions originated with our final redactor.

Given the obvious literary contacts between Hos 1 and 3, the dissimilarities between the two become all the more striking. The variations in the Hos 3 narrative betray the final redactor's interpretive procedures. The primary technique for commentary is paronomasia. While paronomasia in its strict sense refers to puns, i.e. the play on similiar *sounding* words,[40] it has come to be a comprehensive term describing a wide variety of plays on words.[41] We will use the term, paronomasia, in this broader sense. The criteria for recognizing the various types of paronomasia will be those outlined by Casanowitz.[42] Whenever a particular wordplay has a technical designation, such as *antanaclasis* or parasonancy, that designation will be employed.[43]

For Hos 3, paronomasia can be seen chiefly in v. 1. The following comparison of Hos 1:2b and 3:1 will provide us with clues regarding the redactor's interpretive techniques:

Received Tradition

1:2b   *wayyō'mer yhwh 'el-hôšēaʿ*
       lēk qaḥ-lĕkā 'ēšet zĕnûnîm
       wĕyaldê zĕnûnîm
       kî-zānōh tizneh hā'āreṣ
       mē'aḥărê yhwh ·

Redactional Commentary

3:1   *wayyō'mer yhwh 'ēlay 'ôd*
       lēk 'ĕhab-'iššâ 'ăhūbat rēa'
       ûmĕnā'āpet
       kĕ'ahăbat yhwh 'et-bĕnê yiśrā'ēl
       wĕhēm pōnîm 'el-'ĕlōhîm 'ăḥērîm
       wĕ'ōhăbê 'ăšîšê 'ănābîm

1:2b   And YHWH said to Hosea,
       "Go, take for yourself a wife of <u>harlotry</u>
       and bear children of <u>harlotry</u>,
       for the land <u>indeed whores</u>
       away from YHWH."

3:1   And YHWH said to me again,
       "Go, <u>love</u> a wife who <u>has been made love to</u>
       by a lover and is an adulteress,
       as YHWH <u>loves</u> the children of Israel and they
       are turning to other gods and <u>loving</u> raisin
       cakes."

One of the most conspicuous differences in the beginnings
of the two accounts is the substitution of *'hb* for *lqḥ*. Hosea is
commanded to "love" (*'hb*) the wife whom he married (*lqḥ*) in
the Hos 1 narrative. The final redactor's exchange of *'hb* for
lqḥ is due primarily to his concern to reinterpret Hosea's
marriage in light of his own deuteronomistic outlook.[44] He
effects this interpretation through a paronomastic twist on the
four instances of the theologically-loaded word, *'hb*. Andersen
and Freedman have noted that the four occurrences of *'hb* in
3:1 correspond stylistically to the four occurrences of *zny* in
1:2.[45] *Zny* is used in 1:2 to describe the harlotry of the wife
and the land. In 3:1 *'hb* characterizes the love of Hosea and
YHWH *as well as* the unfaithfulness of Gomer and the
children of Israel.

The final redactor achieves his wordplay on *'hb* in two
ways. First, he changes *'hb* from the imperative in YHWH's

command to Hosea (*'ĕhab*) to the passive voice to describe the wife (*'ăhūbat*). The play on a word by means of a change in voice is a recognized paronomastic device.[46] Second, the redactor employs the same root for both the command to Hosea and the characterization of the wife. The final redactor, however, intends a quite different meaning of *'hb* for the latter. This repetition of the same word with a different meaning is termed *antanaclasis* by the rhetoricians.[47] On the one hand, the love that characterizes Hosea's love for Gomer and YHWH's love for the Israelites is a covenantal love. The love portrayed between the wife and her paramour and between Israel and her idols, on the other hand, is an adulterous one.[48] With remarkable economy of words by means of voice change and *antanaclasis*, the redactor accentuates the magnitude of YHWH's command to Hosea. He is bidden to love a wife who has been unfaithful, just as YHWH loves the Israelites who have whored after other gods. One term of the *antanaclasis*, then, corresponds to *zny* of Hos 1:2. The other term of the *antanaclasis* is just the opposite of *zny*. The contrast between the marital partners is made quite obvious through this paronomastic command at the very outset.

In addition to the *zny/'hb* correspondence, the language plays in 3:1 on 1:2 continue in 3:1bB. 1:2bB states that "the land whores away from YHWH," *mē'ăḥărê yhwh*. 3:1bB expands 1:2bB by specifying that the Israelites, in whoring away from YHWH, have turned towards other gods, *pōnîm 'el-'ĕlōhîm 'ăḥērîm*. The wordplay is achieved by the simple transposition of consonants, *m'hry/'hrym*.[49] *Mē'ăḥărê* of 1:2bB which qualifies YHWH becomes *'ăḥērîm* in 3:1bB modifying *'ĕlōhîm*.

The unit concludes in 3:4-5 with a wordplay which has been noted already by a number of scholars.[50] These verses parallel Gomer's acquisition, isolation and implied change of heart in 3:3 by describing Israel's own deprivation of leadership and cultic symbols and her own return to the land:

> 3:4   For many days the children of Israel *will live* (*yēšĕbû*) without king or without prince, without sacrifice

and without pillar, without ephod and (without) teraphim.

3:5   Afterwards, the children of Israel *will repent/return (yāšûbû)* and seek YHWH their God and David their king and come trembling to YHWH and his goodness in the latter days.

The wordplay involves the vowel mutations between *yēšĕbû* in 3:4aA and *yāšûbû* in 3:5aA. The meaning effect of this type of paronomasia, technically referred to as *metaphony*, depends on changes in vowel while the consonants remain the same.[51] Thus, for many days the children of Israel will live (*yšbw/yšb*) apart from their political institutions and cultic symbols. This period of privation, however, has as its objective the return (*yšbw/šwb*) of Israel. The play on *yšb/šwb* is emphasized by the repetition of *yāmîm/hayyāmîm*, "days," and *melek/malkām*, "king" in both verses.

Not only in its metaphonic relationship with *yšb* does the redactor exploit the paronomastic peculiarities of *šûb*. *Šûb* itself is a *double entendre*.[52] On one hand, the root may indicate the return from exile. On the other hand, it may signify repentance, the return to God.[53] For the final redactor, then, repentance on the part of Israel and return to the land are two sides of the same coin. The isolation is emphasized by the fivefold *'ên*, "without." It is designed to effect repentance on Israel's part (*šûb*), the turning away from other gods towards YHWH, which will simultaneously bring about the restoration (*šûb*) of Israel in the land.

The final redactor's addition of 3:1-5 effectively marks the conclusion of the first main section of the Book of Hosea, viz. Hos 1-3. Hos 3:1-5 is essentially an interpretive commentary on the tradition found in Hos 1-2. An openendedness discernible in Hos 1-2 finds its resolution, so to speak, in Hos 3. In the first place, the marriage of Hosea to an adulterous wife is given a "happier ending." Hosea is commanded to "love" this wife in spite of her licentiousness. This love bears fruit. In the disciplinary measures which Hosea must impose upon his wife to isolate her from her lovers, the conversion of the wife and her return to husband are achieved.

The 3:1-5 narrative also resolves the analogous marital relationship between YHWH and Israel in Hos 2 on a note of hope. After a similar period of chastisement when Israel shall exist in exile without leadership or cult, she will repent of her unfaithfulness. She will then be restored in the land, have her leaders returned and, ultimately, be reestablished in her covenantal relationship with YHWH.

With the inclusion of 1:1 and 3:1-5, the final redactor sets off the first main section of the Book of Hosea. He begins the whole book with 1:1, a statement of his understanding of the tradition in a particular context of Israelite history. With the addition of 3:1-5, he gathers part of that tradition into a coherent unit. This tradition dealt with the marriage of Hosea to Gomer (Hos 1) and the marriage of YHWH and his people (Hos 2). In positioning his interpretive commentary after Hos 1-2, the redactor in effect segregates the tradition of Hos 1-2 from that of Hos 4-14. He has imposed a completely new structure onto the tradition which was passed to him. We will support this assumption, that the material which the final redactor received and edited originally formed a unified whole, in our discussion in Chapters 6 and 7 of the redactional stages of Hos 4-14 below.[54]

The tradition of Hos 1-2, which was once structurally connected with that of the latter part of the book, now exists in its final state in quite a different relationship to it. With the final redaction, the tradition of Hosea's marriage to Gomer and YHWH's to Israel becomes the interpretive introduction for the larger section of the book. In other words, at a previous level of the book's transmission the marital traditions of Hos 1-2 were consolidated with the traditions of Hos 4-14. Now, however, they are set apart from Hos 4-14 by the final redactor's inclusion of the 3:1-5 unit.

Through this remolding of the tradition, the redactor intended that Hos 1-3 become the hermeneutical "window" through which the rest of the book must be regarded. For the remainder of the book the message of Hos 1-3 is clear: Despite their infidelity, God loves his people with a covenantal love, a marital love. This fact alone should invite the people to repent and return to their God. In its exilic context, it also means the hope of restoration in the land.

C. *The Reversal of the Children's Names*

1. Hos 1:5 - Jezreel

The work of the final redactor is not only found at the beginning and end of Hos 1-3. His interpretive commentary can be detected within the unit itself in the reversal of the names of Hosea's three children. We begin first with Hos 1:5 which has often been regarded as a late redactional insertion into the text.[55] Even those who maintain the Hosean authorship of the verse would still admit that its present position is secondary.[56]

Received Tradition	Redactional Commentary
Hos 1:4	Hos 1:5

Call his name Jezreel,   And it shall happen on
for in a little while   that day that I *shall*
I shall visit the   *break the bow of*
<u>bloodshed of Jezreel</u>   *Israel* in the
upon the house of Jehu,   <u>valley of Jezreel</u>.
and I shall put an end
to the rule of the house of
Israel

Hos 1:5 interrupts the flow of the birth narrative. In each instance of the birth and naming of the child, YHWH issues a command: "Call his/her name X." This injunction is followed by a *kî* clause which interprets the name (1:4b, 6b, 9b). The command + *kî* clause formula is also the format for YHWH's first order to Hosea to take a harlotrous wife (1:2).

The name of Hosea's son, Jezreel, however, is given a second interpretation in 1:5. This interpretation, furthermore, is prefaced by the eschatological formula, *wĕhāyâ bayyôm hahû'* "on that day," and not by *kî*. There are good reasons for attributing the insertion of 1:5 to the final redactor. In the first place, one should see the eschatological perspective introduced by "on that day," in light of the final redactor's statement in 3:5 where the children of Israel will come trembling before YHWH and his good "in the latter days."

In the second place, the paronomasia characteristic of this redactor's interpretive procedures in 3:1-5 is also evident here. In the redactor's received tradition, 1:4bB, the second half of the *kî* clause interpreting the name Jezreel asserts that YHWH will put an end (*wĕhišbattî*) to the rule of the house of Israel. The final redactor plays upon this statement with a parasonantic pun upon *wĕhišbattî*, viz. *wĕšābartî* (1:5b). Parasonancy is a type of alliterative wordplay involving verbal or nominal roots which differ in one of their three consonants.[57] With a subtle twist the final redactor mitigates the finality of *wĕhišbattî mamlĕkût bêt yiśrā'ēl*, "I will put an end to the rule of the house of Israel." He does this by qualifying it parasonantically with *wĕšābartî 'et-qešet yiśrā'ēl*.[58] Instead of terminating the rule of the house of Israel, YHWH will "break the bow of Israel." According to Waldman, "the breaking of the bow" not only signifies the destruction of military power but also the ending of war and the inauguration of peace.[59] This latter interpretation is certainly the sense of the expression in Hos 2:20 for which, as will be argued, the final redactor is also responsible.[60] In 2:20, in the context of a covenant which YHWH will make with the animals "on that day," YHWH says, "I will break (*šbr*) bow, sword, and weapons of war[61] from the land, and will make them lie down in safety." In the setting of the total literary intent of the final redactor, the tempering of the threat of extermination in 1:5 anticipates the redactor's development of the peace theme in 2:20.

Moreover, the 1:5 addition not only serves to mitigate the threat of 1:4. It also reinterprets *dĕmê-yizrĕʻeʼl*, "bloodshed of Jezreel" (1:4bB). The symbolic "bloodshed of Jezreel" now becomes a location, *bĕʻēmeq yizrĕʻeʼl*, "in the valley of Jezreel." The location, "valley of Jezreel," foreshadows the later paronomasia on *yizrĕʻeʼl* in 2:24-25 which speak about YHWH "sowing" (*zrʻ*) Israel in the land.[62]

2. Hos 1:6bB-7 - Lo Ruhama

Received Tradition Hos 1:6abA	Redactional Commentary Hos 1:6bB-7
Call her name Lo Ruhama For I will never again have compassion upon the house of Israel.	I will surely forgive them (i.e. the house of Israel) and upon the house of Judah I will have compassion. And I will save them by YHWH their God. I will not save them by bow, sword, weapons of war, horses or horsemen.

There is even more agreement among scholars on the secondary character of Hos 1:7.[63] The threat implied against the house of Israel in the birth of Hosea's daughter, Lo Ruhama, is reversed for the house of Judah. Resuming *rḥm*, "to have compassion," from 1:6, the final redactor states in 1:7, "Upon the house of Judah I will have compassion (*'ăraḥēm*)." Terminological and thematic coherences again suggest our final redactor. Hos 1:7 shares with 3:5 the deuteronomic title, *YHWH - 'ĕlōhêhem*, "YHWH their God." Moreover, the final redactor resumes the theme of the "breaking of the bow" in 1:5 and develops it further. No longer will there be a dependence on military might. YHWH alone will deliver his people. Like 1:5, 1:7 anticipates 2:20 where, in the context of a newly ratified covenant, the destruction of the weapons of war will inaugurate peace.

The phrase *kî nāśō' 'eśśā' lāhem* in 1:6bB is problematic. Literally, the phrase means, "I will indeed forgive them."[64] The *sôp pāsûq* in the MT ties *kî nāśō' 'eśśā' lāhem* to the interpretation of the daughter's name, Lo Ruhama. In this context, however, "I will indeed forgive them," is incompatible with the preceding statement, "For, I will never again have compassion on the house of Israel." Moreover, the second *kî* clause deviates from the command + *kî* interpretation pattern found in the other YHWH injunctions, 1:2, 4, 9.

Several explanations have been suggested to resolve the difficulty. The BHS proposes the emendation *śānō' 'eśnā'*, "I will surely hate them." Aquila's *epilēsomai autōn* presumes the rendering *naśōh 'āśśâ*, "I will surely forget them." Sellin would insert a *lo'* after the second *kî* to resolve the difficulties: "I will surely *not* forgive them."[65] Kuhnigk, following Dahood, also departs from the MT by interpreting the consonantal text as *kî nāśō' 'uśśā' lāhem*, "I will surely be deceived by them."[66] Wolff regards the second *kî* following a negative as signifying "rather, on the contrary." He thus renders the clause, "Instead, I will withdraw from them."[67] Andersen and Freedman, on the other hand, think that the *kî* must be resumptive or assertive. They argue that the introductory clause, *kî lō' 'ôsîp 'ôd* (1:6bA), governs all four clauses of 1:6b-7, negating them individually and severally. According to their translation, then, YHWH will neither have pity on the house of Israel nor on the house of Judah together.[68]

The emendations do not fully reckon with the tension which 1:6bB displays, which may very well be the result of the final redactor's work. It is consistent with the editorial mitigation of his received material which we have seen so far. If we were to bracket the *sôp pāsûq*, *kî-nāśō' 'eśśā' lāhem* can be connected to 1:7, making good sense literally. Indeed, Duhm and Wolfe have argued that *kî-nāśō' 'eśśā' lāhem* belongs to 1:7 and originates from the same redactor as 1:7.[69] The second *kî* in 1:6bB would then be an asseverative. Furthermore, the *waw* of *wĕ'et-bêt yĕhûdâ* beginning 1:7 would no longer be an adversative, as it is customarily regarded, but a co-ordinative. In reaction to the negativity of his received text, "I will never again have compassion upon the house of Israel" (1:6abA), the redactor announces on YHWH's behalf, "I will surely forgive them" e.g. the northern kingdom of Israel. Furthermore, he states that the southern kingdom, the house of Judah will also be the object of divine compassion (*rḥm*). While his received text originally prophesied the withdrawal of divine compassion from the

North, the redactor reverses this threat against the North by stating that YHWH will surely forgive Israel. He then applies the compassion which YHWH will again extend to the house of Israel to the southern kingdom of Judah as well.

3. Hos 2:1 - Lo Ammi

Although the threats implied in the names Jezreel and Lo Ruhama find their mitigation or reversal in the redactional insertions 1:5 and 1:6bB-7, as it stands in the MT, Hos 1 ends on a negative note with the judgment pronounced over the birth and naming of Hosea's third child, Lo Ammi (1:9). Scholars customarily group the first three verses of the next chapter, Hos 2:1-3, as a self-contained unit.[70] The majority of them concur as to its secondary character.[71] Those who support the Hosean authorship of Hos 2:1-3 would still admit that its present position was the result of a secondary insertion by a later redactor.[72] The note of hope and eschatological fulfillment as well as the reversal of names in 2:1-3 seem to set it in opposition to the negative tone which ends Hos 1 and begins Hos 2:4.[73] Moreover, Hos 2:2 seems to presume the exile and imminent return of the children of Israel and Judah to the land under one head. In this, it echoes the themes we have found in 3:5. Also, the MT does set 2:1-3 apart structurally from Hos 1 as the beginning of Hos 2.

Problems, however, in grouping 2:1-3 as a unit have already been observed.[74] Why does 2:1 mention only the children of Israel, whereas in the following verse, 2:2, the notion of both Israel and Judah is expressed? Why does 2:1 reverse only the name Lo Ammi among Hosea's children, whereas in 2:2-3 all three names are reversed? Why, furthermore, is an imperative introduced in 2:3 which seems to distinguish this verse from the impersonal style of 2:1-2?

These problems are resolved if we regard Hos 2:1 as the reversal of the name of Hosea's third child, Lo Ammi. Indeed, unlike the MT, there is no textual separation between Hos 1:9 and 2:1 in the Qumran Hosea scroll (4QXIId - Hos 1:7-2:5). Rather, 2:1 immediately follows 1:9.[75] It would thus properly belong to Hos 1 rather than Hos 2. Moreover, in the Vulgate's numbering (followed by the RSV) 2:1-2 is included with Hos 1.

One can explain the MT severance of 2:1 from Hos 1 by the fact that, since 2:1 was similar to 2:2-3 in theme and mood, all three verses were naturally taken together as a group. If 2:1 were understood, then, as belonging to Hos 1, all three names of the children would have their own specific qualification or reversal following the threat. The threat attached to the name Jezreel (1:4) is mitigated by 1:5. The withdrawal of compassion from the house of Israel, embodied in the name Lo Ruhama (1:6abA), is counteracted in 1:6bB-7. God will not only forgive the house of Israel but also extend mercy to the house of Judah. The judgment against the house of Israel implied in Hosea's third child, Lo Ammi, in 1:9 finds its mitigation and reversal in 2:1.

As in 1:5, the final redactor achieves the reversal of Lo Ammi in 2:1 by means of a clever paronomasia. Lo Ammi is so called because the judgment against the house of Israel will be "You are not my people (*lō' 'ammî*) and I am not I AM (*lō'-'ehyeh*) to you." The judgment personified in Hosea's third child is the dissolution of the covenant established between YHWH and the people after their flight from Egypt.[76] The background for this text is Ex 3:14-15 where YHWH reveals his name to Moses in another instance of biblical paronomasia. The Tetragrammaton is brought into a paronomastic relationship with the verb, *hāyâ*, "to be, become."[77]

> And God said to Moses, "I AM WHO I AM" (*'ehyeh 'ăšer 'ehyeh*)...Say this to the people of Israel, 'I AM (*'ehyeh*) has sent me to you...YHWH, the God of your fathers, the God of Abraham, the God of Isaac, and the God of Jacob has sent me to you.'" (Ex 3:14-15)

Our final redactor's paronomasia is noticeable in similar wordplays on the divine appellative, *'ehyeh*. It appears first in his opening word in 2:1, *wĕhāyâ*, "and it will happen." The *wĕhāyâ* initiates a statement recalling God's promise to the patriarchs regarding the multitude of their descendants (Gen 15:5; 22:17; 32:13).[78] Thus, by means of the *'ehyeh/wĕhāyâ* wordplay, the final redactor is able to mitigate the severity of "You are not my people and I am not *'Ehyeh* to you," by recalling the patriarchal promise that "the number of the children of Israel shall be like the sand of the sea, which can be neither measured nor numbered."

Having mitigated the judgment of 1:9 by means of the first paronomastic *wĕhāyâ* in 2:1a, the final redactor achieves its complete inversion in 2:1b. We diagram his paronomastic reversal as follows:

1:9bA	*ky 'tm l' 'my*	⎫ Received
1:9bB	*w'nky l'-'hyh lkm*	⎭ Tradition
2:1bA	*whyh bmqwm 'šr-* *y'mr lhm l'-'my 'tm*	⎫ Redactional
2:1bB	*y'mr lhm bny 'l-ḥy*	⎭ Commentary

1:9bA	For <u>you are not my people</u>	⎫ Received
1:9bB	and I am <u>not I AM</u> to you	⎭ Tradition
2:1bA	And it will happen that in the place where it was said to them, "<u>Not My People are you</u>",	⎫
2:1bB	it will be said of them, "Children of the <u>Living God</u>."	⎭ Redactional Commentary

He begins by introducing another paronomastic *wĕhāyâ* in 2:1b: "And it will happen (*wĕhāyâ*) in the place where (*bimqôm 'ăšer*) it is said of them, 'Not my people are you (*lō' 'ammî 'attem*),' it shall be said of them 'children of the living God (*bĕnê 'ēl-ḥāy*)'." In utilizing *bimqôm 'ăšer* and *lō' 'ammî 'attem*, the final redactor alerts the reader to the text, 1:9, the judgment attached to the name of Hosea's third child in: *'attem lō' 'ammî wĕ'ānōkî lō'-'ehyeh lākem*, "you are not my people and I am not I AM to you." The final redactor reverses this text, not by stating, "it shall be said of them 'My people (*'ammî*),'" as one would expect, especially since *'ammî* is used later in 2:3 and 2:25. Rather, his inversion lies in the expression *běnê 'ēl-ḥāy*, "children of the living God."

Běnê 'ēl-ḥāy has puzzled many commentators. The divine title, *'ēl-ḥāy* is rare.[79] On this basis, some would argue that the expression is Hosea's own creation[80] or that it is older than Hosea.[81] We would suggest that *běnê 'ēl-ḥāy* is another case of paronomasia. The final redactor achieves the inversion of his received text by playing upon the second half of the judgment, *wě'ānōkî lō'-'ehyeh lākem* (1:9b). By transposing the *lamed* and *aleph* of *lō'*[82] and by making an alliterative pun on the divine appellative, *'ehyeh*,[83] the redactor produces another divine appellative, *'ēl-ḥāy*. Moreover, by describing God's people as "sons of Israel" (*běnê-yiśrā'ēl*), the redactor refers to the reestablishment of the covenant between YHWH and his people.[84] The final redactor thus makes the reversal of the covenantal dissolution threatened in 1:9 complete.

D. The Story of YHWH and his People: Hos 2:2-3 and Hos 2:25 - The Redactional Prologue and Epilogue

Since 2:1 should be regarded as the redactional reversal of the judgment of 1:9, Hos 2:2-3 would be the proper beginning of the story of YHWH and his people. The story of their "marital" relationship is placed between the two accounts of the story of Hosea's own marriage. Its central position in the final redactor's structure (Hos 1-3) highlights its importance for the first division of the book and, indeed, for the rest of the book itself.

Just as the redactor provided an outer frame for the first division of the book with the insertions 1:1 and 3:1-5, so too has he given the special story of YHWH's marriage with Israel an upper and lower limit. Hos 2:2-3 is the final redactor's prologue to the story of YHWH and his wife, Israel. Hos 2:25 is his epilogue.

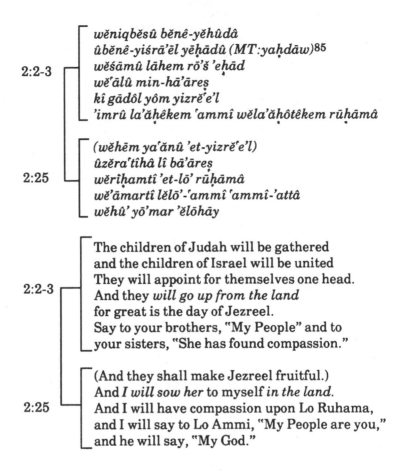

2:2-3

wĕniqbĕsû bĕnê-yĕhûdâ
ûbĕnê-yiśrā'ēl yēḥādû (MT:yaḥdāw)[85]
wĕśāmû lāhem rō'š 'eḥād
wĕ'ālû min-hā'āreṣ
kî gādôl yôm yizrĕ'e'l
'imrû la'ăḥêkem 'ammî wĕla'ăḥôtêkem rūḥāmâ

2:25

(wĕhēm ya'ănû 'et-yizrĕ'e'l)
ûzĕra'tîhâ lî bā'āreṣ
wĕriḥamtî 'et-lō' rūḥāmâ
wĕ'āmartî lĕlō'-'ammî 'ammî-'attâ
wĕhû' yō'mar 'ĕlōhāy

2:2-3

The children of Judah will be gathered
and the children of Israel will be united
They will appoint for themselves one head.
And they *will go up from the land*
for great is the day of Jezreel.
Say to your brothers, "My People" and to
your sisters, "She has found compassion."

2:25

(And they shall make Jezreel fruitful.)
And *I will sow her* to myself *in the land.*
And I will have compassion upon Lo Ruhama,
and I will say to Lo Ammi, "My People are you,"
and he will say, "My God."

Both 2:2-3 and 2:25 contain a paronomasia on Jezreel, as well as a reversal of the two other children of Hosea: Lo Ruhama and Lo Ammi. Moreover, they share common vocabulary, viz. '*rṣ* (2:2aB - *min-hā'āreṣ*; 2:25aA - *bā'āreṣ*) and '*mr* (2:3 - '*imrû*; 2:25b - '*āmartî/yō'mar*). Together, these verses form an inclusio for the story of YHWH's marriage and provide important clues to the final redactor's literary thrust.[86]

Hos 2:2 opens the story with a hope that the children of Israel and the children of Judah will be gathered together.

True to form, the final redactor punctuates this hope by wordplays, the first of which being the parasonancy between *yĕhûdâ* and *yēḥādû*.[87] He fashions 2:2 in a chiasmus:

                    A   B
2:2   *wĕniqbĕṣû bĕnê-yĕhûdâ*

                    B'   A'
           ûbĕnê-yiśrā'ēl yēḥādû

There is a progression implied in this chiasmus: first Judah shall be gathered, then Israel. The two re-formed peoples shall *then* unite by choosing a single leader (*rō'š 'eḥād*) for both, as happened at the first unification under David. We compare this thought with the final redactor's statement in 3:5 that "the children of Israel will seek YHWH their God and David their king" in the latter days. The *yĕhûdâ/yēḥādû* wordplay is continued in *'eḥād*. In keeping with his line of thinking in 1:6bB-7, the final redactor wishes to include Judah with Israel in the history of salvation.

In certain respects, the opening of the story of YHWH's marriage with his people parallels 3:5, the conclusion of the first division of the book. We have already noted the idea of one leader common to 2:2 and 3:5 (*rō'š, melek*). Moreover, just as *šûb* (3:5) frequently means the return from exile, *qbṣ* (2:2) is often used in descriptions of restoration after the exile.[88] One finds the theme of union under a common leader in the exilic texts, Ezek 37:15-19, 21-22, which speak of the gathering (*qbṣ*) of Israel and Judah into one kingdom under one king (*melek*).[89]

When Judah and Israel are gathered together, when they appoint for themselves one head, they shall then, according to our final redactor, *wĕʿālû min-hā'āreṣ*, "go up from the land" (2:2aB). Several suggestions have been put forward to explain this phrase.[90] Two of these, however, are pertinent for our investigation. In the first place, Szabó holds that in tradition *yārad* always denoted going down to Egypt while *ʿālâ* means coming up from Egypt. He thus translates 2:2aB, "they shall go up from the land of exile" or "from the foreign land."[91] This interpretation is buttressed by the fact that the language of 2:2 recalls the exile and the hope of return. In Hos 2:17, the text does state explicitly that Israel will respond "as on the day she came up from the land of Egypt," *'ălōtāh mē'ereṣ miṣrāyim* (cf. Hos 12:14).

In the second place, many scholars point out that *'lh mn-h'rṣ* can also mean "to grow up (like plants) in the land."[92] This interpretation is strongly supported by the fact that Jezreel means "God sows."

'lh mn-h'rṣ in 2:2aB can, therefore, mean a number of things. The multifaceted character of the locution is one that is fully exploited paronomastically by the final redactor. The first hint to the meaning of the expression is provided by the interpretive *kî* clause following it: *kî gādôl yôm yizrĕ'e'l*, "for great is the day of Jezreel." Both Kaatz and Mays have pointed out the alliterative wordplay between *'lh* and the last syllable of *yizrĕ'e'l*.[93] The final redactor paronomastically associates the event of the gathering of Israel and Judah under common leadership and their "going up (*wĕ'ālû*) from the land" with the "great day of Jezreel (*yizrĕ'e'l*)." What the redactor precisely means by this relationship is left pending. He is content simply to allow his received tradition to begin speaking in 2:4. He effects this by a clever patterning of 2:4 by 2:3 which provides a redactional bridge to the tradition.[94] The redactional commentary, 2:3, on the tradition, 2:4, is underlined in the following:

2:3   *'imrû la'ăḥêkem 'ammî wĕla'ăḥôtêkem rūḥāmâ*
2:4   *rîbû bĕ'immĕkem rîbû*

2:3   Say to your brothers, "My people"
          and to your sisters, "She has found
          compassion."
2:4   Plead with your mother, plead...

'ammî and *rūḥāmâ* in 2:3 complete the trio of the now-reversed names of Hosea's children and anchor the verse firmly to the redactor's prologue in 2:2 introducing the story of

YHWH's marriage. However, the imperative *'imrû* beginning 2:3 corresponds stylistically to *rîbû* heading 2:4. The mention of "your brothers" and "your sisters" provides a literary context for the otherwise unnamed addressees implied in "your mother" of 2:4.

Beginning with 2:4, the redactor's received material is primarily in the foreground. The tentativeness in 2:2, the redactor's prologue to the story of YHWH's marriage, regarding the exact meaning of the "great day of Jezreel" finds its resolution only much later in his epilogue to the story, 2:25. This is where the cryptic "day of Jezreel" receives its full explanation. By means of a paronomasia recognized by many on Jezreel in 2:24,[95] the redactor explains that the "day of Jezreel" will be the "day of God's sowing."

The redactor's literary genius is evident in his ability to articulate two levels of meaning by his two paronomasias on the name Jezreel and his *antanaclasis* exploiting the semantic range of *'lh*. The great day of Jezreel is not only the day on which Israel and Judah will go up from the land, *'lh mn-h'rṣ* (2:2). It is also the day when God will sow them in the land, *zr' b'rṣ* (2:25). The redactor's intent can be compared to another exilic text, Jer 31:27:

> "Behold, the days are coming, says the Lord, when I will *sow* (*zr'*) the house of Israel and the house of Judah with the seed of man and the seed of beasts." (Jer 31:27)

From the redactor's exilic point of view, moreover, the people will not only go up from the land of exile (*'lh mn-h'rṣ*). They will also grow up like plants (*'lh*) when they are sown in the land of homecoming (*zr' b'rṣ*). The word *'lh* is open to both levels of interpretation.

The redactor's epilogue to the story of YHWH's marriage, 2:25, ends on the same note as its counterpoint, 2:2-3. This is highlighted in 2:25 by the new names for Jezreel's sister and brother, Ruhama and Ammi, which form a distant chiasmus with Ammi and Ruhama of 2:3. The imperative as well as the designation of brother and sister were used in 2:3 because of the verse's function to provide a redactional transition to the tradition. Now, however, YHWH himself announces his compassion (*rḥm*) over Lo Ruhama. Moreover, the redactor resumes the *'mr* of 2:3 in 2:25: "I will say (*'mr*) to Lo Ammi, "My people (Ammi) are you." Thus liberated, Ammi can also respond, "My God" (*'mr 'ĕlōhāy*). The *'ĕlōhāy* in 2:25 recalls the *bĕnê 'ēl-ḥāy* found in the redactor's reversal of Lo Ammi in 2:2. The epilogue thus closes with the reestablishment of the covenant between YHWH and his people.

The framing prologue and epilogue are the redactional spectacles through which the story of YHWH's marriage is viewed. The final redactor visualizes the marital relationship between YHWH and the people as the renewal of the covenant between them, as well as the return from exile and eventual restoration of the two kingdoms in the land. We have seen this theme through the redactor's eyes before. It appeared in the conclusion to the whole first section of the Book of Hosea, 3:1-5. Here, the redactor articulates the covenantal *'hb*, "love" of YHWH. The united children of Israel will return (*šûb*) to YHWH their God in repentance. This conversion will be the prelude to their return (*šûb*) to the land from exile.

The task remaining is to unveil the final redactor's editing of the tradition of YHWH's marriage with the people in 2:4-24, which he has set within his prologue/epilogue framework. Our next section will demonstrate how the redactor structured his received material in such a way as to link the renewal of covenant with the restoration in the land. In his hands, the story of YHWH's marriage becomes the story of the spiritual journey on which YHWH will lead his people towards conversion.

E. YHWH Leads his People towards Conversion

1. Hos 2:8-9 - The First Step: Barring the Wife's Way to her Lovers

As we have seen in a preceding section, the final redactor has stationed reversals of the tradition at strategic points throughout Hos 1:1--2:1, the story of Hosea's marriage. Here, he has reversed the threats of the three children's names, Jezreel, Lo Ruhama, and Lo Ammi. The same is true also for his treatment of the story of YHWH's marriage, 2:4-24, which he mounts on his 2:2-3, 25 frame. He begins his commentary in 2:4-24 with his insertion, 2:8-9, which describes the first step in the wife/Israel's journey back to YHWH in repentance:

> 2:8 *Therefore, behold, (lākēn hinnēh)*
> I will hedge your way with thorns
> and I will erect a wall against her,
> so that she will not find her paths.
> 2:9 She will pursue her lovers but not overtake them.
> She will *seek (ûbiqšātam)* them but not find them.
> Then, she will say, "I shall go and
> *return (wĕ'āšûbâ)* to my first husband,
> because it was *better (ṭôb)* for me then than it is now."

Commentators have questioned for a long time the position of 2:8-9 in the development of the chapter.[96] First of all, 2:8-9 intrudes with a puzzling shift from third person in 2:7 to second person in 2:8a, "I will hedge *your* way with thorns." Scholars usually resolve the more difficult second person reading by emending the MT in favor of the Gk and Syr which contain a third feminine singular suffix.[97]

Moreover, 2:9b describes the wife's decision to repent and return (*šwb*) to her first husband. She acknowledges that she was better off with her first husband than now. Her repentance in its present position is rather premature in the course of the text. The movement towards repentance clashes with YHWH's resolve to punish his wife for her adultery (2:11-15a). Furthermore, the wife's acknowledgment of the good life with her husband collides with the beginning of 2:10 where YHWH states, "she *did not know* that I gave her grain, wine and oil."

Finally, 2:8-9 seems to interrupt the flow of the oracle between 2:7 and 2:10. In 2:7, the faithless wife states that she will go after her lovers who have given (*ntn*) to her her bread, water, wool, flax, oil and drink. In 2:10, YHWH insists that he has given (*ntn*) her grain, wine and oil. Utilizing the same verb, *ntn*, 2:7 and 2:10 contrast the lovers whom the wife thinks supplies her needs and YHWH who, in fact, provides for her material welfare. The tight connection between 2:7 and 2:10 is thus broken by 2:8-9.[98]

Certain marks indicate our final redactor. The repentance of the wife in 2:9 depends upon the obstruction placed by the husband to separate her from her lovers, described in 2:8. In the isolation from her paramours the wife realizes the beneficence of her husband and decides to return to him. We have observed this strategy to occasion the wife's repentance before from the final redactor's perspective. In 3:4-5 YHWH will isolate the children of Israel for many days. They will then repent/return ($\check{s}wb$) and seek ($bq\check{s}$) YHWH and come trembling before him and his good ($t\hat{o}b$) in the latter days. Hos 2:9 describes the wife's activity with the vocabulary of 3:4-5. Wrongfully, she will seek ($bq\check{s}$) her lovers but will not find them. She will then say, "I will return ($\check{s}wb$) to my first husband because it was better ($t\hat{o}b$) for me than it is now."

Scholars have already observed that in the final text the $l\bar{a}k\bar{e}n$'s introducing 2:8, 11, 16 indicate three moments in YHWH's treatment of Israel: the separation from her lovers (2:8-9), total deprivation (2:11-15), and purification (2:16-17).[99] This three-part movement in the text is due to the redactor's refashioning of his tradition. One of these $l\bar{a}k\bar{e}n$'s was already in the tradition. This $l\bar{a}k\bar{e}n$ begins the judgment in 2:11. To create the journey motif from the tradition, the final redactor inserts a $l\bar{a}k\bar{e}n$ $hinn\bar{e}h$ to introduce his commentary in 2:8-9 and another $l\bar{a}k\bar{e}n$ $hinn\bar{e}h$ to introduce 2:16-17, which we will discuss in the next section. The final redactor is thus able to transform the judgment of 2:11, which begins with $l\bar{a}k\bar{e}n$, into the second stage of a journey in repentance.

The journey of the wife/Israel which the redactor begins to describe in 2:8-9 occurs at two levels. It is the wife's spiritual journey towards conversion. At the same time, it is her physical migration back to the land into which she will ultimately be sown (2:25). The journey starts with the "hedging of *your way* with thorns," 2:8a. By blocking the wife's pursuit of her lovers YHWH initiates her trek back to himself ($\check{s}wb$, 2:9b). The change of suffix to the second person is a hallmark of the redactor's interjection into his received material. We have observed this change of person in the "I" narrative, interpreting the "he" narrative, 1:2-9.[100] We will encounter this switch in person in the final redactor's interpretive commentary in 2:10b, 19-20.[101]

2. Hos 2:16-17: The Final Step: Leading the Wife into the Wilderness

2:16   *Therefore, behold (lākēn hinnēh)*, I will seduce her.
        I will lead her into the wilderness
        and speak to her heart.

2:17   *I will give (wĕnāttatî)* her her vineyards there
        and make the valley of Achor,
        the gateway of hope.
        She will respond (wĕ'ānĕtâ) there as in the days
        of her youth,
        as on the day she came up from the land of Egypt.

Like 2:8-9, the final redactor introduces his next commentary on the tradition in 2:16 with *lākēn hinnēh*.[102] The secondary character of 2:16-17 has already been affirmed by commentators because of the tenor of hope which contrasts these verses with the preceding verses.[103]

Evidence of our final redactor can also be based on other grounds. In the first place, the *lākēn hinnēh* beginning 2:16 continues the journey/*šwb* motif which was inaugurated by his redactional insertion, 2:8-9. After barring the wanton pursuit of her paramours (2:8-9), after despoiling her (2:11-15a), YHWH will then seduce his wife and *lead her into the wilderness* (2:16). Here in the wilderness YHWH will again provide for her. He will give her vineyards and make the valley of Achor, the gateway of hope. Here, too, will Israel respond "as in the days of her youth, as on the day she came up from the land of Egypt (2:17)." In 2:16-17 the author envisages the future return of Israel as a new Exodus, new covenant and new settlement in the land.[104] On one hand, it is the people's return from the land of exile. The *'ălōtāh mē'ereṣ-miṣrāyim*, "she came up from the land of Egypt," echoes the description, *wĕ'ālû min-hā'āreṣ*, "they will go up from the land," found in the redactor's prologue to the story of YHWH's marriage, 2:2.[105] On the other hand, the wilderness to which Israel is led becomes the place where Israel returns in repentance to YHWH. Here in the wilderness of the ancient Mosaic covenant, a covenantal dialogue between Israel and God is reestablished.

In the second place, 2:16-17 contain wordplays which have become the signature of the final redactor. We encounter paronomasia first in 2:16aBb: *wĕhōlaktîhā hammidbār wĕdibbartî ʿal-libbāh*, "I will lead her into the wilderness and speak to her heart." The "Wortspiel" involves the root *dbr* which concludes *hammidbār* and begins the next word, *wĕdibbartî*. Through such a wordplay, the final redactor is able semantically to associate the place where YHWH speaks (*hammidbār*), "the wilderness," with YHWH's speaking, *wĕdibbartî*, "I will speak." The paronomasia is highlighted further by the alliteration of ʿal-libbāh, "to her heart," with *hammidbār wĕdibbartî*.[106]

One can observe another wordplay in 2:17aB: *wĕʾet-ʿēmeq ʿākôr lĕpetaḥ tiqwâ*, "the valley of Achor, the gateway of hope." According to Josh 7:24-26, the "valley of Achor" is so named because Achan (ʿ*kn*) had brought calamity (ʿ*kr*) on the people of Israel in confiscating spoil from Jericho.[107] The final redactor has in mind this paronomastic etymology for his reference to the "valley of Achor" in 2:17.[108] He plays upon the literal sense of the expression as the "valley of trouble" which YHWH will turn into a "gateway of hope" for his wife.[109] The character of the wordplay which transforms the "valley of Achor" into the "gateway of hope" is most likely alliteration which is common to both. The alliteration of the ʿ/ʿ and *q/k* of ʿ*ēmeq ʿākôr* corresponds stylistically to the alliteration of *t/t* and *ḥ/q* of *lĕpetaḥ tiqwâ*.[110]

The parasonantic *jeu de mots* in 2:17 between *wĕnātattî*, "I will give," and *wĕʿānĕtâ*, "she will respond," and *miššām/ šāmmâ*, "there," constitute two more instances of the final redactor's love of paronomasia in 2:16-17. By the skillful manipulation of consonants, the redactor juxtaposes the God who will "give there" (*ntty, mššm*) with the wife who will "respond there" (ʿ*nth, šmmh*). Furthermore, as in 2:16 with *hammidbār wĕdibbartî 'al-libbāh* and in 2:17a with *'ēmeq 'ākôr lĕpetaḥ tiqwâ*, the final redactor punctuates 2:17b by means of alliteration, chiastically arranged:

$$\begin{array}{cccc} A & B & B' & A' \end{array}$$
2:17b   *wĕ'ānĕtâ šammâ kîmê nĕ'ûrêhā*
"And she will respond there
as in the days of her youth."

We point out in A/A' the transposition of the *'ayin/nūn* in *'ānĕtâ* and *nĕ'ûrêhā*. Moreover, we note that in its alliterative connection with *wĕ'ānĕtâ* (A), *kîmê nĕ'ûrêhā* (A'), "as in the days of her youth," differs from the similar expression found in the redactor's received tradition in 2:5aB, viz. *kĕyôm hiwwālĕdāh*, "as on the day of her birth," precisely in this paronomasia. The alliteration of 2:17bA is continued in 2:17bB: *ûkĕyôm 'ălōtāh mĕ'ereṣ-miṣrāyim*, "as on the day she came up from the land of Egypt."

The verb *'nh* which describes Israel's response in the wilderness to YHWH's overtures of love (2:17b) refers to the covenantal response at Sinai. The exodus-wilderness language of 2:16-17 recalls this covenant which was made "in the days of her youth," which is described thus in Ex 19:5-6, 8:

> "If you keep my covenant, you shall be my treasured possession among all the peoples ... You shall be to me a kingdom of priests and a holy nation ... All the people responded (*'nh*) as one." (Ex 19:5-6, 8)

The covenantal *'nh* in 2:17b anticipates the final redactor's antanaclasis on *'nh* in 2:23-24. The renewal of the covenant between YHWH and Israel will result in a similar cosmic response by the whole of creation.[111]

3. The Function of the Triadic *lākēn's*

The present position of the three *lākēn's*, then, is not accidental. Rather, by these signposts the final redactor refashions the tradition which had come into his hands. One of these *lākēn's*, viz. 2:11, was already present in the tradition.

Here, it opened a sentence of condemnation, 2:11-15.
However, framed now between the redactional additions, 2:8-9
and 2:16-17 which begin with *lākēn hinnēh*, 2:11-15 completely changes its sense. The finality of the judgment which
was present in the redactor's tradition is transformed. 2:11-15
now becomes simply the second step in a purifying ordeal
whose purpose is to bring about Israel's return to God.[112]

The redactor articulates this return to grace in three
movements. The wife's journey begins with the obstruction
which bars her lustful wanderings after her lovers (2:8-9). The
second movement towards conversion is marked by the wife's
total devastation (2:11-15). YHWH will strip her of
everything he has given her to make her remember what she
had forgotten: that YHWH is her husband who has given
everything to her. In the third movement of the journey, 2:16-
17, YHWH will seduce his ravaged wife to the place of their
first betrothal. He will bring her into the wilderness and woo
her with tokens of his love. The now-repentant wife will
reciprocate to her spouse as in the earlier days of their
relationship. In the completion of this process of purification,
the covenantal drama can now be re-enacted.

F. YHWH Renews His Covenant With His People

1. The Triadic Occurrences of *nĕ'ūm-yhwh* and *(hāyâ) bayyôm hahû'*

The three redactional moments of the journey towards
conversion find their stylistic counterparts in the portrayal of
the covenantal renewal between YHWH and his people. The
final redactor erects another threefold structure across his
overall framework. This construction can be seen in the three
occurrences of the formulas, *nĕ'ūm-yhwh* ("says YHWH,"
2:15bB, 18aA, 23aA) and *(hāyâ) bayyôm hahû'* ("it will
happen) on that day," 2:18aA, 20aA, 23aA.

The oracular formula, *nĕ'ūm-yhwh* occurs only four times
in Hosea.[113] Besides the three instances cited, the formula
appears again at the close of a major structural division of
Hosea, viz. 11:11.[114] The majority of scholars agree that the

three instances of *nĕ'ūm-yhwh* in Hos 2, if not the verses themselves in which they appear, are due to later redaction.[115] This is also true for the eschatological formula *(hāyâ) bayyôm hahû'*, which likewise appears three times in Hos 2.[116] We have already perceived the redactor's use of *(hāyâ) bayyôm hahû'* in 1:5 to introduce his mollification of the tradition.[117] The task at hand is to demonstrate the final redactor's commentary on his received tradition in Hos 2 by means of these formulas. It is to this task that we now turn.

2. Hos 2:15b - The Forgetting of YHWH

2:15a I will call her to account for the feast
days of the Baals to whom she burns
incense. She adorned herself with her ring
and her ornament and went after her lovers,
2:15b *and me she forgot, says YHWH.*
(wĕ'ōtî šākĕḥâ nĕ'ūm-yhwh)

The first occurrence of *nĕ'ūm-yhwh* appears at the end of the second step of the redactor's educational journey for Israel, 2:15b. YHWH has just announced in v. 15a punishment upon his wife, Israel, because of her cultic faithlessness in running after her baalim-lovers. Marti and, more recently Buss, both regard the two words preceding our formula, *wĕ'ōtî šākĕḥâ*, "and me she forgot," as an addition. Marti notes that the expression, "and me she forgot," is much milder in tone than the judgment in the previous verses. He points out that the expression recurs in 8:14 and 13:6 which, he thinks, are non-Hosean. Moreover, he states that the notion of "forgetting YHWH" is a characteristic theme of the deuteronomistic circles and should thus be attributed to them (cf. Dt 6:12; 8:11, 14, 19; 32:18).[118]

In its present context, the purpose of the redactional addition, 2:15b, is clear. It provides a transition from the received tradition ending with 2:15a to the redactional commentary, 2:16-17. Framed between the redactional 2:8-9 and 2:16-17, the tradition, 2:11-15a which formerly ended in judgment becomes the rite of passage which the wife must

undergo in her return to her first husband (2:9). By means of
2:15b, the redactor can make the transfer from the now
chastised wife who had forgotten YHWH in her wantonness to
the seduction of this wife by YHWH back to himself. The
addition prepares for the renewal of the covenant. As we will
see shortly, the redactor had placed the marital reunion of
YHWH and Israel in a wider context, a *covenantal* context.
The ultimate violation of the covenant was the "forgetting of
YHWH," i.e. the desertion of God in the worship of other gods.

3. Hos 2:10b, 2:18aA, 2:19 - The Elimination of Idolatry

2:18aA   *wĕhāyâ bayyôm-hahû' nĕ'um-yhwh*
2:18aBb *tiqrĕ'î 'îšî wĕlō'-tiqrĕ'î-lî 'ôd ba'lî*
2:19   *wahăsirōtî 'et-šĕmôt habbĕ'ālîm mippîhā*
         wĕlō'-yizzākĕrû 'ôd bišmām

2:18aA   *And it will happen on that day, says YHWH*
2:18aBb You will call me "my husband."
         And you will never again call me "my Baal."
2:19   *I shall remove the names of the baals from her*
         mouth. Never again will they be mentioned by
         their names.

One finds the first occurrence of *hāyâ bayyôm-hahû'* and
the second instance of *nĕ'ūm-yhwh* in Hos 2 in 2:18aA.
Together they introduce a saying, 2:18aBb-19, which is
striking in its internal differences in person. Hos 2:19 accords
with 2:16-17 in referring to Israel in the third person feminine
singular: "I shall remove the names of the baals from *her*
mouth." In 2:18aB, on the other hand, YHWH addresses
Israel directly in the second person feminine singular: "*You*
will call me 'my husband'. And *you* will never again call me
'my Baal.'" Scholars usually resolve the change in person by
harmonizing the text on the basis of the Gk and Syr.[119]
   We would attribute the grammatical and thematic
pluralities in 2:18-19 to our final redactor. One finds his
editing, first, in 2:18aA with the two introductory formulas,
hāyâ bayyôm-hahû' nĕ'ūm-yhwh. Second, the final redactor

expands the tradition, 2:18aBb, by 2:19. We have seen in the discussion of 3:1-5 and 2:8a that the change in person from the second person in 2:18aBb to third person in 2:19 is a clue to the hand of our final redactor commenting on his tradition.[120] Moreover, while 2:18aBb and 2:19 exploit the marital imagery of the previous verses, 2:16-17, they do not treat baalism in the same fashion. Hos 2:18aBb lays the blame on the baalization of the cult of YHWH. 2:19, on the other hand, directly attacks idolatry, the worship of false gods.[121] We shall see that a polemic against idolatry will characterize the final redactor's commentary in the rest of the book.

The purpose of the expansion, 2:19, becomes clear when one regards it in light of the covenantal dimension added by the final redactor. As was pointed out, 2:18aBb criticizes the baalization of the cult of YHWH. Hos 2:19, however, focuses principally upon idolatry, the worship of other gods, whose names YHWH will remove so that they will never be mentioned again. In this, 2:19 concurs with the ideas expressed in the exilic text, Zech 13:2:

> "And on that day, says the Lord of hosts, I will cut off the names of the idols from the land, so that they shall be remembered no more." (Zech 13:2)

Both Hos 2:19 and Zech 13:2 contain the two formulas, "on that day, says the Lord," and the notion that the baalim idols "will be remembered no more."

Moreover, according to the Book of Deuteronomy and the Deuteronomistic History, the transgression of the covenant was defined chiefly in terms of the forgetting of YHWH in the sin of idolatry.[122] Within the deuteronomistic thrust of our final redactor, the period of chastisement in exile, the road to conversion and the renewal of covenantal dialogue necessarily entail the elimination of any vestiges of idolatry.[123] Within this *covenantal* setting provided by the redactor the renewal of the *marriage vows* between YHWH and his people which was present in his tradition can now take place.

For these reasons, therefore, we regard 2:10b, "I lavished silver upon her, and gold which they made into a Baal," also as an insertion by our final redactor.[124] We have already seen that the change of person is characteristic of the final redactor's commentary (Cf. 3:1; 2:8; 2:19). Hos 2:10b focuses the trangression of the people upon the making of baals from their precious metals. In this, the final redactor anticipates in 2:10b his later commentary in 2:19, where YHWH will ultimately remove the names of the baals from his wife's lips.

4. Hos 2:20 - The Cosmic Covenant

2:20   I shall make for them a covenant *on that day*
        (bayyôm hahû')
    with the beasts of the field
    and with the birds of the air
    and the reptiles of the ground.
    Bow and sword and weapons of war I shall
    break (abolish, *'ešbôr*) from the land.
    And I shall make them lie down in safety.

With the second eschatological *bayyôm hahû'* the final redactor in 2:20 explicitly announces the event of the new covenant for which he had been preparing his readers in the previous verses.[125] In the language of covenant making (*krt bryt*)[126] he articulates the form which this new covenant will take resulting from the marital reunion of YHWH and Israel. We have already observed the final redactor's theme of the breaking of the bow, sword and weapons of war from the land in his interpretive additions, 1:5 and 1:7.[127] In 2:20 he develops this theme to its fullest extent. In the new covenant YHWH will not only break the might of the military but bring real peace to the land. The idea of a new covenant here in 2:20 approaches that found in later texts such as Jer 31:31-33, Ezek 16:59-62, and in particular Ezek 34:25-31 which shares with Hos 2:20 the description of the cosmic benefits which will ensue from this covenant.

With the theme of the cosmic reconciliation of Israel with nature, the final redactor reverses 2:14bB. In 2:14bB the tradition threatened that the beasts of the field, *ḥayyat haśśādeh*, will devour Israel. However, in the final redactor's commentary, 2:20, YHWH will make peace between Israel and nature in the establishment of the new covenant, beginning with the beasts of the field, *ḥayyat haśśādeh.*

5. Hos 2:22b - The Knowledge of YHWH

The change in 2:21-22 referring to the wife in the second person indicates that the final redactor's received tradition is again in the foreground. The common marital symbolism and shared direct address to Israel in the second person suggest that 2:18aBb, 21-22 should be grouped as the redactor's tradition.[128]

2:18aBb	*tiqrĕʾî ʾîšî wĕlōʾ-tiqrĕʾî lî ʿôd baʿlî*
2:21	*wĕʾēraśtîk lî lĕʿôlām*
	wĕʾēraśtîk lî bĕṣedeq ûbĕmišpāṭ
	ûbĕḥesed ûbĕraḥămîm
2:22a	*wĕʾēraśtîk lî bĕʾĕmûnâ*
2:22b	*wĕyādaʿat ʾet-yhwh*

2:18aBb	You will call me "my husband."
	You will never again call me "my Baal."
2:21	I shall betroth you to me forever.
	I shall betroth you to me with righteousness
	and with justice
	with love and with compassion.
2:22a	I shall betroth you to me in faithfulness,
2:22b	*And you will know YHWH.*

The only segment which could be questionable as the tradition is the conclusion of the betrothal announcement, *wĕyādaʿat ʾet-yhwh,* "and you shall know YHWH." In the first place, the switch from first person, "I will betroth you to me," in 2:21-22a, to second person, "you will know YHWH," in 2:22b departs stylistically from the *wĕʾēraśtîk lî bĕ* plus substantive pattern of 2:21-22a. Moreover, if YHWH had been speaking in the first person, why does he then refer to himself in the third person, *ʾet-yhwh?* One would expect "and you shall know me," or "you shall know that I am YHWH."[129] Because of these concerns, some scholars would emend the

text from *wĕyādaʿat ʾet-yhwh* to *ûbĕdaʿat yhwh*, "I will betroth
you in faithfulness *and in the knowledge of YHWH.*"[130]
     One is able, however, to reconcile the problems regarding
the relationship between 2:21-22a and 2:22b if one assesses
2:22b as arising from the final redactor. Wolff, Mays, and
Andersen and Freedman have noted that the statement, "you
shall *know* YHWH," reverses 2:15b, "and me she *forgot.*"[131]
We have already suggested that 2:15b, the forgetting of
YHWH, may be a deuteronomistic addition to the tradition,
functioning as a bridge from the tradition to the redactional
commentary.[132] The "knowledge of God" is also a favorite of
the deuteronomist as the opposite of the "forgetting of
YHWH."[133] Moreover, the "knowledge of God" has strong
covenantal connections.[134] It would thus be consistent with
the intention of the final redactor to situate the tradition of
the marital union between YHWH and Israel in a covenantal
context. Finally, like 2:15b the insertion, 2:22b - "and you
shall know YHWH," functions as a redactional bridge. Hos
2:22b is the transition from the redactor's received material,
2:21-22a - the marital union between YHWH and Israel, to his
redactional commentary, 2:23-24. By means of the insertion,
the redactor is able to reflect in 2:23-24 upon the cosmic
proportions which this marital reunion between YHWH and
Israel will take.

6. Hos 2:23-24 - The Cosmic Response

2:23   *wĕhāyâ bayyôm hahûʾ*
          ʾeʿĕneh nĕʾūm-yhwh
          ʾeʿĕneh ʾet-haššāmāyim
          wĕhēm yaʿănû ʾet-hāʾāreṣ

2:24   *wĕhāʾāreṣ taʿăneh*
          ʾet-haddāgān wĕʾet-hattîrôš wĕʾet-hayyiṣhār
          wĕhēm yaʿănû ʾet-yizrĕʿeʾl

2:23   And it will happen on that day
          that I will respond, says YHWH.

I will make the heavens drop rain
and they shall make the earth fruitful.
2:24   And the earth shall produce grain, wine and oil
and they shall make Jezreel fruitful.

With the third occurrence of *hāyâ bayyôm hahû' nĕ'ūm-yhwh* comes the response of the cosmos to the covenant reestablished between God and Israel. Commonly regarded as a later addition[135] or at least a secondary placement of an authentic saying,[136] 2:23-24 is a meditation on the verb, '*nh.* These verses are striking in their five repetitions of '*nh.* Given the final redactor's *antanaclasis* in the fourfold occurrence of the root '*hb* in 3:1,[137] one can reasonably interpret the fivefold meditation on '*nh* as another example of *antanaclasis.* Indeed, Guillaume has pointed out that the targum to Hos 2:2-23-24, which omits '*e'ĕneh nĕ'ūm-yhwh,* "I will respond, says YHWH," in 2:23aA, translates the four remaining '*nh* in four different ways:

> I will *listen* ('*qbyl*) to their prayer. I will command the heavens that they *send down rain* (*yḥtwn mṭr'*) upon the earth. The earth *shall make abundant* (*trby*) the grain, wine and oil, and they *shall supply enough for* (*yspqwn*) the exiles of my people. (Tg. Neb., Hosea 2:23-24)

On the basis of Arabic examples where '*nh* can mean both "to flow" and "to make abundant," Guillaume argues that such nuances are latent in the five MT occurrences of '*nh* in 2:23-24.[138]

Through such a laconic fivefold wordplay on '*nh,* the final redactor is able to deliver the full force of YHWH's own covenantal response ('*nh*) to the wife who will respond ('*nh*) as in the days of her youth, 2:17b. The final redactor begins his meditation on '*nh* with YHWH's explicit statement, "I will respond," says YHWH" (2:23aA, '*e'ĕneh nĕ'ūm-yhwh*). YHWH responds as the creator God who brings fertility to the land. In contrast to Baal who was thought to bring rain, YHWH declares that he will make the heavens drop rain (2:23aB, "*nh '*t-hšmym*).[139] This in turn will make the earth fruitful (2:3ab, *whm y'nw 't-h'rṣ*). The earth will thus produce grain, wine and oil (2:24a, *wh'rṣ ťnh 't-hdgn w't-htyrwš w't-hyṣhr*) which will make Jezreel fruitful (2:24b, *whm y'nw 't-yzr"l*).

Through his *antanaclasis* on ʿnh the final redactor is able to return to the name Jezreel in 2:24b. Then, by means of another wordplay on the location Jezreel, the redactor arrives at the epilogue to his story of the marriage between YHWH and Israel where YHWH will sow (*zr'*) his people in the land:

> 2:25 I will sow her (*ûzĕraʿ tîhā*) for myself in the land. I will have compassion on Lo Ruhama. I will say to Lo Ammi, "My people are you." And he will say, "My God."

The epilogue to the story of YHWH's marriage in 2:25 forms an inclusio with the final redactor's prologue to this story, 2:2-3. Like 2:2-3, our epilogue not only recapitulates and reverses the names of Hosea's children, Jezreel, Lo Ruhama and Lo Ammi. It also explains the enigmatic "day of Jezreel" announced in 2:2b, the prologue to the story of YHWH and his people. After outlining the three-part program for the return journey of the people back to God in 2:8-24, the redactor asserts by means of a double paronomasia that the "great day of Jezreel" (2:2b, *yzr"l*) is not only the day when the children of Israel will "go up from the land of exile" (2:2aB, *'lh mn-h'rṣ*). It is also the day when they will be sown in the land (2:25, *zr' b'rṣ*). Because of their repentance (*šwb*), they will return (*šwb*) to the land of homecoming.[140]

IV. Summary of the Final Redacted State of Hos 1-3

We would now like to summarize our results regarding the final redacted state of Hos 1-3: the story of Hosea's marriage. We begin first with the person of the final redactor. In view of recurring themes of exilic chastisement coupled with the hope of return to the land contingent upon the people's repentance (3:4-5; 2:2, 8-9, 16-17), the final redactor interpreted his received material in all likelihood during the time of the Babylonian exile when the return to the land was a real possibility. Two facets of his interpretive commentary suggest a Judean provenance for him. The first is his emphasis on the Judean kings in the superscription to the work, 1:1. Second, threats or judgments in his tradition appear to have been directed specifically to the northern kingdom (cf. House of Jehu in 1:4 and House of Israel in 1:4, 6). Our redactor, however, takes care not only to reverse the threats against the North, but also to include the Judean nation in the promises of salvation (1:7; 2:2). Moreover, the language and particular theological concerns common to the final redactor's commentary indicate that he probably belonged to the deuteronomistic tradition.

In keeping with the tenor of hope which was possible from his later historical perspective, the final redactor mitigates or reverses his received material. Without seemingly changing a word of this tradition he qualifies it by additions, in which paronomasian links to the tradition may be found. Moreover, he enlarges the tradition through plays on words. The wordplays characteristic of his interpretive commentary are *antanaclasis* (2:2, 23-24; 3:1), double entendres (2:9; 3:5), *metaphony* (3:4-5), parasonancy (1:5a, 2:2, 17, 24-25), transposition of consonants (2:1; 3:1b), alliteration (2:1bB, 16-17), and certain extended wordplays (2:1, 16-17).

Above all else, the final redactor's hand can be detected in the present structure of Hos 1-3. He gives the older tradition in the book a new literary gestalt by restructuring and expanding it with his own interpretive commentary. He refashions his received material first by providing a redactional beginning for it in 1:1. This superscription opens the story of Hosea's marriage, Hos 1-3, as well as the whole Book of Hosea by situating the Hosean tradition in the final redactor's historical framework.

Second, the final redactor supplies the conclusion to the story of Hosea's marriage by adding 3:1-5 to the tradition. This important contribution is an interpretive commentary on both the tradition of Hosea's marriage to Gomer (Hos 1) and of YHWH's marriage to Israel (Hos 2). In placing 3:1-5 after Hos 1-2, the redactor separates the marriage traditions of Hos 1-2 *de facto* from Hos 4-14 where the conjugal theme is not that apparent. In doing so, he creates a structurally new tradition in which the marriages of YHWH and of Hosea become the interpretive perspective for the remainder of the book. As the prism which refracts Hos 4-14, the larger portion of the Hosean tradition, the final redaction of Hos 1-3 converges on the convenantal love of YHWH for Israel, his spouse. This unique love of YHWH forgives the infidelity of his wife when she approaches him in repentance.

The third structural change of the tradition is the paronomastic mitigation or inversion of the threats symbolized by the names of Hosea's children in Hos 1. For Jezreel (1:4), the redactor qualifies the termination of northern sovereignty (wĕhišbattî) with the breaking of the bow of Israel (wĕšābartî) in 1:5. The redactor will develop this theme again in 1:7 and finally in 2:20 where the crushing of military power means simultaneously the establishment of peace in the land. For Lo Ruhama (1:6abA), the redactor asserts in 1:6bB-7 that YHWH will indeed forgive the House of Israel as well as grant compassion (rḥm) to the House of Judah. The redactor's reversal for the third child, Lo Ammi, has not been recognized in the past because structurally it is placed in Hos 2 in the MT. In 2:1 the final redactor inverts the judgment in 1:9, "You are not my people and I am not I AM (lō' 'ehyeh) to you," by means of an ingenious wordplay on lō' 'ehyeh in 2:1 through which Not My People becomes the "children of the living God" (bĕnê 'ēl-ḥāy).

In the fourth structural reformulation of the tradition, the final redactor situates the narrative of YHWH and his unfaithful wife (Hos 2) in a centrally prominent position. He does this by buttressing the marital story of YHWH on either side with a story of Hosea's marriage. One of these stories, Hos 1, was already in the tradition. With Hos 3, the final redactor adds a second story of Hosea's marriage. In this he not only distinguishes the marriage tradition from the rest of the Hos 4-14 traditions, as we have already pointed out, but also dramatizes this special marital relationship between YHWH and his people like a solitaire in its jewelry setting.

The tradition of YHWH and his wife Israel becomes a paradigm, not only for the rest of the book, but also for the earlier tradition of Hosea's marriage depicted in Hos 1. For, highlighted in the final edition of Hos 2 is the forgiving love of YHWH who renews his covenantal vows with his wayward but repentant wife. Following this characterization of YHWH's marriage with Israel is Hos 3, the second narrative of Hosea's marriage added by the final redactor. The conflict entailed in YHWH's command to Hosea to marry a whore in Hos 1 finds its resolution in Hos 3. Here, Hosea is now commanded to love ('*hb*) his harlot wife just as YHWH loves the children of Israel. In the context of the redacted tradition of YHWH's marriage in Hos 2, the earlier tradition of Hosea's marriage in Hos 1 is given a "happier ending" in Hos 3.

Fifth, the final redactor provides the story of YHWH and Israel with a special inclusio-like frame: a prologue, Hos 2:2-3, and an epilogue, Hos 2:25. These verses form a bracket around the narrative of YHWH and his people proper, Hos 2:4-24, which tell of the libidinous rovings of YHWH's inconstant wife and her journey back to her first husband. The redactional prologue and epilogue together articulate the destination and destiny of this wife, the people of God. In travelling the spiritual road of repentance and conversion, the united kingdoms of Israel and Judah will also make a physical trek. They will go up from the land of their exile (2:2, '*lh mn-h'rṣ*) to be sown ultimately in the land of promise (2:25, *zr' b'rṣ*) where they will grow up like plants in that land (2:2, '*lh mn-h'rṣ*). Furthermore, the reversal of the children's names in the prologue and the epilogue underscores, both at the beginning of the story of YHWH's marriage and at its conclusion, the covenantal relationship which will be reinstated between YHWH and his people.

Sixth, the final redactor refashions the tradition of YHWH and his spouse in Hos 2 in such a way that this journey motif is readily perceivable. The directional signs for the journey are the three *lākēn's*: 2:8, 11, 16. The second of the *lākēn's* was already in the tradition. It opened a sentence of condemnation, 2:11-15. The final redactor, however, is responsible for the first and third *lākēn hinnēh's* as well as the verses which they introduce, 2:8-9, 16-17. Framed between these *lākēn hinnēh's*, 2:11-15, the sentence of condemnation of the redactor's tradition, is contextualized as the second step in a process of purification. It no longer possesses the finality it had at the earlier stage of the tradition.

The first step in the final redactor's purgative ordeal is barring the wife's paths to her lovers (2:8-9). The second movement is her complete desolation which results from her infidelities (2:11-15a). At the third stage of the journey YHWH will conduct the now-disciplined wife into the wilderness and seduce her with offers of love. She then will respond to YHWH as she did during the earlier days of their relationship when they pledged themselves to each other on Sinai.

Seventh: Having endured her purgatorial itinerary, the wife is now prepared to reaffirm her marriage vows with her husband. The final redactor situates the renewal of vows found in his tradition in a *covenantal* context. He has just ended the journey of the wife "in the wilderness" (2:16). This is the place where she made her first covenantal response when she came up out of Egypt (2:17, '*nh*). The final redactor communicates the vow ceremony in a threefold structure which corresponds to his three stage journey theme introduced by the three *lākēn*'s. The introductory formulas for the covenantal renewal ceremony are the triadic instances of (*wĕhāyâ*) *bayyôm hahû*' and *nĕ'ūm-yhwh* (2:15b, 18, 20, 23).

Together with the redactional addition, "and me she forgot," the first occurrence of *nĕ'ūm-yhwh* in 2:15b makes a transition from the redactor's received material, ending in 2:15a, to his redactional commentary beginning with 2:16. The thoroughly disciplined wife who had forgotten YHWH can now be wooed into the wilderness by YHWH himself.

In 2:18aA *hāyâ bayyôm hahû*' *nĕ'ūm-yhwh* introduce a saying from the redactor's tradition, viz. "You will call me 'my husband'. And you will never again call me 'my Baal'" (2:18aB). Commenting on this piece of the tradition, the redactor reiterates in 2:19 the *covenantal* dimension which this marital reunion will take. Hos 2:19, "I shall remove the names of the baals from her lips...," directly attacks idolatry which, from the deuteronomistic viewpoint of our final redactor, was the gravest sin against covenant.

With the second occurrence of *bayyôm hahû'* in 2:20 the final redactor expounds on the direction which the vow renewal between YHWH and Israel will take. The covenant between them will have a cosmic dimension. Nature itself will be reconciled with Israel. Moreover, the national peace, to which the final redactor alluded in 1:5 and 1:7, is now conveyed most forcefully in 2:20 as one of the benefits which will result from the covenant. The cosmic covenant and its cosmic peace described in 2:20 together with the strong covenantal associations of the redactor's addition in 2:22b, "and you shall know YHWH," become the context for the earlier tradition of the marriage proposal in 2:21-22a, "I will betroth you to myself forever..."

The final occurrences of *wĕhāyâ bayyôm hahû'/nĕ'ūm-yhwh* introduce a reflection on the cosmic reply to God's own covenantal response, 2:23-24. The redactor carries out this meditation by means of a fivefold *antanaclasis* on the root *'nh*. In direct contrast to the notion that Baal brings rain, the redactor emphasizes in his wordplay that YHWH's covenantal response entails making rain fall upon the earth. This is the response of the creator God who makes the earth fertile. The rain which he causes to fall will insure the earth's yield and ultimately make the valley of Jezreel fecund once more (2:24). By returning to the name Jezreel, the redactor is able, again by means of paronomasia, to conclude the story of YHWH's marriage and come to his epilogue, 2:25. Here, the redactor punctuates the fact that the wife Israel will be sown (*zr'*) back into the land, where she will grow up like plants in the land (*'lh mn-h'rṣ*, 2:2).

CHAPTER FOUR

The Composition of Hos 1-3: Earlier Stages of the Tradition

Having discussed the final redactor's structural organization of and interpretive commentary on the Hos 1-3 tradition, we are now in a better position to take up the question of the earlier traditions in the text. The discussion of the earlier stages of the tradition will necessarily be hypothetical. Opinions regarding these stages are contingent upon one's determination of the final redactor's *selection* and *arrangement* of the tradition.[1] With the nature of the final redaction established to a certain extent, one can, nevertheless, make some judgments about the prior stage(s) of the material which the final redactor chose for his work.

The final redactor's traditional material is located in Hos 1 and Hos 2. We use an asterisk (*) to refer to the chapters at their earlier stages. Minus the commentary of the final redactor, this traditional material is composed of Hos 1*, a narrative of Hosea's marriage to Gomer (1:2-4, 6abA, 8-9) and Hos 2*, an oracle of YHWH (2:4-7, 10a, 11-15a, 18aBb, 21-22a). The following is a text of this tradition. We refer the reader to the chart outlining the editorial history of Hos 1-3 above.[2] Anticipating our results, we have put in *italics* those verses in Hos 2* for which we will argue that the author of Hos 1* is responsible.

I. Hos 1* and Hos 2*: Reconstructed Text

Hos 1*

1:2   *těḥillat dibber-yhwh běhôšēaʿ*
       wayyōʾmer yhwh ʾel-hôšēaʿ
       lēk qaḥ-lěkā ʾēšet zěnûnîm wěyaldê zěnûnîm
       kî-zānōh tizneh hāʾāreṣ mēʾaḥărê yhwh
1:3   *wayyēlek wayyiqqaḥ ʾet-gōmer bat-diblāyim*
       wattahar wattēled-lô bēn

1:4   *wayyō'mer yhwh 'ēlāyw qĕrā' šĕmô yizrĕ'e'l*
        kî 'ôd mĕ'aṭ ûpāqadtî 'et-dĕmê yizrĕ'e'l
        'al-bêt yēhû' wĕhišbattî mamlĕkût
        bêt yiśrā'ēl
1:6   *wattahar 'ôd wattēled bat wayyō'mer lô*
        qĕrā' šĕmāh lō' rūḥāmâ kî lō' 'ôsîp 'ôd
        'ăraḥēm 'et-bêt yiśrā'ēl
1:8   *wattigmōl 'et-lō' rūḥāmâ*
        wattahar wattēled bēn
1:9   *wayyō'mer qĕrā' šĕmô lō' 'ammî*
        kî 'attem lō' 'ammî
        wĕ'ānōkî lō' 'ehyeh lākem

                    Hos 2*
2:4aA   *rîbû bĕ'immĕkem rîbû*
2:4aB   *kî-hî' lō' 'ištî wĕ'ānōkî lō' 'îšāh*
2:4b   *wĕtāsēr zĕnûnêhā mippānêhā*
        wĕna'ăpûpêhā mibbên šādêhā
2:5   *pen-'apšîṭennā 'ărummâ*
        wĕhiṣṣagtîhā kĕyôm hiwwāledāh
        wĕśamtîhā kammidbār
        wĕšattîhā kĕ'ereṣ ṣiyyâ
        wahămittîhā baṣṣāmā'
2:6   <u>*wĕ'et-bānêhā lō' 'ăraḥēm kî bĕnê zĕnûnîm hēmmâ*</u>
2:7a   <u>*kî zānĕtâ 'immām hôbîšâ hôrātām*</u>
2:7b   *kî 'āmĕrâ 'ēlĕkā 'aḥărê mĕ'ahăbay*
        nōtĕnê laḥmî ûmêmay ṣamrî ûpištî
        šamnî wĕšiqquyāy
2:10a   *wĕhî' lō' yādĕ'â kî 'ānōkî nātattî lāh*
        haddāgān wĕhattîrôš wĕhayyiṣhār
2:11   *lākēn 'āšûb wĕlāqaḥtî dĕgānî bĕ'ittô*
        wĕtîrôšî bĕmô'ădô wĕhiṣṣaltî ṣamrî ûpištî
        lĕkassôt 'et-'erwātāh
2:12   *wĕ'attâ 'ăgalleh 'et-nablûtāh*
        lĕ'ênê mĕ'ahăbêhā
        wĕ'îš lō'-yaṣṣîlennâ miyyādî
2:13   *wĕhišbattî kol-mĕśôśāh ḥaggāh ḥodšāh*
        wĕšabbattāh wĕkol mô'ădāh
2:14   *wahăšimmōtî gapnāh ûtĕ'ēnātāh*

'ăšer 'ămĕrâ 'etnâ hēmmâ lî
'ăšer nātĕnû-lî mĕ'ahăbāy
wĕśamtîm lĕya'ar wĕ'ăkālātam ḥayyat haśśādeh

2:15a *ûpāqadtî 'alêhā 'et-yĕmê habbĕ'ālîm*
'ăšer taqṭîr lāhem watta'ad nizmāh
wĕḥelyātāh wattēlek 'aḥărê mĕ'ahăbêhā

2:18 *tiqrĕ'î 'îšî wĕlō' tiqrĕ'î lî 'ôd ba'lî*

2:21 *wĕ'ēraśtîk lî lĕ'ôlām*
wĕ'ēraśtîk lî bĕṣedeq ûbĕmišpāṭ
ûbĕḥesed ûbĕraḥămîm

2:22a *wĕ'ēraśtîk lî bĕ'ĕmûnâ*

1:2   The beginning of YHWH's speaking through
       Hosea.
       And YHWH said to Hosea, "Go, take for yourself
       a wife of harlotry and have children of harlotry,
       for the land surely whores away from YHWH."

1:3   So he went and took Gomer the daughter of
       Diblaim
       and she conceived and bore him a son.

1:4   And YHWH said to him, "Call his name Jezreel,
       for in a little while I shall visit the bloodshed
       of Jezreel upon the house of Jehu and put an
       end to the rule of the house of Israel . . ."

1:6a   And she conceived again and bore a daughter.
       And he said to him, "Call her name Lo Ruhama,

1:6bA for I will no longer have compassion
       upon the house of Israel . . ."

1:8   After she weaned Lo Ruhama,
       she conceived and bore a son.

1:9   Then he said, "Call his name Lo Ammi
       for you are not my people
       and I am not I AM to you . . ."

2:4aA Plead with your mother, plead,

2:4aB *for she is not my wife and I am not her husband*

2:4b   that she remove her harlotry from her face
       and her adultery from between her breasts,

2:5   lest I strip her naked
       and set her out as on the day of her birth.

I will make her like a wilderness,
change her into an arid land,
and slay her with thirst.

2:6   *And upon her children I will have no compassion*
for children of harlotry are they.

2:7a   *For their mother has whored. The one who*
conceived
them has behaved shamefully.

2:7b   For she said, "I will go after my lovers
who give me my bread and my water,
my wood and my flax, my oil and my drink" ...

2:10a   But she did not know that I gave her
the grain, wine and oil ...

2:11   Therefore, I will turn and take back
my grain in its time and my wine in its season.
I will withdraw my wool and my flax which
were to cover her nakedness.

2:12   And now I will expose her genitals
in the sight of her lovers.
No one will rescue her from my hand.

2:13   I will put an end to all her joy,
her feasts, her new moons, her sabbaths,
all of her assemblies.

2:14   I will lay waste her vines and her fig trees,
of which she said, "A harlot's hire are they to
me which my lovers have given me."
I will make them a forest
and the beasts of the field will devour them.

2:15a   I will call her to account for the feast days
of the Baals to whom she burns incense.
She adorned herself with her ring and her
ornament and went after her lovers ...

2:18aBb *You will call me "my husband".*
You will never again call me "my Baal" ...

2:21   *I will betroth you to me forever.*
I will betroth you to me with righteousness
and with justice, with love and compassion.

2:22a   *I will betroth you to me with faithfulness* ...

The question at hand is whether or not this tradition itself is a composite work. Furthermore, if this tradition is a composite one, what is its literary *history* and what are the literary *relationships* among its composite parts?

Arguing against the unity of Hos 1* and 2* and in favor of its heterogeneity are the facts that Hos 1* and Hos 2* contrast each other in style, form and content. Hos 1* is prose while Hos 2* is on the whole more poetic.[3] With respect to form, Hos 1* is a narrative dealing with the marriage of Hosea and the birth and naming of his children. Hos 2*, on the other hand, is an oracle of YHWH. Moreover, while Hos 1* focuses on the marriage between Hosea and Gomer, Hos 2* highlights the conjugal relationship between YHWH and Israel.

Rhetorical difficulties, moreover, present themselves in Hos 2*. Whereas the children are addressed in the 2nd per. pl. in 2:4, "Plead with *your* mother, plead," a shift occurs in 2:6. In 2:6 the children are referred to in the 3rd person, "and upon *her children* I will have no compassion." Furthermore, after extended threats of punishment Hos 2* ends on a note of hope in 2:18aBb, 21-22a, where the wife will call YHWH her husband and where YHWH will betroth himself to his wife once again. Commentators who do detect some sort of literary history in the Hos 1-3 material usually regard Hos 1, the third person account of Hosea's marriage, as the secondary component. For example, a number of commentators suggest that Hos 1 was written by a disciple and was a secondary interpretation of Hos 2 and 3.[4]

If we accept scholarly opinion that Hos 1* is non-Hosean, two possibilities are open to us regarding the literary history of Hos 1* and Hos 2*. The first is that someone wrote a third person account of Hosea's marriage and the ominous births of the children. This account circulated independently from Hos 2*, the sayings of Hosea. It was prefixed to Hos 2* at a later date by another person, a collector who saw a theological connection between the narrative of Hosea's marriage (Hos 1) and the oracle of YHWH (Hos 2).[5] Since Hos 1* appears to be directed against the northern kingdom because of its references to the house of Israel (1:3, 6) and to the dynasty of

Jehu (1:6), this collection most likely occurred before the North's demise in 722 BCE.

The second possibility for the literary history of Hos 1* and Hos 2* is that someone wrote Hos 1* as a veritable introduction to Hos 2*. Hos 1* would thus be this person's intentional composition to give the oracle of YHWH (Hos 2*) a literary correlative in the life of Hosea. From this perspective, there is no "middleman", a collector who saw a relationship between Hos 1* and Hos 2* and joined them together. Instead, the one who actually wrote Hos 1* is responsible for providing it as the literary/theological context for Hos 2*. As with the first possibility, this person probably wrote Hos 1* before the North's demise in 722 BCE.

II. Possibility 1: Hos 1* and Hos 2* as Two Independently Authored Texts Joined Later

Problems present themselves with respect to Possibility 1, i.e. that Hos 1* and 2* are texts by two different authors joined later by a collector. If the units were originally discrete and unrelated, as has been maintained, one should be able to determine more precisely the exact forms of these units. The *persistence* of written and oral forms even when removed from their original *Sitz-im-Leben* has been a dominant presupposition of form critics.[6] Ideally, when the forms are established and with them a grasp of their original intent, one is then in a better position to understand why a collector joined two isolated forms into a new literary unit having a new meaning.

This, however, has not been the case. The precise form of Hos 1* has not been easily pinpointed. Commentators describe Hos 1* variously as a biography,[7] a *memorabile*,[8] an allegory,[9] a vision,[10] a kerygmatic narrative,[11] a call narrative,[12] a sign-act narrative,[13] a naming sermon,[14] a tract,[15] and most recently, an apologetic against a perfunctory dismissal of Hosea's message of judgment.[16] The variety of designations for Hos 1* underscores the problem of treating it as once having been an independent unit. This problem is complicated further by the fact that each particular categorization does not adequately characterize Hos 1* in and of itself.

When one encounters Hos 2*, the problem becomes more complex. Scholars usually regard Hos 2 in its present state as a loose collection of sayings.[17] They generally assume that the redactor who assembled the disparate oracular units in Hos 2 was the one responsible for joining his collection to Hos 1. The question of the form and life setting of the heterogeneous fragments is not taken up. Hence, the unity of Hos 2 is already a secondary one. This unity, furthermore, defies form-critical classification, even in spite of Wolff's efforts to describe it as a "kerygmatic" unity. We have already observed the inadequacies of this ambiguous designation.[18]

III. Possibility 2: Hos 1* as a Secondary Introduction to Hos 2*

Because of the problems just described, Possibility 1 seems to be inadequate as a description of the literary history of Hos 1* and Hos 2*. There are, on the other hand, good reasons to support Possibility 2, i.e. that someone wrote Hos 1* as a later introduction to Hos 2*, the YHWH oracle.

A. Hos 1* as the Interpretive Literary Context of Hos 2*

In the first place, Hos 1* supplies an interpretive literary context for Hos 2*. The change to the 2nd per. pl., "*you* are not my people and I am not I AM to *you*," in 1:9 provides a transition from Hos 1* to the 2nd per. pl. beginning Hos 2*, "plead with *your* mother, plead" (2:4). The children addressed in "your mother" become the symbolically named children of Hosea whose births are described in Hos 1*. The "mother" who is the object of the children's *rîb* in 2:4 is understood to be Gomer bat Diblaim whose marriage to Hosea is also described in Hos 1*. Moreover, Hos 1:2bB interprets 2:5b where the adulterous wife will become like an arid and barren land. With an interpretive *kî* clause 1:2bB gives the *raison d'être* of Hosea's symbolic marriage to a whore: "For the land surely whores away from YHWH."[19]

Thus, the prefatory Hos 1* provides a distinctive interpretive perspective for the Hos 2* tradition. The "mother" depicted in Hos 2* is personified as the prophet's own wife. In her person and character, Gomer becomes the symbol of the harlotrous land. By the same token, the children who are summoned to "plead" with their mother to renounce her harlotry (2:4aA) are concretized as Hosea's children by Gomer (1:3, 6, 8). Their ominous names, Jezreel, Lo Ruhama, and Lo Ammi, embody threats which bolster the impact of their *rib* against their mother.

Many scholars detect in Hos 2 an amalgam of symbols which fuses the marriage of YHWH and Israel and of Hosea and Gomer into one prophetic novella.[20] This is due precisely to the fact that the secondary composition, Hos 1*, provides an *interpretive* commentary for Hos 2*. The possibility for equating the two unions was already inherent in the Hos 2* tradition which the author of Hos 1* explicitates in his commentary. On the basis of the beginning of Hos 2*, "plead with your mother, plead" (2:4), the Hos 1* author was able to provide a narrative prologue which interpreted the "mother" as Hosea's harlotrous wife, Gomer, and the children addressed as Hosea's children. It was, therefore, the author of Hos 1* who was responsible for transforming the Hos 2* tradition concerning the marriage between YHWH and Israel into a corresponding theological portrayal of the *prophet's* marital and parenting mission. Hosea's marriage with Gomer provides, in turn, a heuristic device for gaining further insight into the YHWH/Israel relationship.

Because Hos 1* provides an interpretive literary context for Hos 2*, they should not be considered independent units which were brought together later. Hos 1* exists precisely *in a relational function* with Hos 2*. The difficulty in describing Hos 1* by itself is due principally to its relational character with Hos 2*. Hos 1* is a literary piece composed expressly for Hos 2*. The author of Hos 1* intended that Hos 1* and 2* be read *together* as a unit.

B. Aporiae in Hos 2* Arising from the Author of Hos 1*

There is, moreover, a second argument in favor of Possibility 2. Aporiae in Hos 2* can be attributed to the one who wrote Hos 1* for Hos 2*.

1. Hos 2:4aB: "For she is not my wife and I am not her husband"

We begin first with 2:4aB: *kî hî' lō' 'ištî wĕ'ānōkî lō' 'îšāh*, "for she is not my wife and I am not her husband." Hos 2:4aB is problematic in its present position in 2:4-5. Some scholars maintain that the clause, "for she is not my wife and I am not her husband," is a divorce formula, citing Babylonian divorce formulas and Elephantine marriage contracts in particular as support.[21] The association of the clause with the children's *rîb* which inaugurates the verse emphasizes the legal aspects of a divorce proceedings.

Not a few commentators, however, have questioned the designation of the 2:4aB clause as a divorce formula.[22] In the first place, there are no biblical or rabbinic sources where this divorce formula is used, although such material on the topic of divorce is plentiful.[23] In the second place, the aramaic divorce formulas found at Elephantine and Murabba' at are terminologically different from the Hos 2:4aB formula. At Elephantine, the usual public declaration of divorce involves *śn'*, lit. "to hate":[24] "Should Eshor rise up in an assembly tomorrow or some other day and say, 'I divorce my [wife] Miphtahiah ...'" (*wy'mr śn' 't [l'n]tty mpṭhyh ...* AP 15, 26-27).[25] Murabba' at documents involve the root *šbq*: "I divorce and repudiate of my own free will today ...you my wife X" (*šbq wmtrk mn r'ty ywm' 'nh ... lky 'nyt*).[26] These documents record a marriage formula which articulates 2:4aB in the affirmative: "She is my wife and I am her husband from this day forward" (*hy 'ntty w'nh b'lh mn ywn' znh*).[27] Although Hos 2:4aB reflects this marriage formula to some extent, it is incorrect to assume that its opposite is a divorce formula, especially since these documents already have an expressed pronouncement of divorce.[28]

In the third place, the context of 2:4aB presents difficulties. If 2:4aB is indeed a divorce formula, it is premature in the course of the text. The plea that the wife "remove her harlotries from her face," which follows this alleged divorce formula, would make little sense. Moreover, if the act of stripping the wife naked (2:5) was part of a divorce proceeding, it would not be introduced by *pen*.[29] Hos 2:4aB seems to intrude between 2:4aA and 2:4b. If one were to remove 2:4aB, a logical connection between 2:4aA and 2:4b establishes itself: "Plead with your mother, plead . . .that she may remove her harlotries from her face." For these reasons, some scholars isolate the whole clause as a later secondary interpolation,[30] or regard the clause as authentic and its present placement secondary.[31] Others would delete only the second half of the clause, "and I am not her husband," as a later gloss.[32]

On one hand, then, Hos 2* with the inclusion of 2:4aB, "for she is not my wife and I am not her husband," seems to be a divorce proceeding where YHWH rejects his wife (2:4-5), punishes her unfaithfulness (2:10-15a), and takes her back in marriage after she is suitably chastised (2:18aBb, 21-22). On the other hand, strong arguments militate against the idea that Hos 2* was originally a divorce suit. The purported divorce clause, 2:4aB, is artificial in its present context.

We suggest that both opinions are true to some extent and that the incongruities in the text are due to different redactional stages of the Hos 2* tradition. Hos 2:4aB seems to be a later insertion into the text. The one responsible for this insertion would most likely be the one who provided Hos 2* with the Hos 1* commentary. Indeed, it is in Hos 1* where YHWH commands Hosea to become a prophetic icon of his experience with Israel by choosing a harlot for a wife. The Hos 1* author sets the stage, then, for the repudiation of the wife/Israel in the Hos 2* tradition by this introductory commentary.

Moreover, the actual repudiation of the wife/Israel in 2:4aB echoes his description of the judgment personified in the birth of Hosea's third child, Lo Ammi:

1:9   (qĕrā' šĕmô lō' 'ammî)
      kî 'attem lō' 'ammî
      wĕ'ānōkî lō'-'ehyeh lākem
2:4a (rîbû bĕ'immĕkem rîbû)
      kî hî' lō' 'ištî
      wĕ'ānōkî lō' 'îšāh

1:9   (Call his name Lo Ammi)
      for you are not my people
      and I am not I AM to you.
2:4   (Plead with your mother, plead)
      for she is not my wife
      and I am not her husband.

As was already mentioned, the Hos 1* author connects his commentary, 1:9, with the beginning of his tradition, 2:4a, by means of a switch from third person to second person.[33] Furthermore, 1:9 and 2:4aB are striking in their stylistic similarities. Both begin with the particle *kî*. Both make use of the pronoun: 1:9 - *'attem*, "you"/*wĕ'ānōkî*, "and I"//2:4aB - *hî'*, "she"/*wĕ'ānōkî*, "and I". Moreover, *lō' 'ammî* and *lō'-'ehyeh* correspond stylistically to *lō' 'ištî* and *lō' 'îšāh*.

Expressed in negative terms, 1:9, "for you are not my people and I am not I AM to you," refers to the disintegration of the covenant between YHWH and Israel.[34] With the concomitant insertion of 2:4aB into the Hos 2* tradition, "for she is not my wife and I am not her husband," the Hos 1* author depicts the same deterioration in the relationship between YHWH and Israel symbolically as a divorce. His commentary does not utilize the customary divorce formula. Instead, his marital imagery reflects the reversal of the covenant reflected in 1:9.

It is the Hos 1* author, then, who reworks his tradition into something quite new, namely, the celebrated metaphor of the covenant between YHWH and Israel as a marital union. He does this by providing a narrative framework (Hos 1*) whereby the "mother" expressed in his tradition (2:4aA) becomes the prophet's harlotrous wife, Gomer. She, in turn, represents figuratively the land "who whores away from

YHWH" (1:2b). Moreover, with the judgment inherent in Hosea's third child, Lo Ammi, the Hos 1* author highlights the breakdown of the covenant between God and the people because of their profligacy (1:9). With the 2:4aB interpolation, this author envisions the covenantal dissolution as a matrimonial divorce.

2. *Hos 2:6-7a* - *"and upon her children I will have no compassion, for children of harlotry are they. For their mother has whored. The one who conceived them has behaved shamefully."*

Hos 2:6-7a present contextual difficulties. Prior to the verses in 2:4-5, the children are addressed in the 2nd per. pl. imperative to make a *rîb* against their mother. Hos 2:6-7a, however, shifts to 3 pl. imperfect to refer to these same children who had just been addressed in the 2 pl. It is puzzling that YHWH would enjoin the children to plead, while at the same time state that he will have no compassion upon them either. Moreover, 2:6-7a disrupts a connection between 2:5 and 2:7b, " . . .and I will slay her with thirst . . .for she said, 'I will go after my lovers . . .'" Scholars reconcile the inconsistencies in a number of ways: by maintaining that 2:6-7a is an independent saying attached to 2:4-5 as a gloss,[35] by regarding only 2:6[36] or 2:6b[37] as secondary; by regarding 2:6 as authentic but placing it after Hos 1 together with 2:4aB,[38] and by emending the text to the 2 pl.[39]

Noteworthy for our discussion is the fact that Bewer finds a coherence between 2:6-7a and the intrusive divorce formula already discussed, 2:4aB. He groups 2:4aB and 2:6-7a together with 2:12 into what he thinks is an authentic saying of Hosea:

2:4aB   She is not my wife
         And I am not her husband.
2:6   And her children I do not pity
         Because they are children of harlotry.

2:7a   For their mother has played the harlot.
          She that conceived them has done shamefully.
2:12   And now I will uncover her shame
          Before the eyes of her lovers.
          And no man shall rescue her out of my hand

Bewer thinks that this reconstruction is more punitive in tone
vis-à-vis the surrounding verses into which it is interwoven.
There is no longer a plea that "the mother" stop her infidelity
lest something terrible happen. Rather, a divorce from the
"wife" is definitely announced.[40]
     Sellin, like Bewer, observes that 2:4aB and 2:6 cohere
regarding the unfaithful wife and her children. Moreover, he
thinks that the original location of these verses is just after
1:9. According to Sellin, nothing is said up to 1:9 about the
harlotry of Gomer cited in 1:2. The names of her children in
1:4, 6, 9 are directed at the people and have nothing to do with
her specifically. Placed after 1:9, however, 2:4aB, 6 completes
the narrative by functioning as the judgment against Gomer
and against her children. This judgment against Gomer and
her children which originally formed the climax of Hos 1 was,
according to Sellin, disrupted by the later insertion, 2:1-3.[41]
     Bewer and Sellin note thematic correspondences which
link 2:4aB, our covenantal divorce clause, with 2:6-7a and
these verses with the Hos 1* tradition. We think that these
correspondences are due to a common authorship. The Hos 1*
author is consistent in his editing of Hos 2*. His additions to
the Hos 2* tradition reflect verbally his prefatory statements
in Hos 1*. First of all, the statement of divorce in 2:4aB,
relates back to the taking of Gomer as wife in 1:2bA, as well as
the statement of covenantal breakdown involved in the name
of the third child, Lo Ammi in 1:9b:

	Hos 1*		Hos 2*
1:2bA	*wife* of harlotry	2:4aB	For she is not my *wife*
			and I am not her
			husband
1:9b	For you are not my people		
	and I am not I AM to you		

Second, the threat inherent in the daughter's name, Lo
Ruhama, is also shared by the introductory narrative, Hos 1*,
and the editorial commentary in Hos 2*:

	Hos 1*		Hos 2*
1:6bA	*I will never again have compassion* upon the house of Israel	2:6a	Upon her children *I will have no compassion*

Finally, in the following instances the Hos 2* additions
recapitulate information found previously in Hos 1*:

	Hos 1*		Hos 2*
1:2b	bear children of harlotry	2:6b	for children of harlotry are they
1:2bA	Take for yourself a wife of harlotry	2:7aA	for a harlot is their mother
1:3b, 6a, 8b	she conceived	2:7aB	she who conceived them

Within the interpretive context of the Hos 1* narrative,
the Hos 1* author sets the stage for the divorce metaphor
which he introduces into the Hos 2* tradition. As was pointed
out, this metaphor represents the dissolution of the covenant
between YHWH and the people. The Hos 1* author refashions
the Hos 2* tradition in light of the failure of the covenant on
the people's part. He does this specifically in his reversal of
the covenant formula embodied in Hosea's third son, Lo Ammi
(1:9). Further, he inserts a concomitant formula mirroring the
marital breakdown between God and the people (2:4aB). In
doing so, he creates from the Hos 2* tradition a divorce
proceeding. The original Hos 2* tradition, as we will see
shortly,[42] was probably a legal complaint against adultery
and its subsequent punishment. It was not, strictly speaking,
a divorce. However, it becomes such in the editing of Hos 2*
by the Hos 1* author.

3. Hos 2:18aBb - *"You will call me 'my husband.'*
                   You will never again call me 'my Baal' ...
  2:21-22a - *I will betroth you to me forever.*
               I will betroth you with
                 righteousness
                 and with justice
                 and with love
                 and with compassion.
               I will betroth you to me with
                 faithfulness ...*"*

Hos 2:18aBb and 2:21-22a are formulated as a direct
speech to Israel in the 2nd person. Moreover, they share
distinctly marital imagery in contrast to their adjacent verses,
which we have attributed to our final redactor.[43] On this
basis, Willi-Plein, Renaud, and Ruppert group these verses
into a literary unit.[44] There are good reasons to think that
these verses, too, are additions of the Hos 1* author to the Hos
2* tradition. In the first place, the notion of "husband" in
2:18aBb is consistent with a) Hosea as husband taking a wife
in Hos 1*, and b) with the interpolation, 2:4aB, by the Hos 1*
author: "she is not my wife and I am not her *husband*."

Moreover, a rapport exists between 2:18aBb and Hos 1* in
the "naming" motif involving the word *qārā'*. In Hos 1*,
YHWH commands Hosea to "call" his children by a certain
name, *qĕrā' šĕmô/šĕmāh* ..." (1:4, 6, 9). In 2:18aBb YHWH
announces to Israel that she will "call" (*tiqrĕ'î*) him "my
husband" and not "my Baal." By calling YHWH "husband"
Israel now identifies herself as "wife" (cf. 2:4aB).

Finally, the brideprice involved in the betrothal cited in
2:21-22a is conceptualized in terms of a *covenantal*
relationship between the two parties: YHWH will betroth
Israel with righteousness, justice, steadfast love, compassion
and faithfulness.[45]

On the basis of these coherences, it may be fair to say,
then, that according to the Hos 1* author, the covenant which
Israel transgressed (1:2) and which YHWH abrogated (1:9;
2:4aB) is now to be renewed (2:18aBb, 21-22a). Just as the
annulment of the covenant between YHWH and Israel took

the form of a *divorce* in the eyes of the Hos 1* author in 2:4aB,
so too is the renewal of covenant described as a renewal of
marital commitment in 2:18aBb, 21-22a. It is the Hos 1*
author, then, who first interjects a note of hope into the
original Hos 2* tradition. Unlike the old covenant, this new
covenant, this renewed marital communion, will last forever
(2:21). This note of hope will be taken up later by the final
redactor. As we have seen, this redactor enlarges upon the
marital covenant theme to include the whole cosmos.[46]

IV. The "Collector" of the Sayings Attributed to Hosea: 1:2-4, 6abA, 8-9; 2:4aB, 6-7a, 18aBb, 21-22a

The author of Hos 1*, therefore, played a very important
role in the literary formation of the Book of Hosea. We will
refer to this author from now on as the *collector* (C). It was he
who published the first written *collection* of the sayings
attributed to the prophet Hosea. These sayings begin in Hos
2:4a and continue for the rest of the book. At this stage of
literary formation, no obvious demarcation of the tradition
exists between Hos 1-3 and 4-14. This division, as we have
seen, was created by the final redactor.[47] The task at hand is
to summarize the literary-theological purpose of the collector
and his initial collection of the sayings attributed to Hosea.

The starting point in discovering this purpose is to note
the obvious: that the collector *selects* the sayings of Hosea
which are preserved in the work. He discriminates between
sayings relevant for his composition and those that are not.
Furthermore, he *arranges* these diverse sayings into a literary
production. The sayings of Hosea, then, acquire their first
gestaltist unity in the literary achievement of the collector.
The collector provides the foundation for the subsequent
redaction of the book. He creates the *first written tradition*
regarding Hosea which later editing expands, modifies and
reinterprets. In the hands of later redactors, the collection
becomes a different literary work with a distinct literary-
theological thrust. We have already observed the degree to
which later redaction creates a formally and functionally

different publication from the collection, viz. its *final* gestaltist unity.

In both dual processes of selection and arrangement certain hermeneutical presuppositions of the collector influence the direction of the literary gestalt which he eventually desires to produce. One can infer the character of these suppositions from the collector's literary tailoring of the material.

In the first place, he provides a literary context for the saying in his Hos 1* composition. Introducing the assembled sayings, Hos 1* represents the transgressions of Israel as a breach of *covenant*. Because of their sin, the collector typifies them as Not My People (1:9).[48]

Moreover, C describes the breakdown of covenant in terms of *conjugal union and dissolution.* These motifs take on two basic forms at the hands of the collector. On one hand, one encounters the theme in the prophetic act of Hosea to marry a wife of harlotry and bear children of harlotry. On the other hand, Hosea's sign-act in the collector's eyes mirrors the marital breakdown between YHWH and Israel. His symbolization of the covenant as a marriage underscores the exclusivity and intimacy that should exist between the covenantal partners. C, therefore, represents the violation of covenant as a *divorce*. The land is unfaithful in whoring away from YHWH (1:2). Therefore, YHWH declares, "She is not my wife and I am not her husband" (2:4aB). With the addition of the 2:4aB clause, C alters the character of the *rîb* against the mother which was in the original Hosean tradition.[49] The *rîb* now becomes a divorce proceeding.

A third hermeneutical presupposition of C is the fact that in composing the Hos 1* narrative, he grounds the saying which begins in 2:4a in a moment of a particular prophet's life, viz. the prophet *Hosea*. Without this introductory material there would be no indication that the collection of oracles is to be attributed to the eighth century prophet Hosea. C thus establishes a stronger connection between the saying and the personality of the prophet.

Furthermore, this concern to correlate the sayings in the historical ministry of Hosea (whether a "true" event or otherwise) has important ramifications. Scholars usually presume that YHWH's command to Hosea to marry a harlot is the beginning of Hosea's prophetic ministry. Hos 1*, then, would describe Hosea's "call" to be God's prophet.[50] Commentators typically think that a call narrative is the prophet's attempt to vindicate and legitimate himself in his office before his opponents. However, B. O. Long argues against a *Sitz-im-Leben* of situational conflict for these call accounts. His following remarks have direct relevance for our own conclusions regarding the Collector of the sayings of Hosea:

> In sum, I would suggest that the accounts of call have been shaped much more by a later, reflective concern than by the immediacy of prophetic activity with its potential for contested authority. The accounts reflect a kind of interpretative interest, *an interest in shaping a portrait of the prophet and introducing his "book" with a view possibly toward his vindication as a spokesman for truth.* It is doubtful that they were ever used in such "full dress" form in the life situation of the prophet. More likely that these accounts might be used to support claims of followers, or successors in a certain prophetic tradition, who, lacking deeds of power, might support their own legitimacy by referring to the transcendent warrant of the master, now of course vindicated by events. *In any case, even though we lack detailed information, it seems sufficiently clear that accounts of call relate most directly to problems of authority in the life situations of tradents, persons who looked back on the departed prophet, who were concerned with transmitting a body of vindicated portraits, claims and exhortations.*[52]

On the basis of Long's comments, it may be fair to say that the collector's introduction constitutes a strategy of legitimation - for the prophet and for himself. The collector legitimates the prophet by anchoring the oracles in a selected aspect of Hosea's ministry: Hosea's marriage and parenting which was commanded by God himself.[53] In C's composition, the prophet's divinely decreed marriage becomes the symbolic counterpart to the "marriage" of YHWH and Israel. Because Hosea in his life experience represents YHWH, the husband of Israel, his sayings, in the collector's eyes, obtain authority as the written Word of God. The prophet's oracles still "live" and speak authoritatively in this written collection.

The collector, furthermore, legitimates himself and the collection which he creates. He lacked the call from God and the deeds of power which seemed to support a prophetic ministry.[54] However, he carries on the prophet's work by compiling and assembling the sayings into a literary tradition. By asserting the divine commissioning of the prophet and by portraying his master as the prophetic embodiment of God's experience with Israel in Hos 1*, C claims authority for his "book" which now transmits the prophetic traditions.

A fourth and final hermeutical presupposition of the collector is that he envisions *hope* for the "marriage" between YHWH and Israel. In 2:18aBb, 21-22a he reverses the divorce declaration which looms heavily over the rest of the Hosean oracle. The divorce will ultimately be repealed in favor of a "rebetrothal" to symbolize the new covenant which will be ratified. Contrary to scholars like Marti and Harper who consign all hope passages to the exilic period,[55] the message of hope is introduced by the northern tradent who first assembled the tradition. The dating of the collector should be narrowed to a time when circumstances exerted pressure to form a collection of Hosean oracles and when *hope* of a "rebetrothal" between YHWH and Israel was a real possibility. We tentatively date the Collector after the fall of the northern kingdom in 722/21 BCE.[56] Sentiments of hope could have sprung up during the time of Hezekiah's reform (715-705?). During this time Hezekiah had approached the citizens of the defunct North to participate in the reform program. It was anticipated that religious unification between North and South would serve as a prelude to political unification.[57]

V. *The First Redaction (R1) of the Collection:*
   2:10a, 11, 13-15a

Having identified the work of C, we turn to the remaining verses of the earlier stages of the tradition in Hos 2*. Again anticipating our results, we have put in *italics*, the editorial contribution of the first redactor, R1:

	Hos 2*
2:4aA	*rîbû bě'imměkem rîbû*
2:4b	*wětāsēr zěnûnêhā mippānêhā*
	wěna'pûpêhā mibbên šādêhā
2:5	*pen-'apšîṭennā 'ărummâ*
	wěhiṣṣagtîhā kěyôm hiwwālědāh
	wěśamtîhā kammidbār
	wěšattîhā kě'ereṣ ṣiyyâ
	wahămittîhā baṣṣāmā'
2:7b	*kî 'ăměrâ 'ēlěkā 'aḥărê mě'ahăbay*
	nōtěnê laḥmî ûmêmay ṣamrî ûpištî
	šamnî wěšiqqûyāy
2:10a	<u>*wěhî' lō' yādě'â kî 'ānōkî nātattî lāh*</u>
	<u>*haddāgān wěhattîrôš wěhayyiṣhār*</u>
2:11	<u>*lākēn 'āšûb wělāqaḥtî děgāni bě'ittô*</u>
	<u>*wětîrôšî běmô'ădô wěhiṣṣaltî ṣamrî ûpištî*</u>
	<u>*lěkassôt 'et-'erwātāh*</u>
2:12	*wě'attâ 'ăgalleh 'et-nablūtāh*
	lě'ênê mě'ahăbêhā
	wě'îš lō' -yaṣṣîlennâ miyyādî
2:13	<u>*wěhišbattî kol-měśôśāh ḥaggāh ḥodšāh*</u>
	<u>*wěšabbattāh wěkol mô'ădāh*</u>
2:14	<u>*wahăšimmōtî gapnāh ûtě'ēnātāh*</u>
	<u>*'ăšer 'āměrâ 'etnâ hēmmâ lî*</u>
	<u>*'ăšer nātěnû-lî mě'ahăbāy*</u>
	<u>*wěśamtîm lěya'ar wě'ăkālātam ḥayyat haśśādeh*</u>
2:15a	<u>*ûpāqadtî 'alêhā 'et-yěmê habbě'ālîm*</u>
	<u>*'ăšer taqṭîr lāhem watta'ad nizmāh*</u>
	<u>*wěḥelyātāh wattēlek 'aḥărê mě'ahăbêhā*</u>

2:4aA	Plead with your mother, plead . . .
2:4b	that she remove her harlotry from her face
	and her adultery from between her breasts
2:5	lest I strip her naked
	and set her out as on the day she was born.
	I will make her like a wilderness,

> change her into an arid land,
> and slay her with thirst . . .

2:7b   for she said, "I will go after my lovers,
> who give me my bread and my water,
> my wool and my flax,
> my oil and my drink" . . .

2:10   *But she did not know that I gave to her*
> *the grain, wine and oil.*
> *Therefore, I will turn and take back*
> *my grain in its time and my wine in its season.*

2:11   *I will rescue my wool and my flax*
> *which were to cover her nakedness.*

2:12   And now, I will expose her genitals
> in the sight of her lovers.
> And no one will rescue her from my hand.

2:13   *I will put an end to all her joy,*
> *her feasts, her new moons, her sabbaths,*
> *and all of her assemblies.*

2:14   *I will lay waste her vines and her fig trees*
> *of which she said, "A harlot's hire are they to me*
> *which my lovers have given me."*
> *I will make them a forest*
> *and the beasts of the field will devour them.*

2:15a   *I will call her to account for the*
> *feast days of the baals to whom she burned incense.*
> *She adorned herself with her ring and her*
> *ornament*
> *and went after her lovers . . .*

As with the Hos 1* and Hos 2* discussion, we pose the question whether this tradition is a unity or a composite. In one of the latest redactional analyses of Hos 1-3, Ruppert pinpoints a real disparity between Hos 2:4-5, 7b, 12 and 2:10-11, 13-15a.[58] In the first place, there are changes in form. Hos 2:4-5, 7b exposes the sin of the wife in the form of a *rîb*, while 2:10-11, 13-15a is a threat or judgment speech. Another clue to the disparity between these two blocks of material is the fact that the woman attributes to her lovers different gifts in 2:7 and 2:14. In 2:7b, the lovers give the wife bread, water, wool, flax, oil and drink. In 2:14, the gifts becomes vines and fig trees. Furthermore, 2:11 appears to be a doublet of 2:12 in the repetition of *nsl* which has a different meaning in each verse. On one hand, *YHWH* will *withdraw* the wool and flax (2:11b, *wĕhiṣṣaltî*). On the other hand, *no one* will *rescue* the wife from the hand of YHWH (2:12, *yaṣṣîlennâ*).[59] One can compare this resumption of the same verb to make a contrast with that found in 2:7b and 2:10b which share the same verb *ntn*. On one hand, the wife is under the impression that her *lovers* give (*nōtĕnê*) her all her material goods according to 2:7b. On contrast, *YHWH* declares in 2:10 that he has given (*nātattî*) her good things.

Moreover, Hos 2:10-11, 13-15a appear to be later interpretations of 2:4aA, 5, 7b, 12. They have in common a calculated theological intent, viz. a deuteronomistic attack against abuses in cult.

We point out, first, the most obvious references to cult in 2:13. Here, YHWH will abolish the wife's liturgical feasts, new moons, sabbaths, and cultic assemblies. According to later texts, 2 Chron 8:13 and Ezek 45:17, they constitute the main Mosaic liturgical celebrations. They had been corrupted and no longer make up true worship of YHWH (cf. Isa 2:13-14). Worthy of note are Jeremiah's and Ezekiel's oracles against the people for violation of the Sabbath (Jer 17:21-27; Ezek 20:12-13, 16, 21, 24; 22:26) and especially the connection of feast and new moon with the sin of Jeroboam according to the deuteronomist in 1 Kgs 12:32-33.

Second, in 2:10 the wife did not "know" that YHWH provided for her well-being. We have already witnessed the deuteronomistic notion of "knowing" YHWH in the final redactor's 2:22b, "And you will *know* YHWH."[60]

Third, 2:10 revises the list of natural products in 2:7b which the lovers allegedly provide for the wife. In 2:10 the "bread, water, wool, flax, oil and drink" of 2:7b are converted to "grain, wine, and oil," which YHWH will retract. Several scholars have pointed out that "grain, wine, and oil" seems to be a stereotyped deuteronomic expression, particularly in the context of the cultic tithe.[61]

Fourth, 2:14a parallels 2:7b where the wife's own words count as evidence for her crime against her husband.

2:7b	*kî 'ămĕrâ*	2:14a	*ăšer 'āmĕrâ*
	'ēlĕkâ 'ahărê		*'etnâ hēmmâ lî*
	mĕ'ahăbay		*'ăšer nātĕnû-lî*
	nōtĕnê lahmî		*mĕ'ahăbāy*
	ûmêmay etc.		

2:7b	for she said	2:14a	of which she said,
	"I will go after		"A harlot's hire are
	my lovers who give		they to me which my
	me my bread		lovers have given me."
	and my water etc."		

Hos 2:14a adds an interpretive twist to 2:7b in describing the gifts from the lovers as *'etnâ*, a "harlot's hire." Concerning *'etnâ*[62] the proscriptions regarding the cultic tithe in Dt 23:18-19 are noteworthy:

> There shall be no cult prostitute of the daughters of Israel, neither shall there be a cult prostitute of the sons of Israel. You shall not bring the hire of a harlot (*'etnan zônāh*) or the wages of a dog, into the house of the Lord your God. (Dt 23:18-19)

Thus, 2:10 and 2:14a make the wife's offenses in 2:7b more definite as transgressions due to improper cultic tithes.

Fifth, 2:14b resumes *śym* from 2:5b. In the language of treaty curses 2:14b expands upon the desolation YHWH will make of the wife for her breach of covenant described in 2:5b: "I will make them a forest and the beasts of the field will devour them."[63]

Sixth, 2:15aA identifies the wife's paramours of 2:7a explicitly as the Baalim. These are condemned repeatedly by the deuteronomistic historian (Dt 4:3; Judg 2:11, 13; 3:7; 8:33; 1 Kgs 22:54; 2 Kgs 3:2; 17:16 *et passim*).

And finally, 2:15a condemns the wife for burning incense (*qṭr, hiphil*) to these Baalim.   Deuteronomy and the Deuteronomistic History characteristically denounce the burning of incense to the baals and foreign gods.[64]   In this connection, 1 Kgs 13:1-2 and 2 Kgs 23:5 are particularly germane to our discussion. 1 Kgs 13:1-2 relates the incident when Jeroboam burned incense (*qṭr, hiphil*) upon the altar in his unorthodox sanctuary at Bethel.   A man prophesies against the altar, saying:

> "Behold, a son shall be born to the House of David, Josiah by name: and he shall sacrifice upon you the priests of the high places who *burn incense* (*qṭr, hiphil*) upon you, and men's bones shall be burned upon you." (1 Kgs 13:2, RSV)

2 Kgs 23:5 narrates the fulfillment of this prophecy when Josiah undertakes his reform of the cult:

> He desposed the idolatrous priests whom the kings of Judah had ordained to *burn incense* (*qṭr, piel*) in the high places at the cities of Judah and round about Jerusalem; those also who *burned incense to Baal* (*qṭr lbʿl, piel*), to the sun, and the moon, and the constellations, and all the hosts of heaven. (2 Kgs 23:5, RSV)

VI. The First Redactor (R1) and the Final Redactor (R2)

We have, then, a redaction of the collection of Hosean oracles which seems to be steeped in deuteronomistic ideology but is distinct from and earlier than the deuteronomistic thrust of our final redactor. The final redactor would have inherited his working material from this earlier redactor and built upon it to create the present text. From now on, we refer to the first redactor as R1 vis-à-vis the final redactor, R2.

R1 appears to be preoccupied with cult and the idolatrous worship which has permeated the cult.   His perspective is explicitly deuteronomistic.   His redactional technique includes the resumption of select words (*ntn* - 2:7, 10; *nsl* - 2:11b, 12; *śym* - 2:5b, 14b) or phrases (2:7b, 10a, 14a, 15a) from his tradition and revising them according to his theological intent. Moreover, he arranges his commentary in an order which inverts his tradition. The total effect of his redaction is chiastic:

TRADITION

A	2:4	harlotry from her face adultery from between her breasts
B	2:5	I will make (*šym*) her like a wilderness
C	2:7b	For she said, "I will go after my lovers who give me my bread and water ..."
D	2:12	And now, I will expose her genitals in the sight of her lovers. And no one will rescue (*nṣl*) her out of my hand.

R1

D'	2:11	I will rescue (*nṣl*) my wool and my flax which were to cover her nakedness.
C'	2:14a	Of which she said, "A harlot's hire are they to me which my lovers have given me."
B'	2:14b	I will make (*šym*) them a forest ...
A'	2:15a	her ring her jewelry

We turn to the phenomenon of two deuteronomistic redactions. We wish to suggest here that the literary formation of the Book of Hosea has analogues in the literary evolution of Deuteronomy and the Deuteronomistic History. A number of scholars have recently recognized a double redaction of the Deuteronomistic History,[65] modifying M. Noth's influential single redaction theory of the work.[66]

The first and main redactor of the History, DTR 1, would have edited his work during the time of Josiah. The second redactor, DTR 2, supplemented this history during the exilic period. One of the principal DTR 1 themes commentators note is that of the crimes of Jeroboam and his northern successors.[67] Jeroboam had established alternatives to the Jerusalem cult at the sanctuaries at Bethel and Dan (1 Kgs 12:25-33). Making two calves of gold, he presented them to the people, saying: "You have gone up to Jerusalem long enough. Behold your gods, O Israel, who brought you up out of the land of Egypt" (1 Kgs 12:28). According to DTR 1, this was apostasy against Yahwism in the worst sense. This redactor, a Judean, traced all the problems of the North to this "sin of Jeroboam." The perseverance of this motif in the History up to 2 Kgs 22:1ff, where Josiah attempts to destroy the effects of Jeroboam's sin, has led scholars to conclude that the DTR 1 history was royal Judean propaganda for Josiah's reform.[68]

We point out that the interpretive additions of R1 in Hos 2* have some points of contact with DTR 1. Both would attribute the downfall of the North, not to unsound political policy or to the territorial expansionism of its neighbors, but to religious apostasy, to a polluted cult. This apostasy originated in the sin of Jeroboam. For R1 it shows its face in feasts (*ḥag*), new moons (*hodeš*) and cultic assemblies (*mô'ēd*) which Jeroboam established at the northern sanctuaries (Hos 2:13; 1 Kgs 12:32-33). At these centers, an illegitimate priesthood burned incense to the Baals (Hos 2:15; 1 Kgs 13:1-2). However, like YHWH who will put an end (*šbt*, *hiphil*) to the cultic feast days (Hos 2:13), Josiah will put an end (*šbt*, *hiphil*) "to the idolatrous priests whom the kings of Judah had ordained to burn incense in the high places at the cities of Judah and round about Jerusalem" (2 Kgs 23:5).[69]

VII.   *The Saying Attributed to the Prophet Hosea (H):*
       2:4aAb-5, 7b, 12

Having pinpointed the hand of C, R1 and R2 in the present text, we can now deal with the saying of Hosea preserved in the work. This saying becomes the springboard for the literary evolution of the tradition. From a form critical perspective these verses appear to be a complete unit whose structure presents itself thus:

A. 2:4aAb - *Call to rîb against the mother*

bĕ 'immĕkem rîbû	Plead with your mother, plead . . .
wĕtāsēr zĕnûnêhā mippānêhā	that she remove her harlotry from her face

wĕna 'ăpûpêhā mibbên	and her adultery from
šādêhā	between her breasts,

B. 2:5 - *Threat which accompanies the rîb*

pen-'apšîṭennâ 'ărummâ	lest I strip her naked
wĕhiṣṣagtîhā kĕyôm	and set her out as on the
hiwwālĕdāh	day she was born.
wĕśamtîhā kammidbār	I will make her like a
	wilderness,
wĕšattîhā kĕ'ereṣ ṣiyyâ	change her into an arid land,
wahămittîhā baṣṣāmā'	and slay her with thirst . . .

C. 2:7b - *Accusation or indictment*[70]

kî 'āmĕrâ	For she said,
'ēlĕkâ 'aḥărê mĕ 'ahăbay	"I will go after my lovers
nōtĕnê laḥmî ûmêmay	who have given me my bread
	and my water
ṣamrî ûpištî	my wool and my flax
šamnî wĕšiqqûyāy	my oil and my drink . . ."

D. 2:12 - *Sentence*[71]

wĕ'attâ 'ăgalleh	And now, I will expose
'et-nablūtāh	her genitals
lĕ'ênê mĕ'ahăbêhā	in the sight of her lovers
wĕ'îš lō'-yaṣṣîlennâ	No one will rescue her
miyyādî	from my hand.

The "children" are summoned to *rîb* with their "mother" to persuade her to abandon her adulterous behavior. The clause inserted by the collector, 2:4aB, "for she is not my wife and I am not her husband," created a divorce proceeding from this saying.[72] What, then, is the nature of the *rîb* in this original saying? The primary meaning of the root *ryb* is "to bring legal action" against someone,[73] although the word can be used in pre-legal or extra-legal situations.[74] The forensic overtones of *rîb* suggest that our text is a legal complaint against an adulterous woman. Punishment for adultery according to

Hebrew law is death for both parties (Lev 20:10; Dt 22:22).[75]
However, our Hosean saying, as well as other HB texts,[76]
present an alternative to the death penalty for adultery which
seemed to be current at the time, viz. stripping the guilty
woman naked in public.[77] In 2:5 the speaker threatens to
denude the wayward woman if she does not forswear her
harlotry. In 2:12, he actualizes his threat and disgraces her
before her lovers.[78]

Who are the "children" addressed in this legal complaint
and who is their scarlet "mother"? Who, indeed, is the
speaker? Removed from its secondary literary context, the
saying cannot refer back to Gomer and her children in Hos 1*.
One presumes that the speaker is YHWH. Nevertheless, the
saying is ambiguous enough so that one can see why and how
the collector added Hos 1* to it, securing the oracle in the life
and ministry of Hosea. Some scholars understand the
"mother" to be the land of Israel (which YHWH will make like
a wilderness, 2:5) and the "children" to be the inhabitants of
the land.[79]. Others, the collective personality vis-à-vis the
individual members of the collective.[80] Still others, the whole
people of Israel in contrast to the faithful "children of YHWH"
within the nation who do not agree with the actions of the
whole.[81]

In order to determine the identity of the "mother" and the
"children," we should relate the passage with the remaining
Hosean sayings interwoven with the rest of the book, Hos 4-
14. Consistent with our approach thus far, we must determine
first for Hos 4-14 the contributions of the final redactor (R2),
the first redactor (R1) and the collector (C). Anticipating our
results, however, we think that the Hosean saying beginning
in Hos 2:4a ends with the Jacob tradition in 12:13: "Jacob fled
to the land of Aram; there Israel did service for a wife, and for
a wife he herded sheep." According to Gen 32:29 Jacob is
renamed Israel which becomes the patronymic of the nation.
Dt 26:5 typifies Jacob as the "father" of Israel: "A wandering
Aramean was my father."

In prospect, we suggest that the "mother" in 2:4ff is
Rachel, the favored wife of Jacob,[82] for whom Hos 12:13 states
that Jacob served Laban by tending sheep. Ru 4:1 describes

Rachel and Leah as building up the house of Israel together. In a very striking passage Jer 31:15 speaks of the matriarch as follows:

> A voice is heard in Ramah,
> lamentation and bitter weeping.
> Rachel is weeping for her children;
> she refuses to be comforted for her children
> because they are not. (Jer 31:15, RSV)

Here, Rachel, the mother of Joseph and Benjamin, is bitterly grieving the fate of these northern tribes.

The earliest tradition in the Book of Hosea, then, would have personified the kingdom of Israel as the preferred wife of Jacob/Israel, Rachel. Her "children" become the northern tribes. As ancestress of the northern tribes, she becomes a symbol of their moral corruption. She represents them as an adulterous woman.[83] We mention here that the image of YHWH as husband is not operative at this stage. Jacob is Rachel's husband. The metaphor which Hosea wishes to convey is the image of Rachel as "mother" of Israel who has whored, not Rachel as "wife" of YHWH. However, since the image of "mother" is polyvalent, the collector seized the opportunity later to transform it into a conjugal metaphor for YHWH and Israel.

CHAPTER FIVE

The Redactional History of Hos 1-3: A Summary

We are now in a position to summarize our findings on the redactional history of Hos 1-3. Although we determined this history by working first from the final redaction and then back to the earlier stages of the tradition, we will present our results now in chronological sequence. The following is a table outlining the redactional phases of the tradition:

H	C	R1	R2
			1:1
	1:2-4		1:5
	1:6abA		1:6bB-7
	1:8-9		2:1-3
2:4aA	2:4aB		
2:4b-5	2:6-7a		
2:7b			2:8-9
		2:10a	2:10b
		2:11	
2:12		2:13-15a	2:15b-18aA
	2:18aBb		2:19-20
	2:21-22a		2:22b-25
			3:1-5

I. Hosea (H)

The earliest tradition is a saying attributed to the prophet Hosea which begins in 2:4aA and continues in the rest of the book. It appears to be a legal complaint of YHWH brought against an adulterous woman and her subsequent punishment. We will argue below in our analysis of Hos 4-14 that the harlotrous mother is Rachel, wife of Jacob/Israel, and that her "children" are the northern tribes.

II. The Collector (C)

This saying attributed to the prophet Hosea is preserved
for us by C, the collector of the Hosean tradition. The theme of
the marital union between YHWH and Israel originates in his
brilliant reinterpretation of the original saying. First of all,
he provides the Hosean oracle with a narrative introduction,
Hos 1*. Here, he grounds the oracle in the ministry of Hosea,
focusing on Hosea's infamous marriage to Gomer and the birth
of their children. Hos 1* becomes the literary context of the
original saying whereby the "mother" in 2:4 becomes Gomer,
symbolizing the land which "whores away from YHWH" (1:2).
The "children," in turn, become the "children of harlotry" (1:2;
2:6) personifying threats against the land: Jezreel, Lo
Ruhama, and Lo Ammi.

Secondly, with Hos 1* C creates a structural homology
between the marriages of Hosea and Gomer and YHWH and
Israel. In Hos 2* he extends his marital motif even further.
He transforms the original *rib*, a legal complaint against
adultery, into a *divorce* proceedings by means of his 2:4aB
addition. His overall concern is the covenant and its
dissolution, representing them as a marriage and a divorce.

Thirdly, all is not bleak in the eyes of the Collector. After
the punishment which the Hosean oracle prescribes (2:12), C
interjects a note of hope for the relationship between YHWH
and his wife. In 2:18aBb, 21-22a, he describes the remarriage
between God and Israel, signifying the new covenant which
will be established between them.

The Collector is probably a northerner and a disciple of
Hosea. In all likelihood, he composed his work to legitimate
his beloved master and to legitimate himself and his
collection, telling the story of Hosea's marriage to the harlot
as if it were a prophetic "call" narrative. The tentative date of
his literary activity is after the fall of the North in 722/21
BCE, perhaps during the time of Hezekiah's reform. Here,
hope for a "remarriage" between YHWH and Israel is a real
possibility.

III. The First Redactor (R1)

The sayings of the prophet Hosea achieve their first literary gestaltist unity in the collection. The first two columns of the above table, e.g. *H* + *C*, become the *tradition* which the first redactor (R1) inherits and edits for his own purposes to create another literary gestalt. His editorial work consists in resuming certain words or phrases from his tradition and then making his commentary. He seems to arrange his commentary in a chiastic inversion of his tradition. His interpretive remarks focus on the deterioration of the cult and are typically deuteronomistic. Since our final redactor, R2, also seems to be deuteronomistic, we propose that the literary formation of the Book of Hosea may have a parallel in the double redaction of the Deuteronomistic History. Our R1 has some similarities with DTR 1 who viewed the deterioration and fall of the northern kingdom as the result of the "sin of Jeroboam."

IV. The Final Redactor (R2)

The second redactor, R2, is responsible for the text as we have it in its present state, its final gestaltist unity. *H* + *C* + *R1* become the *tradition* which R2 inherits and revises for his own situation in the exile. Like C and R1 before him, his editorial work reformulates the tradition. He reverses or modifies his tradition principally by means of paronomasia. One recognizes his paronomastic reinterpretations in 3:1-5 which parallels the collector's account of Hosea's marriage (Hos 1*) and his mitigation or reversal of the threats implied in the names of Hosea's three children (1:5, 6bB-7; 2:1).

Besides qualifying the portentous tone of his tradition, R2 makes extensive structural changes in it. First, he provides the tradition with a redactional beginning (1:1) and a redactional conclusion (3:1-5). His conclusion, 3:1-5, segregates the marriage tradition in Hos 1-2 from Hos 4-14. Moreover, it places the marriage between YHWH and Israel, 2:4-24, in a prominent position between the two narratives on Hosea's marriage, providing it with an inclusio-like frame,

2:2-3, 25. In keeping with his theme of repentance and return to YHWH and the land, R2 introduces a journey motif, structuring his tradition to accommodate it. Inserting *lākēn hinnēh* plus commentary both before as well as after the tradition's final verdict, viz. 2:11-15a which was introduced by *lākēn* alone, R2 transforms it into the second step of a three-fold process of purification. Hos 2:8-9 becomes the first step where YHWH will bar the wife's path to her lovers in order to re-route her back to himself. Hos 2:16-17 is the final stage of the journey where YHWH will lead his punished wife into the wilderness of their first love.

Finally, R2 expands the collector's theme of the marriage/covenant between YHWH and Israel by giving it a cosmic dimension. By means of the triadic occurrences of *hāyâ bayyôm hahû' nĕ'ūm yhwh*, he builds to a climax in which all creation participates in the covenantal renewal/remarriage of YHWH and his people.

CHAPTER SIX

The Composition of Hosea 4-11, 12-14: The Final Redacted State

We now begin the redactional analysis of Hos 4-11, 12-14. In dealing with these chapters, we will assume the results of our investigation of Hos 1-3: that the literary formation of the work consists in an initial collection of the oracles of Hosea (C) and two redactions of this collection (R1 and R2). We will identify first the structure and literary thrust of the final stage of the book, the work of R2. We will argue that the final redactor is responsible for the Hos 4-11, 12-14 structure. We will then determine the earlier phases of the tradition, R1, C, and Hosea.

As is well acknowledged, Hos 4-14 is perhaps the most difficult Hebrew text next to the Book of Job. We have argued in the preceding chapters that the tensions in the text are due primarily to interpretive redactional commentary. For this reason, we will try to maintain the correctness of the MT and keep emendations based on other ancient versions to a minimum. It is these tensions in the text which provide clues to the process of composition.

From our analysis of Hos 1-3, we operate under the following working assumptions regarding the final redacted state of Hos 4-14:

1. that R2 is responsible for the overall structure, Hos 4-11, 12-14
2. that the primary literary-theological thrust of R2 is the repentance of the people in exile and their restoration in the land
3. that one of the linking devices R2 uses to mitigate or reverse his tradition is paronomasia.

I. Hos 14:2-10: The Redactional Conclusion

Just as the final redactor closed off the first section of the Book of Hosea with 3:1-5, so too does he conclude the third and

final section of the book, Hos 12-14, with Hos 14:2-10. Not a
few commentators have already suggested that the Hos 14:2-
10 unit is a later secondary addition.[1] We noted above that
with the addition of 3:1-5, the first section, Hos 1-3, thus
became the hermeneutical introduction for the rest of the
work. The marriage metaphor which symbolically portrays
the relationship between YHWH and his people characterizes
Hos 1-3. In dividing off Hos 1-3, R2 highlighted the forgiving
covenantal love of YHWH towards a repentant people. Such a
message offered consolation to a people in exile.[2] Likewise,
the final redactor's conclusion, 14:2-10, recapitulates these
themes and makes the final statement of the work. In order to
facilitate our discussion, we will treat 14:2-10 in sections,
beginning with 14:2-4.

A. *14:2-4 - The final redactor's exhortation to the people to
    repentance*

14:2a   *šûbâ yiśrā'ēl 'ad yhwh 'ĕlōhêkā*
14:2b   *kî kāšaltā ba'ăwônekā*
14:3a   *qĕḥû 'immākem dĕbārîm*
         wĕšûbû 'el-yhwh
14:3b   *'imrû 'ēlāyw*
         kol-tiśśa' 'āwôn
         wĕqaḥ-ṭôb
         ûnĕšallĕmâ pĕrî-m[3] śĕpātênû
14:4a   *'aššûr lō' yôši'ēnû*
         'al sûs lō' nirkāb
         wĕlō' nō'mar 'ôd 'ĕlōhênû
         lĕma 'ăśēh yādênû
14:4b   *'ăšer-bĕkā yĕrūḥam yātôm*

14:2a   Return, O Israel, to YHWH your God,
14:2b   for you have stumbled in your iniquity.
14:3a   Take with you words
         and return to YHWH.
14:3b   Say to him:
         "You forgive all iniquity.

Now accept what is good.
And we will render the fruit of our lips.
14:4a   Assyria will not save us.
Upon horses we will not ride.
And we will never again say, 'our God',
to the work of our hands.
14:4b   For in you the orphan finds compassion."

The final redactor begins 14:2-10 with a summons to repent: *šûbâ yiśrā'ēl 'ad yhwh 'ĕlōhêkā*, "return, O Israel, to YHWH your God." Just as R2 used *antanaclasis* in 3:1-5 and 2:23-24 in the repetition of *'hb* and *'nh* respectively,[4] he conducts a similar wordplay in the fivefold antanaclasis involving the root *šûb*. We have already seen that *šûb* is a favorite word of this redactor in 2:9 and 3:5.[5] In 14:2-10, R2 cleverly manipulates the word within a range of meanings, listed as follows:

14:2	- *šûbâ*	to repent and return to YHWH
14:3	- *šûbû*	
14:5a	- *mĕšûbātām*	faithlessness or apostasy
14:5b	- *šāb*	to turn away or divert anger
14:8	- *yāšūbû*	to return to the land

We point out especially 14:5 where *šûb* is used twice with different meanings: "I will heal their faithlessness *(mĕšûbātām)* ... for my anger has turned *(šāb)* from them." Moreover, in 14:8 the *antanaclasis* is reinforced by metaphony: "They shall return *(yāšûbû)* and dwell *(yēšĕbû)* in my shade."[6] The same use of metaphony by R2 involving *yāšûbû/yēšĕbû* occurs in 3:5: "They shall dwell *(yēšĕbû)* for many days .... Afterwards, they shall return *(yāšûbû)*."[7] The final redactor therefore concludes his work on a theme which is uppermost in his mind as he writes to the exiles, viz. the people's repentance which, for him, will precipitate their return to their beloved homeland. He underscores this theme by means of the five instances of *šûb*.

Besides the striking repetition of *šûb*, we point out other paronomasia and motifs typical of R2 in Hos 14:2-4. In the first place, Israel's declaration in 14:3-4, "You forgive (*tiśśā'*) all iniquity ... for in you the orphan finds compassion (*yĕrūḥam yātôm*),"[8] recalls the final redactor's reversal of the threat against the House of Israel implied in the name of Hosea's daughter, Lo Ruhama, in 1:6bB-7: "I will indeed forgive (*nāśō' 'eśśā'*) them and upon the House of Judah I will have compassion ('*ăraḥēm*)."[9]

A second example of R2's hand is the wordplay on the proper noun, Ephraim, in *pĕrî-m*, "fruit," in 14:3b and 14:9b.[10] The two words are related not only parasonantically but also in etymology.[11] According to Gen 41:52, Joseph's second son is called Ephraim, "because God has made me fruitful (*hiprani*) in the land of my affliction." In Hos 14:9 the play between the words becomes most explicit. Here, YHWH likens himself to a tree from which Ephraim draws its fruit: *'eprayim mah-lî 'ôd lā'ăṣabbîm ... mimmennî peryĕkā nimṣā'*, "Ephraim - what more has he to do with idols ... From me will your fruit be obtained."

Third, in 14:4 the final redactor urges Israel to renounce its dependence upon political alliances (v. 4aA), military might (v. 4aB) and idolatry (v. 4aC). His manner of formulating his exhortation is striking. We point out the alliteration in *'aśśûr lō' yôśî'ēnû*, which picks up the alliterative series of *ś/ś*[12] in the previous lines: *śûbâ, yiśrā'ēl, kāśaltā, śûbû, tiśśā', ûnĕśallĕmâ, śĕpatênû*. Kaatz thinks *'śr* incorporates a pun, not only on *'aśśûr*, "Assyria," but also on *'eśer*, "happiness."[13] Thus, for R2 Assyria (*'aśśûr*), which Israel thinks is a source of happiness (*'eśer*) or good fortune, will not save them (*lō' yôśî'ēnû*). The paronomasia on *'śr* is extended further to 14:9. Assyria will not save Israel/Ephraim but "I (YHWH) will look after him (*wa'aśûrennû*)" (14:9b).

Moreover, in the R2 interpolation, 1:7, YHWH declares that he will save them (*wĕhôśa'tîm*) by YHWH their God and will not save them (*lō' 'ôśî'ēm*) by military means, including horses (*bĕsûsîm*). The redactor's statement here in 14:4, "Assyria will not save us (*lō' yôśî'ēnû*); upon horses ('*al-sûs*) we will not ride," echoes his declaration in Hos 1:7. Note that *sûs* continues the alliteration of *ś/ś*.

The third renunciation, 14:4aBb regarding idolatry, is equally striking. The following represents not only the alliteration of *š/ś* but also of *y*, and *'/':*[14]

14:4aBb   *wĕlō' nō'mar 'ôd 'ĕlōhênû*
              lĕma'ăśēh yādênû
              'ăšer bĕkā yĕrûḥam yātôm

14:4aBb   And we will never again say "our God"
              to the work of our hands
              for in you the orphan finds compassion.

In 14:4aB, the *lĕma'ăśēh* correlates with the redactor's accusation in 2:10b that Israel made (*'āśû*) Baals with the silver and gold which YHWH provided. Hos 14:aBb also echoes his conclusion to the story of YHWH and Israel in 2:25. In the latter, YHWH will have compassion (*wĕriḥamtî*) on Lo Ruhama, and Ammi will declare (*yō'mar*) to YHWH alone, "My God" (*'ĕlōhāy*).

B. *14:5 - The healing of Israel*

14:5a   *'erpā' mĕšûbātām*
           'ōhăbēm nĕdābâ
14:5b   *kî šāb 'appî mimmennû*

14:5a   I will heal their faithlessness.
           I will love them freely,
14:5b   for my anger has turned from them.

After the final author's exhortation to the people to repent comes YHWH's response in the 1st person to the contrite nation. Beginning this response, 14:5 involves the *antanaclasis* on the root *šwb* as well as the alliteration of ', *š*, *b*, *p*, and *m*. The verse is arranged in a chiasmus.[15]

'erpā' mĕšûbātām 'ōhăbēm nĕdābâ kî šāb 'appî mimmennû

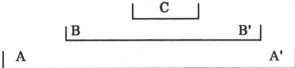

In the structure of the chiasmus, YHWH will heal the apostasy of his people (*mĕšûbātām*), because his anger has turned away (*šāb*) from them. Highlighted by the structure in C is *'ōhăbēm nĕdābâ*, "I will love them freely." The theme of the God who loves his people is picked up from Hos 3:1-5. In the latter, the final redactor makes his point by means of a fourfold *antanaclasis* on *'hb*.[16]

C. 14:6-9 - Israel, the lush plantation of YHWH

14:6a	*'ehyeh kaṭṭal lĕyiśrā'ēl*
	yipraḥ kaššôšannâ
	wĕyak šārāšayw kallĕbānôn
14:7a	*yēlēkû yōnĕqôtāyw*
	wîhî kazzayit hôdô
14:7b	*wĕrēaḥ lô kallĕbānôn*
14:8a	*yāšūbû yēšĕbû bĕṣillî*
	(MT: yōšĕbê bĕṣillô)[17]
	yĕḥayyû dāgān
	wĕyiprĕḥû kaggāpen
14:8b	*zikrô kĕyên lĕbānôn*
14:9a	*'eprayim mah-lî 'ôd lā'ăṣabbîm*
14:9b	*'ănî 'ānîtî wa'ăšûrennû*
	'ănî kibrôš ra'ănān
	mimmennî peryĕkā nimṣā'

14:6a	I will be as the dew to Israel.
	He shall blossom like the lily.
14:6b	He shall strike root like Lebanon.
14:7a	His suckers shall spread out
	His splendor shall be like the olive tree
14:7b	and his fragrance like Lebanon.
14:8a	They shall return and sit in my* shade.

	They shall make grain grow.
	They shall blossom as the vine.
14:8b	His renown will be like the wine of Lebanon.
14:9a	Ephraim - what more has he[18] to do with idols
14:9b	I respond and look after him.
	I am like a luxuriant juniper.
	From me will your fruit be obtained.

Continuing YHWH's 1st person response, 14:6-9 resumes and brings to a climax the agricultural theme which characterized the final redaction of Hos 2. Here in Hos 2, all of creation will participate in the covenant which YHWH will renew with his people (2:20, 23-24). One of the last details concluding Hos 2 is the fact that YHWH will sow Israel in the land (2:25, *zr' b'rṣ*).[19] Hos 14:6-9 develops this image by describing the luxuriant growth of Israel in the land, which follows upon this sowing. Consistent with R2's fondness for three's in restructuring the Hos 2 tradition,[20] this section contains a threefold repetition of "Lebanon," 14:6b, 7b, 8b. Alliteration abounds, particularly with the letters *y*, *š/ś* and *h/g*.

With the statement in 14:6, "I will be as a dew to Israel," R2, on one hand, recalls a Jacob tradition. In Gen 27:28 Isaac, thinking Jacob to be Esau, pronounces a blessing over him, saying:

> "May God give you the dew of heaven (*ṭal haššāmayim*) and the fatness of the earth and plenty of grain and wine." (Gen 27:28. Cf. Gen 27:39; Dt 33:28).

On the other hand, R2 recalls his own description of YHWH's covenantal response (*'nh*) to Israel in 2:23 where he will make the heavens drop rain upon the earth.[21] It is only through God's free gift of rain that the plantation of Israel not only survives but flourishes. For R2, only YHWH the creator God, and not any other god, grants rain. The abundance of rain is a manifestation of God's covenant with his people. R2 will underscore this fact later in 14:9 where, in contrast with idols, YHWH responds (*'ānîtî*) and looks after Ephraim.

Moreover, the *'ehyeh* beginning 14:6 can perhaps be a paronomasia insinuating this notion of the covenantal God into the text. In our discussion of the final redaction of Hos 1-3, we argued that the reversal of Lo Ammi, resided in 2:1. R2 transforms the threat, "I am not I AM (*lō' 'ehyeh*) to you" (1:9), by means of a wordplay on *hyh* such that Not My People becomes "children of the Living God" (*běnê 'ēl-ḥāy*).[22] In view of this discussion, 14:6aA can be translated, "I will be as a dew to Israel" or, using the divine appellative, "I AM will be as a dew to Israel."

Hos 14:8aA describes Israel as returning and sitting "in my shade."[23] This remarkable detail is clarified in 14:9bA where YHWH states, "I am a luxuriant juniper." Thus, in an image unique in the whole HB, YHWH compares himself to a great tree under whose shade the returning exiles will dwell.[24] This image is in contrast to the picture in 4:12-13 where those who play the harlot sacrifice under the oak, poplar, and terebinth because their shade is good (*kî ṭôb ṣillāh*).[25]

In his portrayal of YHWH as a tree, the final redactor not only resumes the agricultural motif of Hos 2, but also the well-known marital imagery of that chapter, albeit in a more subtle fashion. In a perceptive article, Feuillet lists several points of contact between Hos 14:6-9 and the poem celebrating marital love, the Canticle of Canticles. Both agree in comparing the loved one to a lily (*šôšannâ*: Hos 14:6, Cant 2:1-2; 4:5; 5:13) and to Lebanon. We note especially Cant 5:15 - "his appearance is like Lebanon" (*mar'ēhû kallěbānôn*) - which is similar in construction to Hos 14:6b, 7b, 8b. Also, Cant 4:11, "the fragrance of your garments is like the fragrance (*rêaḥ*) of Lebanon," echoes Hos 14:7b, *wěrêaḥ lô kallěbānôn*, "his fragrance like Lebanon." For Feuillet, the dialogue of love between husband and wife in Cant 2:2-3 is particularly pertinent in understanding Hos 14:6-9.

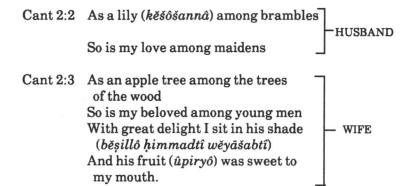

Cant 2:2   As a lily (*kĕšôšannâ*) among brambles ⎤
                                                    ⎬ HUSBAND
           So is my love among maidens   ⎦

Cant 2:3   As an apple tree among the trees ⎤
             of the wood   ⎮
           So is my beloved among young men   ⎮
           With great delight I sit in his shade ⎬ WIFE
             (*bĕṣillô himmadtî wĕyāšabtî*)   ⎮
           And his fruit (*ûpiryô*) was sweet to ⎮
             my mouth.   ⎦

The resemblance between Hos 14:6-9 and Cant 2:2-3 is
noteworthy on four accounts. First, the husband's comparison
of his wife to a lily in Cant 2:2 corresponds to YHWH's
statement in Hos 14:6 that Israel shall blossom as the lily.
Second, both passages speak of the husband as a tree. In Cant
2:3 the wife compares her beloved to an apple tree. In Hos 14:9
YHWH depicts himself as a luxuriant juniper. Third, both
share the expression "to sit in the shade" of the husband, an
expression governed by the assimilation of the husband to a
tree. And finally, both contain the rich metaphor of the wife
procuring her fruit from the tree which is her husband.[26]

By appropriating the language of love in Hos 14:6-9, R2
evokes the marriage motif of Hos 2 which symbolizes the
covenantal relationship between YHWH and Israel.   In
YHWH's final statement, 14:9, R2 sums up the whole literary-
theological design of his editorial work. As usual, it is
artistically constructed:

14:9   A   *'eprayim mah-lî 'ôd lā'ăṣabbîm*

       B   *'ănî 'ănîtî wa'ăšûrennû*
                          ╳
       B'   *'ănî kibrôš ra'ănān*

       A' *mimmennî peryĕkā nimṣā'*

By means of a wordplay on Ephraim in A/A', the final
redactor is able to denounce idols[27] and, at the same time,

insist that YHWH is the true source of everything for Ephraim. Between these two outer cola in B/B', R2 underscores YHWH's bold assertions with the double *'ănî*. Alliteration punctuates the text throughout. Noteworthy, moreover, is the chiastic arrangement in the *'ayin/nun* alliteration of *'ănîtî/ra'ănān* and the *šin/reš* alliteration of *wa'ăšûrennû/kibrôš*. YHWH declares, "I, not idols, respond and look after Ephraim." For R2, YHWH's response is his covenantal response (*'nh*).[28] In contrast to 14:4 where Israel admits, "Assyria will not save us" (*'aššûr lō' yôšî'ēnû*), YHWH insists, "I look after them" (*wa'ăšûrennû*).

D. 14:10 as an R2 composition

14:10a   *mî ḥākām wĕyābēn 'ēlleh*
          nābôn wĕyēdā'ēm
14:10b   *kî-yĕšārîm darkê yhwh*
          wĕṣaddîqîm yēlĕkû bām
          ûpōšĕ'îm yikkāšĕlû bām

14:10a   Whoever is wise, let him understand these things
          Whoever is discerning, let him know them
14:10b   for the ways of YHWH are straight
          and the upright walk in them.
          But the foolish stumble in them.

Although most scholars commonly regard 14:10 as a later Wisdom interpretation of the book as a whole including 14:2-9,[29] there is good reason to think that the author of 14:10 is R2. In the first place, consistent with the final redactor's fondness for framing units,[30] 14:10 balances the very beginning of the book, 1:1, which, as we have argued above, is an R2 composition.[31] In 1:1 he situates the work during a particular time in the deuteronomistic history. In 14:10 he exhorts wise and discerning people to appropriate the truths embodied in the work as they walk in the ways of YHWH.

In the second place, characteristic of R2, 14:10 is formulated in deuteronomistic vocabulary.[32] Those who are wise (*ḥākām*) and discerning (*nābôn*) are held in high esteem according to Dt 4:6:

> "Keep (God's statutes and ordinances) and do them; for that will be your wisdom and your understanding (*ḥokmatkem ûbînatkem*) in the sight of the peoples, who when they hear all these statutes, will say, 'Surely, this great nation is a wise and discerning people" ('*am-ḥākām wĕnābôn*).'" (Cf. Dt 1:13, 15; 32:6; 2 Sam 14:20)

Introducing a passage which is highly reminiscent of Deuteronomy, Jer 9:11 opens in a manner similar to Hos 14:10: "Who is the man so wise that he can understand this? (*mî-hā'îš heḥākām wĕyābēn 'et-zō't*)."

Thirdly, the expression "walking in the way of YHWH" is characteristically Deuteronomic.[33] The expression can refer back to the R2 addition, 2:8-9, where YHWH hedges the wife's "way" with thorns, beginning her journey back to her first husband. Fourth, the theme of stumbling in the ways of YHWH at the very end in 14:10bB, *yikkāšĕlû bām*, has its counterpart at the very beginning of the section, 14:2b - "for you have stumbled in your guilt (*kāšaltā ba'ăwônekā*)." For all these reasons, we prefer to see 14:10 as an R2 composition, rather than a later appendage to the work.

E. *Hos 14:2-10 - Summary*

By composing Hos 14:2-10, the final redactor concludes the Book of Hosea. One can see in the diagram which follows the important structural changes which R2 imposes upon the tradition.

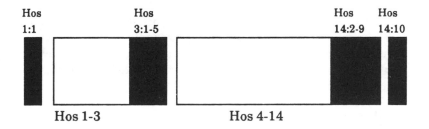

Hos 1:1   Hos 3:1-5   Hos 14:2-9   Hos 14:10

Hos 1-3   Hos 4-14

He provides the book with a redactional beginning (1:1) and end (14:10). Moreover, his literary compositions close off two main sections of the book's macro-structure. Hos 3:1-5, his first major structural change, sections off those traditions which focus on the conjugal theme. In his final statement, 14:2-9, R2 takes up the themes which were characteristic of his redaction of Hos 1-3: repentance and return to the land, the rich growth which results from their being sown in the land, the rejection of political alliances, military might and idols, and the marriage motif typifying the new cosmic covenant between YHWH and Israel.

II. The Macro Structure of Hos 4-11

In his commentary, Wolff observes that the literary formation of the Book of Hosea occurred in the compilation of three large complexes of transmission: Hos 1-3; 4-11; 12-14. All three complexes parallel each other. Each moves from accusation in the form of a *rîb* (2:4; 4:1; 12:3) to threat and then to the proclamation of salvation (3:1-5; 11:8-11; 14:2-9).[34] Wolff's tripartite division of the book is taken up by a number of commentators.[35] We too follow this division, although we argue that it results from the composition of the final redactor.

We saw that R2 concludes two of the three main sections with redactional blocks of material: Hos 1-3 with 3:1-5 and Hos 12-14 with 14:2-9. Anticipating our results, we will see that R2 sections off Hos 4-11 with Hos 11:1-11. He builds up to his Hos 11 climax first by refashioning the traditional beginning of the Hos 4-11 macro structure:

A. Hos 4:3: Refashioning the Traditional Beginning

Both those who maintain the authenticity of 4:1-3 as well as those who argue for its secondary character set these verses apart from the rest of the chapter. From the point of view of content, 4:1-3 is an accusation against the whole people and a more generalized complaint that there is no faithfulness, love or knowledge of God in the land. Hos 4:4-10, on the other hand, focuses on the religious leaders and on more specific offenses.[36] Moreover, a number of scholars characterize 4:1-3 in its present form as a lawsuit (*rîb*) introducing the rest of the oracles.[37]

We detect the final redactor's hand in his addition, 4:3. At the very outset of Hos 4-11, one can see the hand of R2 at work restructuring his tradition:

'al-kēn te'ĕbal hā'āreṣ wĕ'umlal kol-yôšeb bāh
bĕḥayyat haśśādeh ûbĕ'ôp haššāmāyim
wĕgam-dĕgê hayyām yē'āsēpû

Therefore, the land mourns
and all who dwell in it languish.
With beasts of the field, birds of the air
And even fish of the sea they are swept away.

Not a few commentators regard 4:3 as a later interpolation.[38] In the first place, they think that 4:3 misunderstands *hā'āreṣ* in 4:1bB as the "earth," a more cosmic term, rather than the "land," which is its meaning in 4:1.[39] Hos 4:3 interrupts a connection between 4:2 and 4:4 by announcing a punishment which one should encounter first in 4:5b. Hos 4:3 corresponds quite literally with other passages: Am 8:8; Jer 12:4; 23:10; Isa 24:4-6; 33:9. Furthermore, it articulates a later thought, viz. the involvement of nature in the godlessness of humanity.

Hos 4:3, however, recalls the final redactor's insertion in 2:20, where YHWH "will make a covenant on that day with the beasts of the field, birds of the air and reptiles of the ground" (*'im-ḥayyat haśśādeh wĕ'im 'ôp haššāmayim wĕremeś hā'ădāmâ*). In the latter, R2 elevates his tradition by describing the effects of the renewal of God's covenant at the cosmic scale. Similarly, in 4:3 the final redactor raises the evil consequences of Israel's transgressions to a cosmic plane. He portrays the violation of covenant described in his received tradition (4:1-2) as a reversal of creation.[40]

The interpretive principles by which R2 amplifies his traditional material in 4:3 are identical to that which we have observed in other R2 editorials. Contrary to those who think that *hā'āreṣ* as "earth" in 4:3 misunderstands 4:1 where it means "land," the use of *hā'āreṣ* as "earth" is a deliberate *antanaclasis* by R2. In a subtle nuance of *hā'āreṣ* in his tradition, R2 enlarges the *rîb* voiced in 4:1 to include creation. He achieves his literary expansion by means of a chiastic interplay with his tradition:

4:1b   4:3a
'*im yôšĕbê hā'āreṣ . . . te'ĕbal hā'āreṣ wĕ'umlal kol-yôšēb bāh*

| A | B | B' | A' |

Thus, at the very beginning of Hos 4-11, R2 restructures his tradition by his 4:3 commentary. By heightening the repercussions of the breach of covenant to the cosmic level, R2 has in mind the concomitant restoration of universal order in the renewal of covenant (2:20ff and 14:2ff). On one hand, all of creation will mourn and languish because of disruption in the relationship between YHWH and Israel (4:3). On the other hand, all of creation will burst forth in fruitfulness when this relationship is healed (2:20ff; 14:2ff).

B. *Hos 11:11b: nĕ'ūm-yhwh*

The most obvious clue to the final redactor of the tradition is the oracle formula in 11:11b, *nĕ'ūm-yhwh*. We have already encountered his use of the triadic *nĕ'ūm-yhwh* in 2:15b, 18a, and 23a in the first major section, Hos 1-3.[41] In all of Hos 4-14, the formula appears only here in 11:11b. It thus becomes an important structure marker, delimiting the second major section of the literary composition.[42]

C. *Hos 5:15--6:3; 10:12; 11:10-11: The Journey in Repentance*

Within the Hos 4-11 complex we point out three major texts of hope: 5:15--6:3; 10:12 and 11:10-11. They are significant in this complex because their optimism is so seemingly incongruent with their surroundings. Much evidence can be rallied for their R2 authorship. Like the R2 additions in Hos 1-3, these verses function in their particular contexts to mitigate the received material and exhort the people to conversion. Furthermore, by means of these texts of promise, R2 constructs a three-stage journey motif in the Hos 4-11 complex similar to his restructuring of Hos 2. At each stage, R2 recapitulates his theology and provides a commentary framework which serve to unify the complex. Hos 5:15--6:3 begins the journey in repentance. Hos 10:12 exhorts the readers to prepare their hearts for their ultimate sowing back into the land. Concluding the Hos 4-11 complex, 11:10-11 chronicles the future return back to the land itself. We will discuss each of these passages in turn to discover their role in Hos 4-11 subsection.

1. Hos 5:15--6:3: Beginning the Journey

5:15	*'ēlēk 'āšûbâ 'el-mĕqômî*
	'ad 'ăšer-ye'šĕmû
	ûbiqšû pānāy
	bassar lāhem yĕšaḥărunnî
6:1	*lĕkû wĕnāšûbâ 'el-hywh*
	kî hû' ṭārāp wĕyirpā'ēnû
	yak wĕyaḥbĕšênû
6:2	*yĕḥayyēnû miyyōmāyim*
	bayyôm haššĕlîšî yĕqîmēnû
	wĕniḥyeh lĕpānāyw
6:3	*wĕnēdĕ'â nirdĕpâ lāda'at 'et-yhwh*
	kĕšaḥar nākôn môṣā'ô
	wĕyābô' kaggešem lānû
	kĕmalqôš yôreh 'āreṣ

5:15	I will go and return to my place.
	When they accept their guilt,
	They will seek my face.
	In their distress, they will search for me.
6:1	Come, let us return to YHWH.
	Although he has torn us,
	he will heal us.

> Although he has stricken us,
>   he will bind us up.

6:2   He will revive us after two days.
>   On the third day he will raise us up
>   And we will live in his presence.

6:3   Let us know, let us strive to know YHWH.
>   His going forth is as sure as the dawn.
>   He will come to us like rain,
>   Like late rain that gives drink to the earth.

Many scholars have found 5:15--6:3 problematic in its present context. It is a song of repentance and hope incompatible, however, with the series of accusations, threats and judgments which surround it. Those who maintain the text's authenticity usually interpret it as a false or shallow repentance on the people's part which God rejects,[43] or else admit that its present position is due to a collector or redactor.[44] A significant number of commentators regard the text as secondary, not only because the hopeful sentiments are anchored in exilic or post-exilic theology,[45] but also because 5:15--6:3 interrupt a connection between 5:14 and 6:4. In addressing Ephraim and Judah, the objects of God's wrath in 5:14, YHWH states in 6:4: How can I deal with you other than as a lion, to rend you and carry you away?[46]

Commentators, furthermore, have noted that 5:15--6:3 pick up in catchword fashion elements of 5:11-14. However, they regard the presence of catchwords as the principle for the later juxtaposition of separate sayings by collectors who assembled them into a larger composition.[47] We argue instead that the so-called "catchwords" are the deliberate resumption by the final redactor to mitigate or qualify his tradition and to present his own theology. In many ways, these verses reveal the editorial techniques of our R2.

The redactor begins to qualify his tradition in 5:15: "I will go (*'ēlēk*) and return to my place." Here, he takes over the verb *'ēlēk* from 5:14bA, *'ănî 'ănî 'eṭrōp wě'ēlēk*, "I, yes I, will tear up and go away." Moreover, like the *antanaclasis* on *šûb* which we saw in 14:2-8,[48] R2 makes a similar wordplay on *šûb* and *hlk* in 5:15 and 6:1:

5:15   6:1
'ēlēk 'āšûbâ 'el-mĕqômî ... lĕkû wĕnāšûbâ 'el-yhwh
A   B   C   A'   B'   C'

I will go and return   Come, let us return (in
to my place.   repentance) to YHWH.

R2 formulates 5:15--6:3 with the same vocabulary used in
Dt 4:29-30 which a number of scholars assign to an exilic date
of composition:[49]

> "But from there[50] you will seek (bqš) YHWH your God and
> you will find him, if you search after him with all your heart
> and with all your soul. When you are in distress (baṣṣar lĕkā),
> and all these things come upon you in the latter days, you will
> return to YHWH your God (wĕšabtā 'ad-yhwh 'ĕlōhĕkā) and
> obey his voice." (Dt 4:29-30)

> "I will go and return to my place. When they accept their
> guilt, they will seek (bqš) my face. In their distres (baṣṣar
> lāhem), they will search for me. 'Come, let us return to
> YHWH' (wĕnāšûbâ 'el YHWH)." (Hos 5:15--6:1)

Both texts interpret the trials and tribulations of the exile
from a theological perspective: to bring the people to
repentance (cf. 1 Kgs 8:46-50). We have observed the same
theme of a period of chastisement to occasion the repentance of
Israel in the final redactor's journey motif in Hos 2 and in Hos
3:4-5 where Israel, deprived of political leadership and cult
will repent (šûb) and seek (bqš) the Lord their God in the latter
days.[51]

R2 switches from a YHWH speech in 5:15 to his own
summons to the people to repentance in 6:1-3.[52] His parallel
composition, 14:2-9, is structured in the reverse. It begins
with his own exhortation to repent: "Return, O Israel, to
YHWH your God ... (14:2-4)." It then reverts in 14:5-9 to a
YHWH speech: "I will heal their apostasy ... "

As in 14:2, R2 begins in 6:1 with an imperative followed by
a kî clause: "Come, let us return to YHWH. Although he has
torn us, he will heal us." Moreover, he mitigates his tradition

by means of resumption and paronomasia. His received tradition stated in 5:14 that YHWH will tear up, *ṭrp*, Ephraim and Judah like a lion. R2 resumes *ṭrp* and by means of parasonancy qualifies it with *rp'*, "to heal":

| 6:1 | *kî hû' ṭārāp* | Although he has torn us, |
| | *wĕyirpā'ēnû* | he will heal us. |

R2 balances this colon with *yak wĕyaḥbĕšēnû*, "although he has stricken us he will bind us up." Note here the alliteration and assonance of *yak* with the second syllable of *wĕyaḥbĕšēnû*.[53] This assonance and alliteration is continued in 6:2 with *yĕḥayyēnû* and *yĕqîmēnû* to form a poetic structure of rhyme and alliteration:[54]

6:1	*ṭārāp wĕyirpā'ēnû*
	yak wĕyaḥbĕšēnû
	yĕḥayyēnû miyyōmāyim
6:2	*bayyôm haššĕlîšî yĕqîmēnû*
	wĕniḥyeh lĕpānāw

6:1	Although he has torn us
	he will heal us.
	Although he has stricken us,
	he will bind us up.
6:2	He will revive us after two days.
	On the third day he will raise us up
	And we will live in his presence.

The final redactor places the afflictions which YHWH sends upon Israel into perspective. As in the case of the wife in Hos 2,[55] YHWH chastises to bring his people to repentance and into right relationship with him. Such a doctrine of chastisement and correction, which we will encounter again in R2, is characteristic of deuteronomistic and wisdom literature. We refer particularly to Jb 5:17-18 which shares linguistic similarities with Hos 6:1-2:

Behold, happy is the one whom God reproves;
Therefore, despise not the chastisement of the Almighty
   (*mûsar šadday*)
For he wounds, but he binds up (*yak'îb wĕyeḥbāš*)
He smites but his hands heal (*yimḥaṣ wĕyādāw tirpênâ*)
   (Jb 5:17-18)[56]

Although *wĕnēdĕ'â*, "let us know," beginning 6:3 is
sometimes eliminated as metrically superfluous,[57] it appears
to be another instance of the final redactor's parasonancy with
nirdĕpâ, "let us strive":

6:3   *wĕnēdĕ'â nirdĕpâ lāda'at 'et-yhwh*
            kĕšaḥar nākôn môṣā'ô
            wĕyābô' kaggešem lānû
            kĕmalqôš yôreh 'āreṣ

6:3   Let us know, let us strive to know YHWH.
            His going forth is as sure as the dawn.
            He will come to us like rain,
            Like late rain that gives drink to the earth.

The clause, *lāda'at 'et-yhwh*, coheres with the final
redactor's insertion in 2:22 of *wĕyāda'at 'et-yhwh*, "and you
shall know YHWH."[58] It has strong covenantal connotations.
The cryptic phrase in 6:3aB, "his going forth is as sure as the
dawn," on one hand, refers back to 5:15. In 5:15, YHWH
withdraws to his "place" until the people recognize their guilt
and seek his face. The connection between 5:15 and 6:3aB is
strengthened by the fact that *šaḥar*, "dawn" in 6:3A is related
etymologically with the verb *šḥr*, "to seek, inquire," in 5:15.[59]
With the people's repentance, R2 thus declares in 6:3aB that
YHWH will indeed come forth from his place, as certain as the
dawn comes each morning. On the other hand, 6:3aB
anticipates the final redactor's commentary in 6:5. Just as
sure as the dawn is YHWH's going forth from his place
(*môṣā'ô*, 6:3aB), so too does his judgment go forth like a light,
(*yēṣē'*, 6:5).[60]

R2 concludes his exhortation by declaring in 6:3b that
YHWH "will come to us like rain, like late rain that gives
drink to the earth." R2 strategically places this rain motif
here within the total framework of his composition.
Previously, in 2:23-24 R2 described the cosmic ramifications of
YHWH's remarriage with the wife/Israel:

2:23   And it will happen on that day
            that I will respond, says YHWH
            I will make the heavens drop rain
2:24   and they shall make the earth fruitful
            and the earth shall produce grain, wine and oil
            and they shall make Jezreel fruitful.

The rain motif here in 6:3b will continue in 10:12, another
R2 text which we shall discuss shortly,[61] which shares with
6:3b the verb, *yôreh* - "to rain, give drink to." Moreover, the
redactor's conclusion, 14:2-9, will exploit the motif to its
fullness to depict Israel's resettlement in the land in terms of
agricultural lushness: "I will be as a dew to Israel. He shall
blossom as the lily . . . " (14:6aA).[62]

We have in the rain motif, then, a hallmark of the final
redactor's commentary which extends from the beginning of
the composition to its conclusion. In the Hos 4-11 complex the
first R2 text of hope, viz. 5:15--6:3, not only recapitulates the
author's theology found in Hos 1-3, but helps to carry it
through to the end of the Hos 12-14 complex in 14:2-9. The
final redactor's additions, then, are not simply isolated texts
but comprehensive commentaries that pervade the work.

Scholars have, hitherto, singled out 6:1-3 for special study
because of the implications of these verses for a resurrection
theology. We may classify their various interpretations into
the following groups: 1) those who interpret 6:1-3 in light of
the rising from death to life celebrated in Canaanite fertility
cults;[63] 2) those who see a rising to life after sickness and
disease, in other words, a healing;[64] 3) those who think that
6:1-3 evinces a doctrine of the resurrection of the body after
death;[65] 4) those who approach 6:1-3 as a covenantal
resurrection.[66]

Consistent with our redaction-critical approach, we situate 6:1-3 within the broader literary design of our final redactor. From this perspective, the interpretation of 6:1-3 as a covenantal resurrection or renewal is the preferable understanding of the text, in light of what we know of R2 theology thus far. We have already seen in 2:20, 23-24 that R2 envisions a new covenant to be made with Israel when the period of her chastisement is over.[67] This is not to say that other interpretations are illegitimate. Barré has recently criticized Wijngaards's assessment of 6:1-3 as a covenant renewal.[68] He differentiates between a primary and a secondary level of meaning. For Barré, it is only at the "secondary" level, i.e. the applied meaning, that the covenantal renewal interpretation may be correct. Barré admits that he is concerned chiefly with the primary level of meaning. At this level, 6:1-3 envisages a recovery from sickness.

Our own focus, however, is the meaning of the text at the redactional level. R2 utilizes the vocabulary of healing to articulate a hope of deliverance which will take the form of a renewal of God's covenant with Israel - a renewal which he had already characterized in 2:20, 23-24. When Israel recognizes her guilt and seeks the Lord (5:15), when she returns to the Lord in repentance (6:1) and strives to know him (6:3), the Lord will "heal" Israel of the afflictions suffered in exile. He will "revive" Israel after two days. On the "third day" he will raise them up. One should understand the reference to the "third day" in light of the Exodus narrative of the theophany at Sinai:

Ex 19:11   "Be ready on the *third day*; for on the *third day* the Lord will come down upon Mount Sinai in the sight of all the people."

Ex 19:15-17   "Be ready by the *third day*; do not go near a woman." On the morning of the *third day*, there were thunders and lightnings and a thick cloud upon the mountain and a very loud trumpet blast, so that all the people trembled. Then Moses brought the people out of the camp

to meet God, and they took their stand at the
foot of the mountain.

In the Ex 19 Sinai pericope, the ratification of covenant
includes three constitutive elements: 1) the theophany, 2) the
proclamation of YHWH's word, and 3) the response of the
people to adhere to the covenant. The third day of the people's
ritual consecration (Ex 19:11) appears to be the pivotal day on
which God will come and establish his covenant with the
people.[69]

For the final redactor, then, God will renew his covenant
on the third day after he rejuvenates Israel. As in the other R2
commentaries in 2:20, 23-24 and 14:2-9, YHWH, who will
come as the rain to water the earth (6:1), will restore the
fertility that results from good covenantal relations.[70]

2. Hos 10:12: Tilling the Heart

zir'û lākem lişdāqâ
qişrû liprî (MT: lĕpî)[71] ḥesed
nîrû lākem nîr
wĕ'ēt lidrôš 'et-yhwh
'ad-yăbô' wĕyôreh şedeq lākem

Sow for yourselves righteousness.
Reap the fruit* of steadfast love.
Till your untilled earth.
It is time to seek YHWH
Until he comes and rains righteousness for you.

In this second moment of the spiritual journey, R2
encourages the people in 10:12 to prepare the soil of their
hearts to receive the fullness of the creator God who brings
rain upon them. While related to its literary context in its
agricultural imagery, 10:12 is noticeably distinct. In the first
place, 10:12 seems to interrupt a connection between 10:11
and 10:13. Its triadic imperatives, "sow for yourselves
righteousness, reap the fruit of steadfast love, till your
untilled soil," call forth an authentic response in faith for the

reader. A triadic *accusation*, however, follows discordantly in 10:13: "You have plowed iniquity, you have reaped injustice, you have eaten the fruit of lies." In the second place, the use of YHWH in a speech of YHWH betrays a secondary character. Moreover, 10:12aB quotes Jer 4:3a literally: *nîrû lākem nîr*, "Till your untilled land." Thus, some would attribute 10:12 to a later editor.[72]

We perceive the hand of our final redactor in the first word, *zr'*, "to sow," which figured prominently in his redaction of Hos 2: YHWH will sow his people in the land on the great day of Jezreel.[73] Besides *zr'*, R2 recapitulates the notion of inquiring after or seeking YHWH from 3:5 and 5:15,[74] as well as the idea of YHWH coming as the rain in 14:6 and especially 6:3:

6:3   He will come (*yābô'*) to us like rain
         like late rain that gives drink to (*yôreh*)
               the earth.
10:12   Until he comes and rains (*yābô' wěyôreh*)
               righteousness for you.

R2 mitigates the threefold accusation in 10:13a by the urgency of his own threefold summons. Rather than reap iniquity or eat the fruit of lies, he enjoins his readers to reap the fruit of steadfast love. His injunction is artfully fashioned in a chiasmus with *lākem lisdāqâ . . . sedeq lākem* delimiting the unit.[75]

We will discuss the function of 10:12 in the Hos 4-11 complex after we examine the final significant hope passage, viz. 11:10-11. We will then be able to see more clearly the overall strategy of R2 in his three commentaries of promise: 5:15--6:3, 10:12 and 11:10-11.

3. Hos 11:10-11: Journey's End

11:10   *'ahărê yhwh yēlěkû*
         kě'aryēh yiš'āg
         kî-hû' yiš'āg
         wěyeherdû bānîm miyyām

11:11   *yeḥerdû kĕṣippôr mimmiṣrayim*
          ûkĕyônâ mē'ereṣ 'aššûr
          wĕhôšabtîm 'al-bātêhem
          nĕ'ūm-yhwh

11:10   After YHWH they will go.
          Like a lion he will roar.
          Indeed, he will roar
          And the children will come from the west
             trembling.
11:11   They will come trembling like birds from
             Egypt
          And like doves from the land of Assyria
          And I will make them dwell upon their estates,
             says YHWH.

Scholars have long noted the secondary character of
11:10-11.[76] Once again, the clues in the text lead us to
recognize the hand of R2 in these verses. These clues include
the wordplays as well as the exilic deuteronomistic theology.
Hos 11:10 forms an artful chiastic structure.[77]

          A   *'aḥărê yhwh yēlĕkû*
          B   *kĕ'aryēh yiš'āg*
          B'   *kî hū' yiš'āg*
          A'   *wĕyeḥerdû bānîm miyyām*

One finds the notion of "going after YHWH," *'aḥărê yhwh
yēlĕkû*, consistently in Deuteronomy and the Deuteronomistic
History as an expression for keeping the covenant of
YHWH.[78] Thus, R2 reinforces a keynote of his theological
commentary, the renewal of God's covenant with his people.
     Furthermore, the final redactor's concluding remarks to
Hos 11 reverses details found at the beginning of Hos 11.
Although we will discuss his redactional hand in the whole of
Hos 11 in more depth later,[79] we wish to point out here the
chiastic structure of his commentary extending from the
beginning to the conclusion of the chapter:

11:2   11:10

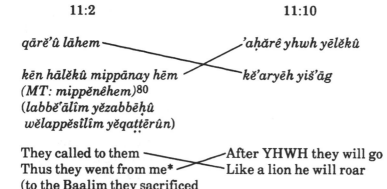

According to 11:2 the people were called and thus went away from YHWH to sacrifice and burn incense to the Baals. In 11:10, however, R2 asserts that the people will go after YHWH. Overriding the "call" to the Baals is the *roaring* of YHWH. This roaring elicits a corresponding response from the people: "The children will come from the west trembling (11:10b)."

Moreover, the notion of the children (*bānîm*) who come from the west links with and mitigates the conception of Israel as God's son (*libnî*, 11:1) who went from YHWH to sacrifice to the Baals. The pluralizing technique of R2 (*bēn/bānîm*) to make more inclusive the future promise for both Israel and Judah was seen in his redactional commentary in Hos 2. Whereas Hos 1 spoke of Hosea's two sons and one daughter who individually represented the North, Hos 2:1-2 speak collectively of the "children of the Living God," and "children of Israel and the children of Judah." Furthermore, whereas Hos 1 refers specifically to two brothers and one sister (Jezreel, Lo Ammi, and Lo Ruhama), Hos 2:3, in reversing Hos 1 declares the promise to "your (pl.) brothers" and "your (pl.) sisters." The fact that the children will come from the west *trembling* (*yeḥerdû*) echoes the final redactor's conclusion to the Hos 1-3 complex. Here in 3:5, the children of Israel (*bēnê yiśrā'ēl*) will come in fear (*pāḥădû*) to YHWH and to his goodness in the latter days.[81]

Hos 11:11 repeats *yeḥerdû* from 11:10 and amplifies the generalized location, *miyyām*, "from the west": "They will come trembling like birds from Egypt and like doves from the land of Assyria." R2 here reverses the condemnation of 11:5a:

11:5a	11:11a
yāšûb 'el-'ereṣ miṣrayim	*yeḥĕrdû kĕṣippôr mimmiṣrayim*
wĕ'aššûr hû' malkô	*ûkĕyônâ mĕ'ereṣ 'aššûr*
He will return to the	They will come trembling
land of Egypt	like birds from Egypt
Assyria will be his king	Like doves from the land
	of Assyria

The shift in the word "land" between cola in 11:5a and 11:10a as well as the contrast of motion (to/from) reinforces the connections between these verses.   Furthermore, 11:11a recalls and mitigates the accusation and threat of 7:11-12, with which it shares literal correspondences:

7:11   Ephraim is like a dove (*kĕyônâ*)
        Silly and without sense
        Calling to Egypt (*miṣrayim qārā'û*)
        going to Assyria (*'aššûr hālākû*)

7:12   ... Like birds (*kĕ'ôp*) of the air
        I will bring them down.

Finally, in 11:11b R2 articulates one of his chief tenets: the resettlement of the exiles back on the land.   The pronouncement, "I will make them dwell (*hôšabtîm*) upon their estates," should be compared with the R2 statement in 14:8: "They shall return and dwell (*yāšûbû*) in my shade."[82] R2 ends his commentary, and indeed, the whole Hos 4-11 complex with his signature, *nĕ'ûm-yhwh*.

D. The Literary Thrust of 5:15--6:3, 10:12 and 11:10-11

We will now investigate the function of these three passages within the Hos 4-11 structural frame. As we had pointed out, the final redactor through his 4:3 addition had elevated the covenantal *rib* announced in 4:1 to a cosmic level. All of creation will suffer the effects of Israel's transgression of covenant. Within his theological vision, however, R2 prepares at the very beginning of Hos 4 the conclusion to his work in 14:2-9. According to 14:2-9, Israel with all of creation will break forth in fertility.[83] R2 epitomizes the movement from barrenness to fertility in the "hermeneutical window" which he provides for Hos 4-14, viz. Hos 1-3, where R2 articulates the theme in terms of the marital covenant between God and Israel. To effect the repentance of the faithless wife, YHWH strips her of the gifts of the land (2:10-11). After the wife undergoes her journey of purification, YHWH will return the gifts of the lands in abundance when the marriage vows between them are renewed (2:23-24).

The three hope passages in the Hos 4-11 section just discussed serve to implement the movement from barrenness to fertility from Hos 4 to Hos 14. As in Hos 1-3, R2 describes the passage which the exiles must undertake as a journey, one not only back to YHWH but also back to the land. Each of our texts contributes to a different stage of the journey.

In 5:15-6:3, YHWH withdraws himself until his people recognize their guilt and *seek* him (5:15). The final redactor's summons in 6:1, "Come, let us return to the Lord," is the clarion call to begin the journey back to the Lord in repentance. Along the way, he will heal those he has rent apart. In describing the process of healing and convalescence, R2 alludes to the renewal of the covenant "on the third day" (6:2). He promises that YHWH will come forth from his place and refresh his people like the rains that water the earth (6:3).

This promise of fertility which will be occasioned by the rains brings us to 10:12 where the rain motif of 6:3 is reiterated. Here, however, R2 enlarges the motif in line with his thoughts in Hos 2:2, 23-24. To prepare for the culmination of the journey, i.e. for being sown back into the land on the

great day of Jezreel, R2 enjoins the people to "sow for
yourselves righteousness; reap the fruit of steadfast love; till
your untilled land." The metaphor relies on the preparatory
agricultural task of plowing land that has lain fallow and thus
needed to be weeded and broken up.   Such agronomic
"groundwork" is essential for a fruitful harvest.   Thus,
following their repentance and healing, the people at this
stage of the journey now "till their hearts" and "sow seeds of
righteousness." Just as spring is the proper time for plowing
and planting, R2 declares, "It is time to seek the Lord." These
planted seeds of righteousness YHWH himself will water with
his own righteousness to help them grow and flourish. R2 is
deliberately building up momentum toward his literary
climax. The image of cultivating and seeding used for the
spiritual preparation of the people anticipates 14:2-9 where
the sowing of the people back into the land results in profuse
foliation and fruition.

Hos 11:10-11 concludes the Hos 4-11 complex. R2
describes the concrete result of the people's return to YHWH,
viz. their concomitant return to the land. He does not portray
the restoration with the agricultural metaphor which he used
in 6:3 and 10:12. Instead, he returns to the familial image of
the returning sons (*bānîm*), which he described in 2:2-3.[84] The
parent/child image, however, is consistent with R2 theology
and with the specific Hos 11 context. With such a context
already steeped in the notion of covenant, R2 exploits this
image to the utmost. The "children" will go after YHWH, i.e.
take up walking in the covenant of YHWH again. As a result,
the "children" will journey back from Egypt and Assyria to be
restored to their homes (11:11). Although the journey ends
here, the story does not. Hos 14:2-9 will describe the
blossoming of Israel as she comes back to the land.

III. The Final Redaction of Hos 4

We have focused on three hope passages in the Hos 4-11
complex for which R2 is responsible. On the basis of these
texts, we have tried to discern the literary movement of R2 in
this second section of the composition. R2 commentary,

however, is not limited in Hos 4-11 to these three texts. We have chosen to examine them first because they are major structural markers in Hos 4-11. Moreover, they are easily identifiable because of their "sore thumb" character along with their immediately recognizable R2 theology.

We will now try to identify the remaining R2 expansions in Hos 4-11. We begin in this section with the final redaction of Hos 4. We will see that there are a few more minor R2 additions of hope which reverse the final redactor's received material. Aside from the positive texts of hope and return from exile, the remaining R2 commentary clusters around other themes which we have already observed in R2 redaction. These themes are:

1) the condemnation of idolatry, particularly graven images (cf. 2:10b, 19; 14:4aA, 9)
2) the abolition of war (cf. 1:5, 7; 2:20b; 14:4aB)
3) a reassessment of cultic and political leadership (cf. 3:4)
4) the reliance on YHWH alone who saves (cf. 14:9)
5) the new exodus (cf. 2:2, 16-17)

These ideas, as well as others which commentators have identified as exilic and deuteronomistic, contribute to the final redactor's literary thrust.

In order to facilitate the discussion of the remaining R2 commentary in Hos 4-11, we will present for each chapter our analysis of its editorial history, although we are primarily concerned in this chapter with R2 additions displayed in the far right column. As we do this, it is important for the reader to understand that we are not simply "tabulating the layers, strata, or accretions" in the text. We have deliberately avoided this terminology, since it does not express adequately the *inter-relatedness* of the editorial stages. Each later stage of the tradition interacts intimately with the earlier stage(s). Each later stage, however, is free to expand upon, mitigate or reverse that earlier tradition by means of certain literary structures and editorial techniques.

A. *The Editorial History of Hos 4*

H	C	R1	R2
		4:1-2	4:3
4:4*		4:4*-5a	
4:5b			4:6a
		4:6b	4:7-12a
4:12bA			4:12bB-13a
		4:13b	4:14
		4:15-16a	4:16b
		4:17a	4:17b
		4:18ab**	
4:18b**-19a		4:19b	

* *kōhēn* = R1
** *qālôn maginnêhā* = H

The textual difficulties of this chapter are commonly recognized. Several scholars explain these difficulties by pointing out the redactional character of the whole Hos 4 chapter. They note its composition as a secondary *literary* joining of different Hosean sayings.[85] We assume, therefore, that the present unity of the chapter is a secondary one. Our task is to determine the extent of R2 redaction which gives the chapter its final form. Earlier, we examined its first R2 expansion, viz. 4:3. This important addition closes off the 4:1-3 unit, making it a heading for the rest of the work. Furthermore, because of 4:3, the covenantal *rîb* announced in 4:1 is raised to a cosmic plane.[86]

B. *Hos 4:6a*

We encounter the next R2 editorial in 4:6a - *nidmû 'ammî mibbĕlî haddā'at*, "my people are destroyed for lack of knowledge." In its present context, 4:6a seems to be isolated, having no conjunctive preceding it. Lohfink explains 4:6a as an asyndetic argumentation sentence to 4:5b.[87] Budde's solution is to supply a *kî* (which he thinks was transposed before 4:6b) to 4:6a: "*For* my people are destroyed for lack of knowledge."[88]   Nowack, Marti, Wellhausen, and Peiser, nevertheless, regard 4:6a as a gloss.[89]

We are first alerted to the final redactor's hand in the wordplay of *nidmû 'ammî*, "my people are destroyed," on 4:5b - *wĕdāmîtî 'immekā*, "I will destroy your mother."[90]   The complaint regarding the people's lack of knowledge is in line with the final redactor's concern for knowledge, seen in 2:22b and 6:3.[91]

Although seemingly isolated, 4:6a maintains verbal links with the preceding (*dmy*) and following (*d't*) discourse.[92]   By means of this short paronomastic addition, R2 is able, first, to interpret "your mother," v. 5b as "my people," an interpretation consistent with the final editing of Hos 1-3. Second, the terms "my people" and "knowledge" have strong covenantal connotations.   Through the addition, then, R2 makes more specific the repercussions of the priestly and prophetic offences which are denounced in his received tradition.   The stumbling of the priest and prophet (v.5a) and their own rejection of knowledge and torah (v.6) will result, according to R2, in the downfall of God's covenanted *people*.

The focus on the *people* is particularly evident in the R2 commentary which follows: 4:7-12a, 13a, and 14.   Significant here are the triadic occurrences of maxims regarding the people:[93]

4:9   Thus it will be like *people* like priest.

4:11   New wine takes away the mind of my *people*.

4:14   A *people* without understanding will be ruined.

These three maxims pertaining to the people, along with their attendant commentary are R2 structural reformulations of his received tradition, similar to his threefold refashioning of Hos 2.[94]   We will discuss each of these in turn.

C. Hos 4:7-10

Although the "I-YHWH" discourse is fairly consistent
throughout 4:4-14, the accusations addressed in the second
person are found principally in 4:6b, 13b and 15. R2 identifies
himself by change of person beginning in 4:7. His received
tradition had just denounced its addressees by declaring:

"Because *you* have rejected knowledge
I will reject *you* from being priest to me.
And because you have forgotten the law of *your* God,
I will reject *your* children." (Hos 4:6b)

By switching to the third person for the accused, R2
comments on these verses in a skillfully constructed editorial,
4:7-10:[95]

4:7   A   *kĕrubbām kēn hāṭĕ'û-lî*
                  kĕbôdām bĕqālôn 'āmîrś
4:8   B   *haṭṭa't 'ammî yō'kēlû*
                  wĕ'el-'ăwônām yiś'û napšô
4:9   C   *wĕhāyâ kā'ām kakkōhēn*
                  ûpāqadtî 'ālāyw dĕrākāyw
                  ûma'ălālāyw 'āšîb lô
4:10   B'   *wĕ'ākĕlû wĕlō' yiśbā'û*
                  hiznû wĕlō' yiprōṣû
         A'   *kî-'et-yhwh 'āzĕbû*
                  lišmōr zĕnût

4:7   A   As they increased so they *sinned* against me
                  their glory into shame I will change;
4:8   B   The *sin* of my people they *eat*
                  and for their iniquity they lift up
                  their gullets
4:9   C   Thus it will be like people like priest:
                  I will punish him for his ways
                  and repay him for his deeds.

4:10   B'   They shall *eat* but not be satisfied;
             They shall *play the harlot*
             but not multiply
        A'   For YHWH they have forsaken
             to cherish *harlotry*.

The structure of these verses is balanced by the use of the roots *ḥt'* in A/B and *znh* in A'/B', while B/B' share *'kl*. Highlighted by the structure in C and punctuated by alliteration is the first of the final redactor's maxims regarding the people: *wĕhāyâ kā'ām kakkōhēn*, "thus it will be like people, like priest." Consistent with his insertion, 4:6a, R2 here in C alligns the ruin of the people with that of the priestly collective. Both resemble each other in their transgressions of covenant which YHWH will ultimately punish.[96]

The structure is interspersed with wordplays - the hallmark of R2. In A we find the assonance between *kĕrubbām/kĕbôdām*,[97] as well as alliteration: *kĕrubbām, kēn, kĕbôdām, bĕqālôn*. De Roche points out that the key to understanding the paronomasia is Hos 9:11, where Ephraim's glory (*kbd*) is identified with its ability to procreate or increase: "Ephraim's glory shall fly away like a bird - no birth, no pregnancy, no conception." Thus, in A, Israel's ability to increase (*kĕrubbām*), in other words her glory (*kĕbôdām*), will be changed by YHWH into shame (*bĕqālôn*).[98] De Roche also identifies other wordplays. In B, even though Israel eats or enjoys sin (*'kl*), in B' she will eat (*'kl*) and not be satisfied. Moreover, though she continues to fornicate (B'-*znh*), she will no longer multiply (B'-*prṣ*), a threat brought home in the paronomasia of A.[99]

With the *kî* clause of A', R2 summarizes the chief offense of which the people and priest are culpable: They have forsaken (*'zb*) YHWH to cherish harlotry (*lšmr znwt*). To "forsake" YHWH is characteristic of Deuteronomy and the Deuteronomistic History to describe the breaking of covenant.[100] "To cherish, keep," on the other hand, specifies the maintenance of the covenant.[101] We note in particular Dt 31:16, a composition of the exilic redactor of Dt:

"And the Lord said to Moses, "Behold, you are about to sleep
with your fathers; then this people will rise up and *play the
harlot (znh)* after the strange gods of the land, where they go
to be among them and they will *forsake me ('zb)* and *break my
covenant*, which I made with them." (Dt 36:16)

True to his deuteronomistic orientation, then, R2 inveighs
against those who, instead of cherishing his law, desert
YHWH in order to cherish harlotry, the worship of other gods.

D. *Hos 4:11-12, 13a, 14*

The next two maxims concerning the people occur in 4:11
and 4:14b. Certain commentators have eliminated them as
glosses, maintaining that they were perhaps once a single
proverb. This proverb would have been written originally in
the margin and separated into two during the process of
transmission.[102] Nevertheless, Lundbom and Mays point out
that these verses function as an inclusio delimiting the 4:11-
14 unit.[103] We would attribute this structure to R2. We
reproduce the structure below, highlighting R2's commentary
on his tradition in underlining:

4:11	A	*wĕyayin wĕtîrôš yiqqaḥ-lēb 'ammî*[104]
4:12	B	*bĕ'ēṣô yiš'āl*
		ûmaqlô yaggîd lô
		kî rûaḥ zĕnûnîm hit'āh (MT: hit'â)[105]
		wayyiznû mittaḥat 'ĕlōhêhem
4:13		*'al-rā'šê hehārîm yĕzabbēḥû*
		wĕ'al-haggĕbā'ôt yĕqaṭṭērû
		taḥat 'allôn wĕlibneh wĕ'ēlâ
		kî ṭôb ṣillāh
	C	*'al-kēn tiznênâ bĕnôtêkem*
		wĕkallôtêkem tĕnā'apnâ
4:14	C'	*lō'-'epqôd 'al-bĕnôtêkem kî tiznênâ*
		wĕ'al-kallôtêkem kî tĕnā'apnâ
	B'	*kî-hēm 'im-hazzōnôt yĕpārēdû*
		wĕ' im-haqqĕdēšôt yĕzabbēḥû
	A'	*wĕ'ām lō' yābîn yillābēṭ*

4:11   A   *New wine takes away the mind of my people.*
4:12   B   *He inquires of his thing of wood.*
             His staff gives him oracles.
             For a spirit of harlotry has led her* astray
             They have played the harlot
             out from under their God.
4:13   *On the tops of mountains they sacrifice*
             And on the hills they burn incense
             Under oak, poplar and terebinth
             because their shade is good
        C   Therefore, your daughters play the harlot
             and your daughters-in-law commit
             adultery.
4:14   C'   *I will not punish your daughters,*
             though they play the harlot
             Nor your daughters-in-law, though they
             commit adultery
        B'   *For they themselves go aside with harlots*
             and with cultic whores they sacrifice.
        A'   *A people without understanding will be ruined.*

The above complex is composed of R2 commentary on the tradition he has received. He has enveloped this tradition and thus modified it in this artistic construction. Like the R2 unit, 4:7-10 discussed above, 4:11-14 containing the two remaining proverbs has a chiastic shape. However, while the first proverb was structurally highlighted in the center of the chiasmus in 4:9, the two maxims in 4:11-14 make up the outer frame, A/A'. Moreover, internally they form a distant chiasmus:

```
              A    B    C
4:11    tîrôš yiqqaḥ-lēb 'ammî
        C'   B'   A'
4:14    wĕ'ām lō' yābîn yillābēṭ106
                   A      B           C
4:11    New wine takes away the mind of my people.
```

C'   B'   A'
4:14   A people without understanding will be ruined.

Hos 4:11-14 has two points of contrast with the R2 conclusion, 14:2-10. In 4:13, R2 criticises an apostate people who sacrifice under oak, poplar and terebinth because their shade is good (*kî ṭôb ṣillāh*). In 14:8-9, on the other hand, YHWH alone is the mighty tree who invites a repentant people to sit in his shade (*bĕṣillî*). In 4:14, R2 portends that a people without understanding (*lō' yābîn*) will come to ruin. In 14:10, however, he advises that whoever is wise should understand (*wĕyābēn*) the truths of his words, lest s/he stumble.

As we examine the poem framed by the two maxims we find R2 deuteronomistic theology come to the fore. Commenting on 4:12bA - "for a spirit of harlotry has led her* astray," R2 interprets this harlotry as idolatry in keeping with Dtr sentiments.[107]   He accuses the people of seeking counsel from lifeless images, a polemic characteristic of exilic times.[108] Furthermore, 4:13a, "on the tops of mountains they sacrifice/and on the hills they burn incense," is considered by scholars as a deuteronomic set-phrase.[109]

R2 expands 4:12bA by means of wordplays:

4:12bA   *kî rûaḥ zĕnûnîm hit'āh**
4:12bB   *wayyiznû mittaḥat 'ĕlōhêhem*

4:12bA   For a spirit of harlotry has led *her* astray
4:12bB   *they have played the harlot out
              from under their God*

R2 resumes *zny* from his tradition and typically switches person from third feminine singular[110] to third masculine plural. Moreover, R2 makes *hit'āh*, "lead her astray," more specific through parasonancy: she is led *mittaḥat 'ĕlōhêhem*, "out from under their God." The word play is carried over into 4:13aB: she is led out from under their God to offer idolatrous sacrifices *taḥat 'allôn wĕlibneh wĕ'elâ kî ṭôb ṣillāh*, "under oak, poplar and terebinth because their shade is good." Note both

the *hit'āh/mittaḥat/taḥat* parasonancy and the alliteration of
the *lamed*'s in 4:13aB.

Hos 4:13b is problematic because of the sudden change to
direct address: "Therefore, *your* daughters play the harlot and
your daughters-in-law commit adultery." Scholars either omit
4:13b as a gloss to 4:14[111] or emend the text to the third
masculine plural.[112] Anticipating our later discussion, we
ascribe the change to the second person to an earlier stage of
redaction continuing the second person address of 4:6.[113] R2
mitigates the accusation of 4:13b by qualifying it in 4:14a:

> "I will *not* punish your daughters though they play
> the harlot,
> *Nor* your daughters-in-law, though they commit adultery
>
> For they themselves (*hēm*) go aside with harlots
> and with cultic whores they sacrifice."

Commentators have been puzzled by the antecedent for
"they" (*hēm*) in 4:14a. Wolff and Andersen and Freedman
think that "they" refers back to the priests who were accused
in 4:6.[114] Rudolph, on the other hand, emends *hēm* to
'ădōnêhem: "For *their lords* go aside with harlots and with
cultic whores they sacrifice."[115] In a sense, both
interpretations would be correct if viewed from the final
redaction. Within the structure of the chiasmus, 4:14a (B')
refers to 4:12-13a (B). The "they" who go aside with harlots
and sacrifice with cultic prostitutes (4:14a) are the *people* who
have played the harlot, sacrificing on the tops of mountains
(4:12-13a). Moreover, since in the scope of R2 commentary,
the priest and people together are guilty before YHWH, the *kî*
hēm of 4:14a refers back to *kî 'attâ* of 4:6b, the denunciation of
the priest: "because you (*kî 'attâ*) have rejected knowledge, I
will reject you from being priest to me." R2, then, places the
accusation, "therefore, your daughters play the harlot," into
perspective. YHWH will not punish the daughters and
daughters-in-law, because the priests and the male laity
themselves go aside with harlots and sacrifice with cult
prostitutes (4:14a).

E. Hos 4:16b, 17b

4:16a   *kî kĕpārâ sōrērâ*
         sārar yiśrā'ēl
4:16b   *'attâ yir'ēm yhwh*
         kĕkebeś bammerḥāb
4:17a   *ḥăbûr 'ăṣabbîm 'eprāyim*
4:17b   *hēnîaḥ (MT: hannaḥ)*[116] *lô*

4:16a   For like a cow is stubborn
         Israel is stubborn
4:16b   *Now YHWH will feed them*
         like a lamb in broad pasture
4:17a   Ephraim is allied to idols
4:17b   *(but) he will provide him rest.*

The remaining R2 redaction in this chapter, 4:16b and
4:17b, is set in *italics* in the above text. Scholars have noted
the incongruity of 4:16b in its present context. They either
interpret it as a question, even though there is no
interrogative particle,[117] or consider it a secondary addition
regarding the optimistic end-times.[118] We follow Willi-Plein
who, highlighting the redactional commentary on the received
tradition, paraphrases the passage as follows:

> "Israel, like a stubborn heifer he is stubborn.
> (But YHWH will now pasture them like a lamb in broad
> pasture.)
> A worshipper of idols is Ephraim.
> (But he-YHWH will provide rest for him.")[119]

With respect to its contents, 4:16b appears to be an R2
commentary mitigating his tradition. The image of YHWH
shepherding or feeding his flock (*r'h*) is consistent with later
exilic thought. We single out Ezek 34:13-15 for special
notice:[120]

> "And I will bring them out from the peoples, and gather them
> from the countries, and will bring them into their own land;

and *I will feed them* (r'h) on the mountains of Israel, by the
fountains, and in all the inhabited places of the country. I will
feed them with good pasture, and upon the mountain heights
of Israel shall be their pasture; there they shall lie down in
good grazing land, and on fat pasture they shall feed (r'h) on
the mountains of Israel. *I myself will be the shepherd of my
sheep, and I will make them lie down, says the Lord God."*
(Ezek 34:13-15, RSV)

As in the many other instances we have seen, R2 mitigates
his tradition by means of paronomasia. YHWH will now feed
his people like a lamb in broad pasture, instead of dealing with
a balky cow (4:16a). In 4:16b he employs another type of
wordplay know as *epanastrophe*. In this type of paronomasia,
the final syllable or syllables are reproduced in the syllables of
the word which immediately follows.[121] In 4:16b *epanastrophe*
can be found in *bammerḥāb*, "in broad pasture," which
connects with the following *ḥăbûr* in 4:17, the redactor's
tradition.[122]

The RSV translation in 4:17b of *hannaḥ-lô*, "leave him
alone," is based on the second meaning of the hiphil of *nwḥ*, "to
leave alone."[123] However, the more usual meaning of *nwḥ* in
the hiphil is "to give rest, to lead, to make quiet."[124] This
reading is confirmed by *anapauō*, "to give rest," in Aquila and
Theodotion. We suggest, then, that for the hiphil imperative,
hannaḥ, one should read *hēnîaḥ*, hiphil indicative pf. 3 ms. sg.

If we are correct, the last R2 commentary of the chapter,
viz. 4:17b, would continue the image of YHWH pasturing his
sheep begun in 4:16b. This notion of pastoral rest is consistent
with Ezek 34:15 just cited: "I myself will be the shepherd of
my sheep and *I will make them lie down, says the Lord God."*
(Cf. also Ps 23:1-3). Moreover, *nwḥ* is used by the
deuteronomist to describe the inheritance of the land:[125]

You will go over the Jordan, and live in the land which
YHWH your God gives you to inherit, when he gives you rest
(*wĕhēnîaḥ lākem*) from all your enemies ... (Dt 12:10).

F. Summary of R2 Commentary in Hos 4

The final redactor had made extensive structural changes in the tradition he received in Hos 4. These changes focus on *the people*. The people perish because of lack of knowledge (4:6a). Furthermore, by means of three proverbs regarding the people, arranged chiastically with their accompanying commentary, he condemns the people's abandonment of YHWH and their harlotrous idolatry (4:7-10, 11-14). He ends his editorial on a note of hope. In spite of Israel's stubbornness which will lead to his downfall, YHWH will shepherd him like a lamb and eventually give him rest (4:16b, 17b).

IV. The Final Redaction of Hos 5

A. The Editorial History of Hos 5

H	C	R1	R2
5:1-2a			5:2b
5:3			5:4
5:5abA		5:5bB-7	
5:8-13a			5:13b
5:14			5:15

B. Hos 5:2b

5:1a	*šim'û zō't hakkōhănîm*	A
	wĕhaqšibû bêt yiśrā'ēl	B
	ûbêt hammelek ha'ăzînû	C
5:1b	*kî lākem hammišpāṭ*	D
	kî paḥ hĕyîtem lĕmiṣpâ	C'
	wĕrešet pĕrûśâ 'al-tābôr	B'
5:2a	*wĕšaḥat baššiṭṭîm he'mîqû*	A'
	(*MT: wĕšaḥătâ śēṭîm he'mîqû*)[126]	
5:2b	*'ănî mûsār lĕkullām*	

5:1a	Hear this, O priests
	Pay heed, O house of Israel
	Listen, O house of the king

5:1b	For the judgment pertains to you
	For you have been a trap at Mizpah
	And a net spread upon Tabor
5:2a	And a pit dug deep in Shittim*
5:2b	*But I am a chastisement to them all.*

The first R2 editorial to be noted in Hos 5 is 5:2b. Structurally, it stands apart from the ABCDC'B'A' pattern in 5:1-2a. Moreover, 5:2b changes conspicuously to the third masculine plural ("to *them* all") in a speech addressed in the second plural to the priests, the house of Israel and the house of the king (5:1).

The final redactor here brings in his *mûsār* theology of YHWH as chastiser. We have seen this thought appear in his redaction of Hos 2 and in 6:1-3 where the purpose of YHWH's chastisement is to occasion the repentance of the people.[127] The notion of *mûsār* is deuteronomic:

> "And you shall remember all the way which the Lord your God has led you these forty years in the wilderness that he might *humble you, testing you* to know what was in your heart, whether you would keep his commandments or not....
> Know then in your heart that as a man *disciplines* (*ysr*) his son, the Lord your God *disciplines* (*ysr*) you." (Dt 8:2, 5. Cf. Dt 4:36,11:2; 21:18; Lev 26:23)

Hos 5:2b, then, furnishes an unmistakable perspective to YHWH's bitter castigation of the nation described in 5:9-14. Indeed, Israel and Judah deserve punishment. They are thoroughly contaminated with infection (v. 13a). However, R2 declares that this punishment has a pedagogical intent: the repentance of the people.

C. Hos 5:4

We witness the final redactor's focus on repentance most clearly in his next editorial, 5:4, which is set off in the following in boldface:

| 5:3 | *'ănî yāda'tî 'eprayim* |
| | *wĕyiśrā'ēl lō' -nikḥad mimmennî* |

kî 'attâ hiznêtā 'eprayim
   niṭma' yiśrā'ēl
5:4   *lō' yittenûm (MT: yittěnû)*[128]
    ma'allêhem lāšûb 'el-'ělōhêhem
    kî rûaḥ zěnûnîm běqirbām
    wě'et-yhwh lō' yādā'û

5:3   I know Ephraim
    Israel is not hidden from me.
    For now you have played the harlot, Ephraim.
    Israel is defiled.
5:4   *Their deeds do not permit them* to return to*
        their God
    For a spirit of harlotry is in their midst
    and YHWH they do not know.

R2 changes from the 1st person YHWH discourse
addressed to "you, Ephraim/Israel" of his tradition in 5:3 to a
3rd person commentary on the relationship between God and
his people in 5:4. Their deeds, which are the primary reasons
for YHWH's punishment according to 4:9 (R2), prevent his
people from returning to him in repentance (*lāšûb*). R2
interacts with his tradition by resuming *znh* from 5:3, (*hznyt*,
"you have played the harlot"), and then laying the blame for
the people's impenitence on "a spirit of harlotry (*rwḥ znwnym*)
in their midst" (5:4b. Cf. 4:12). Moreover, in contrast to the
tradition where YHWH *knows* Ephraim (*'ny yd'ty 'prym*-
5:3aA), the people do not *know* YHWH (*w't-yhwh l' yd'w*,
5:4bB).[129]

D. *Hos 5:13b*

5:13a   *wayyar' 'eprayim 'et-ḥolyô*
      wîhûdâ 'et-mězōrô
      wayyēlek 'eprayim 'el-'aššûr
      wayyišlaḥ 'el-melek yārēb
5:13b   *wěhû' lō' yûkal lirpō' lākem*
      wělō'-yigheh mikkem māzôr

5:13a   Ephraim saw his wound
           Judah, his oozing infection
           Ephraim went to Assyria
           and sent to the great king[130]
5:13b   *But he is not able to heal you*
           or cure you of your infection.

Hos 5:13b presents difficulties because of the surprising
change to the 2nd mas. pl. in a YHWH speech which
consistently refers to Ephraim and Judah in the 3rd person.[131]
However, precisely because of the change in person, Willi-
Plein regards 5:13b as a later gloss. She observes that the
gloss leads into or prepares the way for the thoughts expressed
in 6:1.[132]

The change of person in 5:13b is characteristic of the
insinuation of R2 into the tradition. The independent
personal pronoun, *hû'*, has its antecedent in the ambiguous
mlk yrb in the redactor's received material.[133] R2 insists that
this *mlk yrb* will not heal (*rp'*) or cure "your infection." In
5:13b, R2 interacts directly with his tradition. From 5:13aA
he repeats *mzwr*, "infection," and plays on the words *wayyar'*
'eprayim, "and Ephraim saw," with the infinitive *lrp'*, "to
heal." On the one hand, in 5:13b he confounds any notion that
the *mlk yrb* could possibly remedy the sickness that has
penetrated Ephraim and Judah. On the other hand, in 6:1 R2
using the *same* personal pronoun, *hû'*, asserts positively that it
is YHWH who heals. We recall the idea that YHWH will heal
(*rp'*) Israel of its apostasy in the final redactor's composition,
14:5. Willi-Plein is thus correct in stating that 5:13b prepares
for the thoughts of 6:1. Both originate from the same hand!

E. Hos 5:15 and the Redactional Thrust of Hos 5

Hos 5:15, the last R2 editorial of Hos 5, is part of the major
R2 unit, 5:15--6:3, which we have discussed at length above.
Hos 5:15--6:3 is the first major call to repentance in the three-
stage journey of repentance which R2 imprints upon his
traditional material.[134] In certain ways, the R2 redaction of

Hos 5 prepares for this important divisional marker of the Hos 4-11 macro-structure.

In the first place, 5:2b orients the whole chapter towards the 5:15--6:3 unit. YHWH is the chastisement of the people solely for the purpose of bringing about their repentance. Hos 5:2b has its correlate in 5:15. Here, the people's distress will occasion their seeking the Lord.

Secondly, 5:4a, "their deeds to not permit them *to return to their God*," points ahead to 6:1 where R2 exhorts the chastized people *to return to YHWH*. Furthermore, even though they *did not know YHWH* because of the spirit of harlotry within them (5:4b), R2 still encourages them in 6:3: "Let us *know*, let us strive *to know YHWH*."

Finally, 5:13b looks forward to 6:1. It is not the *mlk yrb* who will heal Ephraim of the disease that afflicts him (5:13a). Rather, it is YHWH alone who heals those he has rent apart, if only they would repent (6:1).

We see, then, that the redactional movement of Hos 5 leads precisely into the exhortation to repentance in Hos 6:1-3. The three editorials of R2 in Hos 5 climax in his first important structural indicator of the Hos 4-11 complex, viz. Hos 5:15--6:3. In contrast to those who see 6:1-3 as an isolated song of repentance, we observe that R2 had laid the groundwork for it even at the beginning of Hos 5.

V. *The Final Redaction of Hos 6*

A. *The Editorial History of Hos 6*

H	C	R1	R2
			6:1-3
		6:4	6:5
		6:6-7	
6:8-10		6:11a	6:11b-7:1aA

B. *Hos 6:1-3*

For Hos 6:1-3, we refer the reader to the more detailed discussion above regarding Hos 5:15--6:3. Suffice it to say at this point that 6:1-3 encapsulates the R2 message of repentance. Within the Hos 4-11 complex, it begins the journey back to YHWH and back to the land. By means of the rain motif (6:3), it continues the movement from barrenness to fertility begun in Hos 2 and ending in Hos 14. Moreover, with the reference to the "third day" it promises the future renewal of God's covenant with his people.[135]

C. *Hos 6:5*

6:4   *mâ 'e'ĕśeh-lĕkā 'eprayim*
       mâ 'e'ĕśeh-lĕkā yĕhûdâ
       wĕhasdĕkem ka'ănan-bōqer
       wĕkaṭṭal maškîn hōlēk

6:5   *'al-kēn ḥāṣabtî bannĕbî'îm*
       hăragtîm bĕ'imrê-pî
       ûmišpāṭî ka'ôr yēṣē'
       (MT: ûmišpāṭêkā 'ôr yēṣē')[136]

6:4   What shall I do with you, Ephraim?
       What shall I do with you, Judah
       Your love is like a morning cloud,
       Like the dew which goes away early.

6:5   *Therefore, I have hewn them[137] by the prophets.*
       I have slain them by the words of my mouth.
       *My judgment is like a light which goes forth.**

Scholars have long suspected the authenticity of 6:5.[138] S. Spiegel describes it as:

> "A dark and delphic verse, out of joint with what precedes and what follows, the type of abrupt and fragmentary utterances which has made many a student of the little book complain with Jerome: *Osee commaticus est et quasi per sententias loquens.*"[139]

We argue that 6:5 is another instance of R2 commentary along with his other editorial of the chapter, 6:1-3. Indeed,

Marti and Robinson place 6:5 after 6:1-3 because of the similarily between 6:3aA and 6:5b:

6:3aA   *kĕšahar nākôn môṣā'ô*
6:5b   *ûmišpaṭî ka'ôr yēṣē'*

6:3aA   As sure as the dawn is his going forth . . .
6:5b   My judgment is like a light which goes forth.[140]

In 6:3 and 6:5, R2 frames and tries to integrate with his tradition in 6:4. He picks themes from 6:4 regarding the morning cloud and the dew which goes away early and associates them with his dawn motif. The switch in person from the "you" addressed to Ephraim and Judah in 6:4 to "them" in 6:5 is another clue to the final redactor's hand. The puzzling connective, *'al kēn*, may have been motivated by its alliteration with the final word of 6:4, the redactor's received tradition, viz. *hōlēk*.

R2 introduces in 6:5 an understanding of prophets and prophecy which will figure prominently in his redaction of Hos 12.[141] In 12:11 he states:

"I spoke to the prophets.
It was I who multiplied visions
And through the prophets gave parables."
     (12:11, RSV)

The text is self-explanatory. YHWH reveals himself and his will through his prophets. They are his mouthpiece. Further, R2 relates in 12:14:

"By a prophet the Lord brought
     Israel up from Egypt,
And by a prophet he was preserved."
     (12:14, RSV)

The reference here, of course, is to Moses, described as a prophet who led Israel out of Egypt.

The final redactor's understanding of prophecy in 6:5, 12:11 and 12:14 is thoroughly deuteronomistic. We cite, first, Dt 18:15-19 which is set in a detailed account of the office of prophet.[142] Moses commands the people that when they enter the land of promise they are to drive out all the diviners, soothsayers, augurs, sorcerers, charmers, mediums, wizards and necromancers who reside there. It is not through these that YHWH will communicate his will to his people. Rather, Moses states:

> "The Lord your God will raise up for you a *prophet like me* from among you, from among your brethren - *him you shall heed* - just as you desired of the Lord your God at Horeb on the day of the assembly, when you said, 'Let me not hear again the voice of the Lord my God, or see this great fire anymore, lest I die.' And the Lord said to me, 'They have rightly said all that they have spoken. I will raise up for them a *prophet like you* from among their brethren; and *I will put my words in his mouth (wĕnātattî dĕbāray bĕpîw)*, and he shall speak to them all that I command him. And whoever will not give heed to my words which he shall speak in my name, I myself will require it of him.'" (Dt 18:15-19)

Moses is portrayed here as the prophet *par excellence* who interceded for the people at Horeb at their request and gave them the words of God's law. He is the prophet who, as R2 illustrates in Hos 12:14, brought Israel out of Egypt. Moreover, instead of consulting alien intermediaries, the people are to seek out the prophet like unto Moses whom God will raise up from them. "*Him* you shall heed," Moses says (Dt 18:15).

Nevertheless, according to the Deuteronomist, the people refused to hear God's word spoken through his chosen agents:

> "YHWH warned Israel and Judah by *every prophet and seer*, saying, 'Repent (*šûb*) of your evil ways and keep my commandments and my statutes, in accordance with all the law which I commanded your ancestors and which I sent to you by *my servants the prophets*.' But, they would not listen, but were stubborn, as their ancestors, who did not believe in YHWH their God .... Therefore, YHWH was very angry with Israel and removed them out of his sight." (2 Kgs 17:13-14. Cf. Jer 35:15)

This distinctive deuteronomistic presentation of the prophets forms the backdrop which helps us understand the final redactor's interpretive exegesis of his tradition in Hos 6:1-3, 5. YHWH sent his prophets with an exhortation to repent and live lives according to *torah* (Hos 6:1-3; 2 Kgs 17:13). Yet, the people refused to heed God's words put into the mouths of his servants. YHWH, therefore, poured out his anger upon them. He has hewn them by the prophets, slain them by the words of his mouth (Hos 6:5; 2 Kgs 17:14).

Our final redactor, then, understood the sayings of the pre-exilic prophet, Hosea, which he received as a tradition, from an explicitly deuteronomistic point of view. Commenting on the 2 Kgs 17:13-14 passage just cited, R. E. Clements makes the following remarks which can describe just as well the literary-theological gestalt of R2's whole composition:

> (2 Kgs 17:13-14) asserts that it was the function of the prophets, who are regarded as a recognizable group, to warn both Israel and Judah to repent and to keep the law (*torah*), which had itself been given to the people by the prophets. *Thus the prophets are presented as preachers of repentance whose message was a call to return to the law.* In line with the entire History this can only refer to the Mosaic law given at Sinai-Horeb. Thus, like Deuteronomy 18:15ff. the prophets are regarded as preachers of the law 'like Moses,' so that they are seen as ministers of the covenant.[143]

D. Hos 6:11b--7:1aA

6:11a	*gam-yĕhûdâ šāt qāṣîr lāk*
6:11b	*bĕšûbî šĕbût 'ammî*
7:1aA	*kĕrop'î lĕyiśrā'ēl*

6:11a	Judah also, he has set a harvest for you,
6:11b	*when I restore the fortunes of my people*
7:1aA	*when I heal Israel.*

The majority of scholars agree on the secondary character of 6:11b--7:1aA.[144] Noteworthy is the fact that some commentators find the redaction occurring at different stages. They regard 6:11a, "Judah also, he has set a harvest for you," as an addition which includes Judah in the destruction of the northern kingdom. Later, an exilic redactor added 6:11b--7:1aA which interpreted the "harvest" positively as a time of restoration.[145]

We will argue below that 6:11a is an R1 addition actualizing the Hosean saying to the southern kingdom of Judah. The harvest image for R1 symbolizes the judgment against Judah who shares guilt with the northern kingdom.[146] This image, however, is transformed by R2. The time of harvest becomes for him a time of. eschatological salvation.[147] He articulates his thoughts in his familiar paronomastic style: *běšûbî šěbût 'ammî kěrop'î lěyiśrā'ēl.* Playing on his favorite word, *šûb,* R2 states that the "harvest" is the time when he will restore (*běšwby*) the fortunes (*šbwt*) of his people and bring healing to Israel. Taking all of his redactional commentary in Hos 6 together, we see his progression of thought through his paronomasia: When the people repent and return to YHWH (*šwb,* 6:1), YHWH, in turn, will return (*šwb*) the fortunes (*šbwt*) of his people (6:11b).

VI. The Final Redaction of Hos 7

A. The Editorial History of Hos 7

H	C	R1	R2
			7:1*
7:1*-3			7:4
7:5-9			7:10
7:11-12a**			7:12a**, 12b
7:13-15***			7:15***
			7:16

*kěrop'î lěyiśrā'ēl = R2
**ka'ăšer yēlēkû = R2
***yissartî = R2

B. Hos 7:4

7:4   *kullām měnā'ăpîm*
           kěmô tannûr bō'ēr hēm
           (MT: bō'ērâ mē'ōpeh)
           'ōpehû[148] *yišbôt mē'îr*
           millûš bāṣēq 'ad-ḥumṣātô

7:4   All of them are adulterers.
           They are like a blazing oven*,
           whose baker ceases to stoke,
           from kneading the dough until it is leavened.

Hos 7:4 is the first of our R2 additions. Its context has been notoriously difficult to interpret because of the ambiguous identity of the *dramatis personae*. This ambiguity is compounded by many textual uncertainties. While we attribute the main bulk of the chapter to Hosea, Hos 7:4 is problematic. Several commentators have regarded it as a gloss to 7:6.[149] The accusation of "adulterers" does not seem appropriate in the present context. Hence, many authors have emended *mn'pym*, "adulterers," to some form of *'np*, "to be angry, furious."[150]

We think, however, that the notion of adultery is a deliberate R2 interpretation, based on a paronomastic interchange with his tradition. In 7:4 R2 resumes key words already present in his received material: *kullām*, "all of them," from 7:7aA, *(kěmô) tannûr*, "like an oven," from 7:6a, 7aA, and *bō'ēr*, "blazing," from 7:4aB. R2 changes from *kattannûr*, "like an oven," in 7:6a, 7aA, to *kěmô tannûr* in 7:4 to strengthen the alliteration of the *mēm*'s:

kullām měnā'ăpîm kěmô tannûr bō'ēr hēm

Furthermore, R2 transforms the original meaning of the oven image in his tradition through paronomasia. The tradition in 7:6 uses the oven image to depict the *anger* of the conspirators:

7:6   *kî qĕrĕbû kattannûr*
      libbām bĕ'orbām
      kol-hallaylâ yāšēn 'appĕhem (MT: 'ōpēhem)[151]
      bōqer hū' bō'ēr kĕ'ēš lehābâ

7:6   For they approached like an oven
      Their hearts with intrigue.
      All night their *anger* smoldered.
      In the morning it blazed like a flaming fire.

R2 plays on *'appĕhem*, "their anger," in 7:6 with the accusation *(kullām) mĕnā'ăpîm*, "(all of them) are adulterers." The oven image which described the heat of anger in the tradition now describes, according to R2 the heat of adulterous lust: "All of them are adulterers; like a blazing oven are they." R2 continues his *'appĕhem/mĕnā'ăpîm* wordplay with *'ōpeh*, "baker," in 7:4b. Although 7:4b furthers the oven imagery of 7:6, its precise meaning, "whose baker ceases to stoke, from kneading the dough until it is leavened," is difficult to ascertain. However, in view of the paronomasia in 7:4a, it may be fair to say that 7:4b could be a sexual *double entendre* elaborating the final redactor's accusation, "all of them are adulterers; like a blazing oven are they."

In his recriminatory addition in 7:4, R2 reinterprets the political intrigue recounted in his traditional material of Hos 7 in light of the people's harlotrous behavior in worshipping strange gods. We have encountered this same transformation of the tradition in 4:11-14. In the latter, R2 reinterprets the "spirit of harlotry" which has led the people astray (4:12bA) as the people's idolatry.[152]

C. *Hos 7:10*

7:9   *'ākĕlû zārîm kōḥô*
      wĕhû' lō' yādā'
      gam-śêbâ zārĕqâ bô
      wĕhû' lō' yādā'

7:10   *wĕ'ānâ gĕ'ôn-yiśrā'ēl bĕpānāyw*
         wĕlō'-šābû 'el-yhwh 'ĕlōhêhem
         wĕlō' biqšūhû bĕkol-zō't

7:9   Aliens devour his strength,
         and he does not know it.
         Even gray hairs are sprinkled upon him
         and he does not know it.
7:10   *The pride of Israel testifies to his face.*
         They do not return to YHWH their God
         And seek him in all this.

Commentators have already noted the secondary
character of our second R2 editorial on Hos 7, viz. 7:10. They
consider 7:10a, "the pride of Israel testifies to his face," as a
later repetition of Hos 5:5. The expression in 7:10b, "YHWH
their God," in a speech of YHWH and the change to the 3 ms.
pl. from the 3 ms. sg. in 7:8-9 argue in favor of its
supplementary nature. Moreover, they think that 7:10 is
rather anticlimactic in its present position after 7:9.[153]
       The notions of returning (*šûb*) to YHWH and seeking (*bqš*)
him have become familiar to us as R2 editorials (Cf. 3:5, 5:15--
6:3). We wish to deal at this point with the motivation which
prompted R2's insertion of 7:10 here in this context. In the
first place, we note the parasonancy between *šêbâ*, "gray
hairs," in R2's tradition in 7:9bA and *šābû*, "return," in
7:10bA. The wordplay becomes a conduit for R2 to insert his
main theological idea of repentance. Second, the two *lō'*s of
7:10 correspond with the two *lō'*s in 7:9. R2 thus resumes the
*lō'*s of his tradition to launch into his own commentary.
       The third motivation for the commentary is one which we
have not as yet encounted in R2 composition. In discussing
7:10, Willi-Plein argues that the exegetical principle which
prompts the addition of 7:10 in the text has analogues with the
second of Hillel's exegetical rules (or *middoth*), viz. *gezerah
shawah*.[154] *Gezerah shawah* consists in a verbal analogy from
one verse to another. Where the same words are applied to
two separate cases it follows that the same considerations
apply to both. According to Willi-Plein, the redactor inserted

Hos 5:5a, "the pride of Israel testifies to his face," here in 7:10a
precisely because of the similarity between 7:9bB and 5:4bB:

7:9bB	Even gray hairs are sprinkled on him
	And he does not know it (*lō' yādā'*)
5:4bB	And YHWH they do not know (*lō' yādā'*)

Both 7:9bB and 5:4bB contain the expression, *lō' yādā'*.
Therefore, according to Hillel 2, the considerations of one
verse would apply to the other verse as well.[155] In order, then,
to illustrate the dynamics of R2's exegetical rationale more
clearly, we present the complete contexts of both verses:

5:4a	*Their deeds do not permit them*	
	to return to their God,	A
	(lāšûb 'el-'ĕlōhêhem)	
	For a spirit of harlotry is in their midst	
5:4bB	And YHWH they do not know (*lō' yādā'*)	B
5:5	The pride of Israel testifies to his face.	C
7:9b	Even gray hairs are sprinkled on him	
	And he does not know it (*lō' yādā'*).	B'
7:10a	*The pride of Israel testifies to his face.*	C'
	They do not return to YHWH their God	A'
	(lō' šābû 'el-yhwh 'ĕlōhêhem)	
	And seek him in all this.	

The R2 commentary is printed in *italics*; the received
tradition which R2 interprets is in regular print. We note the
ABCB'C'A' pattern on the right. The tradition in 7:9b (B')
contains the words *lō' yādā'*. In the final redactor's
hermeneutical reasoning, the presence of *lō' yādā'* in his
tradition permits him to recall another passage, one of his *own*
earlier insertions, which contain these same words, 5:4bB (B).
Moreover, in keeping with his exegetical reasoning, R2
appropriates what was articulated in the earlier text in A/C,
regarding repentance and the pride of Israel, and applies it to
the present 7:10 text in C'/A'.

D. Hos 7:12a**, 12b

7:11   *wayĕhî 'eprayim kĕyônâ*
         pôtâ 'ên lēb
         miṣrayim qārā'û
         'aššûr hālākû
7:12a   *ka'ăšer yēlēkû*
         'eprôś 'ălêhem rištî
         kĕ'ôp haššāmayim 'ôrîdēm
7:12b   *'ayĕsîrēm kĕšēma' la'ădātām*

7:11   Ephraim is like a dove
         Silly and without sense
         They call to Egypt.
         They go to Assyria.
7:12a   *As they go*
         I will spread over them my net
         Like birds of the air I will bring them down
7:12b   *I will chastise them according to the*
              report of their assemblies.

Our third R2 annotation of Hos 7 occurs in 7:12. Commentators have questioned the authenticity of 7:12a, *ka'ăšer yēlēkû*, "as they go," because it seems to disrupt the meter. Some have eliminated it as a gloss,[156] or added another *'aššûr*, "Assyria," for the sake of balance.[157] We see in this R2 insertion a paronomastic interplay between *'aššûr hālākû*, "they go to Assyria," of the tradition (7:11b) and *ka'ăšer yēlēkû*, "as they go," in the redactor's insertion in 7:12a.

Scholars have emended *'ayĕsîrēm* in 7:12b to some form of *'sr*, "to imprison,"[158] or omitted the whole 7:12b clause as a gloss on *'ôrîdēm*, "I will bring them down," in 7:12aA.[159] However, the text need not be emended. With 7:12b, R2 inserts his *mûsār* theology which we have seen in 5:2b.[160] Yes, Ephraim has behaved like a foolish and capricious dove by calling to Egypt and going to Assyria (7:11). And yes, YHWH is indeed given cause to spread his net over this flighty

bird and bring Ephraim down (7:12a). Nevertheless, with
7:12b R2 situates the punishment in perspective: "I (YHWH)
will chastise them (*'ayĕsîrēm*) according to the report of their
assemblies." The purpose of the chastisement is the people's
repentance. Because, as R2 states in 7:10, the people do not
repent and seek YHWH, YHWH must now chastise them.
With 7:12b, R2 mitigates his tradition by means of
paronomasia. The *hiphil* form of *ysr* in 7:12b, *'ayĕsîrēm*, is
unique in the whole HB. Commentators have preferred to
emend the pointing to the *piel*, *'ăyassĕrēm*.[161] However,
'ayĕsîrēm seems to be a wordplay involving rhyme and
parasonancy in the letters ', *r, m* with *'ôrîdēm* of the redactor's
tradition (7:12aB). The parasonancy involving the letters '/*h*,
š, and *m*, is continued in *kĕšēma'*, "according to the report,"
which plays on *kĕ'ôp haššāmayim*, "like birds of the air," of
7:12aB.

E. Hos 7:16

7:14b   '*al-dāgān wĕtîrôš yitgôrārû*
       yāsûrû bî
7:15   *wa'ănî <u>yissartî</u> hizzaqtî zĕrô'ōtām*
       wĕ'ēlay yĕhaššĕbû-rā'
7:16   <u>*yāšûbû lō' 'āl*</u>
       <u>*hāyû kĕqešet rĕmiyyâ*</u>
       <u>*yippĕlû bahereb śārêhem*</u>
       mizza'am lĕšônām
       zô la'gām bĕ'ereṣ miṣrāyim

7:14b   For grain and wine they became sojourners
       They have departed from me.[162]
7:15   *I, yes I, have chastised/trained them.*
       I strengthened their arms,
       But against me they plot evil.
7:16   *They turn to Not Most High.*
       They are like a slack bow.
       Their princes shall fall by the sword
       Because of the stuttering[163] of their tongue.
       This will be their derision in the land of Egypt.

Scholars have already suggested that *yissartî* seems to be a foreign element in 7:15.[164] The insertion has all the earmarks of R2 redaction. *Yissartî*, "I chastised/instructed/ trained," accords with R2's *mûsār* theology which we have just encountered earlier in 7:12b, "I will chastise them according to the report of their assemblies." The springboard for the insertion is the paronomasia, which commentators have pointed out,[165] between *yāsûrû bî*, "they have departed from me," in the redactor's tradition, 7:14b, and *yissartî*. In its present context, *yissartî* takes on a double meaning. On one hand, it interacts paronomastically with *yāsûrû bî* of the tradition (7:14b): "Because they have turned away from me (*yāsûrû bî*), I have chastised them (*yissartî*)." On the other hand, the insertion puts what follows in the tradition in sharper focus: "It was I, YHWH, who trained them,[166] I strengthened their military might. Yet, they plot evil against me!" (7:15aBb).

In his last commentary in Hos 7, R2 reiterates in 7:16 themes which we have already observed in his editing and adds new ones. R2 is able to introduce his comments by means of paronomasia. R2 plays upon the *ḥšb* of the tradition in 7:15b, *wĕ'ēlay yĕḥaššĕbû-rā'*, "they plot evil against me," with his favorite root *šwb*. Instead of repenting of these evil plans and turning to YHWH, the people instead turn to Not Most High, *yāšûbû lō' 'āl*. Although scholars have remarked that *lō' 'āl* may be a corruption of *l-b'l* or *lb'l*, "to Baal,"[167] we prefer to retain the MT. *'al* has been recognized to be a divine name by itself and in combination with other epithets, such as *'āl 'ĕlōhîm* (Ps 7:11) and *'āl yhwh* (Ps 18:42).[168] *Lō' 'āl* is comparable to *lō' 'ēl*, "Not God," in Dt 32:17,21 and *lō' yô'îlû*, "the Non-Helper," in Jer 2:8.

Andersen and Freedman comment that if *lō' 'āl*

"is intended to be a jingle that parodies the name of Baal, it is a little surprising that Hosea did not say **bal 'āl*. Since this negative is in his vocabulary, and, being privative, it would be an even more devastating assertion that Baal is a non-entity." (p. 478)

The epithet *lō' 'āl*, however, accords with the point of the R2 commentary which follows. The name, Not Most High, focuses on the *impotence* of the deity which the people turn to instead of YHWH.[169] R2 makes a vivid contrast with his tradition through his editorial. Although it is YHWH who strengthens the might of the people (7:15), they wander after an impotent god. Indeed, because this god can do nothing for them, R2 goes on to say that the people "are like a slack bow" (7:16), i.e. a bow that has lost its power.[170] In his final exhortation to repentance in Hos 14, R2 enjoins the people to admit that their reliance on military might and a non-god which they make with their hands has no power to save them (14:4).

Bringing his exegetical commentary on Hos 7 to a completion, R2 relates the consequences of the people's military powerlessness in 7:16aBb: "Their princes shall fall by the sword because of the stuttering of their tongue (*mizza'am lĕšōnām*). This will be their derision (*zô la'gām*) in the land of Egypt." One observes the R2 alliteration in *mizza'am lĕ'ōnām* and *zô la'gām* involving the letters *m, z, ', and l*. Noting the secondary character of 7:16aB, Duhm thinks that it was perhaps written later by an Egyptian Jew.[171] We suggest that background for 7:16aBb are the exilic texts, Jer 42-44, which recount Jeremiah's bitter opposition to the flight into Egypt in the face of the Babylonian invasion. There are a number of parallels between the final redaction of Hos 7 and Jer 42-44. We reproduce here a representative passage in Jer 42-44:

Hos 7:14 For *grain and wine* they *become sojourners*
             (*yitgôrārû*)

Hos 7:16 Their princes shall *fall by the sword*
             (*yippĕlû baḥereb*)
             because of the stuttering of their tongue.
             This will be their *derision in the land*
             of Egypt

Jer 44:12 I (YHWH) will take the remnant of Judah
             who have set their faces *to come to the*
             land of Egypt to sojourn, (lābô'
             'eres-misrayim lagûr) and they shall all

> be consumed; in the land of Egypt *they*
> *shall fall (yippōlû)*; by the sword
> and by famine they shall be consumed;
> *from the least to the greatest, they shall*
> *die by the sword (baḥereb)* and by famine;
> *and they shall become an execration, a*
> *horror, a curse and a taunt.*

Both Hos 7:14-16 in its final redaction and Jer 42-44 criticise the people and their leaders for fleeing to Egypt to become sojourners (*gwr*, Hos 7:14; Jer 42:15, 17, 22; 43:2, 44:8, 12, 14). They think that Egypt will provide not only a safe haven for them from the Babylonians but also food to assuage their hunger (Hos 7:14 - grain and wine; Jer 42:14 - bread). However, the people and their leaders will still "fall by the sword" (Hos 7:16; Jer 42:16; 44:12, 27). Instead of having food, they will experience famine. Their derision will ultimately be in the land of Egypt, where they will become an execration, a horror, a curse and a taunt (Hos 7:16; Jer 42:18; 44:8, 12).

In ending Hos 7 with the detail of the people *in Egypt*, R2 anticipates his later commentaries where he describes YHWH bringing Israel *out of Egypt*. (Cf. Hos 11; 12:10, 14; 13:4-5). We will discuss this aspect of R2 redaction in greater length below. Suffice it to say for now that in R2's exilic perspective, the people's experience of derision in Egypt will be reversed when YHWH leads his people out of Egypt again in a new Exodus.[172]

F. The Redactional Thrust of Hos 7

Familiar R2 concepts recur in his redaction of Hos 7: the notion of idolatry as adultery (7:4); the arrogant but futile reliance on military strength and on idolatrous artifacts (7:16); the people's apostasy, impenitence and lack of knowledge (7:10, 16) which provokes YHWH's chastisement (7:12b, 15). R2 exegesis of the tradition in Hos 7 utilizes not only wordplays on the tradition, but also a type of hermeneutical principle similar to Hillel 2 in 7:10, which we have not hitherto seen. Certain words of his tradition in Hos

7:9 recall another passage containing the same words. Because of the similarity of words in both texts, R2 is able to apply the considerations of the earlier passage in his exegesis of Hos 7. R2 adds a new idea at the conclusion of Hos 7, viz. the people's derision in the land of Egypt (7:16). This idea seems to have its background in the events of the exile. He will reiterate this theme again in 8:13 and 9:3. He thus prepares for his later editorials where he affirms that the One who first brought Israel out of Egypt will bring Israel home from exile again in a New Exodus (Hos 11; 12:10, 14; 13:4-5).

VII.   *The Final Redaction of Hos 8*

A.   *The Editorial History of Hos 8*

H	C	R1	R2
		8:1-4a	8:4b-5aA
		8:5aBb-6*	8:6*-7
8:8-10		8:11-12	8:13-14

*kî miyyiśrā'ēl = R1

B.   *Hos 8:4b-5aA, 6**

8:4a	hēm himlîkû wĕlō' mimmennî
	hēśîrû wĕlō' yādā'tî
8:4b	kaspām ûzĕhābām
	'āśû lāhem 'ăṣabbîm
	lĕma'an yikkārēt
8:5aA	zānaḫ 'eglēk šōmĕrôn
8:5aBb	ḥārâ 'appî bām
	'ad-mātay lō' yûkĕlû niqqāyōn
8:6	kî miyyiśrā'ēl
	wĕhû' ḥārāš 'āśāhû
	wĕlō' 'ĕlōhîm hû'
	kî-šĕbābîm yihyeh 'ēgel šōmĕrôn

8:4a   They made kings but not from me.
          They made princes but I did not acknowledge
          them.
8:4b   *With their silver and gold*
          they made idols for themselves.
          So that it will be cut off,
8:5aA   *He has rejected your calf, Samaria.*
8:5aBb   My anger was kindled against them.
          How long will they be unable to be clean,
8:6   even from Israel.
          A workman made it.
          It is Not God,
          for the calf of Samaria will become fragments.

The R2 redaction of Hos 8 centers primarily on the idolatry of Israel, which is personified in the calf of Samaria. We see this first of all in 8:4b which is verbally similar to the R2 insertion, 2:10:[173]

2:10   Silver (*kesep*) I lavished upon her
          and gold which they made into a Baal.
          (*wĕzāhāb 'āśû labbā'al*)

8:4b   With their silver and gold (*kaspām ûzĕhābām*)
          they made idols for themselves (*'aśû lāhem 'ăṣabbîm*)

Similar to R2 use of *antanaclasis* in 2:23-24, 3:1, and 14:2-9, 8:4b begins the final redactor's multiple *antanaclasis* on the root *'śh* in Hos 8. We list these occurrences of *'śh*, each with its nuanced meaning:

8:4b   They made (*'āśû*) idols for themselves.
8:6a   A workman made it (*'āśāhû*).
8:7   (The standing grain) does not yield (*ya'ăśeh*)
          flour. Should it yield (*ya'ăśeh*), foreigners
          would swallow it up.
8:14a   Israel has forgotten his Maker (i.e. his Creator,
          'ōśēhû)

Within the semantic range of the root 'śh, R2 is able to
juxtapose the foolishness of Israel who makes useless idols for
himself (8:4b, 6a) and forgets the One who actually created
him (8:14a). Moreover, by means of 'śh R2 is able to expand
upon his agricultural image which anticipates his second
major hope passage, 10:12. We will discuss these points in
greater detail below.

R2 represents the idolatry of the people in the figure of the
calf of Samaria in 8:5aA. Commentators have found the MT of
8:5 quite difficult. First of all, the third person, zānaḥ, "he
rejects," is incongruous in the YHWH speech which precedes
in 8:4a, "they make kings, but not through *me* . . . ," and
follows in 8:5aA, "*my* anger . . . " Related to this, the change to
the 2nd sg. address, "*your* calf, Samaria," conflicts with the
3rd pl. of the preceding and following statements. Finally, the
object of YHWH's anger expressed in the 3rd pl., "my anger
burns against *them*," is ambiguous. Its immediate antecedent,
"your calf," is singular.

Commentators have endeavored to resolve some of these
difficulties by 1) emending zānaḥ to 1st person[174], 2) or
emending it to the passive[175] or imperative voice,[176] 3)
translating zānaḥ as "your calf *stinks*" [177] 4) emending *bām* to
bô to harmonize with "calf,"[178] 5) placing the clause, "my
anger burns against them," before 8:5,[179] 6) arguing that
'*appî*, "my anger," performs a double duty function as subject
for zānaḥ,[180] 7) assigning the references to the calf of Samaria
in 8:5-6 to later redaction.[181]

We prefer to let the MT stand as is. The third person sg.,
zānaḥ, in a YHWH speech and the second person address to
Samaria are intelligible in view of the final redactor's typical
change of person to distinguish his editorials. Bracketing the
sôp pāsûq after the problematic *lĕma'an yikkārēt* of 8:4bB,[182]
we connect *lĕma'an yikkārēt* to the beginning of 8:5: *lĕma'an
yikkārēt zānaḥ 'eglēk šōmĕrôn*, "so that it will be cut off, he
(YHWH) has rejected your calf, Samaria."[183] Scholars have
viewed *lĕma'an yikkārēt* as an insertion whose terminology is
typical of later texts, such as Zeph 1:11, Zech 9:10, 13:2, Mic
5:9-12, and Nah 1:14.[184]

According to the Deuteronomistic Historian, the installation of the calves of gold at Dan and Bethel by Jeroboam I was *the sin* which led to the deterioration and downfall of both kingdoms, Israel and Judah (I Kgs 12:25--13:34; 2 Kgs 17:14-23).[185] Sharing Dtr sentiments, R2 personifies the idolatry of the people in the figure of the calf of Samaria. In 8:6*, R2 enlarges his 8:4b-5aA description and condemnation of the calf of Samaria. Note how R2 structures his commentary in an ABC/A'B'C' envelope around his tradition, 8:5aBb:

8:4b	*kaspām ûzĕhābām*	A
	'āśû lāhem 'ăṣabbîm	B
	lĕma'an yikkārēt	C
8:5aA	*zānaḥ 'eglēk šōmĕrôn*	
8:5aBb	*hārâ 'appî bām*	
	'ad-mātay lō' yûkĕlû niqqāyōn	
8:6*	*kî miyyiśrā'ēl*	
	$\quad$ D $\qquad$ E	
8:6a	*wĕhû' hārāš 'āśāhû*	A'
	$\quad$ E' $\qquad$ D'	
	wĕlō' 'ĕlōhîm hû'	B'
8:6b	*kî-šĕbābîm yihyeh 'ēgel šōmĕrôn*	C'

The *wĕhû'* beginning the chiastically fashioned bicola, 8:6a, refers directly to the *'eglēk*, "your calf," of the foregoing R2 commentary in 8:5aA. With the second instance of the *'śh* antanaclasis, R2 sarcastically points out that a mere workman (A') has fashioned it out of silver and gold (A). Moreover, like all idols (*'ăṣabbîm* - B), it is Not God (B'). We compare *lō' 'ĕlōhîm*, Not God, to *lō' 'āl*, Not Most High, which we just observed in the R2 editorial, 7:16.[186] Wolff perceptively remarks that *lō' 'ĕlōhîm hû'*, "It is Not God," is precisely the antithesis of Jeroboam I's declaration to the people when he erected the calves: *hinnēh 'ĕlōhêkā*, "Behold your God" (I Kgs 12:28).[187] This argues in favor of the Dtr disposition of R2 redaction. R2 goes on to say that this Not God, the calf of Samaria, will become fragments, since it is simply of human

manufacture (C'). C' parallels C in describing the disastrous
fate of the calf of Samaria.

C. Hos 8:7

8:7a	*kî rûaḥ yizrā'û*
	wĕsûpātâ yiqṣōrû
8:7b	*qāmâ 'ên-lô ṣemaḥ*
	bĕlî ya'ăśeh-qemaḥ
	'ûlay ya'ăśeh
	zārîm yiblā'ûhû
8:8	*nibla' yiśrā'ēl*

8:7a	*Indeed, the wind they sow*
	and the whirlwind they reap.
8:7b	*The standing grain has no shoots to it.*
	It does not yield flour.
	Should it yield, foreigners would swallow it up.
8:8	*Israel is swallowed up . . .*

The following R2 commentary, 8:7, is distinguished by
numerous paronomasia which has been noted by several
scholars.[188] Furthermore, 8:7 anticipates by way of contrast
the R2 hope passage, 10:12, which describes the second
preparatory stage of the journey back to YHWH in the final
redactor's structuring of the tradition.[189] Hos 8:7a accuses the
people: *rûaḥ yizrā'û wĕsupātâ yiqṣōrû*, "They *sow* the wind and
they *reap* the whirlwind." Hos 10:12, on the other hand,
exhorts them: *zir'û lākem liṣdāqâ qiṣrû liprî ḥesed*, "*Sow* for
yourselves righteousness. *Reap* the fruit of steadfast love."
Both passages capitalize on the agricultural imagery
which permeates R2 redaction from the beginning of the Book
of Hosea to its conclusion. Hos 8:7, adopts it to lay bare the
futility of the people's actions. Sowing the wind is a practical
impossibility. With the same agricultural terminology,
however, 10:12 offers concrete ways to restore the people's
relationship with YHWH and culminate their journey in the
land itself: by preparing the soil of their hearts and sowing
into it seeds of righteousness.

Also offering a vivid contrast to 10:12, 8:7b continues the agricultural imagery. In 8:7b, R2 describes the fruitlessness of the people's present agrarian efforts. This fruit*less*ness opposes the fruit*ful*ness portrayed in 10:12 which results from the sowing of righteousness. R2 articulates the people's present infertile condition by means of paronomasia:

> *qāmâ 'ên lô ṣemaḥ*
>   *bĕlî ya'ăśeh qemaḥ*
>   *'ûlay ya'ăśeh*
> *zārîm yiblā'ûhû*

> *The standing grain* has no *shoots*
>   It does not *yield flour*
>   Should it *yield* ⸺
> Foreigners would swallow it up.

We note first the parasonancy in *qāmâ/qemaḥ*, "standing grain/flour," which stands at the beginning and end of the first bicola. The parasonancy passes from *qāmâ* to *qemaḥ* with the help of *ṣemaḥ*, "shoots," which alliterates and rhymes with *qemaḥ*. Moreover, 8:7b contains the third and fourth instances of the *'śh antanaclasis* begun in 8:4.[190] In the latter, *'śh* designates human production, the work of human hands. In 8:7b, however, it describes plant production or yield, or more precisely in our case, the lack thereof.

The final colon of 8:7b contains two more cases of parasonancy: *zārîm yiblā'ûhû niblaʿ yiśrā'ēl*, "*Foreigners would swallow it up.* Israel is swallowed up." *Zārîm*, "foreigners," at the end of 8:7 plays upon *yizrā'û*, "they sow," at the very beginning of 8:7, thus tightly connecting the whole verse. Moreover, R2 provides a transition from his own commentary to the tradition. He anticipates the *blʿ*, "to swallow up," from 8:8, which in the *niphal* refers to *Israel* being swallowed up or engulfed among the nations. Thus anchoring himself in the tradition, he plays upon the word with his own commentary. In the R2 agricultural representation of Israel's moral bankruptcy, *blʿ* now describes the plundering of foreigners who will seize the meager yield, should the grain crop even produce. From the R2 exilic point of view, these foreigners would refer to the invading Babylonian armies.

D. Hos 8:13-14

8:13a   *zibḥê hbhbh (MT: habhābay)*[191] *yizbĕḥû*
          bāśār wayyō'kēlû
          yhwh lō' rāṣām
8:13b   *'attâ yizkōr 'ăwônām*
          wĕyipqōd ḥaṭṭō'wtām
          hēmmâ miṣrayim yāšûbû
8:14a   *wayyiškaḥ yiśrā'ēl 'et-'ōśēhû*
          wayyiben hêkālôt
          wîhûdâ hirbâ 'ārîm bĕṣūrôt
8:14b   *wĕšillaḥtî-'ēs bĕ'ārāyw*
          wĕ'ākĕlâ 'armĕnōtêhā

8:13a   Roast offerings they sacrifice.
          Flesh they eat,
          But YHWH takes no delight in them.
8:13b   And now, he will remember their guilt
          he will punish their sin.
          They will return to Egypt.
8:14a   Israel has forgotten his Maker
          and has built palaces.
          Judah has multiplied fortified cities.
8:14b   But I will send fire into his cities.
          It will devour its fortresses.

The final R2 commentary of Hos 8, 8:13-14 concludes the chapter with a climactic statement of judgment. The authenticity of both verses or parts of them has long since been suspected by scholars.[192] In the first place, the third person reference to YHWH in a speech of YHWH in 8:13 betrays its secondary character as commentary: "Were *I* (YHWH) to write for him (8:12) . . . but *YHWH* takes no delight in them. Now *he* will remember their iniquity (8:13) . . . " Hos 8:14 is even more conspicuous as an addition because

of the reference to Judah in a quotation highly reminiscent of
Am 1:4 and 2:5. Furthermore, the reference to Israel
forgetting his Maker is more characteristic of exilic thought
rather than an 8th century prophet.[193]

R2 themes emerge in 8:13-14. The first is the notion of the
forgetting of YHWH, a deuteronomistic notion we have seen
already in the R2 insertion 2:15bB, "and me she forgot."[194]
Second, the reference to the return (šûb) to Egypt parallels
7:16 describing the people's derision in the land of Egypt
because they turn (šûb) to Not Most High.[195] Both texts insist
that the return to Egypt is due to the people's idolatry. R2
highlights these texts depicting the reversal of the exodus by
situating them prominently at the end of chapters. In this
way R2 thus creates major structural markers for his
composition. Both these concluding statements anticipate the
optimistic R2 commentary in Hos 11 and 12 where YHWH
will surely reverse this judgment and bring this people out of
Egypt again in a new Exodus.[196] Finally, in 7:16 and 8:13-14,
R2 reiterates another theme which we have already observed
in his commentary, viz. the result of an arrogant reliance on
military might instead of YHWH (cf. 1:5, 7 and 14:4).
According to 7:16, the people will become militarily impotent.
Their princes will fall by the sword. All of this will occur
because they turn to Not Most High instead of the One who
really trained and strengthened them. Because Israel and
Judah have made a Not God (8:6) and have forgotten the One
who created them, this One, according to 8:13-14, will
demolish their military strongholds by fire.

R2 links himself to his tradition by taking up its words
and playing upon them. He plays upon the double occurrences
of *mzbḥt lḥṭ'*, "altars for sin offerings," in 8:11 with *zbḥy hbhbh
yzbḥw*, "roast offerings they sacrifice," which is paralleled by
"flesh they eat" in 8:13a. Moreover, with 8:13b he censures
the altars for *sin* offerings described in the 8:10 tradition:
YHWH will punish the people for their sins, *wypqd ḥṭṭ'wtm*.
R2's fifth and final *antanaclasis* on the root *'śh* appears in the
climactic 8:14. In contrast to those who make (*'śh*) idols, 8;4b,
6a, R2 asserts in 8;14 that YHWH is the creator of Israel
(*'ōśēhû*). It is this Creator God whom Israel has forgotten! It is

this Creator god who will turn their military strength to impotence by fire!

E. The Redactional Thrust of Hos 8

R2 unifies his redaction of the chapter by means of antanaclastic repetition of the root '*sh* which he utilizes from beginning to end. Through this *antanaclasis* R2 is able to juxtapose the foolishness of the people's idolatry in the face of the One who made them. In comparison to the other chapters of the Hos 4-11 complex which we have examined, R2's condemnation of idols comes most stringently to the foreground in Hos 8. The final redaction of R2 gives Hos 8 a definite perspective. R2's tradition in Hos 8:1-3 accuses the people of breach of covenant: "They have transgressed my covenant and against my law they have revolted" (8:1b). R2 augments the gravity of this accusation by now including the making of idols. He symbolizes the idolatry of the people in the figure of the calf of Samaria whose installation led to the downfall of Israel. This latter theme betrays his contacts with deuteronomistic circles.

Moreover, R2 anticipates his later editorials with his 8:7 expansion. He contrasts the futility of sowing the wind and reaping the whirlwind with his later exhortation in 10:7 to sow righteousness and reap the fruit of steadfast love. He thus takes up in 8:7 the barrenness/fertility motif which he extends from the beginning of the Book of Hosea to its conclusion.

With 8:7, R2 anticipates later commentary; with 8:13-14, he recalls earlier commentary. In many ways 8:13-14 parallels the final R2 statements of Hos 7, viz. 7:13-16. R2 accuses the people of forgetting their own Creator by creating idols, a Not God, and by building military strongholds. Because of these offenses, YHWH will punish them by fire. For R2, however, the judgment against them is not irreversible. although the people will return to Egypt because of their guilt and sin, R2 asserts ahead in Hos 11 and 12 that YHWH will reverse this decision, if only they would repent.

VIII. The Final Redaction of Hos 9

   A. *The Editorial History of Hos 9*

H	C	R1	R2
		9:1	9:2-4
		9:5	9:6
		9:7	9:8-9
		9:10	
9:11-13			9:14
		9:15	
9:16			9:17

   B. *Hos 9:2-4*

9:2   *gōren wāyeqeb lō' yir'ēm*
       wĕtîrôš yĕkaḥeš bāh
9:3   *lō' yēšĕbû bĕ'ereṣ yhwh*
       wĕšāb 'eprayim miṣrayim
       ûbĕ'aššûr ṭāmē' yō'kēlû
9:4   *lō'-yissĕkû layhwh yayin*
       wĕlō' ye'erbû-lô zibḥêhem
       kĕleḥem 'ônîm lāhem
       kol-'ōkĕlāyw yiṭammā'û
       kî-laḥmām lĕnapšām
       lō' yābô' bêt yhwh

9:2   Threshing floor and wine vat will not keep them.
       New wine will fail from it.
9:3   They will not dwell in the land of YHWH.
       But Ephraim will return to Egypt.
       In Assyria they will eat unclean food.
9:4   They will not pour out their wine as a libation
          to YHWH
       And they will not bring their sacrifices to him.
       For, the bread of mourning is theirs.
       All who eat it will become unclean.
       For their bread is for their hunger.
       It will not come into the house of YHWH.

One is alerted to R2 redaction in these verses by the change of person from the 2nd person address to Israel in 9:1 to 3rd person plural beginning in 9:2. R2 launches into his extended commentary by resuming *gōren*, "threshing floor," from his tradition in 9:1. His commentary takes up, first of all, the barrenness motif: The threshing floor and wine vat will not keep them. New wine will fail from it. We compare the use of *r'h*, "to shepherd, keep," in 9:2a with the R2 insertion, 4:16b: "And now, YHWH will shepherd them like a lamb in broad pasture."[197]

Moreover, through his typical *yšb/šwb* wordplay, R2 announces the exile from the land and the return to Egypt: "They will not dwell *(lō' yēšĕbû)* in the land of YHWH. But Ephraim will return *(wĕšāb)* to Egypt." (Cf. 3:4-5; 10:11; 14:8).[198] R2 thus reiterates the theme of the reversal of the Exodus, which we encountered in the foregoing R2 commentary, 8:13b - "they will return to Egypt." We will discuss "the return to Egypt" further in connection with the R2 addition, 9:6, below.[199]

Several scholars have noted the late character of 9:4.[200] The reference to the house of YHWH presupposes the centralization of cult at the temple in Jerusalem. Furthermore, the barrenness of the land, expressed in 9:3, and the impossibility of cult in the house of YHWH, stated in 9:4, is reflective of the thoughts of the later prophet, Joel:

Jl 1:8   Lament like virgin girded with sackcloth
            for the bridegroom of her youth.
Jl 1:9   The cereal offering and the *drink offering*
            are cut off[201] from the *house of YHWH*
                                    (mibbêt yhwh).
        The priests mourn, the ministers of YHWH.
Jl 1:10   The fields are laid waste,
            the ground mourns;
        because the *grain (dāgān)* is destroyed,
            the *wine (tîrôš)* fails,
            the oil languishes.

Finally, the eating of bread which causes uncleanliness (Hos 9:4aB) accords with Ezek 4:13 regarding the bread eaten in exile:

> And YWHH said: "Thus shall the people of Israel eat their bread unclean (*'et-laḥmām tāmē'*) among the nations whither I drive them." (cf. Am 7:17)

R2 articulates his ideas on the impossibility of cult in the exile by means of parasonancy. We see this first of all in 9:4aB: *kĕleḥem 'ônîm lāhem*, "for, the bread of mourning is theirs.[202] R2 has definite thoughts about this bread of mourning which he delivers in a commentary marked by rhyme and alliteration and repeating the word, *leḥem*:

kol-'ōkĕlāyw yiṭammā'û	"All who eat of it will be unclean"
kî-laḥmām lĕnapšām	"For their bread is for their hunger"
lō' yābô' bêt yhwh	"It will not come into the house of YHWH"

C. Hos 9:6

9:6   *kî-hinnēh hālĕkû miššōd*
         miṣrayim tĕqabbĕsēm
         mōp tĕqabbĕrēm
       maḥmad lĕkaspām
       qimmôś yîrāšēm
       ḥôaḥ bĕ'oholêhem

9:6   For behold, they are fleeing from destruction -
         Egypt shall gather them.
         Memphis shall bury them.
       - with the best of their silver things.
         Weeds will dispossess them,
         Thorns, from their tents.[203]

Commentators have found 9:6 problematic, removing 9:6aA, "For behold, they are fleeing from destruction,"[204] 9:6aB, "Memphis shall bury them,"[205] and/or 9:6bA, "best things of silver,"[206] as later glosses.

We argue that 9:6, along with the notion of the return to Egypt recounted in 9:3, is best explained by Jer 42-44 which forms the background for the final redaction of Hos 7:14-16. We have already shown the parallels between Jer 42-44 and 7:14-16 in the discussion of those verses.[207] We think that Hos 9:6 also relates in brief this flight of the Jews to Egypt from Babylonian reprisals. We display the parallels between Hos 9:3-6 and a representative text from Jer 42-44, viz. Jer 42:11-16, as follows:

"Do not fear the king of Babylon, of whom you are afraid; do not fear him," says YHWH, "for I am with you to save you and to deliver you from his hand. I will grant you mercy, that he may have mercy on you and let you dwell in your own land. But if you say, '*We will not dwell in this land*,' (*l' nšb b'rṣ hz't*) disobeying the voice of YHWH your God and saying, '*No, we will go to the land of Egypt* ('*rṣ mṣrym nbw'*), where we shall not see war, or hear the sound of trumpet, or be hungry for bread (*lḥm*) and we will dwell (*nšb*) there,' then hear the word of the Lord, O remnant of Judah. Thus says the Lord of Hosts, the God of Israel: "If you set your faces to enter Egypt and go to live, then the sword which you fear shall overtake you there in the land of Egypt; and the famine of which you are afraid shall follow hard after you to Egypt; *and there you shall die*." (Jer 42:11-16)

They shall not dwell in the land of YHWH (*l' yšbw b'rṣ yhwh*) But Ephraim shall return to Egypt. (*wšb 'prym mṣrym*) (Hos 9:3)

The *bread* of mourning is theirs. (Hos 9:4)

For behold, *they are fleeing from destruction. Egypt shall gather them. Memphis shall bury them*. (Hos 9:6)

Both passages share the theme of not remaining in the land of YHWH, but fleeing to Egypt. Both insist that in Egypt will be their death. These ideas accord with deuteronomic thought on the return to Egypt as a punishment:[208]

"And YHWH will bring you back (*šûb, hiph*) in ships to Egypt,
a journey which I promised that you would never make again"
(Dt 28:68. Cf. Dt 17:16).

Furthermore, both Hosean and Jeremian texts maintain
that the bread eaten in Egypt is the bread eaten in exile.
According to Hos 9:4, it will be their bread of mourning,
broken for the dead and eaten at the time of funerals; Cf. Dt
26:14 and Jer 16:7. We compare the reference to "Memphis" in
Hos 9:6 to Jer 44:1 where Jeremiah cites Memphis as one of
the Jewish settlements in Egypt. Moreover, Jer 46:14
recounts the devastation wreaked by Nebuchadnezzar at
Memphis.

R2 constructs 9:6 with two obvious paronomasia. The first
is the alliteration, parasonancy, and rhyme between *miṣrayim
tĕqabbĕṣēm/mōp tĕqabbĕrēm*, "Egypt shall gather them/
Memphis shall bury them." The second is the alliteration of
the letters *m/š/ś/h/ḥ* in *qimmôś yîrāšēm/ḥôaḥ bĕ'ohŏlêhem*,
"weeds will dispossess them/thorns, from their tents."

D. *Hos 9:8-9*

9:7   *bā'û yĕmê happĕquddâ*
          bā'û yĕmê hašillūm
      yēdĕ'û yiśrā'ēl
          'ĕwîl hannābî'
          mĕšuggā' 'îš hāruaḥ
          'al rōb 'ăwônĕkā
          wĕrabbâ maśṭēmâ
9:8   *ṣōpeh 'eprayim 'im-'ĕlōhāy nābî'*
          paḥ yāqôś 'al-kol-dĕrākāyw
          maśṭēmâ bĕbêt 'ĕlōhāyw
9:9   *hĕ'mîqû-šiḥētû*
          kîmê haggib'â
      yizkôr 'ăwônām
      yipqôd ḥaṭṭō'wtām

9:7   The days of punishment have come.
          The days of retribution have come.

Israel shall know it.
The prophet is a fool.
The man of the spirit is mad,
Because of your great guilt
and great hostility.
9:8   *The prophet is a watchman of Ephraim with my God.*
A trap set on all his ways.
Hostility in the house of his God.
9:9   *They have deeply corrupted themselves*
as in the days of Gibeah.
He will remember their guilt.
He will punish their sins.

Commentators have deemed Hos 9:8 difficult to interpret. Indeed, this verse have been subject to much emendation.[209] Except for the minor placement of the *athnach* under *nābî̕* , we accept the present MT. We would explain the various cruxes of the verse by R2 redaction.

One can distinguish two different representations of the prophet in 9:7 and 9:8. Hos 9:7 is more pejorative in tone, more in keeping with the description of the stumbling prophet of 4:5. We will argue below that this more damning portrayal of the prophet stems from the hand of R1 at an earlier stage of the book's composition.[210] R2 mitigates this description of the prophet which he has received in his tradition through his 9:8 expansion. We have already encountered his positive deuteronomistic attitude towards the prophets as the instruments of YHWH in his 6:5 insertion.[211]

In 9:8, R2 makes his presence known by the change to the 1st person in *'ĕlōhāy*, "my God." According to R2, the prophet is not a fool or a madman (9:7). Rather, "the prophet is a watchman of Ephraim with my God," *ṣōpeh 'eprayim 'im- 'ĕlōhāy nābî̕*. One can explain the peculiar construction, *'im- 'ĕlōhāy nābî̕*,[212] if one interprets it as a paronomasia on *'ĕwîl hannābî̕*, "the prophet is a fool," in 9:7.[213] To effect this wordplay on 9:7 and thus qualify its negative portrayal of prophets, R2 shifts the definite article, *ha-*, beginning *hannābî̕* in 9:7 to the end of the previous word, *'ĕwîl*, to create the wordplay, *'im-'ĕlōhāy nābî̕*.

R2 expands his characterization of the prophet with *paḥ yāqôš ʿal-kol-děrākāyw*, "a trap set on all his ways." We point out the wordplay: the prophet is a watchman (*ṣōpeh*) of Ephraim; a trap (*paḥ*) set on all his ways. We compare the description of the prophet as a trap on all the ways of Ephraim to Jer 6:27 where YHWH says to Jeremiah

> "I have made you an assayer and tester among the people that you may know *and assay their ways.*

R2 is not only linked to his tradition, 9:7, in the paronomasia between *ʾěwîl hannābîʾ* and *ʾělōhāy nābîʾ*. R2 resumes other words from 9:7 to fashion his own commentary in 9:8-9: *yěmê*, "days," *maśṭēmâ*, "hostility," *ʿawôn*, "guilt," and *pěquddâ/pāqad*, "punishment/to punish." In 9:8bB, R2 locates the great *maśṭēmâ*, "hostility," in the "house of God," which refers back to his 9:4 reference to the "house of YHWH."

Hos 9:9 deserves special comment regarding R2's resumption of words from 9:7 for his editorial. Scholars have regarded 9:9 as a repetitive gloss from 10:9 and 8:13.[214] As with his insertion, 7:10, which we have discussed above,[215] R2 interprets his tradition according to a hermeneutical principle similar to Hillel's *gezerah shawah*.[216] *Gezerah shawah*, we recall, is the verbal analogy from one verse to another, whereby the considerations of one verse is applied to the other verse which shares the same word. *Paḥ*, "trap," in 9:8 recalls for him 5:1-2 where *paḥ* also occurs and which contain *šaḥat hěʿmîqû*, "they have dug a deep pit." R2 is thus able to insert a paraphrase of 5:1-2 in 9:9: *hěʿmîqû-šiḥētû kîmê haggibʿâ*, "they have deeply corrupted themselves as in the days of Gibeah." He interprets the coming "days of punishment" in 9:7 as the result of the people's corruption "as in the days of Gibeah." We will discuss the meaning of "the days of Gibeah" more in depth below when we treat R2's second reference to these days in 10:9.[217] Moreover, the presence of *pěquddâ*, "punishment," and *ʿāwôn*, "guilt," in 9:7 prompts him to quote his own 8:13 insertion literally: *yizkôr ʿăwônām yipqôd haṭṭōʾwtām*, "he will remember their guilt and punish their sins."

E. Hos 9:14, 17

We would like to make a few remarks regarding the
redactional character of the remainder of the chapter, 9:10-17,
before we examine it in depth. At first glance, these verses
seem to contain a heterogeneous mixture of motifs pertaining
to agriculture (vv 10a, 13a, 16a), human conception and birth
or its impossibility (vv 11-12, 13b, 14, 16b), and a polluted cult
resulting in divine rejection (vv 10b, 15, 17). In trying to
resolve the apparently fragmented character of the text,
scholars have sought to rearrange the verses into a more
coherent form. Duhm, for example, suggests the original
arrangement to be 9:10, 13a, 16a, 11, 16b, 12, 13b. Hos 9:14,
15, and 17 would constitute another sayings unit incorporated
into this original one.[218]

We argue that the text should not be rearranged, but
rather, viewed as a composition composed of tradition and
redactional commentary interwoven together. The first
commentary at the final level of redaction would be 9:14:

9:14   *tēn-lāhem yhwh mah tittēn*
         tēn-lāhem reḥem mǎškîl
         wěšāddayim ṣoměqîm

9:14   Give them, YHWH - What will you give?
         Give them a miscarrying womb
         and dry breasts.

One suspects that 9:14 is secondary because of the change
from YHWH speech to a second person address to YHWH. The
speaker of 9:14 emerges as our final redactor whose voice can
be heard in the foregoing R2 commentary, 9:8, where he refers
to "my God." In 9:14, R2 pleas with YHWH to mitigate the
dreadful punishment described in 9:13: "Ephraim must lead
forth his children to slaughter."[219] R2's prayer is that
YHWH's punishment of a deserving people be unfruitfulness
rather than massacre.

R2's voice is heard once again in 9:17 with the declaration, "my God," which also contrasts with the YHWH speech of 9:16:[220]

9:17   *yim'āsēm 'ĕlōhāy kî lō' šāmĕ'û lô*
            wĕyihyû nōdĕdîm baggôyim

9:17   My God will reject them,
            because they have not listened to him.
            They will be wanderers among the nations.

R2 formulates 9:17 in strongly deuteronomistic language. According to Dt 4:1, 30, 36, 5:1 *et passim*, the people are called to hear (*šm'*) and obey the commands and statutes of YHWH's covenant.[221] In a summary statement explaining the events which led up to the Babylonian exile, the Deuteronomist says in 2 Kgs 17:19-20:

> "Judah also did not keep the commandments of YHWH their God, but walked in the customs which Israel had introduced. And YHWH *rejected* (*m's*) all the descendants of Israel, and afflicted them, and gave them into the hand of spoilers, until he has cast them out of his sight." (2 Kgs 17:19-20)

Thus, R2 concludes Hos 9 with his own summary statement. Because the people have not listened to the voice of YHWH, YHWH will reject them, condemning them to their exilic dispersion among the nations.

F. The Redactional Thrust of Hos 9

R2 concludes his commentary in Hos 9 as he began it in 9:3-4. The exile, for him, becomes the reversal of the Exodus. He symbolizes the exile as a "return to Egypt" where true cultic worship of YHWH is impossible. Within the overall context of his received material, the exile becomes the end result of the harlotrous behavior, of which 9:1 accuses Israel:

9:1   Rejoice not, O Israel!
            to exultation, like the peoples.

> For you have played the harlot,
> forsaking your God.
> You have loved a harlot's hire
> upon every threshing floor of grain.

In contrast to the other chapters in the Book of Hosea which we have discussed, R2 articulates much of his commentary in the first person. First of all, this is clear in 9:8 where he qualifies the negative attitude of his received material towards the prophets. This is true, moreover, in his plea to YHWH in 9:14 to mitigate the punishment described in his tradition. Finally, this is evident in his summary statement in 9:17, which explains YHWH's rejection of the people and their subsequent exile as the result of their disobedience.

R2 handles his tradition according to his paronomastic technique, with which we have become familiar, as well as by verbal analogy similar to Hillel's second exegetical principle.

IX. The Final Redaction of Hos 10

A. *The Editorial History of Hos 10*

H	C	R1	R2
		10:1-8	10:9-10
10:11			10:12
10:13a			10:13b-14
		10:15	

B. *Hos 10:9-10*

10:8b   *wĕ'āmĕrû lehārîm kassûnû*
        wĕlaggĕbā'ôt niplû 'ālênû
10:9   *mîmê haggib'â ḥāṭā'tā yiśrā'ēl*
        šām 'āmādû
        lō'-taśśîgēm baggib'â milḥāmâ
        'al-bĕnê 'alwâ
10:10   *ba'ătôtî (MT: bĕ'awwātî)[222] wĕ'essărēm*
        wĕ'ussĕpû 'ălêhem 'ammîm

bĕ'ussĕrām (MT: bĕ'osrām)[223]
lištê 'ăwōnōtām[224]

10:8b   They will say to the mountains, "Cover us!"
       and to the hills, "Fall upon us!"
10:9   *From the days of Gibeah you have sinned, O Israel.*
       There they have remained.
       Surely, war will overtake them in Gibeah,
       because of the wicked ones.
10:10   *When I come*, I will chastise them.*
       The peoples shall be gathered against them,
       When they are imprisoned* for their double guilt.

R2 enters immediately into his commentary through a parasonantic wordplay on *laggĕbā'ôt*, "to the mountains," in his tradition, 10:8, with *haggib'â*, "Gibeah," in 10:9.[225] He also signals his entry into the tradition by a change to a second person singular address: "From the days of Gibeah *you* have sinned, O Israel."[226] The reference to the "days of Gibeah" recalls 9:9 where R2 describes the people as being deeply corrupted "as in the days of Gibeah."[227] According to 10:9, Israel has sinned "from the days of Gibeah."

Wellhausen and Nowack see in the phrase, "days of Gibeah," a reference to the time of Saul, the first king of Israel who had his headquarters in Gibeah. They conclude from this that Hosea had rejected the institution of the monarchy as sinful.[228] It seems, however, preferable to view 9:9 and 10:9 with several commentators as a reference to the events recounted in Judg 19-21, viz. the rape and death of the Levite's concubine in Gibeah which led to the near extermination of the tribe of Benjamin.[229] Indeed, these Gibeah accounts seemed to have figured prominently during the exilic period, the period of our final redactor, since this was the time when the exilic Deuteronomist appended Judg 19-21 to the Book of Judges.[230]

For R2, the "days of Gibeah," which according to Judg 19:30 were unparalleled since Israel came up out of the land of Egypt, becomes a fourfold type for the present sinful condition of the people.[231] First, R2 states in 10:9 that from the days of

Gibeah, they have sinned. *There they have remained.* In other
words, their behavior has remained unchanged since the
crime committed then. Second, the original crime resulted in
a war against the guilty parties in Gibeah (*milḥāmâ*, Judg
20:14, 20, 23). Likewise, R2 remarks that war (*milḥāmâ*) will
indeed overtake the people in Gibeah. Third, the mention of
the wicked ones in 10:9 is an escalation in the typological
comparison. At the earlier time, it would have referred to the
inhabitants of Gibeah. Now, R2 applies it to all of Israel. We
point out, moreover, the R2 wordplay between *'alwâ*, "wicked,"
with the preceding *'al.*[232] Fourth and finally, there is an
escalation in the agents of retribution. According to Judg
20:11, the tribes are gathered (*niph. 'sp*) against the offenders.
According to Hos 10:10, the peoples will be gathered (*pual 'sp*)
against Israel.

In 10:10,[233] R2 situates the imminent war in the context of
his *mûsār* theology: I (YHWH) will *chastise* them. He
articulates 10:10 in a threefold wordplay involving metaphony
and parasonancy:[234]

wĕ'essārēm	I will chastise them.
wĕ'ussĕpû	(The peoples) shall be gathered ...
bĕ'ussĕrām	When they are imprisoned ...

Moreover, one finds alliteration in the consonants, *'ayin/mēm*,
in *'ălêhem 'ammîm*, and *'ăwōnōtām*.

Besides his *mûsār* theology, other elements in 10:10
indicate the R2 pen. The gathering of the peoples should be
seen in light of the invasions that led to the exile. We cite the
following late prophetic texts which speak of this gathering
(*niph. 'sp*) of the nations against Israel:

> Hark, a tumult on the mountains
>   as of a great multitude!
> Hark, an uproar of kingdoms,
>   of nations *gathering together*!
>   (*ne'ĕsāpîm*)
> The Lord of hosts is mustering
>   a host for battle.

(Isa 13:4, RSV)

Now many nations are *assembled* (*ne'espû*)
against you, saying, "Let her be profaned
and let our eyes gaze upon Zion."
(Mic 4:11, RSV)

On that day, says the Lord, I will make
Jerusalem a heavy stone for all the peoples;
all who lift it shall grievously hurt themselves. And all the nations of the earth
will come together against it. (*ne'espû*)
(Zech 12:3, RSV)

R2 makes note of the people's imprisonment with '*sr*,
which in the qal passive designates those deported into exile
according to Is 49:9 and 61:1 (*'ăsûrîm*. Cf. also Zech 9:11). Its
pual form here in 10:10, *bĕ'ussĕrām*, would be due to its
metaphony with *wĕ'essărēm*, "I will chastise them." The
people's imprisonment, R2 explains, results from their "double
guilt" or iniquity, *lištê 'ăwōnōtām*. Scholars have interpreted
the referents for this double iniquity variously.[235] In arguing
for the later editing of 10:10b, Willi-Plein, picking up a cue
from E. Jacob, maintains that the redactor already assumes
the text of Jer 2:13 in this verse without further
explanation:[236]

> "For my people have committed *two evils* (*šĕtayim rā'ōt*): They
> have forsaken me, the fountain of living waters, and hewed
> out cisterns for themselves, broken cisterns, that can hold no
> water."

Indeed, one can point to another text from Jeremiah, set
in a passage filled with deuteronomistic phraseology, which
accords even more with the theological thrust of our final
redactor:

> "For my eyes are upon all their ways; they are not hid from
> me, nor is their iniquity (*'ăwōnām*) concealed from my eyes.
> And I will *doubly recompense their iniquity and their sin*,
> because they have polluted my land with the carcasses of their

detestable idols, and have filled my inheritance with their
abominations." (Jer 16:17-18, RSV)

The dual offense according to this text is explained in terms of
the people's idolatry, also an R2 concern. Although beyond the
scope of the present study, contact points between the final
redaction of the Book of Hosea, Deuteronomy and Jeremiah
are sufficient enough to merit closer examination to determine
more accurately the precise compositional relationship among
the respective books.[237]
One should see the motivation for the R2 insertion in the
tradition's description of the threshing calf described in 10:11:
"Ephraim was a trained heifer that loved to thresh . . . "[238] We
have in Jer 31:18, the exilic Book of Consolation, the
following description:

"I have heard Ephraim moaning, 'Thou hast chastened me
(*yissartanî*) and I was chastened like an untrained calf (*kĕʿēgel
lōʾ lummād*). Bring me back, that I may be restored (*hăšîbēnî
wĕʾāšûbâ*), for thou art the Lord my God.'" (Jer 31:18, RSV)

Given the image of the threshing calf in the tradition, R2
interprets this image in ideas current in exilic times, as is
expressed by Jer 31:18. Both Hos 10:10 and Jer 31:18 exhibit
a *mûsār* theology. Moreover, Jer 31:18 even contains a
paranomasia on the root *šwb*, *hăšîbēnî wĕʾāšûbâ*, "bring me
back, that I may be restored," which typifies our own final
redactor.

C. Hos 10:12

We have already discussed Hos 10:12 at length.[239] This
verse is the second major R2 passage of hope in the Hos 4-11
complex. It constitutes the second phase of the journey back to
YHWH in repentance, which R2 structures from his tradition.
We have seen that R2 anticipates 10:12 by way of contrast
with his insertion 8:7.[240] Moreover, in the insertion, 10:10, R2
describes the chastisement of Israel by YHWH. The exile
becomes their chastisement, which in the *mûsār* theology of
R2 is not simply gratuitous. Its purpose in the mind of R2 is

the repentance of the people, as even our Jer 31:18 text cited
above indicates. Thus, R2 exhorts in 10:12, which follows his
description of the chastisement by the nations:

> Sow for yourselves righteousness,
> Reap the fruit of steadfast love;
> Till your untilled ground,
> For it is time to seek YHWH,
> That he may come and rain righteousness upon you.

D. Hos 10:13b-14

10:13a   *hăraštem-rešaʿ*
         ʿawlātâ qěṣartem
         'ăkaltem pěrî-kāḥaš

10:13b   *kî-bāṭaḥtā bĕdarkěkā*
         běrōb gibbôrêkā

10:14   *wěqāʾm šāʾôn běʿammekā*
         wěkol-mibṣārêkā yûššad
         kěšōd šalman bêt 'arbēʾl
         běyôm milḥāmâ 'ēm ʿal-bānîm ruṭṭāšâ

10:15   *kākâ ʿāśâ lākem bêt-'ēl*
         mippěnê rāʿat rāʿatkem
         baššaḥar nidmōh nidmâ melek yiśrāʾēl

10:13a   You (pl.) have plowed iniquity,
         You (pl.) have reaped injustice,
         You (pl.) have eaten the fruit of lies.

10:13b   *Because you (sg.) have trusted in your (sg.) own
power,*
         *in the large number of your (sg.) crack
troops*[241]

10:14   *The tumult of war will arise among your (sg.)
people,*
         and all your (sg.) fortresses will be destroyed,
         the way Shalman destroyed Beth Arbel.
         *On the day of war mothers will be dashed to pulp
beside children.*

10:15   Thus, he will do to you (pl.), Beth El,
         because of your (pl.) great wickedness.
     In the dawn, the king of Israel shall perish.

This final commentary of R2 in Hos 10 is one that scholars have judged to be secondary principally because of the reference to Shalmaneser IV who lived after Hosea.[242] R2 indicates his hand by the change from second person plural in his tradition, 10:13a, 15, to second person singular in his own commentary, 10:13b-14.

His commentary deals with the "day of war" which, as he had stated in 10:9, will overtake the people in Gibeah. Interpreting the tradition, R2 maintains that the iniquity, injustice, and lies of which the people are culpable (10:13a) result from trusting (bṭḥ) in their power, in the multitude of their crack troops (10:13b). We have seen R2's admonition against an unrealistic confidence in military might in 1:5, 1:7, 2:20, 7:16, 8:14, and 14:4. Trusting in one's military reserves instead of YHWH is particularly denounced by Deuteronomy:[243]

> (The Lord will bring a nation against you from afar ...) they shall besiege you in all your towns, until your high and fortified walls (habbĕṣūrôt Cf. mibṣārêkā in Hos 10:14), in which you trusted ('attā bōṭēaḥ), come down throughout all your land. (Dt 28:49, 52)

Dt 28:53-57 continues with a particularly gruesome picture of the result of the siege of the land, as does R2 in 10:14: "On the day of war, mothers will be dashed to pulp beside children."

R2 paronomasia is also contained in his commentary. Kaatz has noted the play upon š/d of yûššad kĕšōd šalman, "(your fortresses will be destroyed as Shalman destroyed ...") in 10:14.[244] Moreover, Beth Arbel is most likely an interpretive wordplay on Beth El in the tradition, 10:15: As Shalman destroyed Beth Arbel ... so he shall do to you (pl.), Beth El.

E. The Redactional Thrust of Hos 10

We see again that R2 reads and interprets his tradition, particularly the judgments in 10:7-8, 15, in light of his perspective in the exile. The people have too long relied on their own resources, their double iniquity: their idols (cf. Jer 15:17-18) and their military strength (Hos 10:13b). The war that thus results in their imprisonment and deportation is YHWH's chastisement. This chastisement, for R2, is for their return to YHWH. Indeed, this time of exile is "the time to seek the Lord (10:12)."

X. The Final Redaction of Hos 11

A. The Editorial History of Hos 11

H	C	R1	R2
			11:1-4
			11:5-7
			11:8-9
			11:10-11

As one can see, we have assigned the whole Hos 11 chapter to our final redactor for reasons which will become clear in the discussion below. Just as R2 had closed off the Hos 1-3 complex with 3:1-5 and the Hos 12-14 complex with 14:2-10, he concludes the Hos 4-11 complex with 11:1-11. In all three cases, R2 ends each major section on a note of hope. In his hands, the tradition in each section moves from threat, to punishment which, for R2, is a chastisement to evoke the people's repentance, and then on to salvation.[245] To facilitate our discussion of the chapter, we will deal with it in sections, beginning with Hos 11:1-4.

B. Hos 11:1-4

11:1   *kî na'ar yiśrā'ēl wā'ōhăbēhû*
         ûmimmiṣrayim qārā'tî libnî

11:2   qārĕ'û lāhem
        kēn hālĕkû mippānay hēm
        (MT: mippĕnêhem)246
        labĕ'ālîm yĕzabbēḥû
        wĕlappĕsîlîm yĕqaṭṭērûn
11:3   wĕ'ānōkî tirgaltî lĕ 'eprayim
        'eqqaḥēm 'al-zĕrô'ōtāy
        (MT: qāḥām 'al-zĕrô'ōtāyw)247
        wĕlō' yādĕ'û kî rĕpā'tîm
11:4   bĕhablê 'ādām 'emšĕkēm
        ba'ăbōtôt 'ahăbâ
        wā'ehyeh lāhem
        kimrîmê 'ōl 'al lĕḥêhem
        wĕ'aṭ 'ēlāyw 'ôkîl

11:1   When Israel was a youth, I loved him.
        From Egypt, I called my child.
11:2   They invited them.
        Thus they went away from me.*
        To the Baals they sacrificed
           and to images they burned incense.
11:3   But I, yes I, was a guide to Ephraim.
        I took them upon my arms.*
        Yet, they did not know that I healed them.
11:4   With human cords I led them,
           with ropes of love.
        I was to them like those who remove the
           yoke from upon their jaws.
        I bent down to him and fed him.248

Hos 11 is the final redactor's summary of his interpretive
commentary thoughout the Hos 4-11 complex. R2 prepares for
this important chapter by his additions which presage the
return to Egypt because of Israel's apostasy (7:16; 8:13; 9:3, 6).
In an historical retrospect, R2 describes in 11:1-4 not only the
unparalleled redemptive act of the Exodus but also the
covenant in the wilderness where God makes Israel his child
by adoption.249 R2 had characterized these themes before
under the symbol of the marriage in Hos 1-3. Hos 2:16

describes YHWH's seduction of the wife to the wilderness, the place of their first betrothal. In 2:17, the wife/Israel will respond ('nh) "as in the days of her *youth* (*nĕ'ûrêhâ*), as in the time when she came out of the land of Egypt."[250] Here in 11:1-4, R2 resumes the description of the days of Israel's youth (*n'r/h*) during the Exodus and wilderness periods. However, instead of portraying Israel as YHWH's *wife*, R2 now depicts Israel as YHWH's *son*.

Regarding Israel as God's son, R2 states first that YHWH loved him, *wā'ōhăbēhû*. We recall R2's fourfold *antanaclasis* on *'hb*, "to love," in 3:1:

> "And YHWH said to me again, 'Go, *love* a wife who *has been made love to* by a lover and is an adulteress. As YHWH *loves* the children of Israel although they are turning to other gods and *loving* raisin cakes.'"

R2 will repeat the theologically-loaded root, *'hb*, a few verses later in 11:4: YHWH draws Israel with "ropes of love," *ba'ăbōtôt 'ahăbâ*.

R2's idea of the covenantal love of God for his adoptive son is deuteronomic.[251] Dt 1:30-31, in particular, resonates with our final redactor's description of the parental love of YHWH as he supports his son during his exodus and wilderness sojournings:

> "The Lord your God who goes before you will himself fight for you, just as he did for you in Egypt before your eyes, and in the wilderness, where you have seen how the Lord your God bore you, *as a man bears his son*, in all the way that you went until you came to this place." (Dt 1:30-31, RSV. Cf. also Dt 14:1; 32:5-6, 10-11, 18-20 and Jer 3:19; 31:9)

Noteworthy, moreover, is Dt 8:5 which describes the wilderness experience as YHWH's chastisement:

> "Know then in your heart that, as a man disciplines (*ysr*) his son, the Lord your God disciplines you." (Dt 8:5, RSV)

We will see later in our discussion of 11:5 that R2 will take up the deuteronomic notion of YHWH chastising his son: The son must return to the land of Egypt, because he has refused to repent.[252]

Immediately in 11:1, R2 begins his singular paronomastic technique. YHWH proclaims that from Egypt he had called his son, *qārā'tî libnî*. The construction, *qr' l*, signifies both "to summon" and "to name."[253] Thus, one can interpret the R2 *qārā'tî libnî* on two different levels. On one level, R2 describes the summoned assemblage of the people for their exit from Egypt. On the other level, R2 intends that in this act, YHWH "names" them as his adopted children. Moreover, in 11:2 R2 continues his *antanaclasis* on *qr'*, stating, "they called to them (*qārě'û lāhem*)." Here, *qr'* has another sense, viz. "to invite or seduce." Szabó refers especially to Num 25:1-2 which has several contact points with Hos 11:1-2:[254]

> "While Israel dwelt in Shittim the people began to play the harlot with the daughters of Moab. They invited the people (*wattiqre'nā lā'ām*) to the sacrifices of their gods, and the people ate, and bowed down to their gods." (Num 25:1-2, RSV. Cf. Ex 34:15)

Like his *antanaclasis* in 3:1 on *'hb* where R2 contrasts the covenantal love of YHWH with the adulterous love of the people, R2 juxtaposes the covenantal call of YHWH (11:1) with the sexually tempting invitation to the people to worship idols (11:2).

R2 goes on to state that the people, succumbing to the allurement of idolatry, went away (*hlkw*) from YHWH. In 14:10, R2 describes the adherence to the covenant with the characteristically deuteronomic expression, "walking" (*hlk*) in the way of YHWH.[255] Thus in keeping with his covenantal concerns, R2 declares that in their idolatrous practices, the people have transgressed their covenant with YHWH.[256] R2 will reverse 11:2 later in 11:10 in a chiastic structure, which will unify the whole chapter:

11:2	11:10
qārě'û lāhem	*'ahărê yhwh yēlěkû*
kēn hālěkû mippānay hēm	*kě'aryēh yiš'āg*

They called to them.   After YHWH they will go.
Thus they went from me.   Like a lion he will roar.

Although they went away (*hlk*) from YHWH to the Baals
(11:2), the repentant people will go (*hlk*) after YHWH again
(11:10). The "roaring of YHWH" (11:10) will overpower the
"call" to idolatry (11:2). Thus will the covenant between
YHWH and the people be renewed.[257]

Hitherto, the problems in interpreting the meaning of
11:3-4 have been due to the admixture of themes in these
verses. On one hand, the verses seem to describe the parent
YHWH guiding his child and taking him under his protection
(11:3a). On the other hand, this father-son image seems to
meld into the "calf" image in 11:4. This image of Ephraim as
an animal was portrayed in the previous chapter in 10:11.
YHWH as a guide to his son, Ephraim, now draws the animal,
Ephraim, with ropes of love. Moreover, YHWH is likened to
one who raises the yoke from an animal, allowing him to eat.
Thus, the many emendations of these verses have been due to
scholars opting for one interpretation over the other.[258]

We argue, however, that from the vantage point of our
final redactor, both views are not only possible in these verses,
but are deliberately exploited by R2 in his commentary. One
finds the constellation of calf/son/chastisement motifs in Jer
31:18-20, the text which seems to have motivated the R2
commentary in 10:9-10 on the tradition of the threshing calf in
10:11:[259]

v. 18   "I have heard Ephraim bemoaning.
         'Thou has chastened me
             (*yissartanî*)
         and I was chastened, (*wā'iwwāsēr*)
             like an untrained calf.
             (*kĕ'ēgel lō' lummād*)
         Bring me back that I may be restored
             (*hăšîbēnî wĕ'āšûbâ*)
         for thou art the Lord my God.
v. 19   For after I turned away (*šûbî*), I repented.
             and after I was instructed, I smote
                 upon my thigh.

I was ashamed, and I was confounded, because
I bore the disgrace of my youth.'
(*nĕ'ûray*)

v.20   Is Ephraim my dear son? (*bēn*)
Is he my darling child?
For as often as I speak against him,
I do remember him still.
Therefore my heart (*mē'ay*) yearns for him.
I will surely have compassion on him.
(Jer 31:18-20, RSV)

At first glance, one notices the parallels between Jer
31:18-20 and Hos 11:1-8. Both share similar vocabulary and
themes:

Hos 11:1-8		Jer 31:18-20	
v. 1a	*na'ar*, youth	v. 19	*na'ar*, youth
v. 1b	*libnî*, my son	v. 20	*hăbēn lî*, my son
v. 3a	Ephraim	v. 18a	Ephraim
v. 4	calf image	v. 18a	calf image
v. 5, 7	*šwb* antanaclasis	v. 18-19	*šwb* antanaclasis
v. 5-7	chastisement	v. 18a	chastisement
v. 8	portrayal of YHWH as	v. 20	portrayal of YHWH
	compassionate parent:		as compassionate
	libbî, my heart		parent:
	niḥûmay, my compassion		*mē'ay*, my heart
			rḥm, compassion

However, in 11:1-4 (as well as in 11:5-9) R2 expands upon
the ideas of Jer 31:18-20 with his own theological orientation
and style. As we have said in our discussion of 11:1-2, the
youth/Israel is YHWH's adopted son, *whom YHWH loves.* He
is "called" (*qr'*) from Egypt only to be "seduced" (*qr'*) by
idolatry. Thus, he disowns himself as YHWH's son.

Hos 11:3, moreover, continues the R2 picture of the
nurturing parent. Having called him up from Egypt, YHWH
becomes a guide to Ephraim in the wilderness. R2 states that
YHWH took Ephraim "upon his arms," emphasizing the
support and protection of YHWH for his child. Deuteronomy

insistently reminds Israel that YHWH had brought Israel out
of Egypt "with outstretched arm (*bizrōaʿ nĕṭûyâ*)."[260]
Moreover, R2's description in 11:3 of YHWH caring for his son
in the wilderness accords well with Dt 32:10:

> "(YHWH) found (his son)[261] in a desert land,
>   and in the howling waste of the wilderness;
> He encircled him, he cared for him,
>   he kept him as the apple of his eye."
>   (Dt 32:10, RSV)

R2 concludes his father/son theme in 11:3b with "they did
not know that I healed them." Two R2 ideas are contained
here. The first is the deuteronomistic notion of "knowing"
(*ydʿ/dʿt*).[262] The second is the theme of healing (*rpʾ*), which in
11:3b plays upon the word, Ephraim, in 11:3a:
lĕ'eprayim/rĕpā'tîm.[263]

In 11:4, R2 blends the father/son metaphor with the beast
metaphor of Hos 10:11. The verse is filled with R2
paronomasia. With the alliterating letters *ʾ/ʾ/b*, R2 describes
the reins which guide Ephraim as *ba'ăbōtôt 'ahăbâ*, "ropes of
love." The father/son metaphor could still be inferred here in
11:4, since R2 uses *'hb*, "to love," to depict YHWH's parental
response to Israel in 11:1. R2 continues the beast motif in
11:4aB with parasonancy (A/A') and metaphony (B/B'):

> *wā'ehyeh lāhem kimrîmê ʿōl ʿal lĕḥêhem*
>   A   B B' A'
> I was to them like those who remove the yoke upon their
> jaws.

The yoke has a double meaning for R2, as we will see
below in 11:7. On one hand, R2 adopts the literal meaning of
yoke, viz. the harnessing frame placed upon draft animals. On
the other hand, the yoke for R2 is also a symbol of
enslavement.[264] Particularly in exilic texts the yoke describes
the subjugation of Israel by the Babylonians.[265] R2 intends
this latter meaning here in 11:4. As he explains in 11:4aB,
YHWH alone is able to remove the yoke upon them.[266] Yet, as

he will assert in 11:7, the people are appointed to the yoke, i.e. must undergo the exile, because of their apostasy. R2's final impression in the animal/father-son motif in 11:1-4 is also paronomastically constructed, each word beginning with the letter *'aleph*:[267] *wĕ'at 'ēlāyw 'ôkîl,* "I bent down to him and fed him."

C. *Hos 11:5-7*

11:5 *lō' yāšûb 'el-'ereṣ miṣrayim*
      wĕ'aššûr hū' malkô
      kî mē'ănû lāšûb
11:6 *wĕḥālâ ḥereb bĕ'ārāyw*
      wĕkillĕtâ baddāyw
      wĕ'ākālâ mimmō'ăṣôtêhem
11:7 *wĕ'ammî telû'îm limšûbātî*
      wĕ'el 'ōl (MT: 'al)[268] *yiqrā'ûhû*
      yaḥad lō' yĕrômēm

11:5 He will surely[269] return to the land of Egypt,
      Assyria, it will be his king,
      because they have refused to repent.
11:6 The sword will surge throughout his cities.
      It will destroy its strong men.[270]
      It will devour their advisors.
11:7 My people are bent on their apostasy from me.
      To the yoke* they are appointed.
      No one will remove it.

This second section of the chapter resumes in 11:7 the *qr'* *antanaclasis* from 11:1-2. It also begins a fourfold *antanaclasis* on *šwb*, whose range of meanings is similar to R2's fivefold *antanaclasis* on *šwb* in 14:2-9:[271]

11:5a	*yāšûb*	to return to the land (cf. 14:8)
11:5a	*lāšûb*	to repent (cf. 14:2)
11:7	*limšûbātî*	apostasy (cf. 14:5a)
11:9	*'āšûb*	to turn (to destroy, cf. 14:5b)

In 11:5 R2 expresses two of his major concerns by means of this
šwb antanaclasis: The people will return (*šwb*) to the land of
Egypt, because they have refused to repent (*šwb*).[272] R2
portrays the reversal of 11:1 in 11:5. The son whom YHWH
loved, whom he had called from slavery in Egypt, must return
to Egypt because of his impenitence.

We note here the study of Lohfink on Hos 11:5. Lohfink
argues that Hos 11:5 may have been the text upon which the
exilic author of Dt 17:16 based his text:

> "Only (the king) must not multiply horses for himself, or
> cause the people to return (*šwb*) to Egypt in order to multiply
> horses, since the Lord has said to you, 'You shall never return
> that way again.'" (Dt 17:16, RSV)

Interestingly, Lohfink suggests that the situational context of
Dt 17:16 may have been a polemic of the Babylonian exiles
against the Egyptian exiles. He sees this conflict between the
two reflected in the prose passages of Jeremiah.[273]

Departing from Lohfink, we would argue that Hos 11:5
originated during the same period as Dt 17:16, probably in
similar schools of composition. However, Lohfink's
suggestion, that the return to Egypt reflects a conflict between
Babylonian and Egyptian exiles, which is evidenced in
Jeremiah, supports our contention that the R2 insertions
regarding the return to Egypt in Hos 7:16 and Hos 9:6 have
these Jeremiah passages as background.[274]

In 11:6,[275] R2 reiterates his insertions, 7:16 and 8:14,
which depict the princes who have been felled by the "sword"
(*ḥereb*) and the "cities" (*'ārîm*) destroyed by fire. These
terrible events are the consequences of the people's refusal to
repent, described in v. 5b. They constitute, for R2, the
chastisement which is designed not simply as punishment of
the people, but also as instrument for their repentance.

R2 takes up in 11:7 his familiar recital of the
transgressions of "my people" (*'ammî*).[276] He epitomizes the
people's offences with the third *antanaclasis* on *šwb* in Hos 11,
limšûbātî, "apostasy from YHWH." Moreover, in another
antanaclasis on *qr'* of 11:1-2, he intensifies the threat of 11:6:
After the destruction of the cities and their leaders (11:6), the

people, because of their apostasy, "will be appointed to the
yoke," i.e. will be destined for exile.[277] Summarily, we display
the nuances of the *qr' antanaclasis* which R2 uses in Hos 11:

11:1a	*qārā'tî*	to name
		to summon
11:2	*qārĕ'û*	to invite seductively
11:7b	*yiqrā'ūhû*	to appoint

R2 contrasts the condemnation expressed in 11:7b with
the positive description of YHWH in 11:4aB by means of a
chiastic paronomastic interplay:

<pre>
                    A   B   C
11:4aB wa'ehyeh lāhem kimrîmê 'ōl 'al lĕhêhem
            C' B'   A'
11:7b   wĕ'el-'ōl yiqrā'ūhû yaḥad lō' yĕrômēm
                                      A   B
11:4aB I was to them as those who remove the yoke
                            C
                from upon their jaws.
            C'   B'
11:7b   To the yoke they are appointed. No one will
            A'
        remove it.
</pre>

D.   Hos 11:8-9

11:8	*'êk 'ettenkā 'eprayim*
	'ămaggenkā yiśrā'ēl
	'êk 'ettenkā kĕ'admâ
	'ăśîmĕkā kiṣbō'yim
	nehpak 'ālay libbî
	yaḥad nikmĕrû niḥûmāy
11:9	*lō' 'e'ĕśeh ḥărôn 'appî*
	lō' 'āśûb lĕśaḥēt 'eprayim
	kî 'ēl 'ānōkî wĕlō' 'îš
	bĕqirbĕkā qādôš
	wĕlō' 'abô' bĕ'îr

11:8   How can I give you up, Ephraim!
            How can I hand you over, Israel!
         How can I give you up like Admah!
            How can I treat you like Zeboiim
         My heart is turning over inside of me.
            My compassion grows warm all together
11:9   I will not execute my burning anger.
         I will not turn to destroy Ephraim
         For I am God and not man,
         The Holy One in your midst.
         I will not come into the city.

Scholars have already noted the secondary character of 11:8-9.[278] Its immediate context, the one just discussed, is the memorable description of Israel/Ephraim as YHWH's son, called forth out of Egypt only to reject YHWH for the Baalim (11:1-2). Because of Israel's apostasy, the passage declares that he will return to Egypt and Assyria, the sword threatening his cities as well as his fortresses (11:5-6).

The menacing tone switches in 11:8.[279] As many commentators have pointed out, we get a rare glimpse here of the personality of God on the verge of destroying his "son" and yet balking. He eventually announces that he will not wipe out Israel/Ephraim. He is God, not a human being, the Holy One in the midst of them (11:9).

Clues to R2 authorship are the wordplays of the passage as well as its exilic deuteronomistic theology. One observes the first wordplay in 11:8a where all the words begin with or contain the letter 'aleph.[280]

    'êk 'ettenkā 'eprayim
       'ămaggenkā yiśrā'ēl
    'êk 'ettenkā kĕ'admâ
       'ăśîmĕkā kisbō'yim

The unique spelling here of Zeboiim with an 'aleph, sebō'yim, instead of the usual sb(w/y)ym,[281] would support our argument that the final redactor is engaged in a type of visual alliteration involving the letter *'aleph*. The reference to the destruction of Admah and Zeboiim recalls Dt 29:22 in a passage attributed to the exilic redactor of Deuteronomy.[282] In Moses' final words to the people, he warns them that if they forsake the covenant to worship other gods (Dt 29:24-25), YHWH will make the land like Sodom and Gomorrah, Admah and Zeboiim, "which YHWH overthrew in his anger" (*yhwh hāpak bě'appô*, Dt 29:22bB).

In Hos 11:8, however, it is not Admah or Zeboiim which YHWH overthrows in his anger (*hāpak bě'appô*, Dt 29:22bB), but YHWH's heart which is overthrown (or turned over) within him (*nehpak 'ālay libbî*, Hos 11:8b). The compassion (*nīḥūmay*, Hos 11:8b), which YHWH will bestow again upon Lo Ruhama (R2 = 2:3, 23) and upon the orphan (R2 = 14:4), now grows warm in his heart.

With the fourth and final *antanaclasis* on *šwb* in 11:9, R2 states that YHWH will not effect his fierce anger upon Ephraim. We have seen this notion before in the R2 commentary, 14:5b.[283] The terminology of the two texts is similar.

11:9a   *lō' 'e'ĕśeh ḥărôn 'appî*
          lō' 'āšûb lĕšaḥēt 'eprayim

I will not execute *my* burning *anger*.
I will not *turn* to destroy Ephraim.

14:5b   *kî šāb 'appî mimmennû*

For my anger is turned from them.

Like the R2 *šwb/yšb* wordplays which we have noted in a number of places,[284] *šwb* in 11:9a has its paronomastic counterpart in 11:11b. YHWH will not turn (*lō' 'āšûb*) to destroy Ephraim (11:9a). Instead, YHWH will make them dwell upon their estates (*wěhôšabtîm 'al-bātêhem*, 11:11b).

In Hos 2:1, we detected a wordplay involving the transposition of the letters *'aleph/lamed*. 2:1b, *běnê 'ēl ḥāy*, "children of the Living God," reverses the threat of 1:9, *wĕ'ānōkî lō' 'ehyeh lāhem,* "I am not I AM to you."[285] We see a similar paronomastic transpoition of *'aleph/lamed* in 11:9bA: *kî 'ēl 'ānōkî lō' 'îš.* YHWH insists that he is *'ēl,* God. He is, moreover, *lō' 'îš,* "not a man." The whole paronomastic statement is punctuated by alliteration and assonance.

The final statement of 11:9, *wĕlō' 'ābô' bĕʿîr,* "I will not come into the city," reverses the threat of 11:6a, *wĕhālâ ḥereb bĕʿārāyw,* "The sword shall surge against their cities." We point out the rhyme and alliteration of the letters *'/b/ʿ* in *wĕlō' 'ābô' bĕʿîr.*

E. Hos 11:10-11

We have already discussed these major verses in the R2 Hos 4-11 complex.[286] R2 skillfully balances the conclusion of his chapter with its very beginning. Although God's "son" (*bēn*) went away (*hlk*) from YHWH after the seductive Baalim (11:2), his "children" (*bānîm*) will now go (*hlk*) after YHWH (11:10). His call is like a lion's (11:10) which overrides the call of the Baalim (11:2). 11:10-11 constitute the final stage of the three part journey which R2 fashions from his tradition. They recount the journey's end for Israel from the lands of exile to their own land and their own homes. R2 concludes Hos 11 and indeed the whole Hos 4-11 complex with his signature, *nĕ'ūm-yhwh.*

F. The Redactional Thrust of Hos 11 and of the Hos 4-11 Complex

The overriding metaphor of Hos 11 is the famous description of Israel as the "son" of YHWH who calls Israel out of Egypt. Several studies have confirmed the fact that the father-son analogy in 11:1ff is grounded in the technical language of covenant.[287] Hos 11:1-6 would then essentially describe the covenant between YHWH and the people and their transgression of covenant. Moreover, Hos 11:1-6 assumes our knowledge of the law found in Dt 21:18-21,[288] which itself has a complex literary history.[289] The law states that a stubborn and rebellious son who refuses to repent of his behaviour is to be taken to trial by his own parents and then stoned to death.

With this background, the theological thrust of the final redactor is thrown into relief. In 11:8-9, YHWH cannot give over his son to death. He cannot completely forsake his covenant. A parent's compassion prevents him from destroying his son. YHWH transcends the human legal institutions which enforce the death penalty for recalcitrant sons because *He is God, not a human being.* He will instead restore his "children" who in the renewed covenant will "go after YHWH."

Familiar R2 themes emerge in Hos 11. Indeed, one can say that in Hos 11, R2 in many ways recapitulates his redaction of the whole Hos 4-11 complex. These themes are:

1. The love of YHWH (v. 1, 4)
2. The polemic against idolatry (v. 2)
3. YHWH the healer (v. 3)
4. The return to Egypt (v. 5)
5. The *šwb antanaclasis* (vv. 5-9)
6. The chastisement of the exile (vv. 5-7)
7. The return (*šwb*) to the land and dwelling (*yšb*) on it (vv. 10-11)
8. The renewal of covenant (v.10)

In Hos 11, R2 recounts a three-part historical journey. Focusing on the past in 11:1, he describes the first journey from Egypt, the great act of YHWH who called Israel out of Egypt to become his son, his people. The second stage of the journey, 11:5-7, centers on the present. It recounts the tribulations of the exile, symbolized as a return to Egypt. The third stage of the journey, 11:10-11, focuses on the future. Contingent upon the repentance of the people, R2 states that they will come trembling like birds back *from* Egypt and will be returned to their own land and their own homes.

This three-part historical journey motif in Hos 11 is a reflexion of the three-stage journey motif, which R2 structures into the Hos 4-11 complex. R2 depicts this journey as a movement from apostasy to repentance; from barrenness to fertility; from Not My People to My People, Not My Son to My Son. This journey begins, for R2, in 5:15--6:3. R2 summons the people to "Come, let us return to the Lord." He promises YHWH's healing. He pledges YHWH's renewal of covenant, if only they would strive to "know" him. The second phase of the journey occurs in 10:12. Here, R2 reiterates his fertility motif from 6:3 and enjoins the people to prepare the untilled soil of their hearts for YHWH, which, when YHWH comes, will burst forth in fruitfulness. Like the *time of spring* when one usually digs up the earth for sowing, R2 declares, "It is *time* to seek the Lord." The final stage of this journey, 11:10-11, is the return to the land itself from exile. The son, who caused himself to be disowned by going away from YHWH, will come trembling after YHWH in repentance from the land of exile back to the land of YHWH.

In light of our investigation into the Hos 4-11 complex, we are now able to update our diagram of the R2 restructuring of the tradition.[290]

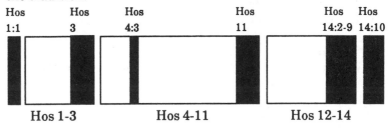

| Hos 1:1 | Hos 3 | Hos 4:3 | Hos 11 | Hos 14:2-9 | Hos 14:10 |

Hos 1-3   Hos 4-11   Hos 12-14

The most obvious change from our previous diagram is that by situating Hos 11 in its present position, R2 closes off another major section in his composition. In R2's reshaping, the book contains three major sections. Each of these sections moves from accusation (*rib*, 2:4, 4:1; 12:3), but finishes on a note of hope, a perspective furnished by our final redactor. R2 has a particular fondness for three's, as is evidenced in his tripartite division of the book, the three-stage journey of chastisement to repentance which one finds in both the Hos 1-3 complex and the Hos 4-11 complex, and triadic repetitions of words or expressions.[291]

The first section, Hos 1-3, becomes the hermeneutical window for the rest of the book. This section documents the journey of the wife/Israel from unfaithfulness to faithfulness, from divorce to the renewal of marriage vows. R2 affirms that God will renew his covenant with Israel if "she returns to her first husband" (2:9). This covenant will affect the whole cosmos by the blessings which will flow from it (2:20-24).

The second section, Hos 4-11, continues the journey in repentance. After modifying his traditional beginning by 4:3, R2 makes it clear that the disruption of covenant effects a disruption in creation, in the natural order itself. Thus, two of the triadic R2 editorials of hope in the Hos 4-11 complex, viz. 5:15--6:3 and 10:12, foretell of the renewal of creation when YHWH will come as life-giving rain to the earth. The journey in Hos 4-11 is, on one level then, a journey from barrenness to fertility.

Moreover, from the concluding Hos 11 commentary it becomes clear that the journey in Hos 4-11 is, for R2, the journey of the son/Israel from Egypt to liberation (Exodus), back to Egypt to slavery (Exile), and then from Egypt again back to the land (New Exodus/Future Restoration). R2 thus depicts the son's journey of adoption, disownment and reconciliation.

Although R2 characterizes the journey back to the land at the end of the Hos 4-11 complex, R2 is not finished with his composition. His conclusion to the Hos 12-14 complex will paint in detail the luxuriant growth of Israel in the land which Hos 4-11 only intimates. It is to this discussion of the final R2 complex, Hos 12-14, that we now turn.

XI. The Final Redaction of Hos 12

A. The Editorial History of Hos 12

H	C	R1	R2
12:1a			12:1b
12:2-4			12:5-7
12:8-9			12:10-12
12:13			12:14
12:15			

B. *Hos 12:1b*

12:1a   *sĕbābūnî bĕkāḥāš 'eprayim*
        ûbĕmirmâ bêt yiśrā'ēl
12:1b   *wîhûdâ 'ôd rād 'im-'ēl*
        wĕ'im-qĕdôšîm ne'ĕmān
12:2a   *'eprayim rō'eh rûaḥ*
        wĕrōdēp qādîm kol-hayyôm

12:1a   Ephraim has encircled me with lies
        The house of Israel with deceit.
12:1b   *But Judah still walks*[292] *with God.*
        And with the Holy One, he is faithful.
12:2a   Ephraim herds the wind
        And pursues the eastwind all day.

Scholars have devoted more investigations on this
important chapter in the Book of Hosea than any of its other
single chapters.[293] Our own analysis of the chapter reveals
that Hos 12 is composed of Hosean tradition and commentary
by the final redactor, R2. Hos 12 is marked by paronomasia
not only in R2 commentary but also in the tradition, which we
attribute to Hosea. The R2 interpretive paronomasia
interacts organically and creatively with that of his received
material.

We see this first of all in R2's first remark, 12:1b.
Problematic is the change in a YHWH speech to the reference
to the deity in the third person, as well as the favorable
depiction of Judah. Scholars have dealt with 12:1b in one of
two ways. They either emend or interpret the text so that
Judah is included in the accusation of 12:1a[294] or regard the
verse as a secondary insertion.[295]

However, besides the change in person and the favorable
statement about Judah, two other signals alert us to R2
commentary. The first are the divine attributes themselves,
'ēl and *qĕdôšîm* which refer back to R2 commentary in 11:9: "I
am God (*'ēl*) not man, the Holy One (*qādôš*) in your midst."

The second is paronomasia, which R2 uses to reinterpret
his tradition. R2 formulates his first description about Judah

with alliteration, *wîhûdâ 'ôd rād 'im-'ēl*, "Judah still walks with God."296 Kaatz notes that *rād 'im-'ēl* also bears an assonantal resemblance to *yiśrā'ēl* of 12:1a.297 Being thus anchored in his tradition by this wordplay permits R2 to insert his commentary on the faithfulness of Judah with God, in contrast to the deceitfulness in the house of Israel. Furthermore, 12:1b not only interacts paronomastically with the tradition in 12:1a. It also plays upon 12:2a, which itself is full of alliteration:298

> 12:1b   *wîhûdâ 'ôd <u>rād</u> 'im-'ēl*
>   *wĕ'im-<u>qĕdôšîm</u> ne'ĕmān*
> 12:2a   *'eprayim rō'eh rûaḥ*
>   *<u>wĕrōdēp qādîm</u> kol-hayyôm*

In 12:1b, *rād/qĕdôšîm* forms a parasonancy with *wĕrōdēp/qādîm* of the tradition in 12:2a. Moreover, R2 uses of the plural, *qĕdôšîm*, rather than the *qādôš* of 11:9, precisely because of the rhyme factor with *qādîm* in his tradition. With 12:1b, R2 sets a positive tone to the chapter. We will see this optimism reflected in the rest of his interpretive commentary.

C. Hos 12:5-7

> 12:4   *babbeṭen 'āqab 'et-'āḥîw*
>   *ûbĕ'ônô śārâ 'et- 'ĕlōhîm*
> 12:5   *<u>wāyyāśar 'ēl</u> (MT: <u>wāyyāśar 'el-mal'āk</u>)*299
>   *<u>mal'āk wayyūkāl</u>*
>   *<u>bākâ wayyithannen-lô</u>*
>   *<u>bêt-'ēl yimṣā'ennû</u>*
>   *<u>wĕšām yĕdabbēr 'immānû</u>*
> 12:6   *<u>wayhwh 'ĕlōhê haṣṣĕbā'ôt</u>*
>   *<u>yhwh zikrô</u>*
> 12:7   *<u>wĕ'attâ bē'lōhêkā tāšûb</u>*
>   *<u>ḥesed ûmišpāṭ šĕmōr</u>*
>   *<u>wĕqawwēh 'el-'ĕlōhêkā tāmîd</u>*

> 12:4   In the womb he grabbed his brother's heel.
>   In his vigor he contended with God.

12:5   *But God ruled.*
        And (the) angel prevailed.
        He wept and sought his favor.
        At Beth-el he met him/us.
        There he spoke with him/us:
12:6   *"YHWH, God of Hosts,*
        YHWH is his memorial.
12:7   *You should return to your God.*[300]
        Cherish steadfast love and justice.
        Wait for your God continually."

These verses begin the so-called Jacob traditions in Hosea, which continue in v. 13-14. Commentators have diverged sharply on their interpretation. It would be beyond the scope of this study to present all possible opinions on these verses. Indeed, Dietrich has written a very lengthy monograph precisely on this subject.[301] We are primarily concerned with clues to the final redaction of the tradition and how this redactor reinterpreted the tradition for his own theological thrust.

Much of the investigations into the Hos 12 Jacob traditions deal with their relationship to the Jacob traditions found in the Book of Genesis. On one hand, the verses seem to depend on the traditions in Genesis. Hos 12:4a combines the tradition regarding Jacob grabbing the heel of his brother, Esau, at birth described in Gen 25:26 with the pejorative etymology on Jacob's name recounted in Gen 27:36:

> Esau said, "Is he not rightly named Jacob (*ya'ăqōb*)? For he has supplanted me (*wayya'qĕbēnî*) these two times. He took away my birthright; and behold, now has taken away my blessing."

Moreover, Hos 12:4b alludes to the struggle at the Jabbok between Jacob and a man, *'îš*, described in Gen 32:24-32.

The problems between the Jacob traditions in Hosea and the Genesis accounts arise precisely in 12:5, which, we argue, begins R2 redaction. Many commentators have questioned the authenticity of Hos 12:5-7.[302] Hos 12:5 seems to continue the account of the nocturnal struggle at the Jabbok, which was

begun in 12:4. The MT, however, is problematic. Assuming
that *wāyyāśar* beginning v. 5a is a repetition of *śrh*, "to strive,"
from v. 4b, the preposition, *'el*, "to," is incongruous. One would
expect *'im* as in Gen 24:24, 28 or *'et* as in Hos 12:4b.[303]

Assuming also that Jacob is the subject of *wāyyāśar* and
wayyūkāl, "Jacob strove(?) and prevailed," the continuation of
the verse presents difficulties. The subject of the following
verbs, "to weep and seek one's favor," is ambiguous. If the
subject is Jacob, one wonders why, after he had just prevailed
over the angel, he would weep and seek his favor. Jacob's
weeping at the Jabbok is not recorded in Genesis. If,
furthermore, the angel is the subject, Hos 12:5b diverges even
more sharply from the Genesis account, which does not relate
that the "man" either wept before Jacob or sought his favor.

Commentators try to resolve these difficulties by arguing
that 1) Hosea has access to a source not preserved by our
Genesis accounts;[304] 2) Jacob's weeping and supplication
refers to Gen 33:4 where Jacob weeps during his reunion with
Esau;[305] 3) Jacob's weeping is parallel to the fast of Moses (Dt
9:9--10:11) where Moses "conquers God by his mighty fasting
and praying;"[306] 4) Jacob's weeping is a kind of midrashic
expansion of the Genesis traditions by the prophet;[307] 5) one
should emend *bākâ*, "to weep," to *bākô* from *bwk*, "to confuse,
perplex," thus: (Jacob) perplexed (the angel) and got mercy for
himself."[308]

The intent of 12:5 becomes much clearer if one views it as
an interpretive commentary of the final redactor. We
compare Hos 12:5a with the Gen 32:29 account where Jacob
receives the name, "Israel," after his struggle with the "man"
at the Jabbok. F. I. Andersen has analyzed the chiastic
structure of this text as follows:

Gen 32:29   *kî-śārîtā 'im 'ĕlōhîm*

            wĕ'im-'ănāšîm wattûkāl

Gen 32:29   For you struggled with God,

            and with men you did succeed.

Andersen explains, "The key to the recovery of this poetic oracle lies in recognition of postpositive *wāw* (so-called *wāw emphaticum*) with the final verb."[309] Furthermore, Eslinger sees the same syntactical structure in Hos 12:5a. He vocalizes *'el* to *'ēl* which has already been suggested by several scholars.[310] He reads *wyśr* from *śrr*, "to rule," with the MT, rather than identifying it with *śrh*, "to strive," from v. 4b.[311] The structure of v. 5a thus becomes:

wāyyāśar 'ēl   But God ruled,

mal'āk wayyūkāl   And (the) angel prevailed.[312]

In an ingenious wordplay, R2 not only reverses his tradition in Hos 12:4, but also the Gen 32:29 tradition regarding the naming of Jacob to Israel. Hos 12:4 and Gen 32:29 both concur that Jacob struggled with God: *śārā 'et-'ĕlōhîm*, Hos 12:4b, *śārîtā 'im 'ĕlōhîm*, Gen 32:29. Thus Jacob is deemed, *yiśrā'ēl*, "he who strives with God." Playing upon *śārā 'et- 'ĕlōhîm* in 12:4, R2 maintains in an ironic twist on the Israel etymology that "God ruled," *wāyyāśar 'ēl*. The divine appellative, *'ēl*, recalls R2's similar use of the word in his preceding 12:1b and 11:9b commentaries. Furthermore, R2 contends that the "angel prevailed," *mal'āk wayyūkāl*, and not Jacob as in Gen 32:29, *wattūkāl*. R2 uses *mal'āk* as a synonym of *'ēl* because of its alliteration value with *wayyūkāl* which follows.[313] Thus reinterpreting both the Hos 12:4 and Gen 32:29 traditions, R2 paints an equally different picture of Jacob's response to his opponent at the Jabbok: in 12:5aB he states that Jacob wept and sought God's favor, *bākā wayyithannen-lô*.

Beginning with 12:5, R2 constructs "a paradigm of repentance" using the important figure of Jacob as archetype.[314] R2 has mitigated the presentation of Jacob in his traditional material to such an extent that the eponymous ancestor becomes a model for Israel to turn back to YHWH. Israel likewise should recognize the sovereignty of God and weep and seek his favor. This repentant posture before YHWH has a deuteronomistic flavor. 1 Kgs 8:33-34 describes

Solomon's prayer to YHWH in the newly constructed temple thus:[315]

> "When your people Israel are defeated before the enemy
> because they have sinned against you, if *they turn again (šwb)*
> to you, and acknowledge your name, and pray and *seek your*
> *favor (wĕhithannenû)* in this house, then hear in heaven, and
> forgive the sin of your people Israel, and *bring them again to*
> *the land which you gave to their ancestors."* (1 Kgs 8:33-34. Cf.
> 1 Kgs 8:47)

The transformation of the patriarch becomes more apparent as R2 continues his portrayal of Jacob in Hos 12:5b-7:[316]

At Beth-el he met him/us. (*bêt-'ēl yimṣā'ennû*)
   There he spoke with him/us
   (*wĕšām yĕdabbēr 'immānû*):
"YHWH, God of Hosts,
   YHWH is his memorial.
You should return (*šwb*)to your God.
Cherish (*šmr*) steadfast love and justice.
   Wait for your God continually."

On one level, this R2 commentary presupposes Gen 28:10-17, Jacob's dream at Bethel where YHWH speaks to Jacob, saying:[317]

> "Behold, I am YHWH, the God of Abraham your father and
> the God of Isaac; the land on which you lie I will give to you
> and to your descendants ... Behold, I am with you and *will*
> *protect (šmr)* you wherever you go, and *will bring you back*
> (*šwb, hiph*) to this land; for I will not leave you until I have
> done that of which *I have spoken (dbr)* to you." (Gen 28:13, 15)

By resuming important words from this Jacob/Beth-el tradition, viz. the revelation of the divine name, YHWH, to Jacob, *šmr, šwb,* and *dbr,* R2 recalls the promise made to Jacob that YHWH has given the land to him and to his descendants and that YHWH *will bring him back* to the land. Such a recollection of hope would offer consolation to R2's readers in the exile.

The deliberately ambiguous suffix on *yms'nw* and *'mnw* in 12:5b permits a double referent, "him" and "us," i.e. Jacob and the present generation.[318] On another level, then, R2 states: "There, he (Jacob) spoke with *us*." R2 therefore places in the mouth of the eponymous ancestor, first, a confession of faith: "YHWH, God of Hosts, YHWH is his memorial." Scholars have noted the similarities between 12:6 and Ex 3:15 where YHWH reveals his name to Moses.[319]

Hos 12:6	Ex 3:15
wyhwh	*yhwh*
'ĕlōhê haṣṣĕbā'ôt	*'ĕlōhê 'ăbōtêkem* ...
	zeh-šĕmî lĕ'ōlām
yhwh zikrô	*wĕzeh zikrî lĕdōr dōr*
YHWH	YHWH
God of Hosts	God of your fathers ...
	This is my name forever.
YHWH is his memorial.	This is my memorial
	throughout all generations.

R2 thus recalls here in Jacob's confession, the God of the Exodus who had revealed himself to Moses on Horeb. We will see in the R2 commentary a few verses later in 12:10, that this same God of the Exodus will reveal his name again to the present generation: "I am YHWH, your God from the land of Egypt."

Besides a confession of faith, R2 puts into the mouth of the founding father of Israel an exhortation to his descendants in the exile *to return to YHWH their God* (*wĕ'attâ bē'lōhêkā tāšûb*). Only then will God's promise to Jacob be fulfilled, viz. the return (*šwb*) to the land from exile, which R2 pictures as a new Exodus.

Moreover, just as YHWH promises to protect (*šmr*) Jacob and his descendants wherever they go (Gen 28:15), the patriarch enjoins his descendants to cherish (*šmr*) steadfast love and justice and wait upon the Lord (Hos 12:7b). R2's deuteronomistic orientation comes to the fore here, since, on one level, *šmr* refers to "keeping" or "observing" the commandments of the covenant.[320] As we will see below, R2 plays upon the different meanings of *šmr* which occur in 12:7, 13, and 14. He thus creates another *antanaclasis*, which he will use to recreate the Jacob of his tradition into a paradigm of repentance for his exilic readers.

D. Hos 12:10-12, 14

12:8   *kĕna'an bĕyādô mō'zĕnê mirmâ*
         la'ăśōq 'āhēb
12:9   *wayyō'mer 'eprayim 'ak 'āšartî*
         māṣā'tî 'ôn lî
         kol-yĕgî'ay lō' yimṣĕ'û-lî
         'āwôn 'ăšer-ḥēṭ'
12:10 *wĕ'ānōkî yhwh 'ĕlōhêkā mē'ereṣ miṣrayim*
         'ōd 'ôšîbĕkā bo'ŏholîm kîmê mô'ēd
12:11 *wĕdibbartî 'al-hannĕbî'îm*
         we 'ānōkî ḥāzôn hirbêtî
         ûbĕyad hannebî'îm 'ădammeh
12:12 *'im-gil'ād 'āwen*
         'ak-šāw' hāyû
         baggilgāl šĕwārîm zibbēḥû
         gam mizbĕḥôtām kĕgallîm
         'al talmê śādāy
12:13 *wayyibraḥ ya'ăqōb śĕdēh 'ărām*
         wayya'ăbōd yiśrā'ēl bĕ'iššâ
         ûbĕ'iššâ šāmār
12:14 *ûbĕnābî' he'ĕlâ yhwh 'et-yiśrā'ēl mimmiṣrāyim*
         ûbĕnābî' nišmār

12:8   Canaan, in whose hands are deceitful scales.
         He loves to exploit.
12:9   Ephraim says, "How rich I become!
         I have acquired wealth for myself!
         None of my crimes will ever catch up with me,
            nor iniquity which I have wrongly committed."
12:10 *I am YHWH your God from the land of Egypt.*
         I will again make you dwell in tents
            as in the days of (the tent) meeting.

12:11   *I spoke through*[321] *the prophets.*
        I multiplied visions.
        So, by the hand of prophets, I shall destroy.[322]
12:12   *If there is iniquity in Gilead,*
                how worthless they will become!
        If in Gilgal they sacrifice bulls,
                their altars will surely become like stone heaps
        upon the furrows of the field.[323]
12:13   Jacob fled to the land of Aram.
        Israel served for a wife,
                and for a wife he tended (sheep).
12:14   *By a prophet YHWH brought Israel*
                up from Egypt,
        and by a prophet he was protected.

There are several parallel points of contact between the two R2 commentaries, 12:6-7 and 12:10.[324] Both contain a revelation of the divine name. In 12:6, Jacob proclaims it in phrasing similar to the Exodus tradition, Ex 3:15, where YHWH reveals his name to Moses: "YHWH God of Hosts. YHWH is his memorial." In 12:10, YHWH himself discloses his name with an explicit reference to the Exodus: "I am YHWH your God from the land of Egypt, (*wĕ'ānōkî yhwh 'ĕlōhêkā mē'ereṣ miṣrayim*)." One should compare YHWH's statement here with the first commandment of the Decalogue: "I am YHWH your God (*'ānōkî yhwh 'ĕlōhêkā*) who brought you out of the land of Egypt (*mē'ereṣ miṣrayim*), from the house of slavery" (Dt 5:6; Ex 20:2). The motivation for this R2 commentary on 12:8-9 may lie in a parasonancy between *mē'ereṣ miṣrayim*, "from the land of Egypt," and the *antanaclasis* on *mṣ'* in the tradition, 12:9:

> *wayyō'mer 'eprayim 'ak 'āšartî*
>   *māṣā'tî 'ôn lî*
> *kol-yĕgî'ay lō' yimṣĕ'û lî*
>   *'āwôn 'ăšer-ḥēṭ'*

Ephraim says, "How rich I become!
I have acquired wealth for myself.

None of my crimes *will ever catch up* with me.
Nor iniquity which I have wrongly committed."[325]

By means of the *šwb/yšb* interplay, R2 asserts that, if the people heed Jacob's exhortation to repent (*šwb*, 12:7a), YHWH will again make them dwell (*yšb*, 12:10b) in tents. The reference to "dwelling in tents as in the days of (the tent) of meeting"[326] suggests the wilderness period. In R2 theology, the wilderness period was the ideal time of honeymoon, the time of the ratification of covenant between YHWH and Israel after God had liberated Israel from Egypt (Cf. Hos 2:16-17). With the adverb, *'ôd*, "again," R2 foretells of a *new* wilderness period, one that will occur, as we will see, after a new Exodus from the lands of exile. R2 unifies YHWH's declaration of the new wilderness period, and thus of a new covenant, with the parasonancy of *'ôd/mô'ēd* at the beginning and end of the line, as well as rhyme with the vowel "o":

12:10b *'ōd 'ôšîbĕkā bo'ŏholîm kîmê mô'ēd*[327]

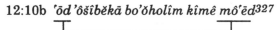

12:10b I will again make you dwell in tents
as in the days of the (tent) of meeting.

According to Ex 33:7, Moses had pitched a tent in the wilderness far from the Israelite campground, which he called "the tent of meeting," *'ōhel mô'ēd*. Inside the tent, Moses would encounter YHWH. YHWH would speak to him, revealing his will for the people. Ex 33:9-11 stresses the privileged intimacy Moses had with YHWH. Their encounter was an occasion of worship for the people.[328]

> "When Moses entered the tent, the pillar of cloud would descend and stand at the door of the tent, and *YHWH would speak with Moses* (*wĕdibber 'im-mōšeh*). And when all the people saw the pillar of cloud standing at the door of the tent, all the people would rise up and worship, every man at his tent door. Thus *YHWH used to speak to Moses face to face* (*wĕdibber yhwh 'el-mōšeh pānîm 'el pānîm*), as a man speaks to his friend." (Ex 33:9-11)

With this background, we are in a better position to understand the theological design of R2 commentary in 12:11-12, 14. By means of his allusion to the earlier days of the tent of meeting, R2 brings to mind the days when YHWH would speak (*dbr*) to Moses. Through Moses he makes his will known to the people. As R2 will remark in 12:14, Moses thus becomes the prophet par excellence, who leads the people out of Egypt and becomes their mediator and intercessor vis-à-vis YHWH.

This notion of Moses as prophet *par excellence* is distinctly deuteronomic. We recall for the reader our discussion of the final redactor's commentary in 6:5 which is relevant here for 12:11-12, 14.[329] According to Dt 18:15-19, Moses informs the people that the agent through whom YHWH will communicate his will is the prophet:

> "The Lord your God will raise up for you *a prophet like me* from among you, from among your brethren - *him you shall heed* - just as you desired of the Lord your God at Horeb on the day of the assembly, when you said, 'Let me not hear again the voice of the Lord my God, or see this great fire anymore, lest I die.' And the Lord said to me, 'They have rightly said all that they have spoken. I will raise up for them *a prophet like you* from among their brethren; and *I will put my words in his mouth, and he shall speak to them all that I command him. And whoever will not give heed to my words which he shall speak in my name, I myself will require it of him.*'" (Dt 18:15-19, RSV)

It is not the diviners, soothsayers, sorcerers and other mediums of Canaan who will be God's mouthpiece to the people. Indeed, the people must rid the land of these (Dt 18:9-14). Instead, YHWH will commission a prophet like Moses: "*Him* you shall heed" (Dt 18:15).

The Deuteronomistic History, however, documents the people's continual rejection of God's word revealed by his chosen agents. Thus,

> "YHWH warned Israel and Judah by *every prophet and seer*, saying, 'Repent (*šûb*) of your evil ways and keep my commandments and my statutes, in accordance with all the law which I commanded your ancestors and which I sent to

you by *my servants the prophets.*' But, they would not listen,
but were stubborn, as their ancestors, who did not believe in
YHWH their God ... Therefore, YHWH was very angry with
Israel and removed them out of his sight ... " (2 Kgs 17:13-14,
18. Cf. Jer 35:15)

R2 commentary reflects this deuteronomistic interpretation of the prophetic office, as "preachers of repentance
whose message was a call to return to the law."[330]   YHWH
maintains in Hos 12:11 that, since the days of the tent of
meeting when he spoke to Moses, the first and foremost
prophet, he has "spoken through the prophets (*wĕdibbartî ʿal
hannĕbî'îm*) and has multiplied visions (*ḥāzôn hirbêtî*)."[331]
Consistent with Dt 18:15ff and 2 Kgs 17:13-14, R2 implicitly
refers to a succession of prophets since the time of Moses
whose mission was the continual conversion of Israel back to
the covenant.   However, since Israel and Judah refused to
repent of their apostasy, the R2 texts, Hos 6:5 and 12:11, are
clear about the consequences. In 6:5 YHWH states: "*Therefore
I have hewn them by the prophets. I have slain them by the
words of my mouth.* Similarly, in 12:11 YHWH declares: "*By
the hand of the prophets I shall destroy.*" The agents of God's
revelation thereby become the agents of God's just
punishment.[332]

In 12:12, R2 augments 12:11 by giving two examples of
trangressions and the punishment which will result from
them.   R2 formulates this expansion with a variety of
wordplays which have been acknowledged by a number of
scholars.[333] According to Eybers, the specific proper names,
Gilead and Gilgal, were selected primarily for their
paronomastic value with each other (the alliteration of
gîmel/lamed), and in combination with the other striking
words of the verse.[334]

The first R2 example in 12:12 is a paronomastic comment
on the tradition, 12:9, where Ephraim boasts about the riches
he has accumulated:

12:9   *wayyō'mer 'eprayim
          'ak 'āšartî māṣā'tî 'ōn lî*
12:12   *'im-gil'ād 'āwen 'ak-šāw' hāyû*

12:9   Ephraim says:
         "How rich I become! I have acquired
         wealth for myself!
12:12   If there is *iniquity* in Gilead,
         How worthless they become!

In 12:12 R2 resumes the particle, *'ak*, from 12:9 and plays upon *'ôn*, "wealth," with *'āwen*, "iniquity."[335] R2 thus equates Ephraim's so-called wealth with iniquity and so judges their capital resources as worthless.

R2 then links the first example of the people's transgression to the second by means of an alliterative wordplay between Gilead and *šāw'*, "worthless," in 12:12aA and Gilgal and *šĕwārîm*, "bulls," in 12:12aB:

v. 12aA   *'im-gil'ād 'āwen 'ak-šāw' hāyû*
                 A   B
v. 12aB   *baggilgāl šĕwārîm zibbĕḥû*
                     B'   A'
v. 12b   *gam mizbĕḥôtām kĕgallîm*

v. 12aB   If in Gilgal they sacrifice bulls,
v. 12b   their altars will surely become
           like stone heaps . . .

This second example intensifies the transgression and punishment of Gilgal by means of a chiastically structured paronomasia: *gilgāl//gallîm* and *zibbĕḥû//mizbĕḥôtām*.

Finally, R2 links his commentary in 12:10-12 to 12:13 by the *śdy/śdh* which concludes v. 12 and occurs in the first line of v. 13:[336]

v.12   *Their altars will surely become like stone heaps*
         upon the furrows of the field (*'al talmê śādāy)*

v.13   Jacob fled to the land of Aram *(śĕdēh 'ărām)*

R2's concluding editorial in Hos 12, viz. 12:14, encapsulates much of his previous commentary in the chapter.[337] He patterns his editorial closely to the Jacob tradition in 12:13, but by means of *antanaclasis* mitigates this tradition to his own advantage:

12:13	*wayyibraḥ yaʿăqōb śĕdēh 'ărām*	
	wayyaʿăbōd yiśrā'ēl bĕ'iššâ	A
	ûbĕ'iššâ šāmār	B
12:14	*ûbĕnābî' heʿĕlâ yhwh 'et-yiśrā'ēl*	
	mimmiṣrayim	A'
	ûbĕnābî' nišmār	B'

12:13	Jacob fled to the land of Aram.	
	Israel served for a wife,	A
	and for a wife he tended (sheep).	B
12:14	*By a prophet YHWH brought Israel*	
	up from Egypt,	A'
	and by a prophet he was protected.	B'

R2's first *antanaclasis* in 12:14 is on the preposition *bĕ* of his tradition in 12:13, *bĕ'iššâ*, "for a wife." R2 repeats the two instances of *bĕ*, but uses the instrumental meaning of the preposition for his own addition: "*bĕnābî'*, "by a prophet."[338]

R2 structures 12:14 as a parallel commentary, A'/B', on his tradition, A/B. The description of the eponymous patriarch in A, *wayyaʿăbōd yiśrā'ēl*, "Israel served," recalls for him the time when the nation of Israel was a slave, *ʿbd*, in the land of Egypt (Cf. Ex 1:13-14 and Dt 5:15). This recollection prompts his own interpretive commentary, A': "By a prophet YHWH brought Israel up from Egypt." R2 is thus able to incorporate and, indeed, to sum up the deuteronomistic Moses traditions implied in his previous editorials, 12:10-11: Moses - to whom YHWH first revealed his name (12:10a), to whom YHWH spoke as a friend (12:10b), who became the first of a succession of prophets through whom God revealed and executed his will (12:11) - was the one whom YHWH chose to lead his people up from Egypt. To highlight this unique relationship between

YHWH and Moses, R2 creates an inclusio-like structure for his commentary in 12:10a and 12:14:

> v. 10a   I am YHWH your God from the land of Egypt . . .

> v. 14   . . . and by a prophet YHWH brought Israel from Egypt.

R2's second *antanaclasis* is on the root *šmr*. In 12:13 (B), *šmr* describes the bride-price which Jacob had to pay for Rachel, viz. shepherding Laban's flocks for seven years (Cf. Gen 30:31). In 12:14, R2 exploits another meaning of *šmr*, "to guard, protect." *Šmr* is used to describe divine protection in particular. In the Jacob/Bethel tradition, Gen 28:15 cited earlier in our examination of 12:5,[339] YHWH says to Jacob, "Behold, I am with you and will *protect (šmr)* you wherever you go and will bring you back to this land." We saw in Hos 12:7 that R2 resumed *šmr* from this promise to Jacob and, creating an *antanaclasis*, made it an injunction put into Jacob's mouth for his descendants to "cherish" or "observe" the covenantal attributes, steadfast love and justice.[340] Furthermore, in connection with the Exodus tradition, which is pertinent to our Hos 12:14 text, Josh 24:17 states:

> "For it is YHWH our God who brought us and our fathers up from the land of Egypt, out of the house of slavery (*mibbêt 'ăbadîm*), and who did those great signs in our sight, and protected (*šmr*) us in all the way that we went, and among all the peoples through whom we passed."

Thus, with this distinctive nuance of *šmr*, R2 declares in 12:14b that by a prophet, the chosen mediator between YHWH and his people, Israel was protected.[341]

E. The Redactional Thrust of Hos 12

The springboard for R2 commentary in Hos 12 is the Jacob tradition presented in his received material. The problem scholars perceive in Hos 12 is the seemingly contradictory portrayals of Jacob one finds here. On one hand, we have an indictment (*rîb*) against Jacob/Israel which traces the offenses of the present day Israel back to its eponymous patriarch (12:1b, 3, 15). In parallel expositions, the texts correlate the past deceitfulness and arrogance of Jacob (12:4) with the people's current corruption (12:8-9). Moreover, 12:13 implies the ultimate humiliation of Jacob/Israel when he became a common slave for a wife.[342] What offense this servitude for a wife parallels in contemporary Israel is not immediately clear.[343]

On the other hand, one finds also a positive characterization of Jacob. We argue that this affirmative portrayal is due to R2 editorial. R2 mitigates the incriminatory depiction of the patriarch by transforming him into a prototype of a repentant Israel (12:5). In R2 redaction, this forebearer of Israel summons the presently exiled nation to turn back to YHWH their God (12:7). Only then will the promise made to him, viz. that he will be brought back to the land (Gen 28:13, 15), be realized for his descendants.

R2 redaction builds up to a climax in 12:14, the interpretive commentary of the Jacob-Rachel tradition in 12:13. Willi-Plein suggests that the logic of 12:13-14 is similar to the first of Hillel's exegetical rules, *qal waḥomer*.[344] According to *qal waḥomer*, what applies in a less important case will certainly apply in a more important case.[345] With an exegetical hermeneutic similar to the *qal waḥomer*, R2 transfigures the account of Jacob/Israel's mortifying enslavement for a wife (12:13) into a bride-rescue story with his 12:14 commentary. Thus, Coote states:

> Just as Jacob travelled to a foreign country to take a wife and bring her back, so YHWH also went to a foreign country to take a wife and bring her back.[346]

The focus of R2, however, is not simply on the past event. The whole thrust of his commentary in 12:5-7, 10-12, 14 is a summons and a promise. If the people listen to their patriarch's injunction to repent (12:7), YHWH will bring his people back in a new Exodus. If Jacob sojourned to a foreign land for a wife and brought her back ..., if YHWH went to Egypt to bring Israel back in the first Exodus ..., how much

more so will YHWH now lead his people back from exile in a
new exodus, if only they would repent.

One can say that R2 makes use of this type of reasoning
also in Hos 3:3-5.[347] R2 describes Hosea as saying to his newly
recovered wife:

> "You must dwell as mine for many days. You shall not play
> the harlot or belong to another man. Then indeed I will be
> yours.

> For the children of Israel shall dwell many days without king
> or prince, without sacrifice or pillar, without ephod or
> teraphim. Afterward, the children of Israel shall return and
> seek YHWH their God and David their king; and they shall
> come trembling to the Lord and to his goodness in the latter
> days." (Hos 3:3-5)

The sexual abstinence between Hosea and Gomer is applied in
a much greater degree to the nation of Israel, cultically and
politically impoverished before YHWH.

For R2, the agent through whom YHWH performed the
first Exodus was the prophet *nonpareil*, Moses. He was the
intimate of YHWH who led the bride up from Egypt to the
wilderness where she bonded herself in a marital covenant
with God. For R2, the agent for the new Exodus is also a
prophet, an heir to the line of Moses. He is the prophet Hosea,
to whom R2 attributes pseudonymously his exilic composition
of exhortation and promise. We saw in our discussion of Hos 1-
3 how R2 structured his tradition so that the marital tradition
of Hos 1-3 becomes the hermeneutical window for the rest of
the book.[348] In his redaction, the model for Hosea's conduct
with his own estranged wife is YHWH's own line of action
with the wife/Israel. To implement her conversion, YHWH led
her through a three stage journey of purification. The fruits of
her conversion, however, far outweighed the pain of her
punishment. Thus, in Hos 3, Hosea is called to love his
unfaithful Gomer and chastise her so that she may become his
again. The rest of the book attributed to him by R2 is a
prophetic call to the wife/Israel to recognize their exile as
YHWH's chastisement and repent, so that a new marriage
may be realized in their time.

By means of his redaction of Hos 12, R2 thus recalls his previous commentary, Hos 1-3. Since Hos 12 is the first chapter of his third major division in the book, this resumption of the marital theme is structurally important. We recall in our examination of 14:2-9, the conclusion to the Hos 12-14 complex, that R2 takes up the marriage motif through imagery reminiscent of the Song of Songs.[349] R2 seems to structure his complexes so that the marriage motif is focused in the two outer complexes, Hos 1-3 and 12-14, framing the middle complex, Hos 4-11, which is dominated more by the image of the youth/Israel.

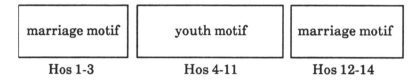

marriage motif	youth motif	marriage motif
Hos 1-3	Hos 4-11	Hos 12-14

Although focusing on different motifs, the complexes are not unrelated. All three complexes contain the journey theme. In Hos 1-3, we become involved with the three-stage journey of the wife/Israel. Hos 4-11 chronicles the three-stage journey of a people summoned to repent. This journey is embodied in the youth/Israel who, in Hos 11, was called by YHWH out of Egypt in the first Exodus, who returned to Egypt in the exile, and who will return from Egypt in the future restoration.

Hos 11 prepares for the Jacob/Israel tradition in Hos 12 in its final redacted state. The youth/Israel who was called from Egypt by YHWH becomes the wife/Israel who is brought out of Egypt by YHWH through a prophet. Hos 12 also records a three-stage journey. The first is Jacob's journey to a foreign land for a wife to bring her back to his land. The second is YHWH's journey to Egypt to rescue the wife/Israel in the first Exodus through the prophet, Moses. The third is YHWH's journey to the lands of exile to rescue his wife again through the agency of a prophet. This prophet is Hosea whose manifesto of summons and promise to Israel in exile is our final redactor's composition.

R2 not only recalls previous commentary, but also anticipates further commentary. We will see shortly that R2 will repeat the Exodus-Wilderness motifs of Hos 12 in Hos 13. Here, however, his *mûsār* theology comes utmost to the fore.

XII. *The Final Redaction of Hos 13*

A. *The Editorial History of Hos 13*

H	C	R1	R2
			13:1-11
13:12-13			13:14
13:15--14:1			

Like Hos 12, Hos 13 is composed of Hosean tradition and commentary on this tradition by the final redactor. We will see in our discussion that R2 will indict his readers for their apostasy in worshipping idols. For R2, the magnitude of their offense against the One who brought them out of Egypt and cared for them in the wilderness necessitates a just punishment. This chastisement, of course, is their exile. Just as R2 had in 4:3 brought the indictment against Israel to a cosmic plane,[350] so in Hos 13 does R2 involve the cosmic powers of Sheol and Death in the chastisement of Israel. The tenor of the chapter appears hopeless. Indeed, R2 is building up to a climax: YHWH is inflicting his just punishment on a people who had broken his covenant. We know, however, that amid this punishment, R2 will call to the people, saying, "Return, O Israel, to YHWH your God . . . (14:2)" Their hope to return to the land of their inheritance is in their repentance.

B. *Hos 13:1-3*

13:1   *kĕdibbēr (MT: kĕdabbēr)*[351] *'eprayim rĕtēt*
        nāśā' hû' bĕyiśrā'ēl
        wayye'šam babba'al wayyāmōt
13:2   *wĕ'attâ yôsîpû laḥāṭō'*
        wayya'ăśû lāhem massēkâ
        mikkaspām kitbûnām 'ăṣabbîm
        ma'ăśēh ḥārāšîm kullōh

lāhem hēm 'ōměrîm zōběhê 'ādām
'ăgālîm yiššāqûn
13:3 *lākēn yihyû ka'ănan-bōqer*
wěkattal maškîm hōlēk
kěmōṣ yěsō'ēr miggoren
ûkě'āšān mě'ărubbâ

13:1 Truly, He had spoken terrifyingly against
Ephraim.
He had lifted up (His voice) against Israel.
But he incurred guilt through Baal and died.
13:2 And now they continue to sin.
They make a cast image for themselves,
from their silver, idols, according to
their skill.
All of it, the product of a craftsman.
They who sacrifice people speak to them.
They kiss calves.
13:3 Therefore, they will be like the morning mist,
like the dew that goes away early,
like chaff which is stirred up from a threshing
floor,
and like smoke from a window.

To understand the problematic 13:1-3, one should regard
these verses as an R2 commentary on 12:15:[352]

12:15 *hik'îs 'eprayim tamrûrîm*
wědāmāyw 'ālāyw yiṭṭôš
wěherpātô yāšîb lô 'ădōnāyw
13:1 *kědibbēr 'eprayim rětēt*
nāśā' hû' běyiśrā'ēl ...

12:15 Ephraim has caused bitter provocation.
He will make him accountable for his bloodguilt.
His Lord will return upon him his disgrace.
13:1 *Truly, He has spoken terrifyingly against*
Ephraim.
He has lifted up (his voice) against Israel ...

R2 commentary in 13:1 presumes for its subject the *'ădōnāyw*, "his Lord," which concludes 12:15. R2 concurs with his tradition that the Lord will hold Ephraim responsible for his bloodguilt and return to Ephraim his disgrace. However, R2 maintains that Ephraim had been warned. The Lord "truly has spoken (*dbr*) terrifyingly against Ephraim." The *dbr* in 13:1 recalls the R2 commentary, 12:11 where YHWH states that he has "spoken (*dbr*) through the prophets," revealing his will and his warning to his people to keep the law.[353] Thus, R2 insists that the people themselves are responsible for any suffering they must undergo.

Hos 13:1-3 contains several parallels with 2 Kgs 17:7-23, regarded as a composition of the exilic deuteronomist which summarizes the decline in the worship of Israel that led to the downfall of both kingdoms.[354] Although YHWH had spoken through the prophets, warning them to keep to his commandments (Hos 13:1a; 2 Kgs 17:13), they still incurred guilt through Baal (Hos 13:1b; 2 Kgs 17:16) and died.[355] They continued to sin (*ḥṭ'*) against YHWH their God (Hos 13:2aA; 2 Kgs 17:1, 14-15). They made cast images for themselves (*'śhw lhm mskh*, Hos 13:2; 2 Kgs 17:16), as well as idols (*'ăṣabbîm*, Hos 13:2; *hebel*, 2 Kgs 17:15). Moreover, they have committed human sacrifice (Hos 13:2b; 2 Kgs 17:16)[356] and paid homage to calves (Hos 13:2b; 2 Kgs 17:16).[357] We recall that in 8:4b, 6, R2 had made an indictment similar to 13:2:

8:4b   With their *silver* and gold *they made* (*'śh*) *idols* for themselves.

8:6   A *craftsman made it* (*wĕhû' hārāš 'ăśāhû*); It is not God. The *calf* of Samaria shall become splinters.

13:2   *They make* (*'śh*) a cast image for themselves. From their *silver*, *idols* according to their skill. All of it, *the product of craftsmen* (*ma'ăśeh hārāšîm*). . . . They kiss *calves*.

These offenses against YHWH did not go unnoticed. According to 2 Kgs 17:18, "therefore, the Lord was very angry with Israel, and removed them out of his sight." Hos 13:3 formulates the verdict by recalling the judgment in Hos 6:4 and expanding upon it:[358]

> Therefore, they will be like the morning mist,
>> like the dew that goes away early,
> like chaff which is stirred up from a threshing floor,
>> and like smoke from a window.
>> (Hos 13:3)

C. *Hos 13:4-8*

13:4   *wĕ'ānōkî yhwh 'ĕlōhêkā mē'ereṣ miṣrāyim*
       wĕ'lōhîm zûlātî lō' tēdā'
       ûmôšîa' 'ayin biltî

13:5   *'ănî yĕda'tîkā bammidbār*
       bĕ'ereṣ tal'ūbôt

13:6   *kĕmô rĕ'îtîm (MT: kĕmar'îtām)*[359] *wayyiśbā'û*
       śābĕ'û wayyārom libbām
       'al-kēn šĕkēḥûnî

13:7   *wa'ĕhî lāhem kĕmô-šāḥal*
       kĕnāmēr 'al-derek 'āšûr

13:8   *'epgĕšēm kĕdōb šakkûl*
       wĕ'eqra' sĕgôr libbām
       wĕ'ōkĕlēm šām kĕlābî'
       ḥayyat haśśādeh tĕbaqqĕ'ēm

13:4   I am YHWH your God from the land of Egypt.
       A god besides me you have never known.
       There is no savior except me.

13:5   I knew you in the wilderness,
          in the land of drought.

13:6   When I pastured them,
          they were satisfied.
       When[360] they were satisfied,
          their heart was lifted up.
       Therefore, they forgot me.

13:7   I will be to them like a lion.
         Like a leopard along the way I will lurk.[361]
13:8   I will fall upon them like a bereaved she-bear.
         I will tear open the cavity of their heart.
         I will devour them there like a lion,
         a wild beast which will rend them.

Like 13:1-2, 13:4-6 is permeated with deuteronomic paraenesis,[362] which harmonizes with what we have seen previously in R2 redaction.[363] While 13:1-2 summarizes the continual sinfulness of the people in the third person, YHWH speaks summarily in the first person in 13:4-6. Like the R2 commentary in 12:10,[364] YHWH begins his declaration by revealing his name: "I am YHWH your God from the land of Egypt." The R2 theme of the God who first liberated his people from Egypt in one paradigmatic act emerges again in his commentary. R2 expands upon this revelation with other deuteronomistic notions. In the first place, his statement in 13:4bB, "A god besides me you have never known," appropriates the deuteronomistic expression, yd^c, "to know," which we have seen in his previous editorials.[365] One should compare Hos 13:4b to Dt 32:17 where the gods which the people do not know are the gods of the land:

"They sacrificed to demons which were no gods,
     to gods they *have never known.*"
('ĕlōhîm lō' yĕdā'ûm, Dt 32:17)

Hos 13:4, moreover, resembles Dt 5:6-7 where YHWH announces the first commandment of the Decalogue:

"I am YHWH your God ('ānōkî yhwh 'ĕlōhêkā), who brought
you out of the land of Egypt (mē'ereṣ miṣrāyim), out of the
house of bondage. You shall have not other gods before me
(lō'-yihyeh lĕkā 'ĕlōhîm 'ăhērîm 'al-pānāy)." (Dt 5:6-7)

"I am YHWH your God from the land of Egypt ('ānōkî yhwh
'ĕlōhêkā mē'ereṣ miṣrayim). A god besides me you have never
known (wē'lōhîm zûlātî lō' tēdā'). There is no savior (môšîa')
except me." (Hos 13:4)

Both texts insist on the primacy of YHWH over any other god. *He* is the One who rescued his people from the land of Egypt. His proclamation in 13;4, "There is no savior (*môšîa'*) except me," correlates with R2 commentary in 14:4 where the people declare, "Assyria will not save us (*lō' yôšî'ēnû*)." R2 will expand upon this notion of no "savior" but YHWH later in 13:9-11.

In 13:5-6 YHWH recounts his beneficent care of the people whose reaction to it is heartless arrogance. Deuteronomic ideas are again apparent in R2 redaction. R2 accords with Dt 8:15-16 and Dt 32:10-14, which describe YHWH's patronage of the people in the arid wilderness. When they became satisfied (*śb'*), Hos 13:6 and Dt 8:13-14 maintain that the people's hearts became proud (Dt 8:14, *wĕrām lĕbābekā*; Hos 13:6, *wayyārom libbām*. Cf. Dt 32:15) and they forgot YHWH (*škḥ*. Cf. also Dt 32:18). We compare 13:6b, "Therefore, they forgot me," with R2's own previous statement in 2:15b, describing the wife/Israel: "And me she forgot."366

Moreover, the R2 description in 13:6a, that in the wilderness YHWH "pastured" his people (*rě'îtîm*), correlates with his 4:16b addition of hope where YHWH will "pasture" Israel (*yir'ēm*) like a lamb in broad pasture.367

In 13:7-8, R2 pronounces the punishment, with which YHWH will now subject the people because of their offenses. His description is reminiscent of R2's tradition, 5:14:

> For I will be like a lion (*kaššaḥal*) to Ephraim,
> and like a young lion (*kakkĕpir*) to the house of Judah.
> I, yes I, will rend (*ṭrp*) and go away.
> I will carry off and none shall rescue.
>   (Hos 5:14)

R2, however, expands this description to include more ravenous beasts. He wishes to intensify the castigation of the people in view of their great suffering and humiliation incurred in the exile:

> I will be to them like a lion (*kĕmô-šāḥal*)
> Like a leopard along the way I will lurk.

> I will fall upon them like a bereaved she-bear.
> I will tear open the cavity of their heart.
> I will devour them like a lion (*kĕlābî*),
>   a wild beast which will rend them.
>   (Hos 13:7-8)

We parallel Hos 13:7-8 with Dt 32:23-24 which, like Hos
13:7-8, describes YHWH's punishment of a people who
arrogantly forgot the One who cared for them in the
wilderness:

> And I will heap evils upon them.
> I will spend my arrows upon them.
> They shall be wasted with hunger
>   and devoured with burning heat
>   and poisonous pestilence:
> And I will send *the teeth of beasts against them*
>   *with the venom of crawling things of the dust.*
>   (Dt 32:23-24)

Scholars have related the imagery of the devouring animals in
both Hos 13:7-8 and Dt 32:23-24 to Ancient Near Eastern
treaty curses which include similar threats, should one of the
parties break the covenant.[368] The language which R2 utilizes
for his vivid description of punishment is thus the language of
covenant, even though he does not explicitly mention the
word, "covenant."[369] At the beginning of his composition in
Hos 2:20a, R2 describes the renewal of covenant in terms of
animal imagery:

> "And I will make for them a covenant on that day with the
> beasts of the field (*ḥayyat haśśādeh*, cf. Hos 13:8), the birds of
> the air, and the creeping things of the ground." (Hos 2:20a)

Here, the renewal of covenant results in the pacification of
nature, while the covenantal breach which R2 describes in
13:7-8 generates the savagery of nature. We further note that
in his 4:3 addition, R2 includes "the beasts of the field (*ḥayyat
haśśādeh*), the birds of the air, and even fish of the sea," as
being affected in the covenantal *rîb* announced in 4:1.[370]

D. Hos 13:9-11

13:9   *šîḥetkā yiśrā'ēl*
        kî-bî bě'ezrekā
13:10   *'ĕhî malkěkā 'ēpô'*
        wěyôšî'ăkā běkol-'ārêkā
        wěšōpěṭêkā 'ăšer 'āmartā
        těnâ-lî melek wěśārîm
13:11   *'etten-lěkā melek bě'appî*
        wě'eqqaḥ bě'ebrātî

13:9   It is your destruction, O Israel,
        that you are against me,
        against your help.[371]
13:10   Where is your king, then, who will save you?
        ('Ehyeh is your king now and he will save you.)
        In all your cities, your judges,
        Of whom you said,
        "Give me a king and princes"?
13:11   I gave you a king in my anger.
        I took him away in my wrath.

These very difficult verses have been the subject of differing opinions and consequent emendations.[372] If we analyse these verses from the point of view of the final redactor, their meaning can be much clearer. In commenting on 13:7a, Andersen and Freedman suggest that the form *'ĕhî*, "I will be," may be a pun on the divine name *'ehyeh* both here in 13:7 and in 13:10 and 13:14, in which it seems to be an interrogative particle.[373] Such wordplays on the divine name is characteristic of R2 commentary.[374] By means of an *'ĕhî/'ehyeh* paronomasia, R2 is able to articulate two different streams of thought in 13:10 (and in 13:14 which we will discuss below).

On one level, he poses a question, "Where is your king who will save you? In all your cities, your judges, of whom you said 'Give me a king and princes'?" During the exile, the people were bereft of their leadership.[375] R2 already had referred to this absence in 3:4: "For the children of Israel shall dwell many days without king or prince, without sacrifice or pillar, without ephod or teraphim."376

On another level, however, R2 makes an assertion: "*Ehyeh* will be your king now, and he will save you (*yôšî'ăkâ*).377 He emphasized already in 13:4 that the people have no savior (*môšîa'*) other than YHWH their God.

Several scholars have pointed out the contact points between Hos 13:10-11 and the 1 Sam 8:6-8 narrative regarding the original institution of the Israelite monarchy:378

> The thing displeased Samuel when *they said, "Give us a king to govern us (ka'ăšer 'ămĕrû tĕnā-lānû melek lĕšopţēnû)."* Samuel prayed to the Lord. And the Lord said to Samuel, "Hearken to the voice of the people in all that they say to you, for they have not rejected you, *but they have rejected me from being king over them.* According to all the deeds which they have done to me, from the day I brought them out of Egypt even to this day, forsaking me and serving other gods, so they are also doing to you." (1 Sam 8:6-8, RSV)

Regarding 1 Sam 8, Clements remarks that "the theocratic ideal expressed in 1 Sam 8:8, and the assumption that this ideal may necessitate a very sharp criticism of the monarchy, represents a viewpoint of the Deuteronomists of the exilic age who were able to consider the institution in retrospect."379 Ezek 20:33-34 expresses similar exilic notions about the kingship of YHWH:

> "As I live, says the Lord God, surely with a mighty hand and an outstretched arm, and with wrath poured out, *I will be king over you ('emlôk 'ălêkem).* I will bring you out from the peoples and gather you out of the countries where you are scattered, with a mighty hand and an outstretched arm, and with wrath poured out." (Ezek 20:33-34, RSV)

In all three texts, Hos 13:10-11, 1 Sam 8:6-8, and Ezek 20:33-34, the concern is not simply that YHWH is king but the fact that he alone *manifests* his kingship through saving acts. According to 1 Sam 8:6-8, the people have rejected YHWH as king, in spite of his saving activity towards them, "from the day I brought them out of Egypt even to this day." In language reminiscent of the first Exodus,[380] Ezek 20:33-34 describes the new Exodus from the lands of exile. YHWH asserts his sovereignty bringing the exiles out "with mighty hand and outstretched arm and wrath poured out."

In Hos 13:10, then, R2 expresses by means of wordplay both a sarcastic disillusionment with the human institution of the monarchy - *Where* is your king then who will save you? - and an affirmation - *"Ehyeh* is your king now." He is king precisely in the fact that he, and he alone, "will save you."

E. *Hos 13:14*

13:14   *miyyad šěʾôl ʾepdēm*
      mimmāwet ʾegʾālēm
     ʾĕhî děbārêkā māwet
     ʾĕhî qoṭobkā šěʾôl
     nōham yissātēr mēʿēnāy

13:14   Shall I ransom them from the clutches of Sheol?
     (From the clutches of Sheol I will ransom them.)
     Shall I redeem them from Death?
     (From Death I will redeem them.)
     Where is your plague, O Death?
     ('Ehyeh will be your plague, O Death.)
     Where is your sting, Sheol?
     ('Ehyeh will be your sting, Sheol.)
     Compassion is hidden from my eyes.
     (Vengeance is hidden from my eyes.)

The equivocatory character of 13:10-11 is also present in R2's final commentary of the chapter, 13:14. The majority of scholars usually emend the ambiguous *ʾĕhî* in v. 14b to the interrogative *ʾayyēh*, "where?," and interpret the whole verse as a question which implies a threat.[381] Together with the interrogative meaning of 13:10-11, R2 does, on one level, intend a question to make a rhetorical point: "Where is your king then that he may save you? Shall *I, YHWH*, ransom them from the power of Sheol? Shall *I, YHWH*, redeem them from

Death?" The mention of Death (*māwet*) here in 13:14 refers
back to the R2 remark at the beginning of Hos 13, that
Ephraim had incurred guilt through Baal and died (13:1,
wayyāmōt). R2 implies in the question that YHWH has the
power to ransom and redeem his people. YHWH can, however,
withhold this power since, given the people's apostasy, their
"death" is justified. This being so, YHWH can summon the
plagues and stings of Death and Sheol to wreak their havoc
upon his faithless people. The ambiguous word, *nōḥam*, in
YHWH's final statement would then suggest that YHWH's
"compassion" is hidden from his eyes.[382]

Nevertheless, on another level, R2 intends the literal
meaning of 13:14 which has no interrogative particle.[383] Read
together with the paronomasia involving *'ĕhî/'ehyeh* in 13:10-
11, R2 states that 'Ehyeh will be their king; that he will save
them; that his sovereignty extends even over the cosmic
powers, Sheol and Death, themselves:

> From the clutches of Sheol I will ransom them.
> From Death I will redeem them.[384]

As in 13:10, *'ĕhî* in 13:14b becomes a wordplay on the divine
appellative:[385]

> 'Ehyeh will be your plague, O Death.
> 'Ehyeh will be your sting, Sheol.

Moreover, the ambiguous *nōḥam* can now mean that
"vengeance" against the people dissolves as YHWH exerts his
kingship over the ultimate powers of Sheol and Death
themselves.[386] R2's representation of YHWH from this
vantage point would accord with his portrayal of YHWH in
Hos 11. Here, YHWH is a father who is unable to contemplate
the thought of his son's final ruin.[387]

F. The Redactional Thrust of Hos 13

The ambiguity of Hos 13, which is reflected in scholars'
various interpretations of it, is intentionally built into the

chapter by our final redactor. R2 achieves this ambiguity
through his characteristic paronomasia. On one hand, the
chapter indicts the people for its history of flagrant
transgressions against their God. This history is the same as
that recorded by the deuteronomistic historians. The God who
had brought Israel out of Egypt, who cared for them in the
wilderness also has the power to destroy them. He had warned
the people through the prophets to forswear their idolatry.
However, their persistence in sin offers YHWH no recourse
but punishment. Their present exile attests to the fact that no
earthly king or leader can rescue them from the just
chastisement of their God.

Although the exile is already a reality at the time of R2's
composition, although the suffering and torment of the exile is
so great that it seems that the powers of Death and Sheol
threaten to annihilate the nation, R2 still offers hints of hope
in this chapter. The equivocality of the R2 redaction permits
another level of interpretation. At this level, R2 affirms the
sovereignty of YHWH which has been manifested throughout
their history, in spite of their apostasy. It began with
YHWH's momentous act, Israel's liberation from Egypt, and
has perdured since then. For R2, the King who has worked
concretely in their past history is YHWH. He is King because
he alone is able to save them from their present condition.
True to his previous redaction to make his tradition more
cosmic in scope,[388] R2 raises the affirmation of YHWH's
sovereignty to the cosmic level. YHWH alone can ransom
Israel from Death itself, from the clutches of Sheol. Indeed,
'Ehyeh will be Sheol's destruction.

CHAPTER SEVEN

The Composition of Hos 4-10, 12-13: Earlier Stages of the Tradition

With the literary structure and theological thrust of our final redactor having been discerned, the task remains to determine the earlier stages of the tradition in Hos 4-14. Minus the two major R2 chapters, Hos 11 and 14 which sectioned off his Hos 4-11 and 12-14 complexes, one will find the earlier stages of the tradition located in Hos 4-10 and 12-13. It is this material which R2 had incorporated into his own work, imposing upon it a completely new structure and literary context. It is this material which R2 had preserved, mitigated, qualified and expanded.

In our discussion of the prior literary stages of the Hos 1-2 complex, we have ascertained three earlier phases of the tradition. Beginning with the latest stage, we have the first redactor, R1. This redactor seems to share the same deuteronomistic Judean orientation as our final redactor, R2, manifesting a particular concern for cult and cult practices. R1, however, seems to be pre-exilic while R2 is exilic. R1 edits a body of material composed of a collector, (C), and of Hosean sayings, (H). The collector was most likely a disciple of the prophet Hosea. His major addition was the call narrative of Hos 1, which, we argued, was geared to legitimate the ministry of his master and, at the same time, his own work in collecting and preserving his sayings.[1]

In our examination of the final redaction, we presented our understanding of the literary history of each chapter. The reader may have noticed that we were not able to detect any appreciable editing by C in Hos 4-14. The texts beyond the Hos 1-3 complex did not give clues to the presence of his hand. It appears that C's major contribution was the call narrative with which he prefaced the book. This addition constituted a fundamental change in C's Hosean tradition. With his call narrative of the prophet commanded to wed a harlotrous wife, C interprets the Hosean tradition as an accusation of YHWH, the faithful *husband*, against Israel, his faithless *wife*. This metaphor is expanded by R1 and R2 and has become the most memorable aspect of the Book of Hosea. Moreover, C is responsible for inserting a note of hope into his tradition. The marriage vows renewed by YHWH in 2:21-22a are picked up and expanded by R2 and, in his hands, raised to a cosmic plane.[2] C may have been responsible for the arrangement of the Hosean sayings. However, at this point this matter would simply be speculation.

What remains of the earlier stages, then, is the contribution of R1 on the sayings which we attribute to Hosea. We will discuss in this chapter the literary-theological motives of R1 and how he had modified the Hosean sayings for his own readership. Moreover, we will try to determine the original intention of the Hosean material to understand how this material became a springboard for later redaction. In order to distinguish the earlier stages from the final stage of composition, we will use the sigla *, as we did in our previous discussion of Hos 1* and 2*. Anticipating our results we have put in *italics* the sayings attributed to Hosea.

I.   The Earlier Stages of Hos 4*

A.   The Editorial History of Hos 4*

H	C	R1	(R2)
		4:1-2	(4:3)
4:4*		4:4*-5a	
4:5b			(4:6a)
		4:6b	(4:7-12a)
4:12bA			(4:12bB-13a)
		4:13b	(4:14)
		4:15-16a	(4:16b)
		4:17a	(4:17b)
		4:18ab**	
4:18b**-19a		4:19b	

* *kōhēn* = R1
** *qālôn maginnêhā* = H

B. *Reconstructed Text of Hos 4**

4:1   *šim'û děbar-yhwh běnê yiśrā'ēl*
   kî rîb lyhwh 'im-yôšěbê hā'āreṣ
   kî 'ên 'ěmet wě'ên-ḥesed
   wě'ên-da'at 'ělōhîm bā'āreṣ

4:2   *'ālōh wěkaḥēš wěrāṣōaḥ*
   wěgānōb wěnā'ōp pārāṣû
   wědāmîm bědāmîm nāgā'û

4:4   *'ak 'îš 'al-yārēb*
   wě'al-yôkaḥ 'îš
   wě'imměkā kim(a) rîbî kōhēn
    (MT:wě'amměkā kîmrîbê kōhēn)[3]

4:5a   *wěkāšaltā hayyôm*
   wěkāšal gam-nābî' 'imměkā lāylâ

4:5b   *wědāmîtî 'immekā*

4:6b   *kî-'attâ hadda'at mā'astā*
   wě'em'āsě'kā mikkahēn lî
   wattiškaḥ tôrat 'ělōhêkā
   'eškaḥ bānêkā gam-'ănî

4:12bA   *kî rûaḥ zěnûnîm hiṭ'āh (MT: hiṭ'â)*[4]

4:13b   *'al-kēn tiznênâ běnôtêkem*
   wěkallôtêkem těnā'apnâ

4:15   *'im-zōneh 'attâ yiśrā'ēl*
   'al-ye'šam yěhûdâ
   wě'al-tābō'û haggilgāl
   wě'al-ta'ălû bêt 'āwen
   wě'al-tiššābě'û ḥay-yhwh

4:16a   *kî kěpārâ sōrērâ*
   sārar yiśrā'ēl

4:17a   *ḥăbûr 'ăṣabbîm 'eprayim*

4:18   *sār sob'ām*
   haznēh hiznû
    'āhăbû hēbû
   qālôn māginnêhā ṣārar

4:19   *rûaḥ 'awwātāh (MT: 'ōtāh)*[5] *biknāpêhā*
   wěyēbōšû mizzibḥôtām

4:1   Hear the word of YHWH, O people of Israel,
For YHWH has a dispute with the inhabitants of
the land.
For there is no faithfulness, no devotion,
    or knowledge of God in the land.

4:2   Swearing, lying, murdering,
    stealing and adultery break out.
One bloody deed follows another . . .

4:4   *Let no one dispute.*
Let no one reprove.
Indeed, with you is my complaint, O Priest!

4:5a   You stumble by day
    and the prophet stumbles with you by night.

4:5b   *I will destroy your mother . . .*

4:6b   Because you have rejected knowledge,
    I will reject you from being priest to me.
Because you have forgotten the law of your God,
    I will also reject your children.

4:12bA   *For a spirit of harlotry has led her* astray . . .*

4:13b   Therefore, your daughters play the harlot
    and your daughters-in-law commit
    adultery . . .

4:15   Though you play the harlot, O Israel,
    let not Judah incur guilt.
Do not go to Gilgal.
Do not go up to Beth Awen.
Do not swear, "As YHWH lives!"

4:16a   For like a cow is stubborn,
    Israel is stubborn . . .

4:17a   Ephraim is allied to idols . . .

4:18   He turns aside with their drunkards.
They surely play the harlot.
    They make love continually.
Shame has wrapped her shields.

4:19a   *A spirit of lust* is in her skirts.*

4:19b   They shall behave shamefully at their altars.

C. The Hosean Tradition: Hos 4:4*, 5b, 12bA, 18**-19a

We had already pointed out the notorious textual difficulties in this chapter when we discussed its final redaction. We had remarked then that scholars acknowledge the redactional nature of the chapter's composition. On this basis, we tried to establish the structure and theological orientation of its present redacted state.[6] The remaining tradition reconstructed above is also not without its textual difficulties. We think, however, that these aporiae indicate different compositional hands.

The chapter concludes with puzzling intrusions of feminine suffixes in 4:18b, *māginnêhā*, "her shields," and in 4:19a, *'ôtāh*, the fem. accusative particle, and *biknāpêhā*, "in her wings" or "skirts". Furthermore, 4:5b contains an equally problematic reference to "your mother," *'immekā*. Commentators try to resolve these difficulties in a number of ways, e.g. by emendation[7] or simply by assigning them to later redaction.[8]

We would agree with Junker that the mention of "your mother" in 4:4 refers back to "your mother" in Hos 2:4.[9] Moreover, we would agree with Budde that the feminine forms in 4:18-19 continue the image of the adulterous woman in Hos 1-3.[10] This image, we think, is also contained in 4:12bA. Here, the MT and the LXX have no suffix: *kî rûaḥ zĕnûnîm hit'â*, "A spirit of harlotry has led astray." Yet, to harmonize the text, scholars would emend the text to read a third masculine plural suffix, *hit'ām*, "has led *them* astray," following the Targ., Syr., and Vul.[11] However, the reference to the "spirit of harlotry," *rûaḥ zĕnûnîm*, accords well with the image of the *rûaḥ* in 4:19, which describes the "spirit of lust in *her* skirts." With a minor repointing which would not change the consonantal text but simply add a *dagesh* in the final *hē* of *hit'â*, we would read *hit'āh*: "a spirit of harlotry has led *her* astray." Furthermore, with Andersen and Freedman, we would also repoint the feminine accusative particle, *'ôtāh* in 4:19 to *'awwātāh*, "her longing, lust."[12] What we have then is a relatively self-contained, rhythmic discourse:

4:4	'ak 'îš 'āl-yāreb	5 syllables
	wĕ'al-yōkaḥ 'îš	5
	wĕ'immĕkā kim(a) rîbî[13]	7
4:5b	wĕdāmîtî 'immekā	7
4:12bA	kî rûaḥ zĕnûnîm hit'āh	8
4:18bB	qālôn māginnêhā ṣārar	8
4:19a	rûaḥ 'awwātāh biknāpêhā	9

4:4	Let no one dispute.
	Let no one reprove.
	Indeed, with you is my complaint!
4:5b	I will destroy your mother,
4:12bA	for a spirit of harlotry has led her astray.
4:18bB	Shame has wrapped her shields.
4:19a	A spirit of lust is in her skirts.

We would attribute this saying to the prophet Hosea. This saying was extensively expanded and certainly modified by two subsequent redactors. Nevertheless, the clues to this saying were already apparent in the transmitted text. Several points would support the attribution to Hosea. The first is the most obvious one, that it continues the motif of the faithless mother ('im) in the Hosean tradition which, we argued, is found in 2:4aA, 4b-5, 7b, 12:[14]

2:4aA	Plead (rîbû) with you mother (bĕ'immĕkem), plead.
2:4b	that she remove her harlotry (zĕnûnêhā) from her face.
	and her adultery from between her breasts,
2:5	lest I strip her naked
	and set her out as on the day of her birth.
	I will make her like a wilderness,
	change her into an arid land,
	and slay her with thirst.
2:7b	For she said,
	"I will go after my lovers,
	who give me my bread and my water,
	my wool and my flax,
	my oil and my drink."

2:12   And now I will expose her genitals
        in the sight of her lovers.
        No one will rescue her out of my hand.
        (wĕ'îš lō'-yaṣṣîlennâ miyyādî)

Hos 4:4 would continue this saying, picking up the indeterminate 'îš, "one" from 2:12b: wĕ'îš lō'-yaṣṣîlennâ, "no one will rescue her," (2:12b)/'ak 'îš 'al-yārēb wĕ'al-yôkaḥ 'îš, "Let no one dispute. Let no one reprove," (4:4a).   The two sayings, furthermore, parallel each other. The rîb which was *commanded* of the hearer in 2:4, "Plead (rîbû) with your mother," is now *addressed* to the hearer in 4:4b: "With *you* is my complaint (rîbî)." At this point in the Hosean text, the identity of the addressee is unclear. We recall that this was the same case for 2:4. In the present redacted context, the addressees became the children of Hosea by Gomer, described in Hos 1:2–2:3.[15] Moreover, the identity of this mother is still uncertain, although, as we stated above, we will suggest that she is Jacob's wife, Rachel, who personifies the harlotrous nation.[16]

D. R1 Redaction

We turn now to the R1 redaction on this Hosean tradition. Scholars already note the secondary character of Hos 4:1-3.[17] We had discussed 4:3 above as an enlargement of 4:1-2 by the final redactor.[18] Hos 4:1-2 forms R1's own introduction to the rest of Hosea's collected sayings. He picks up the rîb from 4:4 and formulates the rîb again, but now expressly in terms of the covenant.   The attributes cited in 4:1b which the inhabitants of the land lack, viz. faithfulness, love, and knowledge of God, should be understood in the context of covenant.[19]   We recall that "knowledge of God" was a particular deuteronomistic concern of our final redactor (Cf. 2:22b, 6:3, 13:5). So, too, does this concern figure prominently with R1 who also shares deuteronomistic sympathies. The infinitive absolutes in 4:2 articulating sins against one's neighbor are all violations of covenantal stipulations.[20] We compare Hos 4:2 with Jer 7:9-10:

"Will you steal (*gānōb*), murder (*rāṣōaḥ*), commit adultery (*nā'ōp*), swear falsely, burn incense to baal, and go after other gods that you have not known, and then come and stand before me in this house, which is called by my name, and say, 'We are delivered!' only to go on doing all these abominations?" (Jer 7:9-10)

According to Cardellini, the secondary hand in Jer 7:9 is very similar to the hand in Hos 4:2 whose chief interest is the morality of the Decalogue.[21] We will see that his concern for the covenant and law, which R1 introduces into the Hosean collection, permeates the rest of his editorials.

This interest in covenant and law appears especially in 4:4*-5, and 6b. R1 focuses the *rîb* which he addressed to Israel in 4:1 on the "priest," *kōhēn*, which he inserts after the *'immēkā kim(a) rîbî* of his Hosean tradition.[22] R1 accuses the priest of "stumbling by day," in 4:5. The use of *kšl*, "to stumble," here has a figurative meaning. We compare it with the final redactor's conclusion to the book in 14:10b:

For the ways of YHWH are straight
and the upright walk in them.
But the foolish stumble (*kšl*) in them.

We noted that "walking in the ways" of YHWH is characteristically Deuteronomic, describing the adherence to the commandments and law of YHWH.[23] R1 accords with R2 in describing the accusation against the priest as "stumbling." True to his deuteronomistic orientation, he specifies in 4:6b that the priest had rejected knowledge (*d't*) and had forgotten (*škḥ*) the *tôrâ* of his God. According to Dt 31:9-13, the priests were entrusted with the *tôrâ* and were responsible for proclaiming it to the people:

"And Moses wrote this law (*hattôrâ*), and gave it to the priests (*hakkōhănîm*), the sons of Levi, who carried the ark of the covenant of the Lord, and to all the elders of Israel. And Moses commanded them, 'At the end of seven years, at the set time of the year of release, at the feast of booths, when all Israel comes to appear before the Lord your God at the place which he will choose, you shall read this law (*hattôrâ*) before all Israel in their hearing.'" (Dt 31:9-11, RSV. Cf. also Dt 33:10; 17:18)

In castigating the priests, Mal 2:7-9 echoes with the priest's role described in Hos 4:4*-5, 6b and Dt 31:9-11:

> For the lips of the *priest* shall guard knowledge (*šmr d't*), and they (the people) should seek *tôrâ* from his mouth, for he is the messenger of the Lord of Hosts. But you have turned aside from the way. You have made many *stumble* (*kšl*) in the *tôrâ*. You have violated the covenant of Levi, says the Lord of hosts, and so I will make you despised and abased before all the people, because you have not kept my ways, but have shown partiality in *tôrâ*. (Mal 2:7-9)

In 4:5aB, R1 includes the prophet in the priest's guilt.[24] The R1 portrayal of the prophet, as we see here and later in 9:7, differs from R2's more positive understanding of the prophets in 6:5, 9:8, and 12:14. R1's description accords more with the pre-exilic situation in the Jerusalem temple where priest and prophet made up the cultic personnel. Jeremiah in particular accuses its priests and prophets of neglecting their duties and leading the people away from YHWH (Jer 2:8; 5:31; 6:13; 8:10; 14:18; 18:18; 23:11. Cf. also Isa 28:7 and Mic 3:11).

R1 commentary in 4:13b is directly linked with his Hosean tradition in 4:12bA: "for a spirit of harlotry (*zĕnûnîm*) has led her astray." Picking up *znh* from 4:12bA, R1 points out to the priest that "therefore, your daughters play the harlot (*tiznênâ*) and your daughters-in-law commit adultery." The spirit of harlotry which has infected "her" now affects the daughters of the priest and his daughters-in-law, e.g. the wives of the priest's sons who, according to 4:6b, will be forgotten by YHWH.

R1's next editorial in 4:15 continues this theme of harlotry. Addressing the northern kingdom of Israel, he exhorts:

> "Though you play the harlot, O Israel,
>   Let not Judah incur guilt.
> Do not go to Gilgal.

> Do not go up to Beth Awen.
> Do not swear, 'As YHWH lives.'"

Because of the reference to Judah and the similarity between Hos 4:15 and Amos 5:4-5, a significant number of commentators think that the verse is partially or entirely the work of a Judean editor to make Hosea's words relevant for a Judean congregation.[25]

More specifically, Day and Fohrer specify the deuteronomic period for the redaction, since the hostility to northern sanctuaries like Bethel and Gilgal seems to indicate a deuteronomic propensity toward the central sanctuary in Jerusalem (Cf. Dt 12:1-14).[26] The resemblance to Am 5:4-5 is striking. Note the wordplays on Gilgal and Bethel in Am 5:5:

> "Seek me and live;
>   But do not seek Bethel,
> And do not enter Gilgal
>   or cross over into Beer-sheba.
> For Gilgal shall surely go into exile.
>   (*kî haggilgāl gālōh yigleh*)
> And Bethel shall come to nought
>   (*ûbêt 'ēl yihyeh lĕ'āwen*)
>   (Am 5:4-5)

Lust and Coote think that Am 5:4-5 is a composition of a later redactor working in the 7th Cent. during the time of Josiah.[27] In fact, some have associated the 7th Cent. redaction of Amos with the first Josianic edition of the Deuteronomistic History (DTR 1).[28] We had suggested earlier that R1 seems to have affinities with the Josianic author of the DH.[29]

Against this background, Hos 4:15 is most intelligible. R1 considers the cult places and practices of the North as "harlotry." For him, Jerusalem is "the place where YHWH your God chooses from all the tribes to set his name there, for his dwelling, (that place) you shall seek and there you shall enter" (Dt 12:15). It is not the illegitimate sanctuaries and priesthood established by Jeroboam at Bethel, Dan and other northern shrines (I Kgs 12:28-33). Thus, R1 enjoins his

readership, "Do not go to Gilgal. Do not go up to Beth Awen.
Do not swear, 'As YHWH lives'".

Scholars have pointed out that Beth-Awen in 4:15, lit.
"house of trouble, iniquity," is a parasonancy on Beth-El,
"house of God" (Cf. the wordplay on 'ēl/'āwen in Amos 5:5).30
Like R2, our first redactor, R1 seems to have a fondness for
paronomasia. This is seen particularly in 4:16a, 17a, 18**,
19b which continue the accusation against *Israel's* harlotry
begun in 4:15a:

4:16a	*kî kĕpārâ sōrērâ*
	sārar yiśrā'ēl
4:17a	*ḥăbûr 'ăṣabbîm 'eprayim*
4:18**	*sār sob'ām*
	haznēh hiznû
	'āhăbû hēbû
	(qālôn māginnêhā sārar
4:19a	*rûaḥ 'awwātāh biknāpêhā)*
	wĕyēbōšû mizzibḥôtām

4:16a	For like a cow is stubborn
	Israel is stubborn.
4:17a	Ephraim is allied to idols.
4:18	He turns aside with their drunkards.
	They surely play the harlot.
	They make love continually.
	(Shame has wrapped her shields,
4:19a	A spirit of lust is in her skirts.)
4:19b	They shall behave shamefully at their altars.

R2 interpretive redaction in 4:16a, 17b had rather
obscured the paronomastic sequence of R1 redaction on H.
With *kî* beginning 4:16a, R1 refers back to his address to *Israel*
in 4:15. With a paronomastic buildup of words, *sōrērâ sārar
yiśrā'ēl*, R1 attacks the stubbornness (*srr*) of Israel. He
continues in 4:17a with a parasonancy between *kĕpārâ*, "like a
cow," and *'eprayim*.31 What follows in 4:18 is a series of three
parasonantic wordpairs: *sār sob'ām, haznēh hiznû, 'āhăbû
hēbû*.32 With a wordplay on *srr*, "stubborn," in 4:16a, R1

describes Ephraim as "turning aside," *swr*, with the inebriated participants in the idolatrous cult. The verb, *swr*, is used frequently in Deuteronomy and the Deuteronomistic History to describe the people "turning aside" from the "ways" of YHWH to worship other gods.[33] The intent of R1 redaction in these verses is to interpret the references to "harlotry" in his Hosean tradition (4:12bA, 18**, and 19a) as Israel's polluted *cult*, even though the Hosean references to harlotry were probably not descriptive of the cultic sphere.[34]

E. Summary

From the clues which the text itself presents to us, we have determined that the core Hosean tradition continues the imagery of the harlotrous mother which was begun in the Hosean tradition in Hos 2:4. Who this woman is or represents, who are those addressed in the saying, and what precisely is the nature of the woman's harlotry are not known at this point.

In the hands of the first redactor of this tradition, R1, the saying becomes an accusation of transgressions of the law (4:1-2). This accusation is focused particularly on leaders in the cultic sphere, the priests and the prophets (4:4*, 5a, 6b, 13b). The "harlotry" described in the Hosean tradition is interpreted by R1 as a polluted cult conducted in the illegitimate shrines of the North, and not in the central sanctuary in Jerusalem (4:15, 16a, 17a, 18**, 19b). The character of the redaction indicates a deuteronomistic provenance around the time of Josiah's reform.

II. The Earlier Stages of Hos 5*

A. The Editorial History of Hos 5*

H	C	R1	(R2)
5:1-2a			(5:2b)
5:3			(5:4)
5:5abA		5:5bB-7	

5:8-13a   (5:13b)
5:14   (5:15)

B. Reconstructed Text of Hos 5*

Since the R1 redaction of this chapter is minimal, we have
placed R1 redaction in *italics* rather than the Hosean
tradition.

5:1a   *šim'û zō't hakkōhănîm*
        wĕhaqšîbû bêt yiśrā'ēl
        ûbêt hammelek ha'ăzînû
5:1b   *kî lākem hammišpāṭ*
        kî-paḥ hĕyîtem lĕmiṣpâ
        wĕrešet pĕrûśâ 'al-tābôr
5:2a   *wĕšaḥat baššiṭṭim he'mîqû*
        (Mt: wĕšaḥăṭâ śēṭîm he'mîqû)[35]
5:3   *'ănî yāda'tî 'eprayim*
        wĕyiśrā'ēl lō'-nikḥad mimmennî
        kî 'attâ hiznêtā 'eprayim
        niṭmā' yiśrā'ēl
5:5a   *wĕ'ānâ gĕ'ôn-yiśrā'ēl bĕpānāyw*
5:5bA   *wĕyiśrā'ēl wĕ'eprayim yikkāšĕlû bĕ'ăwônām*
5:5bB   <u>*kāšal gam-yĕhûdâ 'immām*</u>
5:6   <u>*bĕṣō'nām ûbibqārām yēlĕkû*</u>
        <u>*lĕbaqqēš 'et-yhwh*</u>
        <u>*wĕlō' yimṣā'û ḥālaṣ mēhem*</u>
5:7   <u>*byhwh bāgādû*</u>
        <u>*kî bānîm zārîm yālādû*</u>
        <u>*'attâ yō'kĕlēm ḥōdeš 'et-ḥelqêhem*</u>
5:8   *tiq'û šôpār baggib'â*
        ḥăṣōṣĕrâ bārāmâ
        hārî'û bêt 'āwen
        'aḥărêkā binyāmîn
5:9   *'eprayim lĕšammâ tihyeh bĕyôm tôkēḥā*
        bĕšibṭê yiśrā'ēl hôda'tî ne'ĕmānâ
5:10   *hāyû śārê yĕhûdâ kĕmassîgê gĕbûl*
        'ălêhem 'ešpôk kammayim 'ebrātî

5:11   'āšûq 'eprayim rĕṣûṣ mišpāṭ
        kî hô'îl hālak 'aḥărê ṣāw
5:12   wa'ănî kā'āš lĕ'eprayim
        wĕkārāqāb lĕbêt yĕhûdâ
5:13a   wayyar' 'eprayim 'et-ḥolyô
        wîhûdâ 'et-mĕzōrô
        wayyēlek 'eprayim 'el-'aššûr
        wayišlaḥ 'el-melek yārēb
5:14   kî 'ānōkî kaššaḥal lĕ'eprayim
        wĕkakkĕpîr lĕbêt yĕhûdâ
        'ănî 'ănî 'eṭrōp wĕ'ēlēk
        'eśśā' wĕ'ên maṣṣîl

5:1a   Hear this, O priests!
        Pay heed, O house of Israel!
        Listen, O house of the king
5:1b   for the judgment pertains to you.
        For you have been a trap at Mizpah
        And a net spread upon Tabor
5:2a   And a pit dug deep in Shittim* . . .
5:3   I know Ephraim,
            and Israel is not hidden from me.
        For now, you have played the harlot, Ephraim.
            Israel is defiled . . .
5:5a   The pride of Israel testifies against him.
5:5bA   Israel and Ephraim will stumble in their guilt.
5:bB   *Judah also has stumbled with them*
5:6   *With their flocks and with their herds they go
            to seek YHWH,*
        *but they will not find him. He has withdrawn
            from them.*
5:7   *Against YHWH they have been traitorous,
            for they have engendered foreign children.*
        *And now he will devour them with their portions
            at the New Moon.*
5:8   Blow the horn in Gibeah!
            the trumpet in Ramah!
        Sound the alarm, Beth Awen!
            Behind you, O Benjamin!

5:9   Ephraim, you will become a desolation on the day
of rebuke.
Among the tribes of Israel
I make known what is sure.

5:10   The princes of Judah have become like those
who remove the landmarkers.
Upon them I will pour out
my fury like floodwaters.

5:11   Ephraim is oppressed.
Justice is abused,
for he is intent on going after filth.[36]

5:12   I will be like a moth to Ephraim
and like rot to the house of Judah.

5:13a   Ephraim saw his wound,
Judah, his oozing infection.
Ephraim went to Assyria,
and sent to the Great King . . .

5:14   Yes, I will be like a lion to Ephraim,
and like a young lion to the house of Judah.
I, yes I, will rend and go away.
I will carry off and no one will rescue . . .

C. R1 Redaction: Hos 5:5bB-7

Hos 5:5 has presented several problems to commentators.
Many think that the second reference to "Israel" in v. 5bA is
metrically superfluous. Thus, several omit it as a doublet.[37]
We think, however, that the reference to Israel is authentic.
To remove the second subject, "Israel," would necessitate a
problematic change in the plural forms, *yikkāšĕlû baʿăwônām*,
"*they* will stumble in *their* guilt."

Nevertheless, we are in good company with a number of
scholars who regard 5:5bB as an actualizing addition for a
Judean readership.[38] We would ascribe 5:5bB to the pen of
R1. It shares a structure similar to the R1 editorial in 4:5a:

4:5a   *wĕkāšal gam-nābî' ʿimmĕkā lāylâ*
5:5bB   *kāšal gam-yĕhûdâ ʿimmām*

4:5a   The prophet also stumbles with you at night.
5:5bB   Judah also stumbles with them.

Through his addition R1 includes Judah in YHWH's judgment against Israel and Ephraim. Moreover, R1 expands this judgment with 5:6-7, which is notably distinct in its present context by its third person reference to YHWH in a saying which is otherwise an obviously first person address by YHWH.[39] Like his editorials in Hos 4*, R1 interprets his tradition in light of cult.[40] The people will go with their sacrifical offerings to seek (*bqš*) YHWH. They will not find him, since he has withdrawn from them. We compare Hos 5:6 with Dt 4:29:

Dt 4:29   But from there, you will seek (*bqš*) YHWH your
           God and you will find him (*mṣ'*),
           if you search after him with all your heart.

Hos 5:6   With their flocks and with their herds, they go
           to seek (*bqš*) YHWH, but they will not find
           (*mṣ'*) him.

R2 will later mitigate R1's cynicism in v. 6 by his 5:15--6:3 expansion. For R2, YHWH has departed from his people, but only until (*'ad*) they realize their guilt and seek (*bqš*) him with a repentant spirit (5:15).[41] R2 thus qualifies R1 by adding a conditional note of hope.

D. The Hosean Tradition

In 1919, Alt published a perceptive reading of Hos 5:8--6:6, in which he identified separate oracles which pertained to the events surrounding the 8th century Syro-Ephraimite war.[42] His theory is adopted by a number of scholars.[43] Certainly, Alt did demonstrate that 5:13-14 could reflect the 2 Kgs 15:19-20 account of Menachem's tribute to Pul of Assyria.[44] His argument that Hos 5:8-10 refers to the annexation of Benjaminite territory by Judah is plausible.[45] It is significant, however, that Alt did not include 5:1-7 in his discussion, stating that "no one nowadays joins (5:8--6:6) with the preceding verses."[46] He regards 5:1-7 as a small separate unit consisting of three sayings: 5:1-2, 3-4, 5-7. Nor does he treat Hos 6:7-11, the verses which follow these sayings. In short, he does not deal with 5:8--6:6 in its present literary context.

In 1966, Good wrote, what he called, "an alternative to Alt."[47] Good's main criticism is that Alt overlooked the cultic elements in the texts in favor of the more historical ones. Good relates 5:8--6:6 to a covenant lawsuit form, although he himself admits that all the formal ingredients of such a form are not present in 5:8--6:6.[48] He would thus situate the poem within a liturgical setting, a covenant renewal ceremony.

Both historical and liturgical/covenantal allusions are juxtaposed in the text. We propose that this juxtaposition is due to redaction. A redaction-critical approach would help to explain the diversity in the text, which is Alt's chief difficulty in dealing with a text like 6:1-6, while ignoring 5:1-7 and 6:7-11. Moreover, such an approach would not be forced to fit the text into a particular form, which is Good's problem in interpreting the text in light of a covenant renewal ceremony.

The Hosean tradition which begins in Hos 5:1 will continue through to Hos 13*. Hos 5:3 accuses Ephraim of playing the harlot. The rest of the tradition will give clues to the nature of the "mother's" harlotry, to which Hosea refers in Hos 2* and 4*. This tradition was preserved in two editions of interpretive commentary. Each edition had its own particular readership and historical situation.

The Hosean tradition which we discern in Hos 5* and in the following chapters seems to have a concrete historical referent. The actual historical occasion is difficult to determine precisely, because the historical events are seen from different editorial vantage points which try to explain the history in retrospect. This is also the case for our main source for the history of Israel, viz. the Deuteronomistic History (Josh-2Kgs), which itself had undergone a pre-exilic and exilic redaction.

With this in mind, we tentatively understand the Hosean saying in Hos 5*, viz. 1-2a, 3, 5abA, 8-13a, 14, in light of the

Syro-Ephraimite war, which involved not only Israel, but Judah as well.⁴⁹ The Hosean tradition begins in vv. 1-2a with a threefold summons to the leadership of the northern kingdom to take heed to the proclamation which follows: "Hear this!" (*šim'û zō't*). Since they are responsible for the circumstances of their country, the judgment pertains to them (v. 1b). In 5:3, Hosea accuses Ephraim of "harlotry," which, if we are correct in our identification of the Hosean tradition, is the political intrigue surrounding the events of the Syro-Ephraimite war (5:8-13a, 14). The Hosean saying will find its continuation in 6:10, which, because of its similarity with 5:3 and 7:1b, functions as a bridge between the Hosean tradition in Hos 5* and Hos 7*.⁵⁰

The R1 redaction of this tradition, 5:5b-7, includes Judah in the threat, but from a particular cultic standpoint. R1 interprets the tragedy that came upon the North, and which will come upon Judah, in light of their worship which violates their covenantal relationship with YHWH. This will become clearer particularly in the R1 redaction in Hos 6*.

*III. The Earlier Stages of Hos 6**

   *A. The Editorial History of Hos 6**

H	C	R1	(R2)
			(6:1-3)
		6:4	(6:5)
		6:6-7	
6:8-10		6:11a	(6:11b--7:1*)

   B. Reconstructed Text

6:4   *mâ 'e'ĕśeh-lĕkā 'eprayim*
        mâ 'e'ĕśeh-lĕkā yĕhûdâ
        wĕhasdĕkem ka'ănan-bōqer
        wĕkattal maškîm hōlēk

6:6   *kî hesed hāpastî wĕlō'-zābah*
        wĕda'at 'ĕlōhîm mē'ōlôt

6:7   *wĕhēmmâ kĕ'ādām 'ābĕrû bĕrît*
        šām bāgĕdû bî
6:8   <u>*gil'ād qiryat pō'ălê 'āwen*</u>
        <u>*'ăqubbâ middām*</u>
6:9   <u>*ûkĕḥakkê 'îš gĕdûdîm*</u>
        <u>*ḥeber kōhănîm*</u>
        <u>*derek yĕraṣṣĕḥû-šekmâ*</u>
        <u>*kî zimmâ 'āśû*</u>
6:10   <u>*bĕbêt yiśrā'ēl*</u>
        <u>*rā'îtî ša'ăryyrîyyâ*</u>
        <u>*šām zĕnût lĕ'eprayim*</u>
        <u>*niṭmā' yiśrā'ēl*</u>
6:11   *gam-yĕhûdâ šāt qāṣîr lāk*

6:4   . . .What shall I do with you, Ephraim?
        What shall I do with you, Judah?
        Your love is like a morning cloud,
            Like the dew which goes away early . . .
6:6   Indeed, I desire love, not sacrifice,
            and knowledge of God, rather than offerings.
6:7   But they have walked over the covenant like dirt.
        Lo, they have been traitorous against me.[51]

6:8   *Gilead is a city of evildoers,*
            a deceitful city, because of bloodshed.[52]
6:9   *Like skulking thieves is a gang of priests.*
            They murder along the Shechem road.
        Indeed, they commit atrocities.
6:10   *In the house of Israel*
            I have seen disgusting things.
        Ephraim's harlotry is there.
            Israel is defiled.
6:11a   Judah, also, he has set a harvest for you . . .

C. R1 Redaction

Scholars have noted the connection between 5:14 and 6:4,
which was interrupted by the R2 expansion, 5:15--6:3.[53] Hos
6:4 begins R1 commentary on the Hosean saying, 5:8-13a,

14.[54] With 6:4, YHWH addresses Ephraim and Judah directly, whereas in the Hosean tradition YHWH refers to them in the third person: "What shall I do with *you*, Ephraim? . . . with *you*, Judah?" Immediately, R1 interprets the historical circumstances, to which the Hosean tradition alludes in Hos 5*, in light of transgressions against YHWH's covenant.[55] The covenantal *ḥesed* of Ephraim is fleeting. R1's accusation recalls his introduction to the Hosean tradition in 4:1-2: "There is no *ḥesed*, no knowledge of God (*da'at 'ĕlōhîm*) in the land."[56] However, this is precisely what YHWH demands from his covenanted people, according to 6:6: "Indeed, I desire *ḥesed*, not sacrifice, and knowledge of God (*da'at 'ĕlōhîm*), rather than offerings." We again see the cultic interpretation of R1 coming to the fore. The worship reflects one's covenantal relationship with the deity. If this relationship is ruptured, the cult itself is a sham. R1 articulates this thought expressly in his next statement, 6:7:

> "But they have walked over my covenant (*'br bryt*) like dirt.
> Lo, they have been traitorous against me."[57]

The expression in 6:7, *'br bryt*, is characteristically deuteronomistic, describing the transgression of YHWH's covenant.[58] R1 plays on the double meaning of *'br*. Its common meaning is "to walk over, pass over." Thus, R1 states that "they have walked over (i.e. transgressed) my covenant like dirt." The second colon of 6:7, *šām bāgĕdû bî*, "lo, they have been traitorous against me," recalls R1's editorial in 5:7a, *byhwh bāgādû*, "against YHWH they have been traitorous."[59]

As we had pointed out when we discussed the final redaction of Hos 6, commentators commonly agree that Hos 6:11 is a secondary insertion.[60] A number of them observe that the redaction occurred at different stages.[61] We think that Hos 6:11a, "Judah, also, he has set a harvest for you," is an R1 addition which includes Judah in the description of the northern kingdom. R1 signals his commentary by departing from the first person YHWH speech to refer to YHWH in the third person. Moreover, as in his actualizing addition in 5:5b, R1 uses *gam*, "also," to apply the sayings tradition to Judah:[62]

5:5bB   *kāšal gam-yĕhûdâ 'immām*
6:11a   *gam-yĕhûdâ šāt qāṣîr lāk*

5:5bB   Judah also has stumbled with them.
6:11a   Judah also, he (YHWH) has set a harvest for you.

D. Hosean Tradition

The Hosean tradition begins again in 6:8-9 with a description of the enormities perpetrated by "a gang of priests," *ḥeber kōhănîm*. Hos 6:8-9 resumes the series of accusations against the "priests, the house of Israel, and the house of the king," who were summoned to hear the judgment against them in 5:1-2a. Hos 6:8-9 seems to continue in Hos 7* where the priests evidently instigated the deterioration of the court by debauchery.

Hosea provides a transition from Hos 6* to Hos 7* in 6:10. On one hand, 6:10 recalls 5:3, the accusation which follows the summoning of the defendants in 5:1-2a:

5:3   I know Ephraim,
          and Israel is not hidden from me.
        For now you have played the harlot, Ephraim A
                      (*hiznêtā 'eprayim*)
        Israel is defiled. (*niṭmā' yiśrā'ēl*)   B
6:10   In the house of Israel
          I have seen disgusting things.
        Ephraim's harlotry is there.   A'
          (*šām zĕnût lĕ'eprayim*)
        Israel is defiled (*niṭmā' yiśrā'ēl*)   B'

On the other hand, 6:10 connects 6:8-9 with 7:1*. Hos 6:10 states that YHWH *sees* (*rā'îtî*) Ephraim's crimes. According to 7:1*, these crimes *will be revealed* (*wĕniglâ*). Moreover, Hos 7:1* is linked with 6:8-9 in the repetition of *p'l*:

6:8   Gilead is a city of *evil-doers*. (*pōʿălê ʾāwen*)

7:1*   For they *act in deceit*. (*pāʿălû šāqer*)

and *gdwd*:

6:9   Like skulking thieves (*ûkĕḥakkê ʾîš gĕdûdîm*)
         is a gang of priests.
7:1*   Robbers break in.
         Thieves roam in the street. (*pāšaṭ gĕdûd baḥûṣ*)

Continuing the Hos 5* Hosean tradition, the Hosean
tradition in Hos 6* apparently still refers to incidents that
occurred around the time of the Syro-Ephraimite war. The
exact nature of the events described by Hos 6:8-10 is still
rather obscure.[63] It seems to describe a company or guild of
priests whose crimes of murder and treachery are denounced
by Hosea.

*IV. The Earlier Stages of Hos 7***

A. *The Editorial History of Hos 7**

H	C	R1	(R2)
			(7:1*)
7:1*-3			(7:4)
7:5-9			(7:10)
7:11-12a**			(7:12a**, 12b)
7:13-15***			(7:15***-16)

     * *kĕropʾî lĕyiśrāʾēl* = R2
     ** *kaʾăšer yēlēkû* = R2
     ****yissartî* = R2

B. *Reconstructed Text*

7:1*   *wĕniglâ ʿăwôn ʾeprayim*
         wĕrāʿôt šōmĕrôn
         kî pāʿălû šāqer

	wĕgannāb yābô'
	pāšaṭ gĕdûd baḥûṣ
7:2	ûbal-yō'mĕrû lilbābām
	kol-rā'ātām zākārtî
	'attâ sĕbābûm ma'allêhem
	neged pānay hāyû
7:3	bĕrā'ātām yĕśammĕḥû-melek
	ûbĕkaḥăšêhem śārîm
7:5	yôm malkēnû heḥĕlû
	śārîm ḥămat miyyāyin
	māšak yādô 'et-lōṣĕsîm
7:6	kî-qērĕbû kattannûr
	libbām bĕ'orbām
	kol-hallaylâ yāšēn 'appĕhem (MT: 'ōpēhem)64
	bōqer hû' bō'ēr kĕ'ēš lehābâ
7:7	kullām yēḥammû kattannûr
	wĕ'ākĕlû 'et-šōpĕṭêhem
	kol-malkêhem nāpālû
	'ên-qōrē' bāhem 'ēlāy
7:8	'eprayim bā'ammîm
	hû' yitbôlāl
	'eprayim hāyâ 'ūgâ
	bĕlî hăpûkā
7:9	'ākĕlû zārîm kôḥô
	wĕhû' lō' yādā'
	gam-śêbâ zārĕqâ bô
	wĕhû' lō' yādā'
7:11	wayhî 'eprayim kĕyônâ
	pôtâ 'ên lēb
	miṣrayim qārā'û
	'aššûr hālākû
7:12a**	'eprôś 'ălêhem rištî
	kĕ'ôp haššāmayim 'ôrîdēm
7:13	'ôy lāhem kî-nādĕdû mimmennî
	šōd lāhem kî-pāšĕ'û bî
	wĕ'ānōkî 'epdēm
	wĕhēmmâ dibbĕrû 'ālay kĕzābîm
7:14	wĕlō'-zā'ăqû 'ēlay bĕlibbām
	kî yĕyēlîlû 'al-miškĕbôtām

'al-dāgān wĕtîrôš yitgôrārû
yāsûrû bî

7:15*** wĕ'ănî ḥizzaqtî zĕrô'ōtām
wĕ'ēlay yĕḥaššĕbû-rā'

7:1*   . . .The iniquity of Ephraim will be revealed,
          the wicked deeds of Samaria,
             for they act in deceit.
          Robbers break in.
          Thieves roam the streets.

7:2   They do not consider in their hearts,
             that I remember all their wickedness.
          Now their deeds encompass them.
          They are before me.

7:3   By their wickedness they made the king glad.
          By their deception, the princes . . .

7:5   By day, they made our king sick,
             the princes, with the heat of wine.
          He stretched forth his hand with babblers.65

7:6   For they approached like an oven,
             their hearts with intrigue.
          All night their anger* smoldered.
          In the morning it blazed like a flaming fire.

7:7   All of them became hot like an oven.
          They devoured their judges.
          All of their kings have fallen.
          There is no one among them who calls upon me.

7:8   Ephraim is among the peoples.
          He is shaken back and forth.
          Ephraim has become an unturned cake.

7:9   Aliens devour his strength,
             and he does not know it.
          Even gray hairs are sprinkled upon him,
             and he does not know it . . .

7:11   Ephraim is like a dove,
             Silly and without sense.
          They call to Egypt.
          They go to Assyria.

7:12a**   . . .I will spread over them my net.
          Like birds of the air I will bring them down
. . .
7:13   Woe to them, for they have fluttered away from
          me.
          Violence to them, for they have revolted
          against me.
          It was I who redeemed them.
          But they spoke lies against me.
7:14   They did not cry to me from their hearts.
          They did not[66] wail from upon their beds.
          For grain and wine they became sojourners.
          They have departed from me.
7:15***   I, yes I, . . .strengthened their arms,
          But against me they plot evil.

C. Hosean Tradition

The earlier stage of Hos 7* is composed of Hosean tradition
which seems to continue the Hosean tradition of Hos 6*.[67] The
conspirators, whose crimes Hos 7* depicts, are presumably the
gang of priests cited in Hos 6:8-9.[68]. Hosea describes their
deeds three times as *rā'/rā'â*, "wickedness, evil:"

7:2   I remember all their *wickedness*.
7:3   By their *wickedness* they made the king glad.
7:15   Against me they plot *evil*.
Cf. 7:1 The *wicked* deeds of Samaria.

According to Hos 7:3, 5, these priests are responsible for
the moral deterioration at court. By their instigation the king
and his princes become intoxicated with wine (vv. 3, 5). This
palace-wide state of inebriation ostensibly prepares for an
assassination attempt (vv. 6-7). The identity of the victims
and the conspirators is unknown. Perhaps Hosea is describing
here the assassination of Pekah (2 Kgs 15:30).[69] Perhaps 7:7,
"all their kings have fallen," is simply a general statement
about the series of *coups d'état* that plagued the North after
the death of Jeroboam II (2 Kgs 15:8-31). The text remains
obscure.

In 7:8-11, Hosea attacks Ephraim's mercurial foreign policy. These texts do seem to refer to the political intrigue of the Syro-Ephraimite war. However, it is difficult to fit the texts into any specific reign of the Northern kings around that time.[70] Hosea accuses Ephraim of his involvement in foreign alliances and of not turning to YHWH. As 7:14 states:

> "They do not cry to me in their heart.
> They did not wail from upon their beds.
> For grain and wine they became sojourners.
> They have departed from me."

Herein lies the "harlotry" of Ephraim which the Hosean tradition exposes. It is the political involvement with the nations and a neglect of YHWH, who had strengthened their military forces (7:15***). For Hosea, the nations are the "lovers" who provide the bread, water, wool, oil and drink (Hos 2:7). According to 7:14, Ephraim, who flirts from one foreign power to another (7:11), has become a sojourner for their grain and wine. Hosea will speak more regarding these "harlotrous" liaisons particularly in Hos 8*.

V.   The Earlier Stages of Hos 8*

A.   The Editorial History of Hos 8*

H	C	R1	(R2)
		8:1-4a	(8:4b-5aA)
		8:5aBb-6*	(8:6*-7)
8:8-10		8:11-12	(8:13-14)

* *kî miyyiśrā'ēl* = R1

B.   Reconstructed Text

8:1   *'el-ḥikkĕkā šōpār*
            kanneŝer 'al-bêt yhwh
        ya'an 'ābĕrû bĕrîtî

wĕʿal-tôrātî pāšāʿû
8:2   lî yizʿāqû 'ĕlōhay yĕdaʿănûkā yiśrā'ēl
8:3   zānaḥ yiśrā'ēl ṭôb
        'ôyēb yirdĕpô
8:4   hēm himlîkû wĕlō' mimmennî
        hēśîrû wĕlō' yādā'tî
8:5aB ḥārāh 'appî bām
        'ad-mātay lō' yûkĕlû niqqāyōn
8:6*   kî miyyiśrā'ēl
8:8   nibla' yiśrā'ēl
        'attâ hāyû baggôyim
        kiklî 'ên-ḥēpeṣ bô
8:9   kî-hēmmâ ʿālû 'aššûr
        pere' bôdēd lô 'eprayim
        hitnû 'ăhābîm
8:10   gam kî-yitnû baggôyim
        'attâ 'ăqabbĕṣēm
        wayyāḥēllû mĕ'aṭ
        mimmaśśā' melek śarîm
8:11   kî hirbâ 'eprayim mizbĕḥôt lĕḥaṭṭē'
        (MT: laḥăṭō')[71]
        hāyû-lô mizbĕḥôt laḥăṭō'
8:12   'ektowb-lô rubbēw[72] tôrātî
        kĕmô-zār neḥšābû

8:1   To your mouth a trumpet!
        For an eagle is over YHWH's house.
        Because they have transgressed my covenant,
            and against my law they have revolted.
8:2   Though they cry to me,
        'God of Israel, we know you!,'
8:3   Israel has rejected the good.
        The enemy shall pursue him.
8:4a They made kings but not from me.
        They made princes but I did not
            acknowledge them . . .
8:5aBb My anger was kindled against them.
        How long will they be unable to be clean,
8:6*   even from Israel . . .

8:8   *Israel is swallowed up.*
           Now, they are among the nations
           like an undesirable vessel.
8:9   *For, they have gone up to Assyria.*
           Ephraim is a wild ass
           wandering off by himself.
           They have hired lovers.
8:10   *Indeed, they have hired them among the nations.*
           Now, I will gather them up.
           They will soon writhe in pain.
           Kings and princes,
           on account of the burden.[73]
8:11   When Ephraim multiplied
           altars for sin (offerings),
                      they became for him altars for sinning.
8:12   Were I to write for him
           numerous things of my law,
                      They would be regarded as something
                      strange.

C. R1 Redaction

In 8:1, R1 picks up the bird image of his Hosean tradition
in 7:11-13 and is thus able to reinterpret his tradition in light
of his deuteronomistic concerns.[74] No longer an alarm against
invading hordes (cf. 5:8), the trumpet blast becomes a solemn
call to Israel to confront YHWH for trangressing his covenant
and rebelling against his *tôrâ*. One should now regard 8:3,
"the enemy shall pursue him," as an example of a *covenantal
curse*, rather than a description of an attacking army.[75] Hos
8:1-2 recalls the vocabulary of previous R1 commentary: "to
trangress the covenant" (*'br bryt*, cf. 6:7), the concern for God's
tôrâ or law (cf. 4:6), and the lack of true knowledge of YHWH
(cf. 4:1, 6; 6:6).
  One should view the reference to the illegitimate
installation of kings and princes referred to in 8:4-5 from a
Judean perspective. The northern kings represent an apostate
schism from the divinely ordained Davidic dynasty. This

dynasty exercises its authority in Jerusalem, wherein stands the "house of YHWH" (cf. Hos 8:1 and 2 Sam 7:4-16).

R1 concludes his commentary in Hos 8*, first, with a paronomastic poke against the illicit cult of the North. According to 8:11, the altars upon which Ephraim presents his sin offerings (*lĕḥaṭṭē'*), have become altars for sinning (*laḥăṭō'*).[76] Second, the reference to "my law," *tôrātî*, in 8:12 becomes a framing device with *tôrātî* in 8:1. Even if YHWH were to write numerous things of his *tôrâ*, Ephraim would regard it as something alien.

D. Hosean Tradition

The Hosean tradition, 8:8-10, which is bordered by R1 redaction, continues the theme found in Hos 7*, viz. the political alliances which Israel makes with foreign nations, particularly Assyria. For the first time since Hos 4*, Hosea describes these partnerships as harlotrous:

> "Ephraim has hired lovers.
> Indeed, they hire them among the nations."
> (Hos 8:9b-10a)

However, Hosea predicts that the leadership will writhe in pain under the "burden," which probably refers to the tribute which the North must present to these powers (cf. 4:13).[77]

VI. The Earlier Stages of Hos 9*

A. The Editorial History of Hos 9*

H	C	R1	(R2)
		9:1	(9:2-4)
		9:5	(9:6)
		9:7	(9:8-9)

9:10

9:11-13 (9:14)

9:15

9:16 (9:17)

B. Reconstructed Text

9:1 *'al-tiśmaḥ yiśrā'ēl*
 'el-gîl kā'ammîm
 kî zanîtā mē'al 'ēlōhêkā
 'āhabtā 'etnān
 'al kol-gornôt dāgān

9:5 *māh-ta'ăśû lĕyôm mô'ēd*
 ûlĕyôm ḥag-yhwh

9:7 *bā'û yĕmê happĕquddâ*
 bā'û yĕmê haššillūm
 yēdĕ'û yiśrā'ēl
 'ĕwîl hannābî'
 mĕšuggā' 'îš hārûaḥ
 'al rōb 'ăwônĕkā
 wĕrabbâ maśṭēmâ

9:10 *ka'ănābîm bammidbār*
 māṣā'tî yiśrā'ēl
 kĕbikkûrâ biťēnâ bĕrē'šîtāh
 rā'îtî 'ăbôtêkem
 hēmmâ bā'û ba'al-pĕ'ôr
 wayyinnāzĕrû labōšet
 wayyihyû šiqqûṣîm kĕ'āhăbām

9:11 'eprayim kā'ôp yiťôpēp kĕbôdām
 millēdâ ûmibbeṭen ûmēhērāyôn

9:12 kî 'im-yĕgaddĕlû 'et-bĕnêhem
 wĕšikkaltîm mē'ādām
 kî-gam-'ôy lāhem
 bĕśûrî mēhem

9:13 'eprayim ka'ăšer-rā'îtî
 lĕṣôr šĕtûlâ bĕnāweh
 wĕ'eprayim lĕhôṣî' 'el-hōrēg bānāyw

9:15 *kol-rā'ātām baggilgāl*
 kî-šām śĕnē'tîm

'al rōa' ma'allêhem
　　mibbêtî 'ăgārĕšēm
lō' 'ôsēp 'ahăbātām
　　kol-śōrêhem sōrĕrîm

9:16　hukkâ 'eprayim
　　šoršām yābēš
　　pĕrî bāly-ya'ăśûn
gam kî yēlēdûn
　　wĕhēmattî mahămaddê biṭnām

9:1　Rejoice not, O Israel,
　　　　to exultation like the peoples,
　　For you have played the harlot away from your
　　God.
　　You have loved a harlot's hire
　　　　upon every threshing floor of grain . . .
9:5　What will you do on the day of festival,
　　　　on the day of YHWH's feast? . . .
9:7　The days of punishment have come.
　　The days of retribution have come.
　　　　Israel shall know it.[78]
　　The prophet is a fool.
　　The man of the spirit is mad,
　　　　because of your great guilt,
　　　　and great hostility . . .
9:10　Like grapes I found in the wilderness, O Israel,
　　Like a fig tree's first fruits in its first season,
　　　　I saw your ancestors.
　　　They came to Baal Peor
　　　　and consecrated themselves to Shame.
　　They became detestable as the thing they loved.
9:11　*Ephraim is like a bird.*
　　　Their glory will fly away.
9:12　*No birth, no pregnancy, no conception!*
　　For, if they bring up their children,
　　　I will bereave them from humanity.
　　Indeed, woe to them when I turn away from them!
9:13　*Ephraim, as I see it, is like a palm[79]*
　　　planted in a field.

	Ephraim will lead his children to slaughter . . .
9:15	All of their evil is in Gilgal.
	Indeed, there I began to hate them.
	Because of the wickedness of their deeds,
	I will drive them out of my house.
	I will no longer love them.
	All their princes are rebels.
9:16	*Ephraim is stricken.*
	Their root has dried up.
	They will yield no fruit.
	Even if they do give birth,
	I will slay the darlings of their womb.

C. R1 Redaction

R1 redaction on the Hosean tradition in Hos 9* is characterized in 9:1, 5, 7, and 10 by the second person address to Israel, vis-à-vis the third person in H.[80] Hos 9:1-2, 5 recall R1 redaction in Hos 2:13-15a.[81] In the latter, the wife/Israel speaks of her vines and fig trees as *'etnâ*, "a harlot's hire," which her lovers have given her (cf. 9:1). Furthermore, according to 2:13, YHWH will put an end to her feasts, *ḥaggāh*, and all of her festival assemblies, *môʿādāh* (cf. 9:5). As we have seen, R1 continues to interpret the harlotry of Israel in light of cultic practices which have become corrupted. The "day of festival," *yôm môʿēd*, and the "day of YHWH's feast," *yôm ḥag-yhwh* (9:5), have become the "days of punishment," *yĕmê happĕquddâ*, and the "days of retribution," *yĕmê haššillūm* (9:7a).

Moreover, in 9:7b, he exposes the corruption of the prophet:

> The prophet is a fool.
> The man of the spirit is mad,
>   because of your great guilt,
>   and great hostility.

R1's negative description of the prophet here is consistent with his remark in 4:5, that the prophet also stumbles with the priest.[82]

Hos 9:10 embodies the "election" tradition which is associated with the wilderness wanderings, a tradition found in later works.[83] R1 associates the pollution in the cult in retrospect to Israel's early history, when Israel played the harlot with the daughters of Moab and, by participating in their idolatrous sacrifices, was yoked to Baal Peor (Num 25:1-2. Cf. Dt 4:3).[84]

R1's final commentary in 9:15, as in 4:15,[85] attacks the illegitimacy of the northern shrines: "All of their evil is in Gilgal and there I began to hate them."[86] R1's reference to the "house of YHWH," as in 8:1, focuses upon the deuteronomistic idea of a centralized cult in Jerusalem.[87]

D. Hosean Tradition

The bird imagery which characterizes Ephraim in the Hosean tradition in 7:11-12[88] is resumed again in Hos 9:11:

7:11   Ephraim is like a dove,
            Silly and without sense.
9:11   Ephraim is like a bird.
            Their glory will fly away.

Furthermore, Hosea conjoins birth and plant imagery in 9:12-13, 16, to describe the repercussions that Ephraim's political misalliances will have on his offspring. In view of the Syro-Ephraimite war, Hosea could be describing the tragedy which will befall the North in military conquest. Ephraim must lead his children to slaughter (9:13). The palm which was planted in a field (9:13) is now stricken (9:16).

VII.   *The Earlier Stages of Hos 10**

A. *The Editorial History of Hos 10**

H	C	R1	(R2)
		10:1-8	(10:9-10)
10:11			(10:12)
10:13a			(10:13b-14)
		10:15	

B. *Reconstructed Text*

10:1   *gepen bôqēq yiśrā'ēl*
          pĕrî yĕšawweh lô
       kĕrōb lĕpiryô
          hirbâ lammizbĕḥôt
       kĕṭôb lĕ'arṣô
          hêṭîbû maṣṣēbôt
10:2   *ḥālaq libbām*
          'attâ ye'šāmû
       hû' ya'ărōp mizbĕḥôtām
          yĕšōdēd maṣṣēbôtām
10:3   *kî 'attâ yōmĕrû*
          'ên melek lānû
       kî lō' yārē'nû 'et-yhwh
          wĕhammelek mah-ya'ăśeh lānû
10:4   *dibbĕrû dĕbārîm*
          'ālôt šāw' kārōt bĕrît
       ûpāraḥ kārō'š mišpāṭ
          'al talmê śādāy
10:5   *lĕ'eglôt bêt 'āwen*
          yāgûrû šĕkan šōmĕrôn
       kî-'ābal 'ālāyw 'ammô
          ûkĕmārāyw 'ālāyw yāgîlû
       'al-kĕbôdô kî-gālâ mimmennû
10:6   *gam-'ôtô lĕ'aššûr yûbāl*
          minḥâ lĕmelek yārēb

bošnâ 'eprayim yiqqāḥ
wĕyēbôš yiśrā'ēl mē'ăṣātô
10:7   *nidmeh šōmĕrôn malkāh*
        kĕqeṣep 'al-pĕnê māyin
10:8   *wĕnišmĕdû bāmôt 'āwen*
        ḥaṭṭa't yiśrā'ēl
        qôṣ wĕdardar ya'āleh 'al-mizbĕḥôtām
        wĕ'āmĕrû lehārîm kassûnû
        wĕlagĕbā'ôt nîpĕlû 'ālênû
10:11   <u>*wĕ'eprayim 'eglâ mĕlummādâ*</u>
        <u>*'ōhabtî lādûš*</u>
        <u>*wa'ănî 'ābartî*</u>
        <u>*'ōl-ṭûb (MT: 'al-ṭûb)*[89] *ṣawwā'rāh*</u>
        <u>*'arkîb 'eprayim*</u>
        <u>*yaḥărôš yĕhûdâ*</u>
        <u>*yĕśadded-lô ya'ăqōb*</u>
10:13a <u>*ḥăraštem-reša'*</u>
        <u>*'awlātâ qĕṣartem*</u>
        <u>*'ăkaltem pĕrî-kāḥaš*</u>
10:15   *kākâ 'āśâ lākem bêt-'ēl*
        mippĕnê rā'at rā'atkem
        baššaḥar nidmōh nidmâ melek yiśrā'ēl

10:1   He made Israel, the vine, luxuriant.
        He made it yield fruit for himself.
        The more He multiplied his fruit,
            he multiplied altars.
        The richer He made his land,
            the more generous they were to the pillars.[90]
10:2   Their heart is false.
        Now, they will incur guilt.
        He will break down their altars.
        He will devastate their pillars.
10:3   For, now they say:
        'We have no king,
            for we do not fear YHWH,
            and a king, what will he do for us?'
10:4   They uttered mere words,
            worthless oaths to cut a covenant.

Judgment flourished like poisonous weeds
    upon the furrows of the field.
10:5   The residents of Samaria sojourn
    to the calves of Beth Awen.
Indeed, its people shall mourn over it,
    its idolatrous priests shall wail over it,
    over its glory, for it has departed from it.
10:6   It is brought to Assyria,
    a tribute to the great king.
Ephraim will receive shame.
    Israel will be ashamed because of its image.[91]
10:7   The king of Samaria will be destroyed,
    like a twig upon the surface of the waters.
10:8   The high places of Awen will be wiped out,
    the sin of Israel.
Thorns and thistles will grow up over their altars.
They will say to the mountains, 'Cover us!'
    and to the hills, 'Fall upon us!' . . .
10:11   *Ephraim is a trained calf.*
    I loved to thresh (her)
I placed upon her neck a fine yoke.*
I harnessed Ephraim.
    Judah will plow.
        Jacob will harrow for himself . . .
10:13   *You have plowed iniquity.*
    Lawlessness you have reaped.
        You have eaten the fruit of lies . . .
10:15   Thus he will do to you, Beth-El.
    because of your great wickedness.
At dawn, the king of Israel will be utterly destroyed.

C. R1 Redaction

Hos 10* is the final chapter in which we find R1 commentary. The point of departure for his editorial is the mention of the "calf-Ephraim" in his Hosean tradition, 10:11. In Hos 10*, he makes an important statement on the fall of the

northern kingdom. He interprets the fall in light of the "sin"
of Jeroboam I, i.e. the erection of the calves in Bethel and Dan
to dissuade the populace from pilgrimage to the central
sanctuary in Jerusalem (1 Kgs 13:25-33). His concern for
covenant, *bĕrît*, appears again in 10:4. Israel's covenantal
loyalty is merely words, a worthless oath, which is typified in
the pilgrimages to the calves of Samaria.

R1 begins Hos 10* by reinterpreting the plant motif of the
Hosean tradition in 9:16: "Ephraim is stricken. Their root has
dried up." In 10:1, R1 contrasts the withered plant, Ephraim,
with the fact that YHWH had made Israel, the vine, luxuriant
and made it once yield fruit for himself. This image of
fruitfulness also harmonizes with R1 commentary in 9:10:
"Like grapes I found in the wilderness, O Israel, like a fig
tree's first fruits in its first season, I saw your ancestors."[92] As
in 9:10, however, R1 interprets the transition from
fruitfulness to deterioration as a cultic malaise. Commenting
on "it shall yield no fruit" in his Hosean saying in 9:16, R1
states in 10:1 that even though YHWH multiplied his fruit,
Israel multiplied *altars*. The richer YHWH made the land, the
more generous Israel was to the *pillars*.

Hos 10:2 recalls Dt 7:5 which commands the people to
destroy the idolatrous artifacts of the new land:

> "Thus shall you deal with them. You shall break down their
> *altars* and dash in pieces their *pillars* and hew down their
> Asherim and burn their graven images with fire." (Dt 7:5. Cf.
> Dt 12:3)

Moreover, 10:2 calls to mind the deuteronomist's account of
Josiah's reform, which may be the period of our R1 redactor.[93]
According to 2 Kgs 23:14-15,

> "And (Josiah) broke in pieces the *pillars*, and cut down the
> Asherim, and filled their places with the bones of men.
> Moreover, the *altar at Bethel, the high place* (*bāmâ*, cf. Hos
> 10:8) *erected by Jeroboam, the son of Nebat, who made Israel
> to sin*, that altar with the high place he pulled down and broke
> in pieces its stones, crushing them to the dust." (2 Kgs
> 23:14-15)

Hos 10:7-8 accords with the insistent refrain of the deuteronomistic historian that the sins of Israel can be traced back to the paradigmatic sin of Jeroboam I, viz. the installation of the "calves of Samaria" in northern sanctuaries.[94] Israel shall fall because of this sin. Indeed, R1 asserts in Hos 10:7-8,

> "The king of Samaria will be destroyed,
>   like a twig upon the surface of the waters.
> The high places of Awen will be wiped out,
>   the sin of Israel." (Cf. 2 Kgs 23:14-15)

Finally, in 10:15, R1 again interprets his tradition in light of the sin perpetrated at Beth-El. The king of Israel will be cut off. R1 uses the same expression, *ndm*, (*niph. dmh*), "to be destroyed," here in 10:15 to describe the king's destruction, as he did in 10:7.

D. Hosean Tradition

The Hosean tradition again focuses on Ephraim, as we have seen in H's previous sayings in 5:11-14, 7:1, 8, 11; 9:11-13, 16, which criticise Ephraim's internal and external political intrigues. In 10:11 and 10:13, however, Hosea does not compare Ephraim to the bird (cf. 7:11-12, 9:11) or to the plant (cf. 9:13, 16), but to the calf. Departing from those who would remove "Judah" as a gloss,[95] we think that the Hosean tradition did direct some of its accusation to the South, as we have seen in Hos 5:10-14[96] and will see shortly in Hos 12:3.

VIII. The Hosean Tradition in Hos 12* and 13*

A. The Editorial History of Hos 12* and 13*

H	C	R1	(R2)
12:1a			(12:1b)
12:2-4			(12:5-7)
12:8-9			(12:10-12)

12:13	(12:14)
12:15	(13:1-11)
13:12-13	(13:14)
13:15--14:1	

B. Reconstructed Text

12:1a   *sĕbābūnî bĕkaḥaš 'eprayim*
         ûbĕmirmâ bêt yiśrā'ēl

12:2   *'eprayim rō'eh rûaḥ*
         wĕrōdēp qādîm
         kol-hayyôm kāzāb wāšōd yarbeh
         ûbĕrît 'im-'aššûr yikrōtû
         wĕšemen lĕmiṣrayim yûbāl

12:3   *wĕrîb lyhwh 'im-yĕhûdâ*
         wĕlipqōd 'al-ya'āqōb kidrākāw
         kĕma'ălālāyw yāšîb lô

12:4   *babbeṭen 'āqab 'et-'āḥîw*
         ûbĕ'ônô śārâ 'et-'ĕlōhîm

12:8   *kĕna'an bĕyādô mō'zĕnê mirmâ*
         la'ăšōq 'ahēb

12:9   *wayyō'mer 'eprayim 'ak 'āšartî*
         māṣā'tî 'ôn lî
         kol-yĕgî'ay lō' yimṣĕ'û lî
         'āwôn 'ăšer-ḥēṭ'

12:13   *wayyibraḥ ya'ăqōb śĕdeh 'ăram*
         wayya'ăbōd yiśrā'ēl bĕ'iššâ
         ûbĕ'iššâ šāmār

12:15   *hik'îs 'eprayim tamrûrîm*
         wĕdāmāyw 'ālāyw yiṭṭôš
         wĕḥerpātô yāšîb lô 'ădōnāyw

13:12   *ṣārûr 'ăwôn 'eprayim*
         ṣĕpûnâ ḥaṭṭā'tô

13:13   *heblê yôlēdâ yābō'û lô*
         hû'-bēn lō' ḥākām
         kî-'ēt lō' ya'ămōd
         bĕmišbar bānîm

13:15   *kî hû' bēn 'aḥîm yaprî'*
         yābô' qādîm

rûaḥ yhwh mimmidbār 'ōleh
wĕyēbôš mĕqôrô
wĕyeḥĕrab ma'yānô
hû' yiššeh 'ôṣar
kol-kĕlî ḥemdâ
14:1 te'šam šōmĕrôn
kî mārĕtâ bē'lōhêhā
baḥereb yippōlû
'ōlĕlêhem yĕruttāšû
wĕhāriyyôtāyw yĕbuqqā'û

12:1a Ephraim has encircled me with lies.
       the house of Israel with deceit . . .
12:2   Ephraim herds the wind,
       and pursues the eastwind.
       All day he multiplies lies and destruction.
       They make a covenant with Assyria.
       Oil is carried to Egypt.
12:3   YHWH has a dispute with Judah,
       to punish Jacob according to his ways.
       According to his deeds He will requite him.
12:4   In the womb he grabbed his brother's heel.
       In his vigor he contended with God . . .
12:8   A trader, in whose hands are deceitful scales.
       He loves to exploit.
12:9   Ephraim says, 'How rich I become!
       I have acquired wealth for myself.
       None of my crimes will ever catch up with me
          nor iniquity which I have wrongly
          committed . . .'
12:13 Jacob fled to the land of Aram.
       Israel served for a wife
       and for a wife he tended (sheep) . . .
12:15 Ephraim has caused bitter provocation.
       He will make him accountable for his bloodguilt.
       His Lord will return to him his disgrace . . .
13:12 Ephraim's iniquity is wrapped up.
       His sin is hidden away.

13:13   The pangs of childbirth will come to him.
          He is an unwise child.
          When it is time, he does not appear
             at the womb's opening . . .
13:15   Indeed, he will become a wild one among
          brothers.[97]
          The east wind comes.
             The wind of YHWH is rising up
             from the wilderness.
          His fountain will dry up.
             His springs will become parched.
          He will plunder his storehouse,
             every precious vessel.
14:1   Samaria has incurred guilt,
             for she has rebelled against her God.
          They will fall by the sword.
          Their babies will be dashed in pieces.
          Their pregnant women will be ripped open.

C. The Conclusion to the Hosean Tradition

The Hosean tradition in Hos 12* and 13* forms the climax of the prophet's saying which began in Hos 2*. In Hos 12*, Hosea traces the present decay in Israel back to its eponymous patriarch, Jacob/Israel. He compares the flight of the present day Ephraim to foreign powers to Jacob's flight to a foreign land, Aram. As he describes the treaties which Ephraim makes with these alien nations as harlotrous (8:10), so does he imply that the union between Jacob and his wife, Rachel, was harlotrous. For her, Jacob/Israel brought shame upon himself by becoming a common slave. The wife of Jacob, the matriarch of Israel, represents for Hosea the harlotrous mother ('im) whom YHWH accuses in Hos 2* and Hos 4*.[98] Because of the conditions by which she became Jacob's wife, e.g. Laban's trickery and Jacob's consequent servitude,[99] she symbolizes for Hosea the deceit and harlotry of contemporary Israel.

As Hosea geared his attacks principally against Ephraim/Israel in earlier chapters,[100] Hosea accuses

Ephraim/Israel in 12:1a of lies and deceit. The image of the wind (*rûaḥ*) and the east wind (*qādîm*) in 12:2a is echoed in chiastic fashion at the very end in 13:15, thus unifying the saying:

12:2a	Ephraim herds the wind (*rûaḥ*)	A
	and pursues the east wind (*qādîm*).	B

13:15	The east wind (*qādîm*) comes.	B'
	The wind of YHWH (*rûaḥ-YHWH*) is rising up from the desert.	A'

The wind which Ephraim tries to control (12:2a) will backlash and soon be his destruction (13:15).

In 12:2b, Hosea indicts Ephraim for his imprudent treaties with foreign powers:

> They make a covenant with Assyria.
> Oil is carried to Egypt.[101]

The dispute (*rîb*) of YHWH, which inaugurates Hosea's saying in 2:4 and 4:4 now concludes it in 12:3:

> YHWH has a dispute (*rîb*) with Judah,[102]
> to punish Jacob according to his ways.
> According to his deeds He will requite him.

Hosea begins in 12:4 to compare the contemporary nation with its erstwhile progenitor, Jacob/Israel. The portrayal of Jacob's deceit and contention with God (12:4) is followed immediately by a disclosure of Ephraim's current guilt (12:8-9). Scholars have noted the connection between 12:4 and 12:8, which, as we have seen, is interrupted by R2 commentary in 12:5-7.[103] The connection is supported by wordplays between 12:4 and 12:8, through which Hosea applies the conduct of Jacob to Ephraim:

12:4	In the womb he grabbed his brother's heel (*'āqab*).
	In his vigor (*'ôn*) he contended with God.

12:8   A trader, in whose hands are deceitful (*mirmâ*)
            scales.
            He loves to exploit.
            Ephraim says, 'How rich I become!
            I have acquired wealth (*mṣ' 'ôn*) for myself.
            None of my crimes will ever
                catch up (*mṣ'*) with me.
            Nor iniquity (*'āwôn*) which
                I have wrongly committed (*ḥṭ'*).'

In Hos 12:8, *mirmâ*, "deceit," recalls Gen 27:35, Jacob's
deception in usurping Esau's rights as oldest son:

> "Your brother came with deceit (*mirmâ*) and he has taken
> away your blessing." (Gen 27:35)

Thus, Esau responds with the same paronomasia on the proper
name, Jacob, as in Hos 12:4a:

> "Is he not rightly named Jacob (*ya'ăqōb*). For he has
> supplanted me (*wayya'qĕbēnî*) these two times. He took away
> my birthright. Now he has taken away my blessing." (Gen
> 27:36)

Ephraim's present-day fraud is placed side by side with
that of his ancestor's. Moreover, Hosea intensifies this
accusation by means of a wordplay in 12:4b and 12:9 on
'wn/*'wn*, along with an *antanaclasis* on *ms'*. In his "vigor" (*'ôn*)
Jacob/Israel struggled with God (12:4b). Through dishonest
means, Ephraim boasts of the "wealth" (*'ôn*) he has acquired
(*mṣ'*) for himself.[104] He arrogantly thinks that none of his
crimes will catch up with him (*mṣ'*) or the "iniquity" (*'āwôn*)
which he has wrongly committed (*ḥṭ'*).[105] Hosea will take up
the accusation against Ephraim's iniquity (*'āwôn*) and wrongs
(*ḥṭ'*) in 13:12.
       In 12:13, Hosea reverts back to the life of Jacob. We find
here Hosea's identification of Ephraim's harlotrous flight to
foreign powers with Jacob's flight to a foreign land to serve for
a wife. Hosea invests in the matriarch, Rachel, the present
day harlotry of the nation. According to Dt 26:5, Jacob is

characterized as the "father" of Israel: "A wandering Aramean was my father." Rachel, Jacob's wife from the land of Aram, will become mother (*'im*) of the Israelite nation (cf. esp. Jer 31:15). As ancestress of the northern tribes, she represents their moral corruption.

As offspring of Jacob and Rachel, Hosea will call Ephraim "an unwise son" (13:13). As in his comment in 8:3, that "Ephraim is a wild ass wandering off by himself," Hosea states that Ephraim will become "a wild one among his brothers" (13:15). Moreover, he becomes one of the children addressed at the beginning of the saying in Hos 2:4: "Plead with your mother, plead ...that she may remove the harlotry from her face, and her adultery from between her breasts." Hosea ends his saying on a threatening note. YHWH will bring destruction to the nation, because she has rebelled against her God (14:1).

CHAPTER EIGHT

Conclusion

We have analyzed the whole book of Hosea from its final redaction back to its earlier stages. We are now in a position to summarize our results and bring our work to a conclusion. Although we began with the final redacted state, we will present our results regarding the editorial history of the Book of Hosea chronologically, as we did in Chapter Five on the literary history of Hos 1-3. We have observed four stages in the composition of the Book of Hosea: the stage of the prophet Hosea himself (H), the stage of the Collector (C), the first redactor (R1), and the final redactor (R2).

We took care to see how these different stages interrelated as a book, how later stages revised and reinterpreted the earlier stages. The final form of the work embodies a gestaltist unity from the different phases of the tradition. We therefore deliberately avoided vocabulary like "strata, layers, and accretions" that highlighted the disunity or disconnectedness of the text rather than its unity. The different stages build upon each other and exist in a relational function with each other.

I. Hosea - H

The Hosean tradition in the book begins in 2:4aA and continues until Hos 13. It begins in Hos 2 as a legal complaint lodged against "your mother" for her adulterous behavior. Within the scope of the Hosean tradition in the rest of the book, we realize that the mother who is denounced is Rachel, the favorite wife of Jacob who is the father of Israel. Her children are the northern tribes, the House of Israel, who attribute their ancestry to her line. The Northern tribes are the children addressed in 2:4aA to *rîb* with their mother. Hosea embodies in the person of Rachel the harlotrous behavior of the leaders of the people: the priests (5:1; 6:9), the king (7:3, 5; 8:10) and the princes (7:3, 5; 8:10). Hosea regards as "harlotrous" the northern kingdom's mercurial political alliances with foreign powers and the intrigue which surrounds them. As we have it in the Hosean tradition in Hos 6* and 7*, this intrigue seems to center around a corrupt but influential guild of priests who plot evil at the king's court. In 8:10, Hosea expressly typifies the foreign policy of the North as harlotrous: "Ephraim has hired lovers. Indeed, they hire among the nations."

Hosea's preferred name for the northern kingdom which he condemns is Ephraim. He describes Ephraim by using various metaphors to criticise Ephraim's dealings with other nations. Ephraim, who mixes himself with the peoples, is like a half-baked cake (7:8). He is like a flighty and senseless dove, calling to Egypt, going to Assyria (7:11. Cf. 9:11). He is a wild ass wandering alone who has hired lovers among the nations (8:9. Cf. 13:15). He is a stricken root, whose foreign alliances will destroy the fruit of the womb, his children (9:11-13, 16). He is a trained calf who has plowed iniquity (10:11, 13).

The Hosean tradition reaches its climax in Hos 12*-13*. In his final metaphor, Hosea describes Ephraim as an unwise son (13:13) of notorious parents. These parents are Rachel and Jacob, the matriarch and patriarch of Israel. In the person of Rachel, Hosea symbolizes the adultery of the northern kingdom who seeks from her foreign lovers her bread, water, wool, flax, oil and drink (2:7b. Cf. 12:2). In Jacob, he creates a parallel between his contemporaries and the deceitful actions of their patronymic ancestor, Jacob/Israel. He traces Ephraim's business frauds and desire for wealth (12:8-9) back to Jacob who cheated his brother and strove with God (12:4). He identifies Ephraim's present-day flight to foreign powers with Jacob's flight to a foreign land. In this foreign country, he is lowered to the status of a slave to obtain Rachel, who for Hosea will characterize the moral corruption of the North.

We would date this core Hosean tradition during the time of the Syro-Ephraimite war. This tumultuous time accords well with the historical allusions Hosea makes in 5:8-13a, 14. These allusions also contain references to Judah, precisely because of Judah's significant role as the catalyst of this war. Hence, we think that the core Hosean tradition did contain some direct references to Judah, not only in 5:10-13a, 14, but also in 12:3.

II. The Collector - C

Vindicated by the disastrous events of the fall of Samaria to the Assyrians, the Hosean oracle which prophesied these events is preserved for us by the Collector, C. He creates the first written tradition of the Hosean saying which later editing expands and modifies for its own purposes. For this oracle the Collector composes a narrative, Hos 1*, describing the "call" of Hosea to prophetic ministry by YHWH. With this narrative the Collector, who was probably a disciple of Hosea, legitimates the ministry of his master as well as his own collection of his master's sayings.

His addition of Hos 1 to the oracle and his own editorials on the saying itself dramatically reinterpret the original Hosean saying. By describing Hosea's call in terms of Hosea's marriage to a harlotrous woman, the Collector provides a distinct literary context for the oracle. In the Hosean saying, the "mother" accused in 2:4aA was Rachel. With the addition of Hos 1*, the "mother" now becomes the prophet's adulterous wife, Gomer. In the original Hosean saying, the "children" who were summoned to *rîb* against their mother in 2:4A were the northern tribes, the "children" of Rachel and Jacob. In the literary context provided by C, however, they now become the prophet's own children by Gomer: Jezreel, Lo Ruhama and Lo Ammi.

Moreover, by prefacing this call narrative to the oracle, the collector creates the memorable metaphor of the marriage between YHWH and Israel from his Hosean tradition. YHWH becomes the faithful husband to Israel, his unfaithful wife. He depicts the dissolution of their covenantal relationship as a *divorce*. However, he adds a note of hope to his Hosean tradition by describing their eventual covenantal reunion as a *rebetrothal.*

Our investigation did not find in the rest of the Book of Hosea any other clues to the Collector's pen. His editorial activity seems to be limited to the call narrative of Hos 1* and

the insertions in Hos 2* reinterpreting the original Hosean
saying as a divorce and rebetrothal. Nevertheless, his
interpretive reshaping of the Hosean tradition is pivotal. The
marriage motif describing God's covenant with his people will
be taken up and expanded by later redaction.

We would date the Collector after the fall of the North in
722/21, perhaps around the time of Hezekiah's reform. It was
during this time that the hope of a "rebetrothal" between God
and Israel was a genuine possibility.

III. The First Redactor - R1

We called the first redactor of the collection R1. It is most
likely that R1 is a Judean, since several of his commentaries
reactualize the northern tradition to include Judah (4:15; 5:5b;
6:4, 11a). He appears to be very steeped in deuteronomistic
ideology. He has a significant concern for Torah, as is
witnessed by his allusions to the decalogue in 4:1-2 and his
accusations that the people have violated Torah (4:6; 8:1, 12).
Concomitantly, he denounces the people for their violation of
covenant and all that it implies (6:4, 6-7; 8:1).

In keeping with his deuteronomistic orientation, R1
maintains that the central sanctuary for the nation is the one
in Jerusalem, the "house of YHWH" (8:1. Cf. 9:15). Hence, R1
protests against the pilgrimages to northern sanctuaries such
as Bethel and Gilgal (4:15; 9:15). He has an overriding
concern for cult and cult practices which he sees as becoming
increasingly syncretistic (5:6; 9:10).

R1 reinterprets the "harlotry" of the nation, which in his
Hosean tradition was the nation's foreign treaties. In R1
redaction it now becomes their polluted cult. The *baals*, not
the nations, become the *lovers* of the "mother" (2:13-15a). This
"harlotry" has infected the very worship of YHWH, from the
priests and their kin (4:4, 6, 13b), down to the people
themselves (4:17-19; 5:6-7; 6:6; 9:1).

R1 traces the adulterous contamination of religious
worship back to Israel's enslavement to Baal-Peor just after
the ratification of their covenant with YHWH in the
wilderness (9:10. Cf. 9:15). R1 commentary climaxes in Hos

10* where he attributes the fall of the northern kingdom to the "sin of Jeroboam", the erection of the calves at Bethel and Dan. His commentary warns his Judean contemporaries that the same fate can happen to them.

One other facet of R1 commentary is his low opinion of the prophetic office. He describes the prophet as "stumbling" with the priest in Hos 4:5. He accuses the prophet of being a fool and a madman in Hos 9:7. This base view of prophecy is in direct contrast to the more elevated perception of prophecy in R2 commentary. Here, the prophet becomes the agent through whom YHWH reveals and executes his will.

We have suggested that our first redactor has affinities with DTR 1, who wrote the first edition of the Deuteronomistic History during the time of Josiah and was perhaps a propagandist for Josiah's reform policies. Besides ideological similarities to DTR 1, our R1 obliquely refers to Josiah's destruction of Bethel in 10:1-2, 8 (Cf. 2 Kgs 23:14-15).

IV. The Final Redactor - R2

To be sure, the primary focus of our investigation was on the composition of the final redactor, R2. He is the last editor of the book and the one who is responsible for the present text. Like R1, R2 has a deuteronomistic orientation. However, this orientation has for its perspective the calamitous event of the exile.

The editing of R2 in the whole book is extensive. The final redactor conducts his exegesis of the tradition principally by means of paronomasian links. He utilizes various types of wordplays to mitigate, reverse, or expand his tradition. Some of these wordplays include *antanaclasis*, double entendres, metaphony, parasonancy, consonantal transposition, assonance, epanastrophe, and alliteration. Furthermore, we saw in our discussion of Hos 7, Hos 9, and Hos 12 that R2 employs exegetical techniques similar to the rabbinic *middoth, gezerah shawah* and *qal wahomer*.

Our final redactor is responsible for major structural changes in the tradition. We display this graphically with the motifs characterizing each structural division as follows:

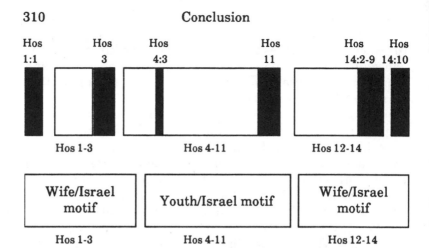

He provides, first, a redactional beginning to the book, viz.
1:1, which situates the tradition in a particular time in the
Deuteronomistic History. He adds a conclusion to the book,
14:10, a word of wisdom which enjoins the reader to take heed
to the word of God presented in it.

R2 inserts blocks of his own editorial, viz. Hos 3, 11, and
14, into the tradition to create a composition having a three-
part structure. We begin with the first major block of
redaction, Hos 3. By adding Hos 3 to Hos 1-2, R2 closes off the
first section of the book. This section is characterized by the
famous metaphor of the marriage between YHWH and Israel.
R2 highlights this marriage structurally by his Hos 3
addition: the poetic story of the the marriage of YHWH and
Israel (Hos 2) is thus buttressed on either side with a narrative
about the marriage of Hosea and Gomer (Hos 1 and 3).
Furthermore, he brackets the story of YHWH and Israel itself
with a redactional prologue (2:2-3) and epilogue (2:25).

The redaction of R2 creates from the tradition a three-part
journey motif of the wife/Israel back to YHWH. This journey
occurs at two levels: it is the wife's spiritual journey in repentance back to her first husband; it is the wife's physical
journey back to her homeland from exile. The first part of the
journey, described by R2 in 2:8-9, is the barring of the wife's
pursuit of her paramours. The second part of the journey is
chronicled in 2:11-15a, which was originally a pronouncement

of judgment against the wife. Framed now between the two R2 additions, 2:8-9 and 2:16-17, this judgment depicts the chastisement of the wife for her infidelity, an ordeal she must endure in her passage back to her spouse. The final redactor then portrays the final stage of the journey in 2:16-17, the leading of the wife into the wilderness, her restoration. This was the place of their first betrothal on Sinai. It is here that they will vow themselves to each other again in a covenantal renewal which will have cosmic ramifications.

The insertion of Hos 11 closes off the second major section of the book, Hos 4-11. This complex is also characterized by a three-part journey motif. By means of the three hope passages, 5:15--6:3, 10:12 and 11:10-11, R2 inspires his readers to return in repentance to YHWH. These three texts articulate a movement from barrenness to fertility. The symbolic barrenness of the people is reflected in the cosmos. R2 depicts in 4:3 the effect of the people's transgression of covenant on all of nature:

> Therefore, the land mourns
> and all who dwell in it languish.
> With the beasts of the field
> the birds of the air
> and even the fish of the sea
> they are swept away. (Hos 4:3)

To prepare for the cosmic covenant which will reverse this sad cosmic state, the three hope passages summon the people to repent and be healed, tilling the soil of their heart to prepare for the fullness and fertility which only YHWH can bring. As 11:10-11 will describe, the repentance of the people will bring them back from the lands of exile to their own homes.

While Hos 1-3 focuses on the wife/Israel, Hos 11 focuses on the youth/Israel.   Like the wife/Israel, the youth/Israel also experiences a three-part journey. The first is a journey from Egypt (the first Exodus), when YHWH first called his child from slavery and cared for him in the wilderness. Because of the youth/Israel's recalcitrance in serving other gods, he

disowns himself as God's child. Thus, he must make a journey
back to Egypt because of his insubordination. For R2, this
journey back to Egypt and slavery is the Exile. Although
YHWH, according to deuteronomic law, is within his rights to
destroy his rebellious son, he transcends these human
institutions. He will not leave his son in exile. The Exile in R2
theology is YHWH's chastisement (*mûsār*) of his people to
make them turn back to Him in repentance. The third part of
the itinerary is the son's return from Egypt. For R2, YHWH
will restore his people and reenact another Exodus, if only his
people would acknowledge their sin and seek Him again.

Hos 14:2-9 concludes the third and final section of the
composition, Hos 12-14. This complex, as well, chronicles a
journey. Moreover, it returns to the wife/Israel motif which
was characterized in Hos 1-3. R2 refashions the Jacob
tradition of Hos 12* in such a way that Jacob, the father of
Israel, becomes a paradigm of repentance for his descendants.
He is no longer the patronymic cheat and liar to whom the
Hosean tradition traces the fraudulent practices of contemporary Israel. Furthermore, the person of Rachel is rehabili-
tated. No longer is she the adulterous mother, but the beloved
wife worthy of rescue. Just as Jacob journeyed to a foreign
land to rescue his wife, and just as YHWH through the
prophet *par excellence*, Moses, rescued the wife/Israel in the
first Exodus, so will YHWH rescue his wife again in a new
Exodus, if she repents, cherishes love and justice, and waits
upon God continually (12:7). For R2, the prophet of the new
Exodus is the prophet, Hosea, to whom he attributes his
composition pseudonymously. He is thus in keeping with his
deuteronomistic understanding of prophecy as a succession of
agents commissioned to do YHWH's will from Moses onward.

Throughout the Hos 4-11 complex, R2 recounts a
movement from barrenness to fertility. In 14:2-9, R2
summarizes this theme. He describes the future result of the
sowing of the wife/Israel in the land, which he depicted back in
2:25: Israel will break forth like a rich plantation. The
garden/Israel will be lush and fruitful. With imagery that
recalls the marital dialogues of the Song of Songs, R2 portrays
the wife/Israel sitting secure in the shade of YHWH and

obtaining her fruit from him alone. The future planting and fruition in the land will only occur, however, when Israel heeds the words of R2: "Return, O Israel to YHWH your God, for you have stumbled because of your iniquity" (14:2).

APPENDIX:

The Redactional History of the Book of Hosea

Hosea 1-3

H	C	R1	R2
			1:1
	1:2-4		1:5
	1:6abA		1:6bB-7
	1:8-9		2:1-3
2:4aA	2:4aB		
2:4b-5	2:6-7a		
2:7b			2:8-9
		2:10a	2:10b
		2:11	
2:12		2:13-15a	2:15b-18aA
	2:18aBb		2:19-20
	2:21-22a		2:22b-25
			3:1-5

Hosea 4-11

H	C	R1	R2
		4:1-2	4:3
4:4*		4:4*-5a	
4:5b			4:6a
		`4:6b	4:7-12a
4:12bA			4:12bB-13a
		4:13b	4:14
		4:15-16a	4:16b
		4:17a	4:17b
		4:18ab**	
4:18ab**-19a		4:19b	

*kōhēn = R1
**qālôn maginnêhā = H

H	C	R1	R2
5:1-2a			5:2b
5:3			5:4
5:5abA		5:5bB-7	
5:8-13a			5:13b
5:14			5:15--6:3
		6:4	6:5
		6:6-7	
6:8-10		6:11a	6:11b--7:1*
7:1*-3			7:4
7:5-9			7:10
7:11-12a**			7:12a**, 12b
7:13-15***			7:15***
			7:16

*kĕrop'î lĕyiśrā'ēl = R2
**ka'ăšer yēlēkû = R2
***yissartî = R2

H	C	R1	R2
		8:1-4a	8:4b-5aA
		8:5aBb-6*	8:6*-7
8:8-10		8:11-12	8:13-14
		9:1	9:2-4
		9:5	9:6
		9:7	9:8-9
		9:10	
9:11-13			9:14
		9:15	
9:16			9:17
		10:1-8	10:9-10
10:11			10:12
10:13a			10:13b-14
		10:15	11:1-4
			11:5-7
			11:8-9
			11:10-11

*kî miyyiśrā'ēl = R1

Hosea 12-14

H	C	R1	R2
12:1a			12:1b
12:2-4			12:5-7
12:8-9			12:10-12
12:13			12:14
12:15			13:1-11
13:12-13			13:14
13:15--14:1			14:2-4
			14:5
			14:6-9
			14:10

ABBREVIATIONS

AB	Anchor Bible
AJSL	*American Journal of Semitic Languages and Literature*
AnBib	Analecta biblica
ANET	J.B. Pritchard (ed.), *Ancient Near Eastern Texts*
AnOr	Analecta orientalia
AOAT	Alter Orient und Altes Testament
ATANT	Abhandlungen zur Theologie des Alten und Neuen Testaments
ATD	Das Alte Testament Deutsch
AusBR	*Australian Biblical Review*
BA	*Biblical Archaeologist*
BASOR	*Bulletin of the American Schools of Oriental Research*
BBB	Bonner biblische Beiträge
BDB	F. Brown, S.R. Driver, and C.A. Briggs, *Hebrew and English Lexicon of the Old Testament*
BHS	*Biblia hebraica stuttgartensia*
Bib	*Biblica*
BibB	Biblische Beiträge
BibOr	Biblica et orientalia
BJRL	*Bulletin of the John Rylands University Library of Manchester*
BK	*Bibel und Kirche*
BKAT	Biblischer Kommentar: Altes Testament
BN	*Biblische Notizen*
BTB	*Biblical Theology Bulletin*
BWANT	Beiträge zur Wissenschaft vom Alten und Neuen Testament
BZ	*Biblische Zeitschrift*
BZAW	Beihefte zur *ZAW*
CAT	Commentaire de l'Ancien Testament
CBQ	*Catholic Biblical Quarterly*
EphCarm	*Ephemerides Carmeliticae*

EvQ	*Evangelical Quarterly*
EvT	*Evangelische Theologie*
FRLANT	Forschungen zur Religion und Literatur des Alten und Neuen Testaments
HAT	Handbuch zum Alten Testament
HKAT	Handkommentar zum Alten Testament
HSM	Harvard Semitic Monographs
HTR	*Harvard Theological Review*
HUCA	*Hebrew Union College Annual*
IB	*Interpreter's Bible*
ICC	International Critical Commentary
IDB	G.A. Buttrick (ed.), *Interpreter's Dictionary of the Bible*
IDBSup	Supplementary volume to *IDB*
Int	*Interpretation*
JAAR	*Journal of the American Academy of Religion*
JB	A. Jones (ed.), *Jerusalem Bible*
JBC	R.E. Brown et al. (eds.), *The Jerome Biblical Commentary*
JBL	*Journal of Biblical Literature*
JETS	*Journal of the Evangelical Theological Society*
JJS	*Journal of Jewish Studies*
JNES	*Journal of Near Eastern Studies*
JPOS	*Journal of the Palestine Oriental Society*
JQR	*Jewish Quarterly Review*
JSJ	*Journal for the Study of Judaism in the Persian, Hellenistic and Roman Periods*
JSOT	*Journal for the Study of the Old Testament*
JSOTSup	Journal for the Study of the Old Testament-Supplement Series
JSS	*Journal of Semitic Studies*
JTSoA	*Journal of Theology for Southern Africa*
JTS	*Journal of Theological Studies*
Jud	*Judaism*
KAT	E. Sellin (ed.), Kommentar zum A.T.
McCQ	*McCormick Quarterly*
Mur	Wadi Murabba'at texts

NAB	New American Bible
NKZ	Neue kirchliche Zeitschrift
NRT	La nouvelle revue théologique
OLZ	Orientalische Literaturzeitung
Or	Orientalia (Rome)
OTA	Old Testament Abstracts
OTL	Old Testament Library
OTS	Oudtestamentische Studiën
OTWSA	Die Ou Testamentiese Werkgemeenskap in Suid-Afrika
RB	Revue biblique
REJ	Revue des études juives
RevExp	Review and Expositor
RevScRel	Revue des sciences religieuses
RHPR	Revue d'histoire et de philosophie religieuses
RSV	Revised Standard Version
SBLSP	Society of Biblical Literature Seminar Papers
SBLDS	SBL Dissertation Series
SBLMS	SBL Monograph Series
SBT	Studies in Biblical Theology
SEÅ	Svensk exegetisk årsbok
SJT	Scottish Journal of Theology
SR	Studies in Religion/Sciences religieuses
ST	Studia theologica
SWJT	Southwestern Journal of Theology
TBl	Theologische Blätter
TBT	The Bible Today
TDOT	G.J. Botterweck and H. Ringgren (eds.), Theological Dictionary of the Old Testament
Tg. Neb.	Targum of the Prophets
TLZ	Theologische Literaturzeitung
TQ	Theologische Quartalschrift
TrinJ	Trinity Journal
T.San	Tractate Sanhedrin, Babylonian Talmud
TSK	Theologische Studien und Kritiken
UF	Ugarit-Forschungen
USQR	Union Seminary Quarterly Review
UUÅ	Uppsala universitetsårsskrift

VT	*Vetus Testamentum*
VTSup	Vetus Testamentum, Supplements
ZAW	*Zeitschrift für die alttestamentliche Wissenschaft*
ZKT	*Zeitschrift für katholische Theologie*

NOTES

Chapter One--Theories of Hosean Composition

[1]F. I. Andersen and D. N. Freedman, *Hosea* (AB 24; Garden City: Doubleday, 1980) 66.

[2]R. H. Pfeiffer, *Introduction to the Old Testament* (New York: Harper, 1948, rev. ed.) 570.

[3]H. Graetz cited in W. R. Harper, *A Critical-Exegetical Commentary on Amos and Hosea* (ICC 18; Edinburgh: T&T Clark, 1905) clix. Cf. Y. Kaufmann, *The Religion of Israel*, trans. and abridged by Moshe Greenberg (Chicago: Univ. of Chicago, 1960) 368-72, who suggests a 1st and 2nd Hosea.

[4]G. H. Ewald, *Commentary on the Prophets of the Old Testament. Vol. I: Amos, Hosea and Zechariah*. J. F. Smith, trans. (London: Williams & Norgate, 1875) 214. Cf. E. G. Kraeling, *The Prophets* (New York: Rand McNally, 1969) 50.

[5]T. K. Cheyne, *Hosea, With Notes and Introduction* (Cambridge: University Press, 1892) 20. Cf. W. Rudolph, *Hosea* (KAT 13/1; Gütersloh: Gerd Mohn, 1966) 26.

[6]Cheyne, in his introduction to W. R. Smith's *The Prophets of Israel and Their Place in History* (London: Adam and Black, 1895) xvii-xxii. The most probable late insertions are 1:7; 2:1-3; 3:5; 4:15a; 5:15--6:4; 6:11; 14:2-10 and the superscription 1:1.

[7]The classic example was that of T. H. Robinson, *Prophecy and the Prophets in Ancient Israel* (London: Gerald Duckworth, 1923) 52-58. On Hosea in particular, see his commentary, *Die zwölf kleinen Propheten* (KAT 14; Tübingen, 1938) 1-2. Cf. the survey by O. Eissfeldt, "The Prophetic Literature," *The Old Testament and Modern Study*, H. H. Rowley, ed. (Oxford: Clarendon, 1951) 126-128, as well as his own literary-critical understanding of Hosean composition in *Einleitung in das Alte Testament* (Tübingen: J. C. B. Mohr, 1943, 1956, 1964) 517-28. Also, A. Weiser, *Das Buch der zwölf kleinen Propheten*, I (ATD 24/1; Göttingen: Vandenhoeck & Ruprecht, 1949) 14; and G. Brillet, *Amos et Osée* (Paris: Éditions du Cerf, 1944) 101-102.

[8]K. Marti, *Das Dodekapropheton: Hosea* (KHAT 13; Tübingen: J.C.B. Mohr, 1904) 1-2.

[9]Marti, *Dodekapropheton*, 8-9: Hos 1:1, 7; 2:2; 4:15; 5:5, 10, 12, 12-14; 6:4, 11; 8:14; 10:11; 12:1b, 3a.

[10]Marti, *Dodekapropheton*, 9-10: Hos 2:1-3, 15b-25; 3:1-5; 5:15-6:3, 5b; 11:10-11; 14:2-10.

[11]Marti, *Dodekapropheton*, 10-11.

[12]Harper, *Amos and Hosea*, clviii-clxii.

[13]Harper, *Amos and Hosea*, clxi, although he disagrees with Marti that Hosea had never referred to Judah.

[14]Harper, *Amos and Hosea*, clxi. Cf. Hos 4:13d; 5:6, 7:4, 16c; 8:8b; 9:1b, 9a, 10; 10:5, 14b; 12:14; 13:4b-7.

[15]E. Day, "Is the Book of Hosea Exilic?" *AJSL* 26 (1909/10) 105-32.

[16]F. E. Peiser, *Hosea. Philologische Studien zum Alten Testament* (Leipzig: J.C. Hinrichs, 1914) III-IV.

[17]Such was E. Sellin's complaint in *Das Zwölfprophetenbuch. Erste Hälfte: Hosea-Micha* (KAT 12; Leipzig: A. Deichertsche, 1929, 2 &3 Aufl.) 22. Moreover, H. Frey, "Der Aufbau der Gedichte Hoseas," *Wort und Dienst* (NF) 5 (1957) 9, felt that Peiser's hypothetical reconstruction was achieved by leveling most of the text as secondary.

[18]K. Budde, "Eine folgenschwere Redaktion des Zwölfprophetenbuchs," *ZAW* 39 (1922) 218-26.

[19]R. E. Wolfe, "The Editing of the Book of the Twelve," *ZAW* 12 (1935) 90-129.

[20]H. S. Nyberg, *Studien zum Hoseabuch* (UUÅ 6; Uppsala: A. B. Lundqvistska, 1935).

[21]See the very perceptive discussion and critique of the Scandinavian debate in D.A. Knight, *Rediscovering the Traditions of Israel* (Missoula: Scholars Press, 1975) 215-399.

[22]Cf. also earlier complaints made by A. Condamin, "Interpolations ou Transpositions Accidentelles?" *RB* 11 (1902) 379-97; S. R. Driver, *An Introduction to the Literature of the Old Testament* (Edinburgh: T&T Clark, 1913, 9th ed.) 306-7; and especially Sellin, *Das Zwölfprophetenbuch*, 18-22. For a later critique, see Mauchline, "The Book of Hosea," 563-64.

[23]H. Birkeland, *Zum hebräischen Traditionswesen* (ANVAO 2, Hist. -Filos. Kl., 1939, No. 1; Oslo: Jacob Dybwad, 1938) 7.

[24]It should be noted here that investigations on the prophets in general were affected by the conclusions of these and other scholars involved in the Scandinavian debate. Consult the overviews by Eissfeldt, "Prophetic Literature," 115-117; 126-134; A.H.J. Gunneweg, *Mündliche und schriftliche Tradition der vorexilischen Prophetenbücher als Problem der neueren Prophetenforschung* (Göttingen: Vandenhoeck & Ruprecht, 1959) 7-20; 51-71; Knight, *Rediscovering*, 215-399.

[25]E. M. Good, "The Composition of Hosea," *SEÅ* 31 (1966) 21-63. His work investigates the mechanical principles by which the collectors joined groups of poems together.

[26]*Hosea* (Neukirchen/Vluyn, 1961, 1965) [ET=*A Commentary on the Book of the Prophet Hosea* (Philadelphia: Fortress, 1974).] The pages cited in the text refer to the English edition.

[27]This is the criticism of G. Fohrer, *Introduction to the Old Testament* (Nashville: Abingdon, 1968) 421-22, and G. M. Tucker, "Commentaries on Hosea: A Review," *Religious Studies Review* 7 (1981) 134.

[28]E. Jacob, *Osée* (Neuchâtel: Delachaux & Niestlé, 1965) 12-13; J. Scharbert, *Die Propheten Israels bis 700 vor. Chr.* (Köln: Bachem, 1965) 136-137. Cf. also, modification of Wolff by J. L. Mays, *Hosea: A Commentary* (Philadelphia: Westminster, 1969) 6; 15-17; and Tucker, "Commentaries on Hosea," 134.

[29]H. Frey, "Der Aufbau der Gedichte Hoseas," *Wort und Dienst* (NF) 5 (1957) 91.

[30]Supra, 4.

[31]Cf. Frey, "Aufbau," 10-13, where Frey posed questions regarding the success of literary and form criticism in analyzing the text. Some of his questions foreshadowed Güttgemanns's critique of the whole literary, form and redaction critical enterprise. Infra, 42-44.

[32]M. Buss, *The Prophetic Word of Hosea* (Berlin: Alfred Töpelmann, 1969).

[33]I. Willi-Plein, *Vorformen der Schriftexegese innerhalb des Alten Testaments* (BZAW 123: Berlin: De Gruyter, 1971).

[34]Supra, 6.

[35]Supra, 5-6.

[36]Supra, 3.

[37]Supra, 4-6.

[38]F. I. Andersen and D. N. Freedman, *Hosea* (AB 24; Garden City: Doubleday, 1980).

[39]Cf. R. Melugin's criticisms of the rhetorical-critical method, "Muilenburg, Form Criticism, and Theological Exegesis," *Encounter with the Text*, M. J. Buss, ed. (Philadelphia: Fortress, 1979) 91-99.

[40]The authors' description is rather vague and misleading. If their statement is taken literally, that the Book of Hosea "offers material from an earlier stage in the process, from the actual deliberations of Yahweh in the divine council," it would presuppose a whole set of theological issues which the authors do not address.

[41]Unfortunately, Grace Emmerson's, *Hosea: An Israelite Prophet in Judean Perspective* (JSOTSup. 28; Sheffield, JSOT, 1984) came too late into my hands to be incorporated into this study.

Chapter Two--Presuppositions in Hosean Scholarship

[1]K. Koch, *The Growth of the Biblical Tradition*, S. M. Cupitt, trans. (London: Adam & Charles Black, 1969) 69.

[2]Cf. W. Richter, *Exegese als Literaturwissenschaft* (Göttingen: Vandenhoeck & Ruprecht, 1971) 49-50.

[3]This is the complaint of J. M. Ward, *Hosea* (New York: Harper & Row, 1966) xviii; and D. J. McCarthy, "God as Prisoner of Our Own Choosing: Critical-Historical Study of the Bible. Why and Whither," *Historicism and Faith*, P.L. Williams, ed. (Scranton: Northeast, 1980) 17.

[4]Cf. Wolff, *Commentary*, 9, where 1:5, 7 are eliminated from the discussion because they are literarily secondary.

[5]Such is J. M. Mays's complaint in *Exegesis as a Theological Discipline*, Inaugural Address delivered April 20, 1960, Schauffler Hall, Union Theological Seminary, Richmond, Virginia, 4-10, and especially McCarthy, "God as Prisoner of Our Own Choosing," 17-19, 26, 37.

[6]Mays, *Exegesis as a Theological Discipline*, 10; Cf. B. W. Anderson, "Tradition and Scripture in the Community of Faith," *JBL* 100 (1981) 7, 16-17

[7]Such was Engnell's complaint against the literary critics. See Knight, *Rediscovering*, 265-266 and I. Engnell, "Prophets and Prophetism in the Old

Testament," *A Rigid Scrutiny*, J. T. Willis, trans. (Nashville: Vanderbilt Univ., 1969) 169. See also McCarthy, "God as Prisoner of Our Own Choosing," 18-19.

[8]Cf. Mays, *Exegesis as a Theological Discipline*, 17-20.

[9]Cf. H. Gunkel, *Die Propheten* (Göttingen: Vandenhoeck & Ruprecht, 1917) 106; Koch, *Growth of the Biblical Tradition*, 72-78; G. M. Tucker, *Form Criticism of the Old Testament* (Philadelphia: Fortress, 1971) 18.

[10]Cf. the complaint of Güttgemanns, *Candid Questions*, 96.

[11]B. O. Long, "Recent Field Studies in Oral Literature and the Question of *Sitz-im-Leben*," *Semeia* 5 (1976) 37. Güttgemanns, *Candid Questions*, 235-257, outlines the philosophical problematics in Gunkel's conception of *Sitz-im-Leben*.

[12]Supra, 10-13.

[13]C. Westermann, *Basic Forms of Prophetic Speech*, H. C. White, trans. (Philadelphia: Westminister, 1967) 27.

[14]J. Jeremias, "Hosea 4-7. Beobachtungen zur Komposition des Buches Hosea," *Textgemäss*, A.H.J. Gunneweg und O. Kaiser, hrsg. (Göttingen: Vandenhoeck & Ruprecht, 1979) 48.

[15]In the structure of Wolff's commentary, the form of the passage is discussed first; the historical setting is discussed second.

[16]Supra, 11-13. Cf. D. Stuart, *Old Testament Exegesis* (Philadelphia: Westminster, 1980) 11. He maintains that some scholars used form criticism to arrive at firm conclusions regarding dating, authorship, genuineness, originality, contextual propriety, historical validity, etc. of passages, which the method, in reality, simply could not support.

[17]This is the understanding of Richter, *Exegese als Literaturwissenschaft*, 165-68; Koch, *Growth of the Biblical Tradition*, 57, would call the last *form-critical process* the redaction history. Cf. H. Barth & O.H. Steck, *Exegese des Alten Testaments* (Neukirchen-Vluyn: Neukirchener, 1971) 48, where redaction criticism takes up the results of literary criticism. The traditional source, form, redaction critical procedure is also characteristic of New Testament methodology. Cf. H. Zimmermann, *Neutestamentliche Methodenlehre* (Stuttgart: Katholisches Bibelwerk, 1976), and the survey of the literature on NT form and redaction criticism in Güttgemanns, *Candid Questions*, 95-114.

[18]Infra, 47-49.

[19]J. Muilenburg, "Form Criticism and Beyond," *JBL* 88 (1969) 1-18.

[20]Infra, 35-37.

[21]Robinson, *Prophecy and the Prophets*, 52; G. Hölscher, *Die Profeten* (Leipzig: J.C. Hinrichs, 1914) 89. On the nature of ecstasy, see H.H. Rowley, "The Nature of Old Testament Prophecy in the Light of Recent Study," *The Servant of the Lord and Other Essays on the Old Testament* (London: Lutterworth, 1952) 91-128; Eissfeldt, "Prophetic Literature," 134-45; and R.R. Wilson, "Prophecy and Ecstasy: A Reexamination," *JBL* 98 (1979) 321-37.

[22]Cf. Ewald, Cheyne and Marti.

[23]Cf. not only the scholars on Hosea already discussed, but particularly I. Engnell, who is most closely identified with the Scandinavian tradition, "Prophets and Prophetism," 168-169.

[24]This was not without its critique from among their own numbers. Cf. S. Mowinckel, *Prophecy and Tradition* (ANVAO, II. Hist-Filos. Kl., 1946, No. 3; Oslo: J. Dybwad, 1946) 19-36; and H. Ringgren, "Oral and Written Transmission in the Old Testament," *ST* 3 (1950) 34-59.

[25]Cf. I. Engnell, "Methodological Aspects of Old Testament Study," *VTSup* 7 (1960) 21-22; E. Nielsen, *Oral Tradition* (SBT, 11; London: SCM, 1954) 63.

[26]Thus, Birkeland, *Traditionswesen*, 6; Nyberg, *Studien zum Hoseabuch*, 8-9; Engnell, "Prophets and Prophetism," 163.

[27]Cf. the image of the smelting-oven of the community in Birkeland, *Traditionswesen*, 23-24 and the charge of Engnell, "Methodological Aspects," 21, against the "anachronistic bookish mode of view" among literary critics.

[28]Knight, *Rediscovering*, 4.

[29]Tucker, *Form Criticism*, 6. The literature on the form critical study of the prophets is vast. Cf. the bibliography in W.E. March, "Prophecy," *Old Testament Form Criticism*, J.H. Hayes, ed. (San Antonio: Trinity University, 1974) 141-177.

[30]Koch, *Growth of the Biblical Tradition*, 33; Tucker, *Form Criticism*, 9.

[31]Koch, *Growth of the Biblical Tradition*, 57-58. Cf. Richter, *Exegese als Literaturwissenschaft*, 153; and R.P. Carroll, *When Prophecy Failed* (London: SCM, 1979) 52-53.

[32]In criticizing literary criticism for making an analytical method subservient to a particular literary theory, the Scandinavian critic, R.A. Carlson, (*David, the Chosen King*, E.J. Sharpe & Stanley Rudman, trans. [Uppsala: Almqvist & Wiksells, 1964] 10), cautioned against a similar abuse of the tradition-historical method.

[33]So argue Nyberg and Birkeland. See also the discussion of Engnell on this in Knight, *Rediscovering*, 267-68.

[34]I. Engnell, "The Traditio-Historical Method in Old Testament Research," *A Rigid Scrutiny*, J.T. Willis, trans. (Nashville: Vanderbilt Univ., 1969) 9. The incongruity of maintaining both the reliability of the oral tradition, as well as the development of the tradition in the community, has been pointed out by Mowinckel, *Prophecy and Tradition*, 66; A.H.J. Gunneweg, *Mündliche und schriftliche Tradition der vorexilischen Prophetenbücher als Problem der neueren Prophetenforschung*, (Göttingen: Vandenhoeck & Ruprecht, 1959) 69-70; Knight, *Rediscovering*, 383-392; W. McKane, "Prophecy and Prophetic Literature," *Tradition and Interpretation*, G.W. Anderson, ed. (Oxford: Clarendon, 1979) 184.

[35]Engnell, cited in Knight, *Rediscovering*, 264. Italics mine.

[36]Koch, *Growth of the Biblical Tradition*, 57-58.

[37]Tucker, *Form Criticism*, 19; Koch, *Growth of the Biblical Tradition*, 58.

[38]H. Gunkel, *The Legends of Genesis* (New York: Schocken, 1964) 39; Koch, *Growth of the Biblical Tradition*, 72-73; Cf. M. Dibelius, *From Tradition to Gospel*, B.L. Wolff, trans. (New York: Charles Scribner's Sons, 1935) 1.

[39]See the opinion of Baudissin, cited in Westermann, *Basic Forms of Prophetic Speech*, 15, regarding the deterioration of the power of the oral stage when put into writing.

[40]Eissfeldt, "Prophetic Literature," 117.

[41]Nielsen, *Oral Tradition*, 33, 60-61, here adopts Engnell's explanation of the written stage of the tradition as a "crisis of credit." The ambiguity surrounding this "crisis" has been pointed out by Gunneweg, *Mündliche und schriftliche Tradition*, 13.

[42]Koch, *Growth of the Biblical Tradition*, 58. Italics mine.

[43]See Long, *Semeia* 5 (1976) 35-49; R. Knierim, "Old Testament Form Criticism Reconsidered," *Int* 27 (1973) 449.

[44]B.O. Long, "Recent Field Studies in Oral Literature and their Bearing on OT Criticism," *VT* 26 (1976) 188. See also Knierim, "Old Testament Form Criticism Reconsidered," 444.

[45]A.B. Lord, *The Singer of Tales* (Cambridge, MA: Harvard Univ., 1964) 99-101.

[46]Long, *VT* 26 (1976) 189-93.

[47]Lord, *Singer of Tales*, 101; Long, *VT* 26 (1976) 193. Cf. R. C. Culley, "An Approach to the Problem of Oral Tradition," *VT* 13 (1963) 119-21.

[48]Lord, *Singer of Tales*, 101. Cf. Culley, "An Approach to the Problem of Oral Tradition," 121.

[49]Infra, 40.

[50]Cf. Knight's discussion in *Rediscovering*, 383-92.

[51]Culley, "An Approach to the Problem of Oral Tradition," 122-123; Knight, *Rediscovering*, 388; Cf. Mowinckel, *Prophecy and Tradition*, 84-87.

[52]Long, *Semeia*, 5 (1976) 36-37.

[53]Knight, *Rediscovering*, 391.

[54]W. Harrelson, "Life, Faith and the Emergence of Tradition," *Tradition and Theology in the Old Testament*, D. A. Knight, ed. (Philadelphia: Fortress, 1977) 11.

[55]D.A. Knight, "Introduction: Tradition and Theology," *Tradition and Theology in the Old Testament* (Philadelphia: Fortress, 1977) 4; cf. *Rediscovering*, 13.

[56]W. Kelber, *The Oral and Written Gospel and the Hermeneutics of Speaking and Writing in the Synoptic Tradition, Mark, Paul, and Q* (Philadelphia: Fortress, 1983) 14. Italics mine.

[57]R. Lapointe, "Tradition and Language: The Import of Oral Expression," *Tradition and Theology in the Old Testament*, D.A. Knight, ed. (Philadelphia: Fortress, 1977) 133.

[58]Lord, *Singer of Tales*, 124-25.

[59]Ibid., 127-28.

[60]Ibid., 125.

[61]Güttgemanns, *Candid Questions*, 197.

[62]Thus, Güttgemanns, *Candid Questions*, 209-11.

[63]Ibid., 339-40.

[64]Cf. the discussion of redaction criticism, supra, 35-36.

[65]Such was Birkeland's insight into the work of the tradents, *Zum hebräischen Traditionswesen*, 23-24.

[66]Güttgemanns, *Offene Fragen*, 88. Italics his, translation mine.

[67]Güttgemanns, "Foundations of a New Testament Theology," 202-204. Cf. also *Candid Questions*, 118.

[68]Güttgemanns, *Candid Questions*, 287-92.

[69]Cf. Particularly W.E. March, "Redaction Criticism and the Formation of Prophetic Books," *SBLSP* 11 (1977) 89-101.

[70]Ibid., 91-94.

[71]Cf. N. Perrin, *What is Redaction Criticism?* (Philadelphia: Fortress, 1969).

[72]Supra, 41-44.

[73]Cf. Perrin, *Redaction Criticism*, 66.

[74]W. Schottroff, "Jeremiah 2:1-3: Erwägungen zur Methode der Prophetenexegese," *ZTK* 67 (1970) 293. See also J. T. Willis' review of Knight's *Rediscovering*, in *JBL* 94 (1975) 284.

[75]Cf. Ewald, cited on p. 2, supra.

[76]Cf. Andersen and Freedman, supra, 22.

[77]Cf. supra, 7-8.

Chapter Three--Hos 1-3: Final Redacted State

[1]Wolff, *Commentary*, xxix-xxxi. Those following Wolff's divisions are Buss, *The Prophetic Word*, 33-34; Scharbert, *Die Propheten Israels*, 135; and Jacob, *Osée*, 12.

[2]Ewald, *Commentary on the Prophets of the Old Testament*, 214-28.

[3]Kaufmann, *The Religion of Israel*, 368-77. See also C. H. Toy, "Note on Hosea 1-3," *JBL* 75-79 and H. Graetz cited in Harper, *Amos and Hosea*, clix.

[4]Kraeling, *The Prophets*, 50. As a young prophet, he wrote Hos 1-3 based on his marriage. As a mature prophet, he composed Hos 4-14 which was a separate collection of his oracles.

[5]G. L. Robinson, *The Twelve Minor Prophets* (Grand Rapids: Baker Book House, 1974) 21-22.

[6]Cf. Eissfeldt, *Old Testament: An Introduction*, 384, and Andersen and Freedman, *Hosea*, 52.

[7]Cf. Harper, *Amos and Hosea*, clix-clxi.

[8]For an excellent summary and critique of the earlier literature on the subject, see H.H. Rowley, "The Marriage of Hosea," *Men of God* (London: Nelson, 1963) 66-97. See also G. W. Anderson, "Hosea and Yahweh," *REx* 72 (1975) 425-36; S. Bitter, *Die Ehe des Propheten Hosea* (Göttingen: Vandenhoeck & Ruprecht, 1975); H. L. Ellison, "The Message of Hosea in the Light of His Marriage," *EvQ* 41 (1969) 3-9; J. R. B. McDonald, "The Marriage of Hosea," *Theology* 67 (1964) 149-56; F. S. North, "A Solution to Hosea's Marital Problems by Critical Analysis," *JNES* 16 (1957) 128-30; Rudolph, *Hosea*, 86-90; idem, "Präparierte Jungfrauen? (Zu Hosea 1)," *ZAW* 75 (1963)

65-73; L. Waterman, "Hosea, Chapters 1-3, in Retrospect and Prospect," *JNES* 14 (1955) 100-109; Wolff, *Commentary*, 13-15.

[9]Mauchline, "The Book of Hosea," *IDB* 6 (1956) 563; Waterman, "Hosea, Chapters 1-3, in Retrospect and Prospect," 193-98; R. Gordis, "Hosea's Marriage and Message: A New Approach," *Poets, Prophets, and Sages: Essays in Biblical Interpetation* (Bloomington: Indiana Univ., 1971) 239-42.

[10]So, A. Condamin, "Interpolations ou Transpositions Accidentelles?" *RB* 11 (1902) 380, 388, who places 2:8-9 after 2:15. He thinks that a later scribe accidentally transposed the text into its present position. The *NAB* adopts his rearrangement of 2:8-9. Cf. the radical rearrangement of the text by the *JB*: Hos 2:1-3 is placed after Hos 3. Hos 2:8-9 is put after 2:15. Hos 2:13 and 2:14 are transposed. Also, F. S. North, "Hosea's Introduction to his Book," *VT* 8 (1958) 429-32.

[11]Engnell, "Prophets and Prophetism," 167-68, explains the phenomenon of threat/hope juxtapositions in the prophetic books by referring to the Arabic *diwān* compositional model. In the *diwān* the words of a poet are arranged, not chronologically, but according to an alternating schema. Cf. also, E. M. Good, "The Composition of Hosea," *SEÅ* 31 (1966) 29-30; Buss, *Prophetic Word*, 33-34; Birkeland, *Traditionswesen*, 61.

[12]J. A. Bewer, "The Story of Hosea's Marriage," *AJSL* 22 (1905-6) 20; A. Weiser, *Das Buch der zwölf kleinen Propheten, I* (ATD 24/1; Göttingen: Vandenhoeck & Ruprecht, 1949) 14; G. Brillet, *Amos et Osée* (Paris: Éditions du Cerf, 1944) 101-102; Eissfeldt, *The Old Testament: An Introduction*, 391; Wolff, *Commentary*, xxix-xxx; Rudolph, *Hosea*, 25; Andersen and Freedman, *Hosea*, 58; G. V. Blankenbaker, *The Language of Hosea 1-3* (Ann Arbor: Xerox Univ. Microfilms, 1976) 227. Cf. Mays, *Hosea*, 15, who prefers to describe the secondary author of Hos 1-3 as the collector of Hosea's oracles rather than the more specific designation of disciple. While Willi-Plein's thesis is that the whole book is the product of redactional efforts extending to the post-exilic period, her understanding of Hos 1-3 is that it was formed in the narrow circle of Hosea's own disciples, *Vorformen*, 127, 244, 252.

[13]Marti, *Dodekapropheton*, 8-10; Wolfe, "The Editing of the Book of the Twelve," 90-129; C. H. Toy, "Note on Hosea 1-3," *JBL* 32 (1913) 77-78; Harper, *Amos and Hosea*, clviii-clxii; Peiser, *Hosea*, 60-63. B. Renaud, "Genèse et unité rédactionnelle de Os 2," *RevScRel* 54 (1980) 1-20; idem., "Le Livret d'Osée 1-3," *RevScRel* 56 (1982) 159-178; L. Ruppert, "Erwägungen zur Kompositions -und Redaktionsgeschichte von Hos 1-3," *BZ* 26 (1982) 208-223.

[14]Robinson, *Die zwölf kleinen Propheten*, 1.

[15]Budde, "Eine folgenschwere Redaktion," 219-227.

[16]E. Galbiati, "La struttura sintetica di Osea 2," *Mélanges Rinaldi. Studi sull'Oriente e la Bibbia* (Genova, 1967) 317-28; H. Krszyna, "Literarische Struktur von Os 2, 4-17," *BZ* 13 (1969) 41-59; U. Cassuto, "The Second Chapter of the Book of Hosea," *Biblical and Oriental Studies, I: Bible,* I. Abrahams, trans. (Jerusalem: Magnes, 1973) 101-40; D. Lys, "J'ai deux amours ou l'amant jugé. Exercice sur Osée 2, 4-25," *ETR* 51 (1976) 59-77; D. J. A. Clines, "Hosea 2: Structure and Interpretation," *Studia Biblica 1978, I:*

Papers on Old Testament and Related Themes (JSOTSup 11; Sheffield: JSOT, 1979)83-103.

[17]W. Vogels, "'Osée-Gomer' car et comme 'Yahweh-Israël' Os 1-3," *NRT* 103 (1981)711-27.

[18]Cf. B. Renaud, "Osée 1-3: analyse diachronique et lecture synchronique, problèmes de méthode," *RevScRel* 57 (1983)249-260.

[19]S. R. Driver, *An Introduction to the Literature of the Old Testament* (Edinburgh: T&T Clark, 1913), 9th ed.) 302; Harper, *Amos and Hosea,* 201.

[20]Marti, *Dodekapropheton,* 8, 13-14; Duhm, "Anmerkungen," 18; Harper, *Amos and Hosea,* clx; Wolff, *Commentary,* 3-6; Mays, *Hosea* 20-21; Willi-Plein, *Vorformen,* 8-9; Andersen and Freedman, *Hosea,* 143-44; J. Jeremias, *Der Prophet Hosea* (ATD 24/1; Göttingen: Vandenhoeck & Ruprecht, 1983) 23, among others regard the whole verse as a later addition. There are, of course, exceptions. Driver, *An Introduction,* 302, for example, thought that the reference, "in the days of Jeroboam", originally referred only to Hos 1-3. When a title was needed for the whole book which derived from a later period, the names of the Judean kings contemporary with and subsequent to Jeroboam were added. Cheyne, *Hosea* 12, regards 1:1 as a thoughtless combination of two distinct traditions which did not refer to the same body of writing.

[21]On *dbr,* cf. Mays, *Hosea,* 20-21, and G. M. Tucker, "Prophetic Superscriptions and the Growth of a Canon," *Canon and Authority,* G. W. Coats and B. O. Long, eds. (Philadelphia: Fortress, 1977) 63-64.

[22]So, T. Lescow, "Redaktionsgeschichtliche Analyse von Micha 1-5," *ZAW* 84 (1972) 62.

[23]For investigations of literary superscriptions, see Tucker, "Prophetic Superscriptions," 56-70; Lescow, "Redaktionsgeschichtliche Analyse von Micha 1-5," 61-64; H. M. I. Gevaryahu, "Biblical Colophons: A Source for the 'Biography' of Authors, Texts and Books," *VTSup* 28 (1975) 42-59. Cf. Andersen and Freedman, *Hosea,* 143-149.

[24]Harper, *Amos and Hosea,* 203-204; Day, "Is the Book of Hosea Exilic?" 117-118; Mays, *Hosea,* 20.

[25]So. Wolff, *Commentary,* 4; Jacob, *Osée,* 18; W. H. Schmidt, "Die deuteronomistische Redaktion des Amosbuches; zu den theologischen Unterschieden zwischen dem Prophetenwort und seinem Sammler," *ZAW* 77 (1965) 170-171; Willi-Plein, *Vorformen,* 115; Lescow, "Redaktionsgeschtliche Analyse von Micha 1-5," 62; Tucker, "Prophetic Superscriptions," 62-63,69.

[26]Cf. Blankenbaker, *The Language of Hosea 1-3,* 208-209; Wolff, *Commentary,* xxix; Andersen and Freedman, *Hosea,* 292.

[27]Nowack, *Die kleinen Propheten,* 28; Robinson, *Die zwölf kleinen Propheten,* 16; Harper, *Amos and Hosea,* clx; Cheyne, in W. R. Smith, *The Prophets of Israel and their Place in History* (London: Adam and Charles Black, 1895) xvii; Willi-Plein, *Vorformen,* 126.

[28]Wolff, *Commentary,* 57; Mays, Hosea, 16; Sellin, *Das Zwölfprophetenbuch,* 49; Weiser, *Das Buch der zwölf kleinen Propheten,* 23. Eissfeldt, *The Old Testament: An Introduction,* 389, thinks only "David their king" is secondary.

[29]Buss, *Prophetic Word,* 10, 70.

[30]Peiser, *Hosea*, 11-13.

[31]J. Schreiner, "Hoseas Ehe, ein Zeichen des Gerichts," *BZ* NF 21 (1977) 163-83. Cf. Ruppert, "Erwägungen," 216, 220 and Renaud, "Le Livret d'Osée 1-3," 163-166.

[32]Marti, *Dodekapropheton*, 9; Day, "Is the Book of Hosea Exilic?" 113; Toy, "Note on Hosea 1-3," 77; P. Haupt, "Hosea's Erring Spouse," *JBL* 34 (1915) 42; L. W. Batten, "Hosea's Message and Marriage," *JBL* 48 (1929) 270-72; Wolfe, "The Editing of the Book of the Twelve," 93; W. F. Stinespring, "Hosea, the Prophet of Doom," *Crozer Quarterly* 27 (1950) 202; North, "Solution to Hosea's Marital Problems," 128-129; P. G. Borbone, "Il Capitolo terzo di Osea," *Henoch* 2 (1980) 257-66.

[33]Stinespring, "Hosea, the Prophet of Doom," 202. Cf. Frey, "Aufbau," 35-36.

[34]Cf. especially those scholars cited in fn. 32 above.

[35]Wolff, *Commentary*, 60-61.

[36]That this Davidic leadership is an exilic theme, see D. C. Greenwood, "On the Hope for a Restored Northern Kingdom," *ZAW* 88 (1976) 377-78. Also Marti, *Dodekapropheton*, 9.

[37]Regarding the lateness of *'hb* as an expression of the relationship between Israel and God, see G. Wallis, "*ʾāhabh*," *TDOT* 1 (1974) 112-113.

[38]Cf. Dt 4:30. F. J. Helfmeyer, "*ʾaḥărê*," *TDOT* 1 (1974) 206.

[39]We find convincing the arguments of Andersen and Freedman, *Hosea*, 304-305, that *wĕgam - 'ănî 'ēlāyik* means here, "then indeed I will be yours." Their arguments do greater justice to the Hosea/YHWH and wife/Israel parallelism in the unit. Thus, implied in the text is the eventual return of Gomer to Hosea. Cf. other explanations, which, however, emend the text, recapitulated in Willi-Plein, *Vorformen*, 124.

[40]Cf. *Oxford English Dictionary*; F. P. Donnelly, *Persuasive Speech* (New York: P. J. Kennedy & Sons, 1931) 37, 171. With respect to Hosea, S. Kaatz, "Wortspiel, Assonanz und Notarikon bei Hosea," *Jeschurun* 11 (1924) 434, thus distinguishes paronomasia from "Wortspiel" which combines not only similarity of sound but also meaning effect. Cf. also W. Bühlmann und K. Scherer, *Stilfiguren der Bibel* (BibB 10; Schweizerisches Katholisches Bibelwerk, 1973) 19-22, who make a similar differentiation between "Paronomasie" and "Wortspiele." However, W. L. Holladay, "Form and Word-Play in David's Lament over Saul and Jonathan," *VT* 20 (1970) 157-58, uses the term "word-play" in the sense in which Kaatz and Bühlmann use "paronomasia."

[41]This was true for many of the ancient Latin and Greek rhetoricians. See also I. M. Casanowitz, *Paronomasia in the Old Testament* (Boston: Norwood, 1894); B. J. Beitzel, "Exodus 3:14 and the Divine Name: A Case of Biblical Paronomasia," *TrinJ* 1 NS (1980) 5-12; J. J. Glück, "Paronomasia in Biblical Literature," *Semitics* 1 (1970) 50-78; J. J. Glück, "Assonance in Ancient Hebrew Poetry: Sound Patterns as a Literary Device," *De Fructu Oris Sui: Essays in Honor of Adrianus van Selms*. I. H. Eybers et al. eds. (Leiden: Brill, 1979) 69-84; J. M. Sasson, "Wordplay in the OT," *IDBSup*, 968-70; D. F. Guillaume, "Paronomasia in the Old Testament," *JSS* 9 (1964) 282-290; Cf. G.

R. Driver, "Problems and Solutions," *VT* 4 (1954) 240-245. Regarding paronomasia as a traditional principle of rabbinic exegesis, see W. Chomsky, "Some Traditional Principles in Biblical Exegesis," *Essays on the Occasion of the Seventieth Anniversary of the Dropsie University* (Philadelphia: Dropsie Univ., 1979) 34-35.

[42]Casanowitz, *Paronomasia in the Old Testament*, 26-43.

[43]Cf. the descriptions of these wordplays in Sasson, "Wordplay in the OT," 968-70; Beitzel, "Exodus 3:14," 5-12; Glück, "Paronomasia," 50-78; and Casanowitz, *Paronomasia in the Old Testament*. For other studies in paronomasia, see F. M. T. Böhl, "Wortspiele im Alten Testament," *JPOS* 6 (1926) 196-212; J. H. Charlesworth, "Paronomasia and Assonance in the Syriac Text of the Odes of Solomon," *Semitics* 1 (1970) 12-26; M. Fishbane, "The Qumran Pesher and Traits of Ancient Hermeneutics," *Proceedings of the VIth World Congress of Jewish Studies* (Jerusalem: World Union of Jewish Studies, 1977) 97-114; I. Gabor, *Der Hebräische Urrhythmus* (BZAW 52; Giessen: A. Töpelmann, 1929); S. Gevirtz, "Of Patriarchs and Puns: Joseph at the Fountain, Jacob at the Ford," *HUCA* 46 (1975) 33-54; G. B. Gray, *Studies in Hebrew Proper Names* (London: Black, 1896); W. Holladay, "The Covenant with the Patriarchs Overturned," *JBL* 91 (1972) 305-20; A. F. Key, "The Giving of Proper Names in the Old Testament," *JBL* 83 (1964) 55-59; D. F. Payne, "Characteristic Word-Play in 'Second Isaiah': A Reappraisal," *JSS* 12 (1967) 207-226; L. Peeters, "Pour une Interprétation du Jeu de Mots," *Semitics* 2 (1971/72) 127-42; J. Porter, "Samson's Riddle: Judges 14:18," *JTS* 13 (1962) 106-109; O.S. Rankin, "Alliteration in Hebrew Poetry," *JTS* 31 (1930) 285-91; H. Reckendorf, *Über Paronomasie in den semitischen Sprachen. Ein Beitrag zur allgemeinen Sprachwissenschaft* (Giessen: Töpelmann, 1909); J. M. Sasson, "Word-Play in Gen 6:8-9," *CBQ* 37 (1975) 165-66; E. A. Speiser, "Word Plays on the Creation Epic's Version of the Founding of Babylon," *Or* 25 (1956) 317-23; W. F. Stinespring, "Humor," *IDB*, Vol. E-J (1962) 660-62.

[44]See Wallis, "'āhabh," *TDOT* 1, 114-117.

[45]Andersen and Freedman, *Hosea*, 295.

[46]See Casanowitz, *Paronomasia in the Old Testament*, 16, 35.

[47]Ibid., 34; Sasson, "Wordplay in the OT," 969-70; Beitzel, "Exodus 3:14," 11-12.

[48]Regarding the licentious connotation of '*hb*, see Wolff, *Commentary*, 60; A. D. Tushingham, "A Reconsideration of Hosea Chapters 1-3," *JNES* 12 (1953) 151; Cf. W. Thomas, "The Root '*āhēb* 'love' in Hebrew," *ZAW* 57 (1939) 64.

[49]Cf. Casanowitz, *Paronomasia in the Old Testament*, 35. Regarding transposition as an exegetical technique of the rabbis, see Chomsky, "Traditional Principles," 33-34.

[50]Andersen and Freedman, *Hosea*, 307; Blankenbaker, *The Language of Hos 1-3*, 221; Rudolph, *Hosea*, 93-94; Jacob, *Osée*, 37.

[51]Cf. Isa 7:9: '*im lō' ta'ămînû kî lō' tē'āmēnû*, "If you will not believe, surely you shall not be established." On *metaphony*, see Beitzel, "Exodus 3:14," 9; Sasson, "Wordplay in the OT," 969; Glück, "Paronomasia," 61-66; Cf. Casanowitz, *Paronomasia in the Old Testament*, 35.

[52]Rudolph, *Hosea*, 93-94.

[53]W. L. Holladay, *The Root Šûbh in the Old Testament* (Leiden: Brill, 1958) 146-47; Glück, "Paronomasia," 58.

[54]In the meantime, see Marti, *Dodekapropheton*, 1-2, who had argued quite early that the present Hos 1-3, 4-14 arrangement is a later structure and that there is a unified level of tradition which Hos 1-3 and 4-14 shared in common.

[55]Day, "Is the Book of Hosea Exilic?" 112; Peiser, *Hosea*, 2; Haupt, "Hosea's Erring Spouse," 48-50; Wolfe, "The Editing of the Book of the Twelve," 104₇105; Pfeiffer, *Introduction*, 573; J. M. Ward, *Hosea: A Theological Commentary* (New York: Harper & Row, 1966) 5-6; Schreiner, "Hoseas Ehe," 170; Renaud, "Genèse et unité rédactionnelle de Os 2," 15, fn. 25; Ruppert, "Erwägungen," 216, 220; Jeremias, *Der Prophet Hosea*, 34. Buss, *Prophetic Word*, 7, thinks that only "it will happen on that day" of 1:5 is secondary.

[56]Wolff, *Commentary*, 19; Mays, *Hosea*, 28; Rudolph, *Hosea*, 52; Willi-Plein, *Vorformen*, 116-117; Blankenbaker, *The Language of Hos 1-3*, 50-51.

[57]Glück, "Paronomasia," 66-70; Sasson, "Wordplay in the OT," 969; Beitzel, "Ex 3:14," 9-10. Cf. Casanowitz, *Paronomasia in the Old Testament*, 35. For an example of parasonancy, see Isa 5:7: "He expected justice (*mišpaṭ*) but behold, bloodshed (*mišpah*); righteousness (*ṣĕdāqâ*) but behold, a cry (*sĕʿāqâ*)!"

[58]Note also the *šbt/šbr* wordplay in Isa 14:4b-5a.

[59]N.M. Waldman, "The Breaking of the Bow," *JQR* 79 (1978) 82-86. Cf. Ps 46:10: "(YHWH) makes wars cease to the end of the earth; he breaks the bow (*qšt yšbr*) and shatters the spear; he burns the chariots with fire!" (RSV)

[60]Infra, 86-87.

[61]See W. Kuhnigk, *Nordwestsemitischen Studien zum Hoseabuch* (BibOr 27; Rome: Biblical Institute, 1974) 3, fn. 9, who renders *mlḥmh* as a synecdoche to mean "weapons of war."

[62]Infra, 75.

[63]Duhm, "Anmerkungen," 18; Wellhausen, *Die kleinen Propheten*, 99; Nowack, *Die kleinen Propheten*, 15-16; Marti, *Dodekapropheton*, 8, 19; Cheyne, in W. R. Smith's *The Prophets of Israel*, xvii; Peiser, *Hosea*, 5; Haupt, "Hosea's Erring Spouse," 50-51; Harper, *Amos and Hosea*, 212-213; Sellin, *Das Zwölfprophetenbuch*, 29; Wolfe, "The Editing of the Book of the Twelve," 93; Weiser, *Das Buch der zwölf kleinen Propheten*, 8; Wolff, *Commentary*, 20-21; Mays, *Hosea*, 29; Jacob, *Osée*, 22; Rudolph, *Hosea*, 53-54; Willi-Plein, *Vorformen*, 117; H. McKeating, *The Books of Amos, Hosea and Micah* (Cambridge: University Press, 1971) 75-79; Buss, *Prophetic Word*, 33-34; Schreiner, "Hoseas Ehe," 170; Jeremias, *Der Prophet Hosea*, 34.

[64]*nāśāʾ lĕ*, "to take away guilt" = "to forgive". Cf. Gen 18:24, 26; Num 14:19; Is 2:9; Ex 23:21. *Pace* Blankenbaker, *The Language of Hosea 1-3*, 94.

[65]Sellin, *Das Zwölfprophetenbuch*, 29. Cf. Weiser, *Das Buch der zwölf kleinen Propheten*, 8.

[66]Kuhnigk, *Nordwestsemitischen Studien*, 4.

[67]Wolff, *Commentary*, 8-9, fn. f.

[68]Andersen and Freedman, *Hosea*, 189-192.

[69]Duhm, "Anmerkungen," 18; Wolfe, "The Editing of the Book of the Twelve," 93. Cf. Praetorius, *Gedichte des Hosea*, 1; Renaud, "Le Livret d'Osée 1-3," 163, and Ruppert, "Erwägungen," 120. Marti, *Dodekapropheton*, 19, considers 1:6bB an insertion which anticipates 2:1-3. We will argue shortly that 2:1-3 is also an interpretive addition by our final redactor.

[70]Cf. H. W. Wolff, "Der Grosse Jesreeltag (Hosea 2, 1-3). Methodologische Erwägungen zur Auslegung einer alttestamentlichen Perikope," *Gesammelte Studien zum Alten Testament* (München: Chr. Kaiser, 1964) 159, who describes the unit form-critically as an unconditional salvation oracle (2:1-2) with messenger exhortation (2:3).

[71]Duhm, "Anmerkungen," 18; A. P. Misener, *The Place of Hosea 1-3 in Hebrew Literature* (Ph.D. Diss. University of Toronto, 1909) 14-16; Nowack, *Die kleinen Propheten*, 14; Marti, *Dodekapropheton*, 8, 20-22; Day, "Is the Book of Hosea Exilic?" 126-27; Harper, *Amos and Hosea*, clx, 246-48; Peiser, *Hosea*, 4-5; Batten, "Hosea's Message and Marriage," 269; Wolfe, "The Editing of the Book of the Twelve," 93-94; 115-116; F. Nötscher, *Zwölfprophetenbuch oder Kleine Propheten* (Würzburg: Echter, 1948) 8; Eissfeldt, *The Old Testament: An Introduction*, 388; Ward, *Hosea: A Theological Commentary*, 23-24; Buss, *Prophetic Word*, 8; Willi-Plein, *Vorformen*, 120; Renaud, "Le Livret d'Osée 1-3," 166-68; idem, "Osée II, 2: '*lh mn h'rṣ*: Essai d'interprétation," *VT* 22 (1983) 496-97; Ruppert, "Erwägungen," 209.

[72]Cf. Wolff, "Der Grosse Jesreeltag," 162-64; idem, *Commentary*, 25, who thinks that 2:1-3 originally belonged with 2:23-25. Condamin, "Interpolations ou Transpositions Accidentelles?" 386-91; Blankenbaker, *The Language of Hosea* 1-3, 122.

[73]Cf. Wolff, "Der Grosse Jesreeltag," 157. Because of its abrupt change in tone from what precedes and what follows, Condamin, "Interpolations ou Transpositions Accidentelles?" 379; Harper, *Amos and Hosea*, 245-46; Sellin, *Das Zwölfprophetenbuch*, 379; Ward, *Hosea: A Theological Commentary*, 23-24, and others would reposition 2:1-3 in the hope sections of 2:16-25 or even at the end of Hos 3. Cf. *NAB* and *JB*.

[74]See survey of scholarship by Blankenbaker, *The Language of Hosea 1-3*, 119-122.

[75]G. W. Nebe, "Eine neue Hosea-Handschrift aus Höhle 4 von Qumran," *ZAW* 91 (1979) 293, and L. A. Sinclair, "A Qumran Biblical Fragment Hos 4QXIId (Hos 1:7-2:5)" *BASOR* 239 (1980) 63.

[76]Cf. Ex 6:5-7; Lev 26:12-13; Jer 7:21-23; 11:4; Ezek 11:20; 14:11; 37:26-27.

[77]Beitzel, "Exodus 3:14," 5-20; Andersen and Freedman, *Hosea* 143, fn. e, 198-99. Cf. D. J. McCarthy, "Exod 3:14: History, Philology and Theology," *CBQ* 40 (1978) 317.

[78]Among the commentators who have observed the similarity of Hos 2:1 and the promise to the patriarchs are Weiser, *Das Buch der zwölf kleinen Propheten*, 12; Rudolph, *Hosea*, 56; Wolff, *Commentary*, 26; Mays, *Hosea*, 31-32; Blankenbaker, *The Language of Hosea 1-3*, 137-38; Andersen and Freedman, *Hosea*, 202.

[79]Ps 42:3; 84:3; Josh 3:10.

[80]Wolff, *Commentary*, 27; idem, "Der Grosse Jesreeltag," 167; Mays, *Hosea*, 32; Blankenbaker, *The Language of Hosea 1-3*, 140. Cf. Andersen and Freedman, *Hosea*, 206-207.

[81]Rudolph, *Hosea*, 56-57. Cf. Sellin, *Das Zwölfprophetenbuch*, 49-50.

[82]Similar to his consonantal transposition *m'ḥry/'ḥrym* in 3:1 commenting on 1:2, supra, 61.

[83]Regarding the alliterative paronomasia between *ḥāy* and *hāyâ*, Casanowitz, *Paronomasia in the Old Testament*, 55, cites Prov 3:22: "They will be life (*wĕyihyû ḥayyim*) to your soul."

[84]See F. C. Fensham, "Father and Son as Terminology for Treaty and Covenant," *Near Eastern Studies in Honor of W. F. Albright*, H. G. Goedicke, ed. (Baltimore: John Hopkins, 1971) 132-133.

[85]Cf. Kunigk, *Nordwestsemitischen Studien*, 5-8.

[86]Galbiati, "La struttura sintetica di Osea 2," 327, Renaud, "Genèse et unité rédactionnelle de Os 2," 15-16, and Jacob, *Osée*, 32, argue for the redactional framing of 2:4-22 by 2:1-3 and 2:23-25. Cassuto observes the same correspondence between 2:1-3 and 2:23-25 in "The Second Chapter of the Book of Hosea," 104-106, although he thinks that these framing verses are authentic rather than redactional. Cf. Sellin, *Das Zwölfprophetenbuch, 51*. Although synchronic studies on Hos 2 move in the right direction in observing an overall unity in Hos 2, the main problem of these studies is that 2:1-3 is overlooked in the structural framework. They begin their analyses with 2:4: See Frey, "Aufbau," 22-26; Krszyna, "Literarische Struktur von Os 2, 4-17," 41-59; Lys, "J'ai deux amours ou l'amant jugé. Exercice sur Osée 2, 4-25," 59-77; and Clines, "Hosea 2: Structure and Interpretation," 83-103.

[87]MT: *yāḥdāw*. For this reading, see Kunigk, *Nordwestsemitischen Studien*, 5-8.

[88]Cf. Dt 30:3; Isa 11:12; Jer 23:3; 29:14; 32:37; Ezek 28:25; 37:21-22; Zech 10:8 among others.

[89]Cf. the study of Greenwood, "On the Hope for a Restored Northern Kingdom," 378.

[90]See the six different possibilities outlined by Rudolph, *Hosea*, 57-58. Wolff, "Der Grosse Jesreeltag," 170-71 and Willi-Plein, *Vorformen*, 119-120, think that "they shall go up from the land" refers to a pilgrimage, perhaps to Jezreel itself. On the basis of Ex 1:9b-10, M. Lambert, "Notes exégétiques," *REJ* 39 (1899) 300, takes the expression to mean "to gain ascendancy over the land." Wolff, revising his earlier opinion of a pilgrimage, states in his *Commentary*, 28, that the expression means "to take possession of the land." H. Gressman, *Der Messias* (Göttingen: Vandenhoeck, 1929) 235, suggests "to swamp or flood the land." Blankenbaker, *The Language of Hos 1-3*, 147, feels that the expression means "to go up in battle from the land." Its "underworld" connotation in Gen 2:6, 1 Sam 28:13 and in some Ugaritic texts prompts W. L. Holladay, "'*ereṣ* - 'Underworld': Two More Suggestions," *VT* 19 (1969) 122-123, Kuhnigk, *Nordwestsemitischen Studien*, 8-10, and Andersen and Freedman, *Hosea*, 209, to interpret *'lh mn-h'rṣ* as a national resurrection of the one nation from the underworld. Against all of these interpretations, K.

Rupprecht, "*'lh mn h'rṣ* (Ex 1:10; Hos 2:2): 'sich des Landes bemächtigen'?" *ZAW* 82 (1970) 446-47, argues that the expression should just be translated literally: "and they shall go up from the land" for both Hos 2:2 and Ex 1:10. Most recently Renaud, "Osée 2,2," 498, nuances Rupprecht by seeing in Hos 2:2 an interpretation of 1:10 in light of the exile.

[91]A. Szabó, "Textual Problems in Amos and Hosea," *VT* 25 (1975) 5-8.

[92]Cf. Isa 53:2; 55:13; Ezek 47:12; Hos 19:8; Dt 29:22. Day, "Is the Book of Hosea Exilic?" 127; Harper, *Amos and Hosea* 247; Jacob, *Osée*, 25; Mays, *Hosea*, 33; Rudolph, *Hosea*, 58; Wolff, *Commentary*, 28.

[93]Kaatz, "Wortspiel," 435; Mays, *Hosea*, 33.

[94]Scholars have found 2:3 problematic with regard to their understanding of 2:1-3 as a unit. Although observing the imperatives that are common to the beginnings of 2:3 and 2:4, Wolff, "Der Grosse Jesreeltag," 157-59, states that the differing contents preclude any other connection. He questions, however, the relationship of 2:3 with 2:1-3 because of differences in style. He concludes that two independent sayings were grouped secondarily into a unit. One was an unconditional salvation oracle (2:1-2), the other, an exhortation (2:3). Blankenbaker, *The Language of Hosea 1-3*, 122, thinks that 2:1-2 should be connected to 1:2-9, while 2:3 is to be joined with 2:4. Andersen and Freedman, *Hosea*, 210-11, think that 2:3 provides a transition to 2:4.

[95]Casanowitz, *Paronomasia in the Old Testament*, 55; Day, "Is the Book of Hosea Exilic?" 127; Harper, *Amos and Hosea*, 244; Kaatz, "Wortspiel," 435; Robinson, *Die zwölf kleinen Propheten*, 15; Weiser, *Das Buch der zwölf kleinen Propheten*, 22-23; Jacob, *Osée*, 32-33; Mays, *Hosea*, 33; I. H. Eybers, "The Use of Proper Names as a Stylistic Device," *Semitics* 2 (1971) 83; Y. Hoffman, "The Day of the Lord as a Concept and a Term in the Prophetic Literature," *ZAW* 93 (1981) 43; Lys, "J'ai deux amours ou l'amant jugé," 74; Blankenbaker, *The Language of Hosea 1-3*, 195.

[96]See the state of the question on these verses by Krszyna, "Literarische Struktur von Os 2, 4-17," 42. We add to his list of those who consider 2:8-9 a later insertion, Nowack, *Die kleinen Propheten*, 20; Harper, *Amos and Hosea*, 236-37; Robinson, *Die zwölf kleinen Propheten*, 11; Weiser, *Das Buch der zwölf kleinen Propheten*, 10; Tushingham, "A Reconsideration of Hosea Chapters 1-3," 158. Marti, *Dodekapropheton*, 25, thinks that only 2:9b is an exilic insertion.

[97]Harper, *Amos and Hosea*, 236; Nowack, *Die kleinen Propheten*, 19; Marti, *Dodekapropheton*, 24; Weiser, *Das Buch der zwölf kleinen Propheten*, 10; Sellin, *Das Zwölfprophetenbuch*, 33-34; Robinson, *Die zwölf kleinen Propheten*, 10; Frey, "Aufbau," 22; Wolff, *Commentary*, 30-31, fn. d; Rudolph, *Hosea*, 63; Mays, *Hosea*, 34; Willi-Plein, *Vorformen*, 121; Buss, *Prophetic Word*, 8; Blankenbaker, *Language of Hos 1-3*, 168, fn. 434. Kuhnigk, *Nordwestsemitischen Studien*, 14, suggests an emphatic *kî* for the *k* suffix.

[98]Renaud presents a good case for the connection between 2:4-7 and 2:10-15 in "Genèse et unité rédactionnelle," 7-10. See also, Clines, "Hosea 2," 83.

[99]Clines, "Hosea 2," 83-86 and especially the excellent analysis by Renaud, "Genèse et unité rédactionnelle," 18-19. Although Renaud perceives the redactional character of 2:8-9 and 2:16-17, the main difficulty with his

analysis is that he thinks that these verses are authentic rather than redactional compositions. A redactor simply arranged these Hosean sayings in their present position and introduced them with *lākēn hinnēh*.

[100]Supra, 58.

[101]Infra, 84-87.

[102]Renaud, "Genèse et unité rédactionnelle," 12-13.

[103]Marti, *Dodekapropheton*, 27-28; Harper, *Amos and Hosea*, clx, 238-39; Day, "Is the Book of Hosea Exilic?" 127; Batten, "Hosea's Message and Marriage," 269; Nowack, *Die kleinen Propheten*, 22; Peiser, *Hosea*, 8-9; Haupt, "Hosea's Erring Spouse," 51; Wolfe, "Editing of the Book of the Twelve," 93-94, 115; Mowinckel, *Prophecy and Tradition*, 74, and others. Cf. Buss, *Prophetic Word*, 8, 72. Willi-Plein, *Vorformen*, 122, and Renaud, "Genèse et unité rédactionnelle," 12-13, think that only the *lākēn hinnēh* of 2:16 is redactional, while the rest of the verse is authentic. Nevertheless, both admit that the placement of 2:16 in its present position is clearly redactional. To a certain extent, this is also Wolff's position, *Commentary*, 388.

[104]Andersen and Freedman, *Hosea*, 269-70.

[105]Supra, 72-74.

[106]Regarding alliteration as a paronomastic device, see Casanowitz, *Paronomasia in the Old Testament*, 28-32, and O. S. Rankin, "Alliteration in Hebrew Poetry," *JTS* 31 (1930) 285-91.

[107]Casanowitz, *Paronomasia in the Old Testament*, 38.

[108]Cf. I.H. Eybers, "The Use of Proper Names as a Stylistic Device," *Semitics* 2 (1971) 82; Mays, *Hosea*, 45; Jacob, *Osée*, 30; Wolff, *Commentary*, 43; Rudolph, *Hosea*, 77; and Andersen and Freedman, *Hosea*, 275, who relate 2:17aB to the Josh 7 tradition.

[109]Nowack, *Die kleinen Propheten*, 22, actually translates 2:17aB, "I will make the valley of trouble into a door of hope."

[110]Cf. Casanowitz, *Paronomasia in the Old Testament*, 28-29, on the alliteration of consonants.

[111]Infra, 88-90.

[112]Renaud, "Genèse et unité rédactionnelle," 18.

[113]In contrast to Hosea, the formula can be found in numerous instances in some prophets, particularly Jeremiah. See, R. Rendtorff, "Zum Gebrauch der Formel *nĕ'ūm jahwe*," *ZAW* 66 (1954), and F. Baumgärtel, "Die Formel *nĕ'ūm jahwe*," *ZAW* 73 (1961) 277-290.

[114]Wolff, *Commentary*, 40-41.

[115]Cf. Marti, *Dodekapropheton*, 28, 30, 32; Robinson, *Die zwölf kleinen Propheten*, 1, 12; Peiser, *Hosea*, 9; Buss, *Prophetic Word*, 9-10; Ruppert, "Erwägungen," 220; Renaud, "Genèse et unité rédactionnelle," 17. Cf. also Mays, *Hosea*, 47-48; Wolff, *Commentary*, 41; Willi-Plein, *Vorformen*, 122; Andersen and Freedman, *Hosea*, 262, who affirm the secondary character of the formula, although provisionally. Nowack, *Die kleinen Propheten*, 23-25, regards only 2:18, 20 as later, but maintains the authenticity of 2:21-25 for the most part.

[116]Cf. Marti, *Dodekapropheton*, 30, 32; Peiser, *Hosea*, 9; Harper, *Amos and Hosea*, 234; Robinson, *Die zwölf kleinen Propheten*, 12, 15; Wolfe, "Editing

of the Book of the Twelve," 105; Wolff, *Commentary*, 32, 47-48; Jacob, *Osée*, 31; Willi-Plein, *Vorformen*, 123; Buss, *Prophetic Word*, 9; Renaud, "Genèse et unité rédactionnelle," 14; Ruppert, "Erwägungen," 220. Cf. Mays, *Hosea*, 47-48.

[117]Supra, 64-65.

[118]Marti, *Dodekapropheton*, 28; Buss, *Prophetic Word*, 9. Also, M. Weinfeld, "Appendix B: Hosea and Deuteronomy," in *Deuteronomy and the Deuteronomic School* (Oxford: Clarendon, 1972) 368.

[119]Cf. Marti, *Dodekapropheton*, 30; Weiser, *Das Buch der zwölf kleinen Propheten*, 10; Sellin, *Das Zwölfprophetenbuch*, 38-39.

[120]Supra, 58, 77-79.

[121]So, Renaud, "Genèse et unité rédactionnelle," 13-14; Willi-Plein, *Vorformen*, 123; and Buss, *Prophetic Word*, 9. Although noting the subtle thematic dissimilarities between 2:18aBb and 2:19, the baalization of YHWH in the former and actual baal worship in the latter, Nowack, *Die kleinen Propheten*, 23, and Harper, *Amos and Hosea*, 234, attribute 2:18 to the glossator and 2:19 to Hosea.

[122]Dt 17:2-3; Josh 23:16; Judg 3:19-20; 2 Kgs 18:12; Dt 6:12-14; Judg 3:7. Cf. also Appendix B of Weinfeld, *Deuteronomy and the Deuteronomic School*, 366-70, on the affinities between Hosea and Deuteronomy.

[123]Cf. the discussion of Hos 3:1, "turning away from YHWH" towards "other gods," supra, 61.

[124]Many commentators have regarded 2:10b as a secondary addition: Marti, *Dodekapropheton*, 25; Nowack, *Die kleinen Propheten*, 20; Harper, *Amos and Hosea*, 230; Sellin, *Das Zwölfprophetenbuch*, 36; Wolfe, "Editing of the Book of the Twelve," 109; Pfeiffer, "Polemic," 232, fn. 9; Mays, *Hosea*, 41; Buss, *Prophetic Word*, 9; Wolff, *Commentary*, 37; Willi-Plein, *Vorformen*, 121.

[125]2:20 has been considered an exilic or post-exilic insertion by Marti, *Dodekapropheton*, 9, 30; Harper, *Amos and Hosea*, 236; Nowack, *Die kleinen Propheten*, 23-24; Wolfe, "Editing of the Book of the Twelve," 105-106; Buss, *Prophetic Word*, 71; Renaud, "Genèse et unité rédactionnelle," 14-15; Ruppert, "Erwägungen," 218-220.

[126]See M. Weinfeld, "*běrith*," *TDOT* 2 (1975) 259-60.

[127]Supra, 64-68.

[128]See infra, 111-112 for a more detailed discussion.

[129]Found in certain MT texts, Cyril of Alexandria, and the Vulgate.

[130]Marti, *Dodekapropheton*, 31; Robinson, *Die zwölf kleinen Propheten*, 12; Peiser, *Hosea*, 10, fn. h.

[131]H. W. Wolff, "'Wissen um Gott' bei Hosea als Urform von Theologie," *Gesammelte Studien zum Alten Testament* (München: Kaiser, 1964) 188-89; Mays, *Hosea*, 43-44; Andersen and Freedman, *Hosea*, 283.

[132]Supra, 83-84.

[133]Dt 4:39; 7:9; 8:5-11; 9:3, 6-7. In this connection regarding "knowledge of God", Wolff, "'Wissen um Gott'", 192 and idem, "Hoseas geistige Heimat," *TLZ* 81 (1956) 92, thinks that Hosea was from the levitical circles which generated the deuteronomistic schools. On the other hand, R. Crotty, "Hosea and the Knowledge of God," *AusBR* 19 (1971) and E. Nicholson, *Deuteronomy*

and Tradition, 73-80, think that the Book of Hosea and Deuteronomy were inheritors of the prophetic party in Israel. Although the writers observe that Hosea has close associations with Deuteronomy and the Deuteronomistic circles, no one to date would attribute extensive redaction of Hosea to these circles. Cf. G. von Rad, "Hosea und das Deuteronomium," *Das Gottesvolk in Deuteronomium* (BWANT III/I; Stuttgart: Kohlhammer, 1929) 80-81.

[134]Cf. Dt 7:9 and the discussion in Wolff, "'Wissen um Gott,'" 203-204; idem, *Commentary*, 53.

[135]Renaud, "Genèse et unité rédactionnelle," 15; Jacob, *Osée*, 31-32; Buss, *Prophetic Word*, 71; Rudolph, *Hosea*, 82; Harper, *Amos and Hosea*, clx; Marti, *Dodekapropheton*, 32; Wolfe, "Editing of the Book of the Twelve," 105; Day, "Is the Book of Hosea Exilic?" 127.

[136]Wolff, *Commentary*, 48; Robinson, *Die zwölf kleinen Propheten*, 15; Willi-Plein, *Vorformen*, 123-124.

[137]Supra, 60-61.

[138]A. Guillaume, "Note on Hosea 2:23, 24 (21, 22)," *JTS* 15 (1964) 57-58. Cf. also G. Rendsburg, "Hebrew *rḥm* = 'rain,'" *VT* 33 (1983) 359-60, who argues that the occurrences of *rḥm* in 2:25 mean "to cause rain upon": "I will sow her to me in the land/And I will have pity on/cause rain to fall upon Lo Ruhama." If Rendsburg is correct, it would support the *antanaclasis* in 2:23-24.

[139]With Guillaume, "Hosea 2:23, 24," 58, I read three of the five instance of *'nh* as hiphil.

[140]Supra, 75-76.

Chapter Four--Hosea 1-3: Earlier Stages

[1]See our discussion regarding the proper methodological approach, supra, 42.

[2]Supra, 55.

[3]Cf. Andersen and Freedman, Hosea, 62. They find the prose markers, *'šr*, *'t*, and *h* principally in those passages which we think are attributable to the final redactor.

[4]J. A. Bewer, "The Story of Hosea's Marriage," *AJSL* 22 (1905-6) 120; W. Caspari, "Die Nachrichten über Heimat und Hausstand des Propheten Hosea und ihre Verfasser," *NKZ* 26 (1915) 144-47; Wolff, *Commentary*, xxix, 11-12; Eissfeldt, *The Old Testament: An Introduction*, 390-91; Mays, *Hosea*, 24. Cf. Budde, "Eine folgenschwere Redaktion," 218-26, who thinks that Hos 2 is the later addition.

[5]Cf. Willi-Plein, *Vorformen*, 129; Ruppert, "Erwägungen," 212.

[6]Cf. Koch, *Growth of the Biblical Tradition*, 34-38.

[7]Andersen and Freedman, *Hosea*, 123, 126; Eissfeldt, *The Old Testament: An Introduction*, 390; J. Wilcoxen, "Narrative," *Old Testament Form Criticism*, J. H. Hayes, ed. (San Antonio: Trinity Univ., 1974) 77.

[8]Wolff, *Commentary*, 10. Cf. the qualification of Wolff's designation by Ruppert, "Erwägungen," 212.

[9]See those scholars cited in Wolff, *Commentary*, 10, fn. 8 and Rowley, "Marriage of Hosea," 79, fn. 1. Renaud, "Le Livret d'Osée 1-3," 162, thinks that Hos 1 originally was a sign-act narrative regarding the birth and naming of Hosea's children. With the addition of 1:2b (describing the wife and children as harlotrous and the *kî* clause interpretation) the sign-act narrative became an *allegory*.

[10]See those cited in Harper, *Amos and Hosea*, 108, and Rudolph, *Hosea*, 40-41.

[11]Mays, *Hosea*, 23-24.

[12]Harper, *Amos and Hosea*, 205; W. Vogels, "Les Récits de Vocation des Prophètes," *NRT* 95 (1973) 5; Mowvley, *Guide to Old Testament Prophecy*, 16-18.

[13]G. Fohrer, *Die symbolischen Handlungen der Propheten* (ATANT 54; Zürich: Zwingli, 1953) 25-28; idem, "Die Gattung der Berichte über symbolischen Handlungen der Propheten," *BZAW* 99 (1967) 95-96; Robinson, *Die zwölf kleinen Propheten*, 7; Willi-Plein, *Vorformen*, 127; March, "Prophecy," *Old Testament Form Criticism*, 172; B. Lang, "Prophetie, prophetische Zeichenhandlung und Politik im Israel," *TQ* 161 (1981) 275-80; M. P. Matheney, Jr., "Interpretation of Hebrew Prophetic Symbolic Act," *Encounter* 29 (1968) 263-267. Schreiner, "Hoseas Ehe," 170-174, Ruppert, "Erwägungen," 212-13, and Renaud, "Le Livret," 161-163, think that Hos 1 was originally a sign-act narrative only in the birth and naming of the children, not in the marriage to Gomer.

[14]Buss, *Prophetic Word*, 55.

[15]Ward, *Hosea*, 9-10.

[16]Blankenbaker, *Language of Hosea 1-3*, 109-111.

[17]Harper, *Amos and Hosea*, 225; Robinson, *Die zwölf kleinen Propheten*, 1; Weiser, *Das Buch der zwölf kleinen Propheten*, 11; Wolff, *Commentary*, 129; Mays, *Hosea*, 37; Buss, *Prophetic Word*, 34; Willi-Plein, *Vorformen*, 126; Blankenbaker, *Language of Hosea 1-3*, 129, and others.

[18]Supra, 11-13.

[19]Cf. Wolff, *Commentary*, 15-16; also Marti, *Dodekapropheton*, 23 and Nowack, *Die kleinen Propheten*, 18, who note the connection between 2:5b and 1:2b where the adulterous wife appears as the "land."

[20]Cf. W. Vogels, "'Osée-Gomer' car et comme 'Yahweh-Israel' Os 1-3," *NRT* 103 (1981) 711-27; Ruppert, "Erwägungen," 211.

[21]de Vaux, *Ancient Israel*, 35; Cassuto, "Second Chapter of the Book of Hosea," 120-122; C. H. Gordon, "Hos 2:4-5 in the Light of New Semitic Inscriptions," *ZAW* 54 (1936) 277-80; Wolff, *Commentary*, 33-34; M. Fishbane, "Accusations of Adultery," *HUCA* 45 (1974) 40; R. Yaron, "Aramaic Marriage Contracts from Elephantine," *JSS* 3 (1958) 30-31; M. J. Geller, "The Elephantine Papyri and Hos 2:3. Evidence for the Form of Early Jewish Divorce Writ," *JSJ* 8 (1977) 139-148. Although aware that Hos 2:4aB has no precise extra-biblical parallel, C. Kuhl, "Neue Dokumente zum Verständnis von Hosea 2:4-15," *ZAW* 52 (1934) 102-109, emends the text to read "(Contest with your mother, contest), for *she said*, 'You are not my husband.'" The woman will be punished because *she* initiated the divorce.

[22]Gordis, "Hosea's Marriage and Message," 249, fn. 30a; Rowley, "Marriage of Hosea," 92; Rudolph, *Hosea*, 65; Mays, *Hosea*, 37-38; Buss, *Prophetic Word*, 8, 87-88; Szabó, "Textual Problems in Amos and Hosea," 509; Andersen and Freedman, *Hosea*, 222-24; J. A. Fitzmyer, "A Re-Study of an Elephantine Marriage Contract (AP 15)," *Near Eastern Studies in Honor of W. F. Albright*, H. Goedicke, ed. (Baltimore: John Hopkins Univ., 1971) 150.

[23]So Gordis, *loc. cit.* against Gordon. Rudolph, Rowley and Szabó concur with Gordis.

[24]For a discussion of *šn'* as a *terminus technicus* for divorce, see Yaron, "Aramaic Marriage Contracts," 32-34.

[25]Cf. also, *BMAP* 2, 7-10; 7, 21-28.

[26]*Mur* 19 ar, 1-3, 12-14, in J. A. Fitzmyer and D. J. Harrington, *A Manual of Palestinian Aramaic* (Rome: Biblical Institute, 1978) 138-141.

[27]*AP* 15, 4; *BMAP* 2, 4; 7, 4. Cf. *Mur* 20 ar 3-4, "[yo]u shall be my wife according to the law of M[oses and] forever."

[28]So, Fitzmyer, "An Elephantine Aramaic Marriage Contract," 150.

[29]So Gordis, "Hosea's Marriage and Message," 249, fn. 30a, against Gordon. Also, Misener, *The Place of Hos 1-3 in Hebrew Literature*, 17; Mays, *Hosea*, 37-38; and Rudolph, *Hosea*, 65.

[30]Harper, *Amos and Hosea*, 226; Budde, "Hosea 1-3," 31-32; Buss, *Prophetic Word*, 8, and others cited by Kuhl, "Neue Dokumente," 102.

[31]Sellin, *Das Zwölfprophetenbuch*, 34-35; Bewer, "Hosea's Marriage," 126.

[32]Marti, *Dodekapropheton*, 22; Robinson, *Die zwölf kleinen Propheten*, 8-9; Haupt, "Hosea's Erring Spouse," 50.

[33]Supra, 103.

[34]Ex 6:5-7; Lev 26:12-13; Jer 7:21-23; 11:4; Ezek 11:20; 14:11; 37:26-27.

[35]Weiser, *Das Buch der zwölf kleinen Propheten*, 13-14; Bewer, "Hosea's Marriage," 126; Wolff, *Commentary*, 34; Willi-Plein, *Vorformen*, 121.

[36]Harper, *Amos and Hosea*, clx; Budde, "Hos 1-3," 34; Peiser, *Hosea*, 7.

[37]Marti, *Dodekapropheton*, 23; Praetorius, *Gedichte des Hoseas*, 4.

[38]Sellin, *Das Zwölfprophetenbuch*, 34-35.

[39]Budde, "Hos 1-3," 34-35 and Sellin, *Das Zwölfprophetenbuch*, 33, 36, both emend 2:7 to read in the 2 pl., while Peiser, *Hosea*, 7, changes only 2:6a.

[40]Bewer, "Hosea's Marriage," 126-27.

[41]Sellin, *Das Zwölfprophetenbuch*, 29-31, 34-35.

[42]Infra, 123-24.

[43]Supra, 84-87.

[44]Willi-Plein, *Vorformen*, 123; Renaud, "Genèse et Unité Rédactionnelle," 14; Ruppert, "Erwägungen," 209. Cf. Rudolph, *Hosea*, 80.

[45]On the covenantal nature of these attributes, see Wolff, *Commentary*, 53. Mays, *Hosea*, 50-52; Ward, *Hosea*, 42; Blankenbaker, *Language of Hos 1-3*, 190-192.

[46]Supra, 86.

[47]Supra, 91-92.

[48]Supra, 107-108.

[49]See infra, 123-124, where we argue that the original Hosean tradition was a legal complaint against an adulterous woman.

[50]Harper, *Amos and Hosea*, 205; Vogels, "Les Récits de Vocations," 5; Mowvley, *Guide to Old Testament Prophecy*, 16-18. Regarding the relationship between the call narrative and the sign-act narrative, a genre which scholars think also describes Hos 1*, consult Wolff, *Commentary*, 10-11 and March, "Prophecy," *Old Testament Form Criticism*, 172-73.

[51]Thus, von Rad, *Message of the Prophets*, 34: "The call commissioned the prophet: the act of writing down an account of it was aimed at those sections of the public in whose eyes he had to justify himself." Also, K. Baltzer, "Considerations Regarding the Office and Calling of the Prophet," *HTR* 61 (1968) 567-81; M. Buss, "An Anthropological Perspective Upon Prophetic Call Narratives," *Semeia* 21 (1982) 16-17; N. Habel, "The Form and Significance of the Call Narratives," *ZAW* 77 (1965) 297-323; J. Lindblom, *Prophecy in Ancient Israel* (Oxford: Blackwell, 1962) 182; T. Overholt, "Prophecy: the Problem of Cross-Cultural Comparison," *Semeia* 21 (1982) 70-71; W. Vogels, "Les Récits de Vocations des Prophètes," *NRT* 95 (1973) 3-24. Cf. R. Kilian, "Die prophetischen Berufungsberichte," in *Theologie im Wandel* (München: Erich Wewel, 1967) 356-76 and W. Zimmerli, "Form-und Traditionsgeschichte der prophetischen Berufungserzählungen in Ezechiel," *BK* 8 (1955) 16-21.

[52]B. O. Long, "Prophetic Authority as Social Reality," in *Canon and Authority*, G. W. Coats and B. O. Long, eds. (Philadelphia: Fortress, 1977) 13. Italics mine.

[53]Although this study focuses on the traditioning process in the formation of the work rather than on the historicity of the account, there may be some historical basis in Hos 1*. According to Long, "Prophetic Authority," 19, deviant behavior, such as a conjugal union with a prostitute, seems to be a societal expectation which played a role in the prophet's legitimacy. Regarding the important interrelationship between the prophet and the society in which he prophesies, see R. Wilson, *Prophecy and Society in Ancient Israel* (Philadelphia: Fortress, 1980) 21-88.

[54]See, T. W. Overholt, "Seeing is Believing: The Social Setting of Prophetic Acts of Power," *JSOT* 23 (1982) 3-31; Long, "Prophetic Authority," 13-16; idem, "Social Setting for Prophetic Miracle Stories," *Semeia* 3 (1975) 46-63.

[55]Marti, *Dodekapropheton*, 9-10; Harper, *Amos and Hosea*, clviii-clxi.

[56]Willi-Plein, *Vorformen*, 129.

[57]John Bright, *A History of Israel* (Philadelphia: Westminster, 1981), 3rd. ed.) 283. See also, R. E. Clements, "Patterns in the Prophetic Canon," 47-51.

[58]Ruppert, "Erwägungen", 208-223. For other opinions regarding the redaction of Hos 2, see Willi-Plein, *Vorformen*, 120-121, and Renaud, "Genèse et Unité Rédactionnelle," 6-11.

[59]Earlier, Harper, *Amos and Hosea*, 231, noticed the difficulty in 2:11 and 2:12, but removed 2:12 as a gloss repeating 2:11b and interrupting the connection between 2:11b and 2:13.

[60]Supra, 87-88.

[61]Dt 7:13; 11:14; 12:17; 14:23; 18:4; 28:51. Besides these, note also the cultic context of the expression in later books: Jer 31:12; Hag 1:11; Neh 10:40; 13:5, 12; 2 Chron 31:5. Cf. U. Cassuto, "The Prophet Hosea and the Books of the Pentateuch," *Biblical and Oriental Studies, I: Bible*, I. Abrahams, trans. (Jerusalem: Magnes, 1973) 93-94; von Rad, *Das Gottesvolk*, 80; Wolff, *Commentary*, 37.

[62]A *hapax legomenon*. With Wolff, *Commentary*, 38 and Willi-Plein, *Vorformen*, 122, we accept the MT rather than emend the text to the more common 'etnan. 'etnâ appears to be a wordplay on t'nh, "fig tree," in 2:14a. The wordplay could well be continued in nātěnû, "which my lovers *have given* me," which follows 'etnâ.

[63]See D. R. Hillers, *Treaty Curses and the Old Testament Prophets* (Rome: Pontifical Biblical Institute, 1964) 44-56, regarding devouring beasts and treaty curses. Also, cf. Blankenbaker, *Language of Hos 1-3*, 178.

[64]*Hiphil*: 1 Kgs 3:3; 11:8; 12:33; 13:1, 2. Cf. Jer 48:35. *Piel*: 1 Kgs 22:44; 2 Kgs 12:4; 14:4; 15:4, 35; 16:4; 17:11; 22:17; 23:5, 8. Cf. Jer 1:16; 7:9; 11:12, 13, 17; 19:4; 32:29. Cf. Weinfeld, *Deuteronomy and the Deuteronomic School*, 321-322. He cites Hos 2:15 as a prophetic prototype in Hosea for its equivalent in the Book of Deuteronomy (p. 364). We argue, however, that 2:15 originates precisely from deuteronomistic circles as a redactional expansion of the tradition.

[65]See F. M. Cross, "The Themes of the Book of Kings and the Structure of the Deuteronomistic History," in *Canaanite Myth and Hebrew Epic* (Cambridge: Harvard University, 1973) 274-289; R. D. Nelson, *The Double Redaction of the Deuteronomistic History* (JSOT 18; Sheffield: JSOT, 1981); R. E. Friedman, *The Exile and Biblical Narrative: The Formation of the Deuteronomistic and Priestly Works* (Chico, CA: Scholars Press, 1981); A.D.H. Mayes, *The Story of Israel between Settlement and Exile. A Redactional Study of the Deuteronomistic History* (London: SCM, 1983).

[66]M. Noth, *Überlieferungsgeschichtliche Studien* (Tübingen: Max Niemeyer, 1957, 2 Aufl.) 1-110 [= ET: *The Deuteronomistic History* (JSOTSup 15; Sheffield: JSOT, 1981)].

[67]1 Kgs 15:26, 34; 16:25-26, 30; 22:52; 2 Kgs 13:2, 11; 14:24; 15:9, 18, 24, 28, *et passim*.

[68]Cross, "Themes of the Book of Kings," 274-89; Nelson, *Double Redaction*, 32-36, 120-23; Friedman, *Exile and Biblical Narrative*, 4-10.

[69]Cf. Ezek 16:41; 23:27, the allegories of the harlots.

[70]See J. Muilenburg, "The Linguistic and Rhetorical Usages of the Particle kî in the Old Testament," *HUCA* 32 (1961) 157, regarding kî introducing an accusation.

[71]See Isa 5:5; 2 Sam 12:10; 14:15, where the sentence begins with wĕ'attâ.

[72]Supra, 107-108.

[73]See K. Nielsen, *Yahweh as Prosecutor and Judge: An Investigation of the Prophetic Lawsuit* (Sheffield: JSOT, 1978); G. W. Ramsey, "Speech-Forms in Hebrew Law and Prophetic Oracles," *JBL* 96 (1977) 45-58; J. Limburg, "The Root ryb and the Prophetic Lawsuit Speeches," *JBL* 88 (1969) 291-304; B. Gemser, "The *Rib* Controversy-Pattern in Hebrew Mentality," *VTSup* 3

(1969) 129; W. H. Clark, "Law," and W. E. March, "Prophecy," both in *Old Testament Form Criticism*, J. H. Hayes, ed. (San Antonio: Trinity University, 1974) 135-36, 165-68.

[74]Buss, *Prophetic Word*, 76-77. Blankenbaker, *Language of Hosea 1-3*, 152-156, doubts that *ribû* in 2:4 should be understood in terms of a court case. He thinks that 2:4 describes a family scene where the children of a family prevail upon their mother to change her adulterous behavior. The legal connotations of *rib*, however, militate against the passage being a completely private family affair. The conduct of the woman is public and thus will be her disgrace.

[75]Cf. Laws of Eshnunna 28 (*ANET*, p. 135); Middle Assyrian Laws 13 (*ANET*, p. 181).

[76]See Jer 13:22, 26f; Ezek 16:39; 23:26, 29 and Nah 3:5.

[77]According to *Sf* I, A, 40-41, the punishment of a prostitute was public denudation. See J. A. Fitzmyer, *The Aramaic Inscriptions of Sefire* (Rome: Pontifical Biblical Institute, 1967) 15, 157. Regarding the laws against adultery, see the provocative discussion of H. McKeating, "Sanctions Against Adultery in Ancient Israelite Society, with Some Reflections on Methodology in the Study of Old Testament Ethics," *JSOT* 11 (1979) 52-72, and the response to McKeating by A. Phillips, "Another Look at Adultery," *JSOT* 20 (1981) 3-25. Cf. also, Gordis, "Hosea's Marriage and Message," 250, fn. 30a; W. Kornfeld, "L'adultère dans l'orient antique," *RB* 57 (1950) 92-109; S. E. Loewenstamm, "The Laws of Adultery and Murder in Biblical and Mesopotamian Law," *Comparative Studies in Biblical and Ancient Oriental Literature* (AOAT 204; Neukirchen-Vluyn: Neukircher, 1980) 146-153.

[78]Rudolph, *Hosea*, 70.

[79]Budde, "Der Abschnitt Hosea 1-3," 30; Marti, *Dodekapropheton*, 22-23; Misener, *The Place of Hos 1-3 in Hebrew Literature*, 16-17

[80]Harper, *Amos and Hosea*, 226; Robinson, *Die zwölf kleinen Propheten*, 8-9; Cheyne, *Hosea*, 17; Keil, *Twelve Minor Prophets*, 51-52; Mays, *Hosea*, 37.

[81]Rudolph, *Hosea*, 64-65, and Wolff, *Commentary*, 33.

[82]So suggested by L.W. Batten, "Hosea's Message and Marriage," *JBL* 48 (1929) 266. Cf. L. Watermann, "Hosea, Chapters 1-3, in Retrospect and Prospect," *JNES* 14 (1955) 102.

[83]A full-scale feminist critique is beyond the scope of this study. However, we wish to point out here that the symbolization of religious corruption as a harlotrous *woman* reflects a male-dominated society which thinks in terms of a male God, and thus, a *husband* whose wife has been unfaithful. In such a context, it would be quite surprising if Jacob, to whom Israel owes its patronymic, represented the adulterous nation, and not his *wife*. Cf. P. A. Bird, "Images of Women in the Old Testament" in *Religion and Sexism*, R. R. Ruether, ed. (New York: Simon and Schuster, 1974) 41-88 and H. Balz-Cochois, "Gomer oder die Macht der Astarte. Versuch einer feministischen Interpretation von Hos 1-4," *EvT* 42 (1982) 37-65.

Chapter Six--Hosea 4-11, 12-14: Final Redacted State

[1]Duhm, "Anmerkungen zu den zwölf Propheten," 42; Wellhausen, *Die kleinen Propheten*, 134; Cheyne in W.R. Smith's, *Prophets of Israel* xviii; Marti, *Dodekapropheton*, 10; Harper, *Amos and Hosea*, clx-clxi, 408-409; Wolfe, "Editing of the Book of the Twelve," 93; Day, "Is the Book of Hosea Exilic," 131, among others. Rudolph, *Hosea*, 249, holds that the unit is authentic but its present position results from later redaction. Willi-Plein, *Vorformen*, 228-232, thinks that 14:3-4, 10, is later redaction while 14:2, 5-9 is authentic.

[2]Supra, 129-130.

[3]With LXX and R. Gordis, "The Text and Meaning of Hosea 14:3," *VT* 5 (1955) 88-90; Wolff, *Commentary*, 231; Mays, *Hosea*, 184, and others.

[4]Supra, 59-61, 89-90.

[5]Supra, 62, 78.

[6]Regarding the emendation of the text, see fn. 17 below.

[7]Supra, 61-62.

[8]See Andersen and Freedman, *Hosea*, 646, regarding the linkage between 14:3 and 14:4.

[9]Supra, 67-68.

[10]Cheyne, *Hosea*, 129; Kaatz, "Wortspiel," 437; Casanowitz, *Paronomasia*, 72, #338; Driver, *Introduction to the Literature of the Old Testament*, 306; Lippl, *Die zwölf kleinen Propheten*, 19; Wolff, *Commentary*, 237; Feuillet, "'S'asseoir à l'ombre' de l'époux: Os 14:8a et Cant 2:3," *RB* 78 (1971) 391-405. Regarding the change in pointing, see fn. 3 above.

[11]Also, scientific etymology, see BDB.

[12]Regarding the alliteration of *š/ś*, see Casanowitz, *Paronomasia*, 29.

[13]Kaatz, "Wortspiel," 437.

[14]See Casanowitz, *Paronomasia*, 28, on the alliteration of *'aleph* and *'ayin*.

[15]Cf. Kaatz, "Wortspiel," 437.

[16]Supra, 59-61.

[17]MT: *yōšĕbê bĕṣillô*. Regarding emendation, see Feuillet, "'S'asseoir à l'ombre'," 393-94; Rudolph, *Hosea*, 248-49; Wolff, *Commentary*, 232; Mays, *Hosea*, 184; Jacob, *Osée*, 95, and others. We prefer the emendation because it accords with the *yāšūbû/yĕšĕbû* metaphony that we saw in the R2 commentary, 3:4-5. Moreover, the "my" suffix of the emendation coheres with 14:9bA where YHWH describes himself as "a luxuriant juniper," under whose shade Israel will sit.

[18]Regarding *lî* as 3 per. sg., see Kuhnigk, *Nordwestsemitischestudien zum Hoseabuch*, 156. Cf. Wolff and Rudolph who emend the text with the LXX, *lô*.

[19]Supra, 75.

[20]Cf. the three stage process of purification utilizing three *laken's* and the triadic occurrences of *(wĕhāyâ) bayyôm hahû' nĕ'ūm-yhwh*, supra, 81-83.

[21]Supra, 89-90.

[22]Supra, 69-71.

[23]We have already pointed out that R2 made use of the metaphony, *yāšūbû/yēšēbû* in Hos 3:4-5.

[24]Feuillet, "'S'asseoir à l'ombre'," 392-94, points out the many instances of sitting in "the shadow of his wings" or "the shadow of his hands," but none where YHWH is compared to a tree in whose shade one sits.

[25]Cf. Jer 2:20; 3:6; Dt 12:2.

[26]Feuillet, "'S'asseoir à l'ombre'," 397-98.

[27]Cf. Hos 2:10b, 19 and 14:4 which are R2 editorials.

[28]Cf. the R2 editorials, Hos 2:17, 23-24.

[29]Nowack, *Die kleinen Propheten*, 86-87; Robinson, *Die zwölf kleinen Propheten*, 54; Good, "Composition of Hosea," 53; Wolff, *Commentary*, 239; Jacob, *Osée*, 98; Mays, *Hosea*, 190; Buss, *Prophetic Word*, 27; Willi-Plein, *Vorformen*, 235-36; G. T. Sheppard, *Wisdom as a Hermeneutical Construct* (BZAW 151; Berlin: Walter de Gruyter, 1980) 129-135.

[30]Cf. 2:2-3, 25; 1:1; 3:1-5.

[31]Supra, 55-57.

[32]So noted Wolff, *Commentary*, 239, and Mays, *Hosea*, 190.

[33]Dt 8:6; 10:12; 11:22, 28; 19:9; 26:17; 28:9; 30:16; 31:29. Cf. the other occurrence of the plural, "ways of YHWH," found in Ps 18:22 which appears to be deuteronomistic.

[34]Wolff, *Commentary*, xxix-xxxi.

[35]Mays, *Hosea*, 15-16; Jacob, *Osée*, 12-13; Rudolph, *Hosea*, 26; Buss, *Prophetic Word*, 32-33; Willi-Plein, *Vorformen*, 206; Scharbert, *Die Propheten Israels*, 135; Jeremias, "Hosea 4-7," 47; Andersen and Freedman, *Hosea*, 331-332.

[36]Weiser, *Das Buch der zwölf kleinen Propheten*, 28; W. Harrelson, "Knowledge of God in the Church," *Int* 30 (1976) 12-13; Andersen and Freedman, *Hosea*, 331-335.

[37]J. Jeremias, "Hosea 4-7. Beobachtungen zur Komposition des Buches Hosea," in *Textgemäss*, A.H.J. Gunneweg & O. Kaiser, hrsg. (Göttingen: Vandenhoeck & Ruprecht, 1979) 48-49; I. Cardellini, "Hosea 4:1-3. Eine Strukturanalyse," *Bausteine Biblische Theologie*, H.-F. Fabry, hrsg. (Köln-Bonn: Peter Hanstein, 1977) 259-270; H. Junker, "Text-kritische, formkritische und traditionsgeschichtliche Untersuchung zu Os 4, 1-10," *BZ* 4 (1960) 165-73; J. A. Wharton, "Hosea 4:1-3," *Int* 32 (1978) 79; H. Huffmon, "The Covenant Lawsuit in the Prophets," *JBL* 78 (1959) 294; K. Nielsen, *Yahweh as Prosecutor and Judge*, F. Cryer, trans. (JSOTSup 9; Sheffield: JSOT, 1978) 32-34; Willi-Plein, *Vorformen*, 129-130; Jacob, *Osée*, 39-40; Mays, *Hosea*, 60-62; Wolff, *Commentary*, 65-66; Rudolph, *Hosea*, 99-102. But, see M. De Roche, "The Reversal of Creation in Hosea," *VT* 31 (1981) 400-409, who argues against 4:1-3 as a covenant lawsuit.

[38]K. Budde, "Zu Text und Auslegung des Buches Hosea," *JBL* 45 (1926) 283; Marti, *Dodekapropheton*, 39; Wolfe, "Editing of the Book of the Twelve," 105-106; Pfeiffer, *Introduction to the Old Testament*, 570-73. Sellin, *Zwölfprophetenbuch*, 52; and Cardellini, "Hos 4:1-3," regard only 4:3aBb as secondary.

[39]Marti, Budde. Cf. Szabó, "Textual," 511, who translates 'eres in 4:1 as "earth" instead of land, precisely because it is more cosmic.

[40]For a complete discussion, see De Roche, "Reversal of Creation in Hosea," 400-409. Furthermore, consult M. De Roche, "Zephaniah 1:2-3: The 'Sweeping of Creation'," VT 30 (1980) 104-109 and idem. "Contra Creation, Covenant and Conquest," VT 30 (1980) 280-290, for a treatment of 'sp = "to sweep away," which describes not only destruction but also the reversal of creation in the later texts of Jeremiah and Zephaniah.

[41]Supra, 82-83.

[42]This is the opinion of Wolff, Commentary, 196-197; Rudolph, Hosea, 219; Willi-Plein, Vorformen, 206; and Andersen and Freedman, Hosea, 576. But cf. Good, "Composition of Hosea," 48-49.

[43]A. Alt, "Hosea 5:8--6:6. Ein Krieg und seine Folgen in prophetischer Beleuchtung," Kleine Schriften zur Geschichte des Volkes Israel, II. (München: Beck, 1953) 184-85; H. Schmidt, "Hosea 6:1-6," Beiträge zur Religionsgeschichte und Archäologie Palastinas: Sellin Fs., A. Jirku, hrsg. (Leipzig: 1927) 111-26; Harper, Amos and Hosea, 283-83; Jacob, Osée, 51.

[44]Cf. Mays, Hosea, 87.

[45]Cheyne, in W. R. Smith's, Prophets of Israel, xx; Marti, Dodekapropheton, 9, 52; Wolfe, "Editing of the Book of the Twelve," 93; Day, "Is the Book of Hosea Exilic?" 129; Pfeiffer, Introduction to the Old Testament, 573. Willi-Plein, Vorformen, 146-149, regards 5:15b--6:3 as secondary.

[46]Marti, Dodekapropheton, 55. Cf. Willi-Plein, Vorformen, 149, who joins 5:15b to 6:4.

[47]Mays, Hosea, 87; Wolff, Commentary, 109; Good, "Composition of Hosea," 37-38; and Buss, Prophetic Word, 14.

[48]Supra, 133.

[49]Cf. F.M. Cross, "The Themes of the Book of Kings and the Structure of the Deuteronomistic History," Canaanite Myth and Hebrew Epic (Cambridge, MA: Harvard University, 1973) 287; R. E. Friedman, The Exile and Biblical Narrative (Chico, CA: Scholars Press, 1981) 16-18; R.D. Nelson, The Double Redaction of the Deuteronomistic History (JSOTSup 18; Sheffield: JSOT, 1981) 94.

[50]I.e., the nations where YHWH will scatter his people. Cf. Dt 4:27.

[51]Supra, 62-63.

[52]Contrary to the number of scholars who think that 6:1-3 is an independent penitential song of the people or the priests inserted here secondarily. Cf. Wolff, Commentary, 116-117 and Mays, Hosea, 87.

[53]See Casanowitz, Paronomasia, 29, for other examples of the consonantal alliteration of ḥ/k.

[54]This assonantal and alliterative structure has already been noted by Kaatz, "Wortspiel," 435.

[55]Supra, 81-82.

[56]Cf. Prov 3:11.

[57]So Sellin, Das Zwölfprophetenbuch, 72, and Lippl, Zwölf kleinen Propheten, 50.

[58]Supra, 87-88.

[59]*BDB*, 1007. Cf. also A. Ceresko, "A Note on Psalm 63: A Psalm of Vigil," *ZAW* 92 (1980) 435-436.

[60]Infra, 175-176.

[61]Infra, 152-153.

[62]Supra, 136-137.

[63]For a bibliographical survey of the literature, see J. Wijngaards, "Death and Resurrection in Covenantal Context," *VT* 17 (1967) 227-228.

[64]Ibid., 228-30; Also, see M. Barré, "New Light on the Interpretation of Hos 6,2," *VT* 28 (1978) 129-41; idem., "Bullutsa-Rabi's Hymn to Gula and Hosea 6:1-2," *Or* 50 (1981) 241-245, who has recently argued for this position. O. Loretz, "Tod und Leben nach altorientalischer und kanaanäischbiblischer Anschauung in Hos 6, 1-3," *BN* 17 (1982) 37-42, defines different redactional stages for 6:1-3. The later insertion of 6:1aBb speaks of healing.

[65]Andersen and Freedman, *Hosea*, 420-21.

[66]Wijngaards, "Death and Resurrection," 230-39; C. Barth, "Theophanie, Bundschliessung und neuer Anfang am dritten Tag," *EvT* 28 (1968) 521-533.

[67]Supra, 86-87.

[68]Barré, loc. cit.

[69]Barth, "Am dritten Tag," 527-532. Cf. W. Brueggemann, "Amos 4:4-13 and Israel's Covenant Worship," *VT* 15 (1965) 1-15.

[70]Wijngaards, "Death and Resurrection," 237.

[71]Read with LXX, *karpon*. Thus, Sellin, Harper, Robinson.

[72]Marti, *Dodekapropheton*, 84; Duhm, "Anmerkungen," 34; Wolfe, "Editing of the Book of the Twelve," 91. Willi-Plein, *Vorformen*, 192, regards 10:12aBb as secondary.

[73]Supra, 71-76 regarding 2:2-3, 24-25.

[74]Supra, 62. Cf. Dt 4:29 where *drš* and *bqš* are used together.

[75]Andersen and Freedman, *Hosea*, 569.

[76]Wolfe, Day, Wellhausen, Nowack, J.M.P. Smith, Harper, Duhm, Marti, Good, Mays, Buss, Willi-Plein. Scharbert, Wolff, Lippl, and Rudolph (v. 10b) understand 11:10 as a secondary expansion.

[77]Andersen and Freedman, *Hosea*, 591.

[78]Dt 13:5; 1 Kgs 18:21; 2 Kgs 23:3. Cf. also Dt 8:6; 10:12; 11:22, 28; 19:9; 26:17; 28:9; 30:16; 31:29; Judg 2:22 for the expression "walking in the way of YHWH". See also Dt 4:3; 6:14; 8:19; 11:28; 13:3, 6; 28:14; 29:5 etc. where "going after other gods" is a transgression of the covenant.

[79]Infra, 214-229.

[80]For our reading, see LXX, Wolff, *Commentary*, 191; Rudolph, *Hosea*, 209; Kuhnigk, *Nordwestsemitische Studien zum Hoseabuch*, 129; Andersen and Freedman, *Hosea*, 578.

[81]Supra, 62.

[82]Supra, 138-139.

[83]Supra, 136-140.

[84]Supra, 72-73.

[85]See especially, Jeremias, "Hos 4-7," 49-52; Willi-Plein, *Vorformen*, 248; Junker, "Os 4,1-10," 168; and Wolff, *Commentary*, 74-75; M. De Roche, "Structure, Rhetoric and Meaning in Hos 4:4-10," *VT* 33 (1983) 185, fn. 2.

[86]Supra, 142-144.

[87]N. Lohfink, "Zu Text und Form von Os 4,4-6," *Bibl* 42 (1961) 327.

[88]K. Budde, "Zu Text und Auslegung des Buches Hosea (Hos 4:1-19)," *JBL* 75 (1926) 286.

[89]Nowack, *Die kleinen Propheten*, 33; Marti, *Dodekapropheton*, 40; Wellhausen, *Die kleinen Propheten*, 110; Peiser, *Hosea*, 14-15.

[90]So noted by Junker, "Os 4, 1-10," 170.

[91]Supra, 87-88, 149.

[92]Andersen and Freedman, *Hosea*, 353.

[93]The proverbial character of these verses has been recognized by C. L. Seow, "Hosea 14:10 and the Foolish People Motif," *CBQ* 44 (1982) 215-218. Wolfe, "Editing of the Book of the Twelve," 112 regards all three proverbs as secondary.

[94]Supra, 73-74.

[95]I am indebted to M. De Roche, "Hosea 4:4-10," 194-195, for his verse analysis which I reproduce here. Many of these verses have already been regarded as secondary insertions. Sellin, *Das Zwölfprophetenbuch*, 57; Lippl, *Die zwölf kleinen Propheten*, 18; and Wolff, *Commentary*, 71,74, all regard 4:9 as a secondary addition. Wolfe, "Editing of the Book of the Twelve," 91, see 4:9b as a later Judaistic addition. Buss, *Prophetic Word*, 36 and Jeremias, *Der Prophet Hosea*, 68, see 4:10 as a later expansion, whereas Marti, *Dodekapropheton*, 42; Wolfe, "Editing of the Book of the Twelve," 91; and Pfeiffer, *Introduction*, 570, think 4:10b a gloss.

[96]For an extended discussion on the nature of the comparison, see Andersen and Freedman, *Hosea*, 359-361.

[97]Noted by Budde, "Hos 4:1-19," 287, and Andersen and Freedman, *Hosea*, 355.

[98]De Roche, "Hos 4:4-10," 196.

[99]Ibid., 197.

[100]Cf. Dt 29:24; Jos 24:16,20; Judg 2:12,13; 1 Sam 8:8; 12:10; 1 Kgs 11:33; 18:18 *et passim*.

[101]Dt 4:2,3,40; 6:2,3; Jos 1:7,8; 2 Kgs 17:13,19,37 *et passim*.

[102]Ruben cited in Harper, *Amos and Hosea*, 260; Wolfe, "Editing of the Book of the Twelve," 112; Nowack, *Die kleinen Propheten*, 35-36; Pfeiffer, *Introduction*, 572.

[103]J. L. Lundbom, "Poetic Structure and Prophetic Rhetoric in Hosea," *VT* 29 (1979) 304-305; Mays, *Hosea*, 72-73.

[104]Regarding the textual problems in this verse, See Lundbom, "Poetic Structure," 303-304.

[105]Infra, 265.

[106]Lundbom, "Poetic Structure," 303.

[107]Day, "Is the Book of Hosea Exilic?" 124. Cf. Dt 31:16; Ex 34:15.

[108]Hab 2:18-19; Isa 44:9-20.

[109]See W. L. Holladay, "On Every High Hill and Under Every Green Tree," *VT* 11 (1961) 170-171, for a complete list of passages. Also, Weinfeld, *Deuteronomy and the Deuteronomic School*, 322,366.

[110]Cf. discussion, infra, 265.

[111]Budde, "Hos 4:1-19," 291.

[112]Cf. BHS; Marti, *Dodekapropheton*, 44; Robinson, *Die zwölf kleinen Propheten*, 20; Budde, "Hos 4:1-19," 291.

[113]We will discuss this stage more thoroughly below, p. 269.

[114]Wolff, *Commentary*, 87; Andersen and Freedman, *Hosea*, 370.

[115]Rudolph, *Hosea*, 106-107.

[116]See infra, 169.

[117]Cf. RSV, Wolff, *Commentary*, 91; Harper, *Amos and Hosea*, 264; Rudolph, *Hosea*, 107; Nowack, *Die kleinen Propheten*, 36-37; Duhm, "Anmerkungen," 21, and others.

[118]Marti, *Dodekapropheton*, 45; Wolfe, "Editing of the Book of the Twelve," 93; Pfeiffer, *Introduction*, 570, 572; Willi-Plein, *Vorformen*, 136-137.

[119]Willi-Plein, *Vorformen*, 136-137.

[120]Cf. Ezek 34:24 where Ezekiel refers to David who will be their shepherd and prince over the people. This accords with the R2 commentary 3:5 where the people will seek YHWH their God and David their king in the latter days. For other passages regarding YHWH as shepherd, see Ezek 34:31; Jer 31:10; Is 40:11. Note also D. N. Freedman, *Pottery, Poetry, Prophecy*, 284-285 on this same topic in Ps 23. He also characterizes this theme as exilic.

[121]For example, *tākōssû 'al hasseh/seh tamîm*, "you should compute for the lamb/(your) lamb should be whole" (Ex 12:4-5); *welir'ôt šehem-behemâ hemmâ lāhem*, "to show to them that they are but beasts" (Eccl 3:18); *pāraš rešet leraglay*, "he has spread a net for my feet" (Lam 1:13; Prov 25:13). For other examples, see Beitzel, "Exodus 3:14 and the Divine Name: A Case of Biblical Paronomasia," 8, and Sasson, "Wordplay in the OT," 969.

[122]Kaatz, "Wortspiel," 435, very early on pointed out the assonance between *bmrhb* and *hbwr*.

[123]Cf. the imperative with *lĕ* in 2 Sam 16:11; 2 Kgs 23:18; Ex 32:10.

[124]BDB, 628.

[125]Cf. Dt 3:20; 25:19; Jos 1:13, 15; 22:4; 23:1.

[126]Hos 5:2a has been a difficult text for a number of commentators. Cf. the different solutions of scholars listed in Harper, *Amos and Hosea*, 267-68. Until a more satisfactory solution presents itself, we follow Wellhausen, Harper, Wolff, Weiser, Mays, Jeremias, and K. Elliger, "Eine verkannte Kunstform bei Hosea (Zur Einheit von Hos 5, 1f)," *ZAW* 69 (1957) 159, in this emendation of the text, interpreting *he'miqû* as an asyndetic relative clause.

[127]Supra, 81-82, 148-149.

[128]See Andersen and Freedman, *Hosea*, 391, and Wolff, *Commentary*, 95.

[129]Commentators have questioned the authenticity of 5:3-4, because of the change of person and repetition of vocabulary. For example, Wolfe, "Editing of the Book of the Twelve," 91, regards both 5:3 and 5:4 as originating from the Judaistic editor. Wellhausen, Nowack, Marti, Peiser, and Pfeiffer think 5:3b is a gloss, perhaps from Hos 6:10. Moreover, Marti and Pfeiffer look upon 5:4b as an unnecessary explanatory gloss from 4:12. Cf. Day, "Is the Book of Hosea Exilic?" 124.

[130]See Andersen and Freedman, *Hosea*, 413-414, regarding "the great king."

[131]Cf. BHS; Marti, *Dodekapropheton*, 51; Robinson, *Die zwölf kleinen Propheten*, 22; Weiser, *Das Buch der zwölf kleinen Propheten*, 40, who try to homogenize the text to the 3rd mas. pl.

[132]Willi-Plein, *Vorformen*, 146. Cf. Peiser, *Hosea*, 22-23. Andersen and Freedman, *Hosea*, 413, must leave out 5:13b to show the structural connection between 5:13a and 5:14a.

[133]The identity of this king is problematic. Cf. all the possible interpretations listed by Harper, *Amos and Hosea*, 277-278.

[134]Supra, 93-94.

[135]Supra, 151-152.

[136]Regarding the emendation, see LXX, Wolff, *Commentary*, 105, g; Kuhnigk, *Nordwestsemitische Studien*, 81.

[137]Understanding the suffix of the parallel *hăragtîm* to be serving double duty. Cf. Andersen and Freedman, *Hosea*, 428.

[138]Nowack, *Die kleinen Propheten*, 44, states that 6:5 is obviously a remnant from another speech which much have been in a statement regarding the sins of Israel from which the *'al kēn* resulted. Wolfe, "Editing of the Book of the Twelve," 115, and B. Duhm, "Anmerkungen zu den zwölf Propheten," *ZAW* 31 (1911) 23, regard 6:5a as a gloss. On the other hand, Marti, *Dodekapropheton*, 9, 52, and Buss, *Prophetic Word*, 14, think that 6:5b is a later insertion. For the opinions of other authors, see S. Spiegel, "A Prophetic Attestation of the Decalogue: Hos 6:5. With Some Observations on Psalms 15 and 24," *HTR* 27 (1934) 105-116, and I. Zolli, "Note on Hosea 6:5," *JQR* 31 (1940-41) 79-81.

[139]Spiegel, "A Prophetic Attestation of the Decalogue: Hos 6:5," 105.

[140]Marti, *Dodekapropheton*, 52; Robinson, *Die zwölf kleinen Propheten*, 25.

[141]Infra, 240-244.

[142]For an in-depth examination of Dt 18, see J. Muilenburg, "The 'Office' of the Prophet in Ancient Israel," in *The Bible in Modern Scholarship*, J. P. Hyatt, ed. (New York: Abingdon, 1965) 74-97.

[143]Clements, *Prophecy and Tradition*, 50. Italics mine. He also observes that the redaction of the Book of Hosea occurred in circles closely connected with the Deuteronomists (pp. 43-51).

[144]Marti, *Dodekapropheton*, 58; Cheyne, in W. R. Smith's, *The Prophets of Israel*, xvii; Harper, *Amos and Hosea*, clx, 291-292; Nowack, *Die kleinen Propheten*, 47; Wolfe, "Editing of the Book of the Twelve," 91-93; G. A. Smith, *The Book of the Twelve Prophets*, I, 225; Pfeiffer, *Introduction to the Old Testament*, 573; Lippl, *Die zwölf kleinen Propheten*, 18, 52; Rudolph, *Hosea*, 141; Willi-Plein, *Vorformen*, 153-54, all regard 6:11-7:1aA as a later Judean exilic or post-exilic insertion. Mauchline, "Hosea," 631; Jacob, *Osée*, 56-57; Nötscher, *Das Zwölfprophetenbuch*, 21; Sellin, *Das Zwölfprophetenbuch*, 78, think that 6:11 originates from a Judean redactor, while Mays, Hosea, 102; Buss, *Prophetic Word*, 15, and Wolff, *Commentary*, 106, attribute only 6:11a to this redactor. Wellhausen, *Die kleinen Propheten*, 117 and Duhm, "Anmerkungen," 24, describe 6:11b as a gloss to the beginning of 7:1.

McKeating, *Amos, Hosea, Micah*, 112, leaves the question of authenticity open.

[145]Marti, *Dodekapropheton*, 58; Wolfe, "Editing of the Book of the Twelve," 91, 93; Willi-Plein, *Vorformen*, 153-54. Cf. Nowack, *Die kleinen Propheten*, 47.

[146]Infra, 280-281.

[147]Willi-Plein, *Vorformen*, 154.

[148]For our reading, see Kuhnigk, *Nordwestsemitische Studien*, 90.

[149]Marti, *Dodekapropheton*, 59; Harper, *Amos and Hosea*,, 295; Wellhausen, *Die kleinen Propheten*, 118; Duhm, "Anmerkungen," 25; Pfeiffer, *Introduction*, 570. Nowack, *Die kleinen Propheten*, 48, thinks only 7:4aBb is a gloss to 7:6.

[150]Cf. Sellin, *Das Zwölfprophetenbuch*, 79; Robinson, *Die zwölf kleinen Propheten*, 26; Lippl, *Die zwölf kleinen propheten*, 53; Rudolph, *Hosea*, 147; G. R. Driver, "Linguistic and textual problems: Minor Prophets I," *JTS* 39 (1938) 156; T. H. Gaster, "Hosea 7:3-6," *VT* 4 (1954) 78; S. M. Paul, "The Image of the Oven and the Cake in Hos 7:4-10," *VT* 18 (1968) 115; Szabó, "Textual Problems in Hosea," 513-514.

[151]MT: "their baker." For our reading, see Syr and Targ; Harper, *Amos and Hosea*, 297; Wolff, *Commentary*, 107; Marti, *Dodekapropheton*, 60; Nowack, *Die kleinen Propheten*, 49; Rudolph, *Hosea*, 147-148; Paul, "The Image of the Oven and the Cake," 115-116, and others. The reading of "their baker" in 7:6 was probably influenced by the '*ōpeh* in 7:4 which we argue is an R2 addition.

[152]Supra, 164-167.

[153]Marti, *Dodekapropheton*, 62; Sellin, *Das Zwölfprophetenbuch*, 82; Duhm, "Anmerkungen," 26; Lippl, *Die zwölf kleinen Propheten*, 18; Mays, *Hosea*, 109; Willi-Plein, *Vorformen*, 159; Jeremias, *Der Prophet Hosea*, 98. Ehrlich, *Randglossen*, 185 and Wolff, *Commentary*, 107, regard 7:10a as a secondary insertion from Hos 5:5.

[154]The seven *middoth* of Hillel are cited in *Sifra* 3a and *T.San.* vii.11.

[155]Willi-Plein, *Vorformen*, 159.

[156]Duhm, "Anmerkungen," 26; Peiser, *Hosea*, 28-29; Lippl, *Die zwölf kleinen Propheten*, 55.

[157]Sellin, *Das Zwölfprophetenbuch*, 82. Cf. Andersen and Freedman who reads an emphatic *kaph* for *k'šr* and repoints '*šr* to Assyria, *Hosea*, 469-470.

[158]Cf. Marti, *Dodekapropheten*, 62; Rudolph, *Hosea*, 151-152.

[159]Peiser, *Hosea*, 28-29

[160]Supra, 170-171.

[161]Cf. Wolff, *Commentary*, 107, fn. u.

[162]Cf. Andersen and Freedman, *Hosea*, 475-476.

[163]Regarding *z'm* = "stuttering," see, G. R. Driver, "Linguistic and Textual problems," 157.

[164]Wolfe, "Editing of the Book of the Twelve," 93; Wolff, *Commentary*, 108; Jacob, *Osée*, 58; Willi-Plein, *Vorformen*, 162. The LXX reads only one verb for the verse.

[165]Especially Willi-Plein, *Vorformen*, 162: "Die Wahl der Wz. *ysr* durch den Glossator zeigt, dass auch bei der Glossierung Assonanz als Verankerung im Text gelten konnte." Also, Kaatz, "Wortspiel," 436; Duhm, "Anmerkungen," 27; Rudolph, *Hosea*, 152; Andersen and Freedman, *Hosea*, 476, who note the paronomasia.

[166]*ysr* = to instruct, see Pr 4:1; 8:10; 8:33; 10:17; 23:12.

[167]Marti, *Dodekapropheten*, 64; Sellin, *Das Zwölfprophetenbuch*, 83; Wolfe, "Editing of the Book of the Twelve," 121; Lippl, *Die zwölf kleinen Propheten*, 56.

[168]M. Dahood, *Psalms I* (AB 16; Garden City: Doubleday, 1966) 45-46; idem. *Psalms III* (AB 17a; Garden City: Doubleday, 1966) 188, 201, 229, 293 etc.; Kuhnigk, *Nordwestsemitische Studien*, 100-101; Andersen and Freedman, *Hosea*, 477.

[169]Cf. the translation of *lō' 'āl* as *Ohnmacht*, "the Impotent One," by Jeremias, *Der Prophet Hosea*, 91.

[170]Cf. G. R. Driver, "Problems of the Hebrew Text and Language," *BBB* 1 (1950) 53-64, who relates *qšt rmyh* to its corresponding Assyrian phrase and thus concludes: "The Hebrew expression then means that in Hosea's view Ephraim has become like such a bow, i.e. feeble and useless..."

[171]Duhm, "Anmerkungen," 27. Marti, *Dodekapropheton*, 64; Harper, *Amos and Hosea*, clxi, 308; K. Budde, "Hosea 7:12" *ZAW* 26 (1912) 32; Jeremias, *Der Prophet Hosea*, 92, also regard 7:16b as a gloss.

[172]Infra, 326-329.

[173]Supra, 85-86. Duhm, "Anmerkungen," 27, has questioned the authenticity of 8:4b-6, stating that it is a post-exilic sermon regarding the foolishness of idol worship which has nothing to do with Hosea's poem which speaks of *politics*. Wolfe, "Editing of the Book of the Twelve," 109; Pfeiffer, *Introduction*, 572; Day, "Is the Book of Hosea Exilic?" 124, all regard 8:4b as a later insertion.

[174]Robinson, *Die zwölf kleinen Propheten*, 32; Weiser, *Das Buch der zwölf kleinen Propheten*, 52; Nowack, *Die kleinen Propheten*, 54; Harper, *Amos and Hosea*, 312; Marti, *Dodekapropheten*, 66; Wellhausen, *Die kleinen Propheten*, 120; Lippl, *Die zwölf kleinen Propheten*, 57.

[175]Cf. LXX; Mays, *Hosea*, 113; Rudolph, *Hosea*, 157; Jeremias, *Der Prophet Hosea*, 102.

[176]Wolff, *Commentary*, 132, i; Jacob, *Osée*, 60.

[177]R. Gnuse, "Calf, Cult, and King: The Unity of Hosea 8:1-13," *BZ* 26 (1982) 83, fn. 5, 86-87.

[178]Marti, *Dodekapropheton*, 66; Nowack, *Die kleinen Propheten*, 55; Robinson, *Die zwölf kleinen Propheten*, 32; Lippl, *Die zwölf kleinen Propheten*, 57.

[179]Harper, *Amos and Hosea*, 315.

[180]J. R. Lundbom, "Double-duty subject in Hosea 8, 5," *VT* 16 (1966) 228. But, see Jeremias, *Der Prophet Hosea*, 102, fn. 3.

[181]Marti, *Dodakapropheten*, 66-67; Peiser, Hosea, 33; Duhm, "Anmerkungen," 27; Pfeiffer, *Introduction*, 572 and "Polemic against Idolatry," 230-232; Wolfe, "Editing of the Book of the Twelve," 110-111.

[182]With its present punctuation, the subject of the niphal 3 ms. sg., *yikkārēt*, is unclear, as its immediate antecedents are formulated in the 3 ms. pl. With LXX and Syr, Nowack, *Die kleinen Propheten*, 54; Marti, *Dodekapropheton*, 66; Lippl, *Die zwölf kleinen Propheten*, 57; Jacob, *Osée*, 60, emend the text to the 3 ms pl, *yikkaretû*.

[183]Cf. Andersen and Freedman, *Hosea*, 493.

[184]Harper, *Amos and Hosea*, 312; Weiser, *Das Buch der zwölf kleinen Propheten*, 52; Willi-Plein, *Vorformen*, 164.

[185]Regarding the sin of Jeroboam I as a major theme of the Deuteronomistic History, see Cross, *Canaanite Myth and Hebrew Epic*, 278-285; Friedman, *The Exile and Biblical Narrative*, 4-6; Nelson, *The Double Redaction of the Deuteronomistic History*, 32-35; J. Debus, *Die Sünde Jeroboams. Studien zur Darstellung Jeroboams und der Geschichte des Nordreiches in der deuteronomistischen Geschichtsschreibung* (FRLANT 93; Göttingen: Vandenhoeck und Ruprecht, 1967).

[186]Supra, 186-187.

[187]Wolff, *Commentary*, 141.

[188]Casanowitz, *Paronomasia in the Old Testament*, 74, #362; S. R. Driver, *Introduction*, 306; Kaatz, "Wortspiel," 436; Lippl, *Die zwölf kleinen Propheten*, 19; Stinespring, "Humor," 661; Seow, "Hosea 14:10," 219.

[189]Supra, 152-153.

[190]Supra, 190-191.

[191]The MT of 8:13a is notoriously difficult. C. Harper, *Amos and Hosea*, 313, for a list of different suggested emendations. With modification, we read the text with E. W. Nicholson, "Problems in Hos 8:13," *VT* 16 (1966) 355-358.

[192]Duhm, "Anmerkungen," 28-29; Marti, *Dodekapropheton*, 69-70; Nötscher, *Das Zwölfprophetenbuch*, 25; Pfeiffer, *Introduction*, 570; Lippl, *Die zwölf kleinen Propheten*, 18; Wolfe, "Editing of the Book of the Twelve," 91; Harper, *Amos and Hosea*, clxii, 324; Wellhausen, *Die kleinen Propheten*, 122; Nowack, *Die kleinen Propheten*, 57; Buss, *Prophetic Word*, 18; Willi-Plein, *Vorformen*, 170, 244; Wolff, *Commentary*, xxxi, 136, and several others.

[193]See Isa 44:2; 51:13; 54:5.

[194]Supra, 83-84.

[195]Supra, 187-188.

[196]Infra, 225-226, 238-244. Lundbom, "Poetic Structure and Rhetoric in Hosea," 307-308, and Andersen and Freedman, *Hosea*, 502, both point out that "the return to Egypt" forms the second half of an inclusio which has its counterpart in 8:9: "They have gone up to Assyria (*hēmmâ 'ālû 'aššûr*)...They will return to Egypt (*hēmmâ miṣrayim yāšûbû*)." We argue that this structure would have occurred at the redactional level. The secondary nature of the whole verse, 8:13, and the R2 focus on the journey to and from Egypt which seems to be typical of his editorials argue in favor of later redaction.

[197]Supra, 168-169.

[198]Marti, *Dodekapropheton*, 70; Sellin, *Das Zwölfprophetenbuch*, 92 and Wolfe, "Editing of the Book of the Twelve," 91, regard 9:3a as a later addition. Buss, *Prophetic Word*, thinks 9:3bB is a secondary expansion.

[199]Infra, 200-202.

200Wolfe, "Editing of the Book of the Twelve," 92, Day, "Is the Book of Hosea Exilic," 124, and Pfeiffer, *Introduction*, 572, think 9:4 is a later gloss reminiscent of Deuteronomy. Sellin, *Das Zwölfprophetenbuch*, 92; Marti, *Dodekapropheton*, 71; Peiser, *Hosea*, 36-37; Lippl, *Die zwölf kleinen Propheten*, 61; Nowack, *Die kleinen Propheten*, 58; Wolff, *Commentary*, 150, 155; Rudolph, *Hosea*, 176; Buss, *Prophetic Word*, 18, fn 39; Willi-Plein, *Vorformen*, 172-73, 245; Mays, *Hosea*, 127, and Jeremias, *Der Prophet Hosea*, 116, all regard various parts of 9:4 as later expansions.

201Cf. the use of *krt*, "to cut off," in the R2 insertion, 8:4bB.

202Pace, BHS; Marti, *Dodekapropheton*, 71; Wellhausen, *Die kleinen Propheten*, 123; Weiser, *Das Buch der zwölf kleinen Propheten*, 57; Robinson, *Die zwölf kleinen Propheten*, 34; Lippl, *Die zwölf kleinen Propheten*, 61, who would emend *lāhem* to *lahmām*.

203For our translation of Hos 9:6, see Andersen and Freedman, *Hosea*, 514, 531-532.

204Duhm, "Anmerkungen," 29. Cf. RSV, Wellhausen, Nowack, and Harper who emend the text to "Assyria.

205Sellin, *Das Zwölfprophetenbuch*, 93, and Lippl, *Die zwölf kleinen Propheten*, 61.

206Duhm, "Anmerkungen," 29. Cf. Sellin, *Das Zwölfprophetenbuch*, 94, and Lippl, *Die zwölf kleinen Propheten*, 61, who eliminate *lĕkaspām* as a gloss.

207Supra, 187-188.

208As noted by Weinfeld, "Hosea and Deuteronomy," *Deuteronomy and the Deuteronomistic School*, 369.

209Cf. the different interpretations and renderings outlined by R. Doobie, "The Text of Hosea 9, 8," *VT* 5 (1955) 199-203.

210Infra, 292-293.

211Supra, 177-178.

212Nowack, Harper, Marti, and Duhm doubt the authenticity of *'im 'ĕlōhāy* because of its peculiarity.

213Marti, *Dodekapropheton*, 73, had already noted the "graphische Wiederholung" of *'ēwil hannābî'* in *'ĕlōhāy nābî'*.

214Duhm, "Anmerkungen," 30; Wellhausen, *Die kleinen Propheten*, 123; Harper, *Amos and Hosea*, 333; Nowack, *Die kleinen Propheten*, 60; Marti, *Dodekapropheton*, 75; Willi-Plein, *Vorformen*, 176-78; McKeating, *The Books of Amos, Hosea, Micah*, 128.

215Supra, 182-183.

216So also does Willi-Plein, *Vorformen*, 176-78, explain the exegetical motivation of the 9:9 glossator.

217Infra, 208-209.

218Duhm, "Anmerkungen," 30. For Willi-Plein, *Vorformen*, 179-183, the original Hosean saying is composed of 9:10, 13a, and 15, which was augmented by a redactor with the authentic sayings fragments, 9:11, 16, 12, 13b-14, 17. Cf. also the reconstructions of Sellin, *Das Zwölfprophetenbuch*, 97-98; Harper, *Amos and Hosea*, 337-338; Marti, *Dodekapropheton*, 76; Nowack, *Die kleinen Propheten*, 61-62; Lippl, *Die zwölf kleinen Propheten*, 64, and Buss, *Prophetic Word*, 19-20.

[219]Such is the opinion of Ewald, Nowack, and Cheyne regarding the interpretation of 9:14. Marti concurs with this interpretation but thinks that the plea is due to a later glossator who shudders before the terrible description of the consumption of the people.

[220]Marti, *Dodekapropheton*, 78, and Wolfe, "Editing of the Book of the Twelve," 91, both attribute 9:17 to later editing. Although she thinks 9:17 is part of an authentic Hosean sayings fragment composed of 9:15bB, 17, Willi-Plein, *Vorformen*, 183, opines that 9:17 can be understood from the exile event as a prophetic oracle of doom regarding this exile and the diaspora situation which resulted from it.

[221]Cf. Weinfeld, *Deuteronomy and the Deuteronomic School*, 337.

[222]See Andersen and Freedman, *Hosea*, 565-66.

[223]Read pual inf. of *'sr* with Rudolph, *Hosea*, 199, and Jeremias, *Der Prophet Hosea*, 132.

[224]Read the *qere*.

[225]The wordplay is noted by Good, "Composition of Hosea," 47, who views it as an oral catchword connection for separate poems.

[226]Contra Nowack, *Die kleinen Propheten*, 65; Robinson, *Die zwölf kleinen Propheten*, 40; Harper, *Amos and Hosea*, 351, who emend the text for the purpose of harmonization. Marti, *Dodekapropheton*, 81-82, and Wolfe, "Editing of the Book of the Twelve," 116, regard 10:9 as the addition of a later editor.

[227]Supra, 204.

[228]Wellhausen, *Die kleinen Propheten*, 125-26; Nowack, *Die kleinen Propheten*, 65. Cf. also, Good, "Composition of Hosea," 47.

[229]Cf. Marti, *Dodekapropheton*, 81; Sellin, *Das Zwölfprophetenbuch*, 106; Rudolph, *Hosea*, 199-200; Willi-Plein, *Vorformen*, 177-78; Jeremias, *Der Prophet Hosea*, 133-34.

[230]Cf. R. G. Boling, *Judges. Introduction, Translation, and Commentary* (AB 6A; Garden City: Doubleday, 1975) 36-38.

[231]Cf. Jeremias, *Der Prophet Hosea*, 133-134.

[232]As noted by Kaatz, "Wortspiel," 436.

[233]Harper, *Amos and Hosea*, clx, 349, 352-353, and Wolfe, "Editing of the Book of the Twelve," 110, both have assigned 10:10 to a later editor. Wellhausen, *Die kleinen Propheten*, 126; Marti, *Dodekapropheton*, 82-83; Nowack, *Die kleinen Propheten*, 66; and Willi-Plein, *Vorformen*, 189-190, consider 10:10b as originating from a redactor.

[234]This threefold paronomasia has been observed by Casanowitz, *Paranomasia*, 47, #34, Rudolph, *Hosea*, 199, and Willi-Plein, *Vorformen*, 190.

[235]Cf. the list of Harper, *Amos and Hosea*, 353.

[236]Willi-Plein, *Vorformen*, 189.

[237]Consult the following for those who have dealt with this question to some extent: A. Alt, "Die Heimat des Deuteronomiums," *Kleine Schriften zur Geschichte des Volkes Israel* (München: C. H. Beck, 1959, 2 Aufl., Band II) 250-275; R. E. Clements, *Prophecy and Tradition* (Oxford: Basil Blackwell, 1975); R. Davidson, "Orthodoxy and the Prophetic Word. A Study in the Relationship between Jeremiah and Deuteronomy," *VT* 14 (1964) 407-416; A. Deissler,

"Das 'Echo' der Hosea-Verkündigung im Jeremiabuch," in *Künder des Wortes. Beiträge zur Theologie der Propheten. Josef Schreiner zum 60. Geburtstag*, L. Ruppert, P. Weimar, E. Zenger, hrsg. (Würzburg: Echter, 1982); K. Gross, "Hoseas Einfluss auf Jeremias Anschauungen," *NKZ* 42 (1931) 241-256; 327-343; idem. *Die literarische Verwandschaft Jeremias mit Hosea* (Borne and Leipzig, 1930); B. Lindars, "'Rachel Weeping for her Children' - Jeremiah 31:15-22," *JSOT* 11 (1979) 47-62; E. W. Nicholson, *Preaching to the Exiles. A Study of the Prose Tradition in the Book of Jeremiah* (Oxford: Blackwell, 1970); G. von Rad, "Hosea und das Deuteronomium," in *Das Gottesvolk in Deuteronomium* (BWANT III/11; Stuttgart: Kohlhammer, 1929) 78-883; H. H. Rowley, "The Prophet Jeremiah and the Book of Deuteronomy," *From Moses to Qumran. Studies in the Old Testament* (London: Lutterworth, 1963) 187-208; I. L. Seeligmann, "Die Auffassung von der Prophetie in der deuteronomistischen und chronistischen Geschichtsschreibung (mit einem Exkurs über das Buch Jeremia)," *VTSup* 29 (1978) 254-284; M. Weinfeld, "*Deuteronomy and Hosea*," *Deuteronomy and the Deuteronomic School* (Oxford: Clarendon, 1972); H. W. Wolff, "Hoseas geistige Heimat," *TLZ* 81 (1956) 83-84.

[238]So also, Willi-Plein, *Vorformen*, 189, regarding the insertion of 10:10b by a glossator.

[239]Supra, 152-153.

[240]Supra, 191.

[241]Regarding this translation, see M. Dahood, "Minor Prophets and Ebla," *The Word of the Lord Shall Go Forth*, Carol L. Meyers and M. O'Connor, eds. (Winona Lake, IN: Eisenbrauns, 1983) 49.

[242]Marti, *Dodekapropheton*, 84; Nowack, *Die kleinen Propheten*, 68; Wellhausen, *Die kleinen Propheten*, 126; and Wolfe, "Editing of the Book of the Twelve," 91, judge 10:13b to be secondary. Moreover, Harper, *Amos and Hosea*, clxi, 358; Day, "Is the Book of Hosea Exilic?" 132; Marti, *Dodekapropheton*, 85; Nowack, *Die kleinen Propheten*, 68; Duhm, "Anmerkungen," 34; Wolfe, "Editing of the Book of the Twelve," 115, 118, regard 10:14 as later.

[243]See also 2 Kgs 18:5 in which the Deuteronomist describes Hezekiah as trusting in YHWH. Cf. 2 Kgs 18:19-24.

[244]Kaatz, "Wortspiel," 436.

[245]Cf. Wolff, *Commentary*, xxxi.

[246]Cf. LXX; Wolff, *Commentary*, 190-191; Kuhnigk, *Nordwestsemitische Studien*, 129; Andersen and Freedman, *Hosea*, 578.

[247]For this very difficult text, see LXX, Syr, Targ; Wolff, *Commentary*, 191; Willi-Plein, *Vorformen*, 197.

[248]The suffix on *'ēlāyw* performs a double duty function for the verb *'ōkil*, "to make eat."

[249]Wolfe, "Editing of the Book of the Twelve," 110, 115, regards 11:2, 3b and 4b as glosses inserted by an anti-idol polemist and by later scribes. Nowack, *Die kleinen Propheten*, 70 omits 11:3bB-4aA as secondary expansions. Cf. also Pfeiffer, "Polemic," 232, fn. 19 = 11:2; Wellhausen, *Die*

kleinen Propheten, 127 = 11:3b; and Sellin *Das Zwölfprophetenbuch*, 113 = 11:4aB.

250Supra, 79-81.

251Dt 4:37; 7:8, 13; 10:15; 23:5 on the love of YHWH. For studies on this topic, see especially D. J. McCarthy, "Notes on the Love of God in Deuteronomy and the Father-Son Relationship Between Yahweh and Israel," *CBQ* 27 (1965) 144-147, responding to W. L. Moran, "The Ancient Near Eastern Background of the Love of God in Deuteronomy," *CBQ* 25 (1963) 77-87. See also, D. J. McCarthy, *Old Testament Covenant. A Survey of Current Opinions* (Atlanta: John Knox, 1978) 32-34, and L. E. Toombs, "Love and Justice in Deuteronomy," *Int* 19 (1965) 389-411.

252Infra, 221-222.

253Andersen and Freedman, *Hosea*, 577.

254Szabó, "Textual Problems in Hosea," 518.

255Cf. supra, 140-141, on Hos 14:10. Also see the citations of Weinfeld, *Deuteronomy and Deuteronomic School*, 332-334, regarding walking in the way of YHWH in Dt and the Deuteronomistic History.

256*pĕsilîm*, "graven images," occurs only here in Hosea. However cf. the Dtr polemic against *pĕsilîm* in Dt 4:16, 23, 25; 5:8; 7:5, 25; 12:3; 27:15.

257Cf. the discussion of 11:10-11, supra, 153-156.

258Cf. for example, Weiser, *Das Buch der zwölf kleinen Propheten*, 69; G. R. Driver, "Linguistic and Textual Problems," 161; Wolff, *Commentary*, 191; and Jacob, *Osée*, 79, who interpret the 11:1-4 as a father/son portrayal, while Robinson, *Die zwölf kleinen Propheten*, 43; Rudolph, *Hosea*, 215-16; and Jeremias, *Der Prophet Hosea*, 142, maintain both themes in the text.

259Supra, 210-211.

260Dt 5:15; 7:19; 9:29; 26:8. Cf. 2 Kgs 17:36.

261Cf. Dt 32:5, 6.

262Cf. R2 = Hos 2:22b; 4:6a; 6:3; 14:10.

263Cf. R2 = 5:13b; 6:1; 7:1a; 14:5.

264Cf. Gen 27:40; Lev 26:13; 1 Kgs 12:4-14.

265Cf. Jer 27:2, 8, 11-12; 28:2, 4, 11, 14; Isa 47:6; Lam 1:14; Ezek 34:27.

266Cf. Ezek 34:27; Jer 28:2, 4, 11, 14; 30:8.

267So noted by Kaatz, "Wortspiel," 436.

26811:7b is indeed difficult. Our own translation is provisional. See Aquila, Sym, Targ which read "yoke," followed by the RSV, Harper, *Amos and Hosea*, 367; Rudolph, *Hosea*, 211-12; Willi-Plein, *Vorformen*, 202-203; and Szabó, "Textual Problems in Hosea," 519.

269Reading an asseverative *lō'* with Kuhnig, *Nordwestsemitische Studien zum Hoseabuch*, 133, and others.

270Cf. Andersen and Freedman *Hosea*, 585-586.

271Supra, 133.

272S. R. Driver, *Introduction*, 306, and Nowack, *Die kleinen Propheten*, 70, have noted this wordplay. Wolfe, "Editing of the Book of the Twelve," 116, thinks the whole 11:5 verse is secondary, while Marti, *Dodekapropheton*, 88 and Jeremias, *Der Prophet Hosea*, 143, attribute v. 5b to a later editor.

[273]N. Lohfink, "Hos 11:5 als Bezugstext von Dtn 17:16," *VT* 31 (1981) 226-228.

[274]Supra, 187-188, 196.

[275]G. A. Smith, *Book of the Twelve Prophets*, 297, fn. 1, would regard 11:6 as an insertion. Jeremias *Der Prophet Hosea*, 143, sees 11:6b as an exilic addition.

[276]R2 = 4:6a, 8, 9, 12, 14; 6:11b.

[277]*BDB*, 896.

[278]Wolfe, "Editing of the Book of the Twelve," 93, and Day, "Is the Book of Hosea Exilic?" 125 assign the whole passage, 11:8-11 to exilic composition. Wellhausen, *Die kleinen Propheten*, 128 and Nowack, *Die kleinen Propheten*, 71, regard 11:8b-11 as secondary. J.M.P. Smith, *A Commentary on the Books of Amos, Hosea, and Micah*, 72, sees 11:9-11 as later, while Harper, *Amos and Hosea*, clx, 372, regards 11:8b, 9a, 10b-11 as additions.

[279]Because the note of promise beginning with 11:8 is seemingly incongruous in the present context, commentators variously interpret 11:8-9 so that it will be more consistent with the punitive tone. Thus, Marti, *Dodekapropheton*, 89, reads: "How shall I abandon you . . ." e.g. "In what way will I abandon you?," or G. S. Glanzman, "Two Notes: Am 3:15 and Hos 11:8-9," *CBQ* 23 (1961) 231, who thinks that '*êk* is used as an affirmative exclamation: "How (gladly) will I surrender you, O Ephraim ... How (gladly) will I make you like Admah." Both Glanzman and Andersen and Freedman, *Hosea*, 589, read the *lō'* of 11:9a not as a negative but an asseverative: "I will certainly act out my fierce anger."

[280]So noted by Kaatz, "Wortspiel," 436.

[281]Compare Gen 10:19; 14:2; Dt 29:22.

[282]Friedman, *The Exile and Biblical Narrative*, 18-19. Cf. Day, "Is the Book of Hosea Exilic?" 125. The only other passages mentioning Admah and Zeboiim are Gen 10:19 and Gen 14:2.

[283]Supra, 135-136.

[284]Cf. 3:4-5; 9:3; 14:8.

[285]Supra, 69-71.

[286]Supra, 153-156.

[287]Besides those authors cited in fn. 251 above, add F. C. Fensham, "Father and Son as Terminology for Treaty and Covenant," *Near Eastern Studies in Honor of W. F. Albright*, H. Goedicke, ed. (Baltimore: Johns Hopkins University, 1971) 121-135; R. G. Boling, "Prodigal Sons on Trial: A Study in the Prophecy of Hosea," *McQ* 19 (1965) 13-27, 38.

[288]Boling, "Prodigal Sons," 22.

[289]E. Bellefontaine, "Deuteronomy 21:18-21 - Reviewing the Case of the Rebellious Son," *JSOT* 13 (1979) 13-31.

[290]Supra, 141.

[291]Cf. *ně'ūm-yhwh* and *hāyâ bayyôm hahû'* in 2:15-23, and Lebanon, 14:6-8.

[292]From the root *rwd*. Cf. Wolff, *Commentary*, 205-206. Also see C. H. Reines, "Hosea 12:1," *JJS* 2 (1951) 156-57, who relates *rād* to the Assyrian verb *redu*, "to walk after, to follow." We part ways with Reines, however, in

his interpretation of 12:1b: that Judah is also culpable of deviating from true religion.

[293]P. R. Ackroyd, "Hosea and Jacob," *VT* 13 (1963) 245-259; A. Bentzen, "The Weeping of Jacob, Hos 12:5a," *VT* 1 (1951) 58-59; R. B. Coote, "Hosea 12," *VT* 21 (1971) 389-402; D. Cornill, "Hosea 12:1," *ZAW* 7 (1887) 285-89; K. Deller, "*šmn bll* (Hosea 12:2). Additional Evidence," *Bib* 46 (1965) 349-352; F. Dietrich., *Die Anspielungen auf die Jakob-Tradition in Hosea 12:1-13:3.* (Würzburg: Echter, 1977); F. Dreyfus, "'L'Araméen voulait tuer mon père': L'actualisation de Dt 26, 5 dans la tradition juive et la tradition chrétienne," *De la Tôrah au Messie.* Maurice Carrez, Joseph Doré, Pierre Grelot, eds. (Paris: Desclée, 1981) 147-161; Lyle M. Eslinger, "Hosea 12:5a and Genesis 32:29: A Study in Inner Biblical Exegesis," *JSOT* 18 (1980) 91-99; F. Foresti, "Hos 12: A Prophetical Polemic against the Proto-Elohistic Patriarchal Tradition," *EphemCarm* 30 (1979) 179-200; M. Gertner, "The Masorah and the Levites. Appendix on Hos 12," *VT* 10 (1960) 241-284; H. L. Ginsberg, "Hosea's Ephraim, More Fool than Knave. A New Interpretation of Hosea 12:1-14," *JBL* 80 (1961) 339-47; E. M. Good, "Hosea and the Jacob Tradition," *VT* 16 (1966) 137-151; Robert Gordis, "Midrash in the Prophets," *The Word and the Book: Studies in Biblical Language and Literature* (New York: KTAV, 1976) 108-113; D. Grimm, "Erwägungen zu Hosea 12, 12 'in Gilgal opfern sie Stiere,'" *ZAW* 85 (1973) 339-347; W. L. Holladay, "Chiasmus, the Key to Hosea 12: 3-6," *VT* (1966) 53-64; Edmond Jacob, "La Femme et le Prophète. A propos d'Osée 12:13-14," *Hommage à Wilhelm Vischer*, Jean Cadier, ed. (Montpellier: Cause Graille Castelnau, 1960) 83-87; D. J. McCarthy, "Hosea 12:2: Covenant by Oil," *VT* 14 (1964) 215-221; Reines, "Hosea 12:1," 156-157; L. Ruppert, "Herkunft und Bedeutung der Jakob-Tradition bei Hosea," *Bib* 52 (1971) 488-504; N. Schmidt, "The Numen of Penuel," *JBL* 45 (1926) 260-279; T. C. Vriezen, "Hosea 12," *Nieuwe Theologische Studien* 24 (1941) 144-149; T. C. Vriezen, "La tradition de Jacob dans Osée 12," *OTS* 1 (1942) 64-78; Julien Weill, "Osée 12:13-13:1 et le prétendu Martyre du Moise," *REJ* 87 (1929) 89-93; A. Zillessen, "Eine Frage zu Hos 12:1," *ZAW* 49 (1931) 150.

[294]Cf. Sellin, *Das Zwölfprophetenbuch*, 118, and Lippl, *Die zwölf kleinen Propheten*, 73, who reads "baal" for '*im-'ēl*, "with God," and *qĕdēšîm*, "whores," for *qĕdôšîm*, "Holy One," and Zillessen, "Eine Frage zu Hos 12:1," 150 and Szabó, "Textual Problems," 520, who emends *rād* to *rāb*, "Judah litigates with God." Moreover, consult Reines, "Hosea 12:1," 156-57; Kuhnigk, *Nordwestsemitischen Studien*, 143-144; Coote, "Hosea 12," 390; Foresti, "Hos 12," 182; and Andersen and Freedman, *Hosea*, 603, who interpret '*ēl* and *qĕdôšîm* as members of the Canaanite pantheon.

[295]Marti, *Dodekapropheton*, 92-93; Harper, *Amos and Hosea*, clx, 376; Nowack, *Die kleinen Propheten*, 73-74; Peiser, Hosea, 48-49; Wolfe, "Editing of the Book of the Twelve," 91; Mays, *Hosea*, 160; Good, "Composition of Hosea," 49; Ginsberg, "Hosea's Ephraim," 340; Jeremias, *Der Prophet Hosea*, 151.

[296]Coote, "Hos 12," 391.

[297]Kaatz, "Wortspiel," 436.

[298]Coote, "Hos 12," 392.

[299]Cf. Eslinger, "Hosea 12:5a and Genesis 32:29," 93-94. We will treat the textual problems of v. 5 in more detail below.

[300]See Andersen and Freedman, *Hosea*, 615, and Kuhnigk, *Nordwestsemitische Studien*, 147-148, regarding the syntax of *bĕ* on *bē'lōhĕkā*.

[301]Cf. F. Dietrich, *Die Anspielungen auf die Jakob-Tradition in Hosea 12:1-13:3. Ein literaturwissenschaftlicher Beitrag zur Exegese früher Prophetentexte.* (Würzburg: Echter, 1977).

[302]Wellhausen, *Die kleinen Propheten*, 129; Marti, *Dodekapropheten*, 92-95; Duhm, "Anmerkungen," 37; Pfeiffer, *Introduction*, 570-71; Nowack, *Die kleinen Propheten*, 74-75; J.M.P. Smith, *A Commentary on the Books of Amos, Hosea, and Micah*, 72; Wolfe, "Editing of the Book of the Twelve, 93, 115, 121; Harper, *Amos and Hosea*, clxi, 380-81; Schmidt, "Numen of Penuel," 267-68, Mauchline, "Hosea," 696, among others think that 12:5-7 is secondary.

[303]So Gertner, "Masorah and the Levites," 277. Cf. BHS; Wellhausen, *Die kleinen Propheten*, 129; Marti, *Dodekapropheten*, 95; Schmidt, "Numen of Penuel," 266; Weiser, *Das Buch der zwölf kleinen Propheten*, 74; Harper, *Amos and Hosea*, 381; and Lippl, *Die zwölf kleinen Propheten*, 74, who suggest emending *'el* to *'et*.

[304]Good, "Hosea and the Jacob Tradition," 150, and Foresti, "Hos 12: A Prophetical Polemic," 193-194.

[305]Holladay, "Chiasmus, the Key to Hos 12:3-6," 56.

[306]Bentzen, "The Weeping of Jacob, Hos 12:5a," 59.

[307]Gordis, "Midrash in the Prophets," 419-420; Gertner, "Masorah and the Levites," 273-282. Cf. Vriezen, "La Tradition de Jacob dans Osée 12," 76.

[308]Coote, "Hosea 12," 395-96.

[309]F. I. Andersen, "Note on Gen 30:8," *JBL* 88 (1969) 200.

[310]Sellin, *Das Zwölfprophetenbuch*, 122; Nyberg, *Studien zum Hoseabuche*, 94-95; Bentzen, "The Weeping of Jacob, Hos 12:5a," 58; Gertner, "The Masorah and the Levites," 277-78; Holladay, "Chiasmus, The Key to Hosea 12:3-6," 56; Wolff, *Commentary*, 206; Ruppert, "Herkunft und Bedeutung der Jakob-Tradition bei Hosea," 495; Foresti, "Hos 12: A Prophetical Polemic," 189; Andersen and Freedman, *Hosea*, 613; Eslinger, "Hos 12:5a and Genesis 32:29," 93-94; Jeremias, *Der Prophet Hosea*, 153.

[311]If *wyśr* was from the root *śrh*, "to strive," one would expect a vocalization of *wayyiśar*. Regarding those who read *śrr* rather than *śrh*, see Gertner, "The Masorah and the Levites," 277; Wolff, *Commentary*, 212; Ackroyd, "Hosea and Jacob," 250; Rudolph, *Hosea*, 222; Ruppert, "Herkunft und Bedeutung der Jakob-Tradition bei Hosea," 495-96; Coote, "Hosea 12," 395; Eslinger, "Hosea 12:5a and Genesis 32:29," 94; Jeremias, *Der Prophet Hosea*, 153.

[312]Eslinger, "Hosea 12:5a and Genesis 32:29," 94, who translates *mal'āk* as "messenger."

[313]Because of its strategic position in the chiasmus as well as its alliterative relationship with *wayyūkāl*, we maintain the authenticity of the MT and would not eliminate *mal'āk* as a gloss as Wolff, *Commentary*, 206; Gertner, "The Masorah and the Levites," 281; Jacob, *Osée*, 86; Ruppert,

"Herkunft und Bedeutung der Jakob-Tradition bei Hosea," 495; Holladay, "Chiasmus, the Key to Hos 12:3-6," 56, and others.

[314]So Eslinger, "Hosea 12:5a and Genesis 32:29," 94-95, although we argue that this paradigm of repentance occurs at the final redactor's level, rather than with the prophet, Hosea, himself.

[315]Cf. also 2 Kgs 20:3, describing Hezekiah weeping (*bkh*) before YHWH in response to Isaiah's words. YHWH consoles Hezekiah in 20:5: "I have heard your prayer. I have seen your tears (*bkh*); behold, I will *heal* you." Jer 50:4 states, "The people of Israel and the people of Judah shall come together, *weeping* as they come; and they shall seek YHWH their God."

[316]Sellin, *Das Zwölfprophetenbuch*, 122; Weiser, *Das Buch der zwölf kleinen Propheten*, 74; Wolff, *Commentary*, 213; Jeremias, *Der Prophet Hosea*, 154, think that 12:6 is a late doxology which was added secondarily. Willi-Plein, *Vorformen*, think both 12:6 and 12:7 originate from later redaction.

[317]Wolff, *Commentary*, 214.

[318]Cf. Good, "Hosea and the Jacob Tradition," 144-145, for all of the possible interpretations of 12:5b. Also Ackroyd, "Hosea and Jacob," 251-52, who thinks that the ambiguity in the suffixes could be deliberate, referring to the patriarch and his descendants equally.

[319]Cf. Gertner's "Masorah and the Levites," 279; Foresti, "Hos 12: A Prophetical Polemic," 184-185.

[320]Cf. Dt 13:19; 15:5; 17:19 etc. See also, Weinfeld, *Deuteronomy and the Deuteronomic School*, 336-37.

[321]Cf. Andersen and Freedman, Hosea, 618, regarding the syntax of '*al*. Also, Harper, *Amos and Hosea*, 388.

[322]From the root *dmh*, "to cease, cut off, destroy." Cf. Hos 4:5, 6; 10:7, 15. Robinson, *Die zwölf kleinen Propheten*, 46; Weiser, *Das Buch der zwölf kleinen Propheten*, 75; Wellhausen, *Die kleinen Propheten*, 18; and Mays, *Hosea*, 166, interpret *dmh* in 12:11 as "I destroy." Others correlate *dmh* with *dmh*, "to compare, liken."

[323]Cf. Dahood, "Minor Prophets," 50-51, regarding this verse.

[324]See especially Marti, *Dodekapropheton*, 96, who thinks that 12:10 is an exilic description and expansion of 12:6-7. Wolfe, "Editing of the Book of the Twelve," 115, also regards 12:10 as a later addition.

[325]Cf. Andersen and Freedman, *Hosea*, 614, 617, and A. Ceresko, "The Function of *Antanaclasis* (*mṣ'* "to find"//*mṣ'* "to reach, overtake, grasp") in Hebrew Poetry, especially in the Book of Qôheleth," *CBQ* 44 (1982) 558-559 on the nuances of *mṣ'* in 12:9.

[326]For Andersen and Freedman, *Hosea*, 618, *mô'ēd* is an abbreviation for '*ōhel mô'ēd*, "tent of meeting." Cf. the widely differing interpretations of *kimê mô'ēd* outlined in Harper, *Amos and Hosea*, 387.

[327]So noted by Kaatz, "Wortspiel," 436.

[328]For further study, see K. Koch, "'*ōhel*," *TDOT*, Vol. 1, 118-130.

[329]Supra, 175-178.

[330]Clements, *Prophecy and Tradition*, 50.

[331]Marti, *Dodekapropheton*, 97, argues that 12:11 is an exilic gloss to 12:10, explaining that YHWH through his prophets often announced the

deliverance from the exile. The noun, ḥāzôn, "vision," is found predominantly in later texts. Cf. Dan 1:17; 8:2, 15, 26,; Ezek 12:21-24, 27; Hab 2:2-3; Jer 14:14; 1 Chron 17:15; Lam 8:9. Noteworthy is that Isa 1:1, Nah 1:1, and Ob 1:1 describe the prophets' revelation as a vision, ḥāzôn. These texts are superscriptions attached to the work later by deuteronomistic theologians. (See our analysis and documentation of the final redactor's superscription, Hos 1:1, supra, 55-57.) The final redactor's statement in 12:11, "I multiply visions," thus reflects the deuteronomistic understanding of YHWH's modes of revelation to his prophets.

332Cf. Jer 1:9-10.

333Casanowitz, Paronomasia, 51, #71; S. R. Driver, Introduction, 306; Stinespring, "Humor," 661; Kaatz, "Wortspiel," 436; Eybers, "Proper Names," 85; Coote, "Hos 12," 399; Mauchline, "Hosea," 702, and many others.

334Eybers, "Proper Names," 85.

335'ôn, "wealth," in 12:9a interplays paronomastically with 'āwôn, "iniquity," in 12:9b.

336So noted by Good, "Hosea and the Jacob Tradition," 148.

337Harper, Amos and Hosea, clxi, 389; Duhm, "Anmerkungen," 37; Marti, Dodekapropheton, 98; Wellhausen, Die kleinen Propheten, 130; Robinson, Die zwölf kleinen Propheten, 48-49; Day, "Is the Book of Hosea Exilic?" 125; Nowack, Die kleinen Propheten, 78-79; Willi-Plein, Vorformen, 214-15, regard 12:14 as a secondary insertion. Cf. Lippl, Die zwölf kleinen Propheten, 18.

338So, Mays, Hosea, 169 and Jeremias, Der Prophet Hosea, 157.

339Supra, 235.

340Supra, 236-237.

341For other examples of šmr = divine protection, see Ex 23:20; Num 6:24; 1 Sam 2:9, 30:23; Jer 31:10 and practically every occurrence of the word in the Psalms.

342Cf. Vriezen, "La Tradition de Jacob dans Osée 12," 75-76. Also, Jacob, "La Femme et le Prophète," 84, who states that Israel according to the flesh is characterized by the wife and the pursuit of the wife.

343Scholars have offered differing opinions regarding this subject. Good, "Hosea and the Jacob Tradition," 149, and Ackroyd, "Hosea and Jacob," 247, think it is an allusion to the political alliances with foreign powers. The predominant view is that the servitude for a wife refers to the cultic prostitution which has infiltrated Israelite worship. See Cassuto, "Hosea and the Pentateuch," 86; Jacob, "La Femme et le Prophète," 84; Wolff, Commentary, 216; Mays, Hosea, 168; Rudolph, Hosea, 231; Ruppert, "Herkunft und Bedeutung der Jakob-Tradition bei Hosea," 500-501; Jeremias, Der Prophet Hosea, 157. We will discuss this question in more detail, infra, 303-304, when we treat the earlier stages of the tradition.

344Willi-Plein, Vorformen, 214-215. To a certain extent, also Gordis, "Midrash in the Prophets," 111.

345Cf. the a fortiori argument in Latin rhetoric.

346Coote, "Hosea 12," 401.

347Cf. the discussion, supra, 361-362.

348Supra, 63-64.

[349]Supra, 138-139.

[350]Supra, 142-144.

[351]With Andersen and Freedman, *Hosea*, 629, we read an asseverative *kaph* with a finite *piel* form for *dbr*.

[352]So, Driver, "Linguistic and Textual Problems," 163. Cf. Andersen and Freedman, *Hosea*, 629. Sellin, *Das Zwölfprophetenbuch*, 120, inserts 13:1 between 12:15a and 12:15b. Willi-Plein, *Vorformen*, 220-222, regards 13:1-3 as a later composition by Hosea's disciples introducing the last sayings of the book. Pfeiffer, *Introduction*, 571-72, thinks that 13:1-3 was inserted later by an anti-Samaritan Jew. Wolfe, "Editing of the Book of the Twelve," 110, attributes 13:1-2 to the anti-idol polemist. Cf. Marti, *Dodekapropheton*, 99-100, and Day, "Is the Book of Hosea Exilic?" 124.

[353]Supra, 240-241.

[354]Nelson, *Double Redaction of the Deuteronomistic History*, 55-65.

[355]Wijngaards, "Death and Resurrection," 238, suggests that 13:1 may refer to covenantal "death," just as 6:1-3 may refer to covenantal resurrection.

[356]Cf. also Dt 18:10; 2 Kgs 16:3; 21:6; Jer 32:35.

[357]Dt 9:12. Cf. also 1 Kgs 19:18: "Yet I will leave seven thousand in Israel, all the knees that have not bowed to Baal, and every mouth that has not *kissed* him (*nšq* as in Hos 13:2b)."

[358]Nowack, *Die kleinen Propheten*, 81; Duhm, "Anmerkungen," 40; Wellhausen, *Die kleinen Propheten*, 131, all think that 13:3a was inserted here secondarily under the influence of Hos 6:4.

[359]With Andersen and Freedman, *Hosea*, 634-35.

[360]*Kēmō* performs a double-duty function for the second colon.

[361]Cf. Jer 5:26.

[362]Thus, Wolff, *Commentary*, 226.

[363]Wolfe, "Editing of the Book of the Twelve," 115, thinks 13:4-6 is a secondary addition by an early scribe.

[364]Supra, 239-240.

[365]Hos 2:22b; 4:6a; 5:4; 6:3; 11:3 which are all R2 insertions.

[366]Supra, 83-84.

[367]Supra, 168-169.

[368]Hillers, *Treaty Curses and the Old Testament Prophets*, 56; Mays *Hosea*, 175-176; T. Wittstruck, "The Influence of Treaty Curse Imagery in the Beast Imagery of Daniel 7," *JBL* 97 (1978) 101.

[369]One of the conclusions Hillers draws in *Treaty Curses and the Old Testament Prophets*, 88, is that "the importance of the covenant idea to the prophets needs to be restudied, since in quite a number of places where the prophetic books, especially *Hosea* and Isaiah 1-39, do not explicitly mention 'covenant,' they nevertheless use parallels in treaty curses" (Italics mine).

[370]Supra, 142-144.

[371]Cf. Horton, *The Minor Prophets*, 69-70, and Cassuto, *Hosea and the Pentateuch*, 98.

[372]Cf. Harper, *Amos and Hosea*, 399-401. Pfeiffer, *Introduction*, 572, questions the authenticity of 13:9-11. Wolfe, "Editing of the Book of the Twelve," 91, 116, ascribes 13:9 to the Judaistic editor and 13:10b to an early

scribe. Cf. Day, "Is the Book of Hosea Exilic?" 125. Marti, *Dodekapropheton*, 102, thinks 13:10b is a prosaic gloss borrowed from 1 Sam 8:6.

[373]Andersen and Freedman, *Hosea*, 635.

[374]Cf. Hos 2:1-2; 7:16; 8:4; 11:9; 14:6.

[375]2 Kgs 24:14-16.

[376]Supra, 61-62.

[377]So, Cheyne, *The Book of Hosea*, 123; and Knight, *Hosea*, 118.

[378]Cf. A. Gelston, "Kingship in the Book of Hosea," *OTS* 19 (1974) 83-84; Mays, *Hosea*, 178; Lippl, *Die zwölf kleinen Propheten*, 80. For this reason, Marti, *Dodekapropheton*, 102 and Wolfe, "Editing of the Book of the Twelve," 116, regard Hos 13:10b as a gloss borrowed from 1 Sam 8:6.

[379]R. E. Clements, "The Deuteronomist's Interpretation of the Founding of the Monarchy in 1 Sam viii," *VT* 24 (1974) 399.

[380]Cf. Dt 7:34; 5:15; 7:19, etc.

[381]Harper, *Amos and Hosea*, 404-406, outlines the various interpretations of this verse.

[382]Cf. Mays, *Hosea*, 181, who points out the ambiguity of the text focussed particularly on the meaning of *nōḥam*. On one hand, it has been interpreted as "vengeance." On the other hand, "compassion, sympathy."

[383]For this reason, Wolfe, "Editing of the Book of the Twelve," 93-94, regards 13:14a as an addition of hope.

[384]Thus Cheyne, *The Book of Hosea*, 124; Horton, *The Minor Prophets*, 71; Knight, *Hosea. God's Love*, 120-121; and Buss, *Prophetic Word*, 26.

[385]Cf. Andersen and Freedman, *Hosea*, 639. Cheyne, *The Book of Hosea*, 124; Knight, *Hosea. God's Love*, 121; and Buss, *Prophetic Word*, 26: "I will be your plague, O Death."

[386]Cf. Sellin, *Das Zwölfprophetenbuch*, 132-134, who translates *nḥm* as "vengeance" and thinks that 13:14 and 13:15a should be placed after 14:5 because of their note of hope.

[387]Thus, Cheyne, *The Book of Hosea*, 124.

[388]Hos 2:20-24; 4:3; 14:2-9.

Chapter Seven--Hos 4-10, 12-13: Earlier Stages

[1]Supra, 114-115.

[2]Supra, 86-90.

[3]With Andersen and Freedman, *Hosea*, 347-350, we read for *km* an asseverative *kaph* with an enclitic *mēm* and emend and repoint to read *wĕ'immĕkā*. They provide a list of the various renderings of the verse, 347-48.

[4]See discussion below, 265.

[5]See Andersen and Freedman, *Hosea*, 376, regarding the pointing of *'wth*.

[6]Supra, 160-170.

[7]The following emend *māginnêhā*, "her shields," to *miggĕ'ônām*, "their pride": Robinson, *Die zwölf kleinen Propheten*, 20; Marti, *Dodekapropheton*, 45; Nötscher, *Zwölfprophetenbuch*, 16; Lippl, *Zwölf kleinen Propheten*, 44; Weiser, *Das Buch der zwölf kleinen Propheten*, 37; J. Zolli, "Hosea 4:17-18,"

ZAW 15 (1935) 175. Cf. Budde, "Zu Text und Auslegung (Hos 4:1-19)," 295, who emends *mgn* to *mg'n* but retains the feminine suffix.

⁸Marti, *Dodekapropheton*, 40, thinks the whole verse, 4:5, along with 4:6a is a supplement. Wolfe, "Editing of the Book of the Twelve," 91, 109, attributes 4:18 to the Judaistic editor, 4:19a to the anti-idol polemicist, and 4:19b to the anti-high place editor. Pfeiffer, *Introduction*, 570, simply states that 4:19 is secondary. Knight, *Hosea. God's Love*, 71, thinks that "her rulers, her shields, or her protectors" is an editorial addition.

⁹Junker, "Os 4, 1-10," 170. Cf. also Mays, *Hosea*, 68; Cheyne, *The Book of Hosea*, 64; Horton, *The Minor Prophets*, 28, who leave this interpretation open as a possibility.

¹⁰Budde, "Zu Text und Auslegung des Buches Hosea (Hos 4:1-19)," 295-297.

¹¹BHS; Wellhausen, *Die kleinen Propheten*, 111; Nowack, *Die kleinen Propheten*, 35; Harper, *Amos and Hosea*, 260; Sellin, *Das Zwölfprophetenbuch*, 58; Lippl, *Zwölf kleinen Propheten*, 42; Weiser, *Das Buch der zwölf kleinen Propheten*, 30 Cf. Duhm, "Anmerkungen," 21; Marti, *Dodekapropheton*, 43; Nötscher, *Zwölfprophetenbuch*, 15; Rudolph, *Hosea*, 106; and Willi-Plein, *Vorformen*, 134, who reads *ht'hw*.

¹²Andersen and Freedman, *Hosea*, 376. Cf. Robinson, *Das zwölf kleinen Propheten*, 20, who emends *'ōtāh* to *tā'awātām*, "their desire, craving."

¹³Regarding *kōhēn* as an R1 addition, see infra, 268.

¹⁴See discussion, supra, 122-125.

¹⁵Supra, 103-105.

¹⁶Supra, 134 135.

¹⁷Cf. especially, Jeremias, "Hos 4-7," 48-49; Willi-Plein, *Vorformen*, 129-30. Wolff, *Commentary*, 66, thinks that 4:1a is secondary, written probably by the same redactor of 1:1. Wolfe, "Editing of the Book of the Twelve," 91, thinks 4:1bA originates from the Judaistic editor.

¹⁸Supra, 142-144.

¹⁹DeRoche, "Reversal," 403; McKenzie, "Knowledge of God in Hosea," 26.

²⁰Cf. DeRoche, "Reversal," 402.

²¹Dt 5:1-21; Ex 20:2-17. Cf. Cardellini, "Hos 4, 1-3," 269.

²²Sellin, *Das Zwölfprophetenbuch*, 52; Jacob, *Osée*, 39, and Lippl, *Zwölf kleinen Propheten*, 41, delete *kōhēn* as a gloss.

²³Supra, 140-141. Cf. Dt 8:6; 10:12-13; 11:22, etc.

²⁴Marti, *Dodekapropheton*, 40; Budde, "Zu Text und Auslegung des Buches Hosea (Hos 4:1-19), 284-85; Wolff, *Commentary*, 70-71; Lohfink, "Os 4, 4-6," 330; Pfeiffer, *Introduction*, 570; and Jeremias, *Der Prophet Hosea*, 66, think that the reference to the prophet in 4:5 is secondary.

²⁵Duhm, "Anmerkungen," 21; Marti, *Dodekapropheton*, 44; G. A. Smith, *The Book of the Twelve Prophets*, 224; Weiser, *Das Buch der zwölf kleinen Propheten*, 36; Wolfe, "Editing of the Book of the Twelve," 92; Rudolph, *Hosea*, 113; Scharbert, *Die Propheten Israels*, 136; Willi-Plein, *Vorformen*, 135, 244; Jeremias, *Der Prophet Hosea*, 71, regard the whole verse as a later Judean addition. For Harper, *Amos and Hosea*, 262-63; Cheyne, in W. R. Smith's *Introduction*, xx; Nowack, *Die kleinen Propheten*, 36, and Lippl, *Zwölf kleinen*

Propheten, 18, 43, Hos 4:15a is an addition of a Judean editor. For Sellin, *Das Zwölfprophetenbuch*, 60; Pfeiffer, *Introduction*, 570; Budde, "Zu Text und Auslegung des Buches Hosea (Hos 4:1-19)," 292, 4:15aB is a Judean gloss. Finally, Wolff, *Commentary*, 72, and Mauchline, "Hosea," 563, 611-12, a Judean editor simply added "Judah" to 4:15 and thus actualized the gloss for a southern readership.

[26]Day, "Is the Book of Hosea Exilic?" 123-24; Fohrer, *Introduction*, 423-24. Cf. Willi-Plein, *Vorformen*, 135.

[27]J. Lust, "Remarks on the Redaction of Amos 5:4-6, 14-15," *OTS* 21 (1981) 146; R. B. Coote, *Amos among the Prophets*, 52.

[28]Cf. Coote, *Amos among the Prophets*, 63.

[29]Supra, 121-222.

[30]Glück, "Paronomasia," 68; S. R. Driver, *Introduction*, 306; Eybers, "Proper Names," 83.

[31]So, Willi-Plein, *Vorformen*, 137.

[32]Noted by Kaatz, "Wortspiel," 435, and Torczyner, "Dunkle Bibelstellen," 277.

[33]Dt 4:9; 5:32; 9:16; 11:16; 11:28; 17:20; 28:14; 31:29; Josh 1:7; 23:6; 1 Kgs 15:5; 22:44, *et passim*.

[34]Infra, 289.

[35]Cf. fn. 126, in our discussion of the final redaction of Hos 5, supra,

[36]Cf. Andersen and Freedman, *Hosea*, 409-410, regarding ṣāw.

[37]Wellhausen, *Die kleinen Propheten*; Sellin, *Das Zwölfprophetenbuch*, 62; Lippl, *Zwölf kleinen Propheten*, 18, 46; Wolff, *Commentary*, 95; Mauchline, "Hosea," 617; Mays, *Hosea*, 82; Willi-Plein, *Vorformen*, 142.

[38]Marti, *Dodekapropheton*, 8; Sellin, *Das Zwölfprophetenbuch*, 62; Day, "Is the Book of Hosea Exilic?" 115-116; G. A. Smith, *The Book of the Twelve Prophets*, 225; Wolfe, "Editing of the Book of the Twelve," 91; Pfeiffer, *Introduction*, 570; Peiser, *Hosea*, 18; Lippl, *Zwölf kleinen Propheten*, 18, 46; Mauchline, "Hosea," 617; Fohrer, *Introduction*, 423-24; Scharbert, *Die Propheten Israels*, 136; Jacob, *Osée*, 48; Wolff, *Commentary*, 95; Mays, *Hosea*, 16, 84; H. J. Cooke, "Pekah (2 Kgs 15:27, Hos 5:3-5)," *VT* 14 (1964) 132-33; Buss, *Prophetic Word*, 13; Willi-Plein, *Vorformen*, 142; Jeremias, *Der Prophet Hosea*, 76.

[39]Thus, Wolfe, "Editing of the Book of the Twelve," 91, thinks 5:6-7 is secondary.

[40]Supra, 269-272.

[41]Supra, 144-152.

[42]A. Alt, "Hosea 5:8--6:6. Ein Krieg und seine Folgen in prophetischer Beleuchtung," *Kleine Schriften zur Geschichte des Volkes Israel, II* (München: Beck, 1953) 163-187.

[43]Cf. Wolff, *Commentary*, 110-112; Jacob, *Osée*,, 49; Rudolph, *Hosea*, 125; Mays, *Hosea*, 86-87. Willi-Plein, *Vorformen*, 248-251, accepts it with qualification, acknowledging the redactional context of the saying.

[44]Alt, "Hosea 5:8--6:6," 179.

[45]Alt, "Hosea 5:8--6:6," 164-76.

[46]Alt, "Hosea 5:8--6:6," 165.

[47]Good, "Hos 5:8--6:6. An Alternative to Alt," *JBL* 85 (1966) 273-86.

[48]Good, "Hos 5:8--6:6," 284.

[49]Cf. the references to Judah in vv. 10, 12, 14. This is where we would part company with Marti, Nowack, Wolfe, Harper, etc., who would see the references to Judah as secondary substitutions for an original "Israel."

[50]Infra, 281-282.

[51]For this translation, see D. J. McCarthy, "*Běrît* in Old Testament History and Theology," *Bib* 53 (1972) 113, who takes his cue from Dahood in translating *kě'ādām*, "like dirt." See also, Kuhnigk, *Nordwestsemitische Studien*, 82.

[52]Cf. Andersen and Freedman, *Hosea*, 440-41.

[53]Marti, *Dodekapropheton*, 55; Willi-Plein, *Vorformen*, 150; Mays, *Hosea*, 96.

[54]Marti, *Dodekapropheton*, 9; Nowack, *Die kleinen Propheten*, 44; Robinson, *Die zwölf kleinen Propheten*, 24; Ehrlich, *Randglossen*, 179; Wolfe, "Editing of the Book of the Twelve," 91; Buss, *Prophetic Word*, 14, would all replace "Judah," in 6:4aB with Israel. However, we argue that "Judah" in 6:4 is an R1 Judean commentary on a tradition which contained "Judah."

[55]Cf. Day, "Is the Book of Hosea Exilic?" 125, who would date the book of Hosea during the time of the deuteronomists because of the references to covenant as in Hos 6:4, 6-7, which are typically deuteronomistic.

[56]Supra, 267-268.

[57]Wolfe, "Editing of the Book of the Twelve," 115, regards Hos 6:6-7 as editing by early scribes.

[58]Dt 17:2; Josh 23:16; Judg 2:20; 2 Kgs 18:2. Cf. Dt 17:2. Also, Weinfeld, *Deuteronomy and the Deuteronomic School*, 340, and L. Perlitt's discussion of Hos 6:7 in *Bundestheologie im Alten Testament*, 141-144.

[59]Supra, 276.

[60]See supra, 178, fn. 144.

[61]See supra, 179, fn. 145.

[62]Supra, 275-276.

[63]Cf. Wolff, *Commentary*, 122-123, and Mays, *Hosea*, 101-102, for their opinions.

[64]See supra, 181, fn. 151 regarding the reading of "their anger" for 7:6.

[65]See H. N. Richardson, "Some Notes on *lyṣ* and its Derivatives," *VT* 5 (1951) 166.

[66]With Andersen and Freedman, *Hosea*, 474, we interpret the *lō'* in v. 14aA with the verb in v. 14aB.

[67]Supra, 281-282

[68]Cf. Andersen and Freedman, *Hosea*, 447

[69]Cf. Wolff, *Commentary*, 124; Mays, *Hosea*, 104.

[70]Thus, Wolff, *Commentary*, 127.

[71]Cf. Rudolph, *Hosea*, 160; Mays, *Hosea*, 114; Jeremias, *Der Prophet Hosea*, 103.

[72]Read *qere*.

[73]Cf. Andersen and Freedman, *Hosea*, 506-508, regarding the translation of 8:10.

[74]So, Perlitt, *Bundestheologie*, 129-30, who regards 8:1 as inauthentic. Also, Harper, *Amos and Hosea*, 308; Day, "Is the Book of Hosea Exilic?" 124; Nowack, *Die kleinen Propheten*, 53; and Jeremias, *Der Prophet Hosea*, 104, who think Hos 8:1b is a later secondary insertion. Marti, *Dodekapropheton*, 64-65 and Wolfe, "Editing of the Book of the Twelve," 115, think that 8:1-2 are both additions.

[75]See G. I. Emmerson, "The Structure and Meaning of Hosea VIII 1-3," *VT* 25 (1975) 704-706. Also, Hillers, *Treaty Curses and the Old Testament Prophets*, 26-27.

[76]Casanowitz, *Paronomasia*, 34, 55; Kaatz, "Wortspiel," 436; Jacob, *Osée*, 64.

[77]Andersen and Freedman, *Hosea*, 507.

[78]Cf. D. W. Thomas, " Note on the Meaning of *yd'* in Hosea 9:7 and Isaiah 9:8," *JTS* 41 (1940) 43, who translates *yd'*, "to be humiliated," on the basis of an arabic root.

[79]Cf. the arab. ṣ̌awr. Rudolph, *Hosea*, 182-83, and Jeremias, *Der Prophet Hosea*, 119, adopt this interpretation for the MT ṣ̌ôr.

[80]Because of the direct address in 9:5, Marti, *Dodekapropheton*, 71, regards it as secondary.

[81]Supra, 117-120.

[82]Supra, 268.

[83]Dt 32:10; Jer 2:2. Cf. R2 = Hos 11.

[84]Wolfe, "Editing of the Book of the Twelve," 110-111, and Pfeiffer, "Polemic," 232, fn. 19, think that 9:10b is a secondary insertion against idolatry. Cf. Day, "Is the Book of Hosea Exilic?" 125.

[85]Supra, 269-270.

[86]Cf. Am 4:5.

[87]Cf. Day, "Is the Book of Hosea Exilic?" 124.

[88]Supra, 286.

[89]Cf. Andersen and Freedman, *Hosea*, 567.

[90]See Andersen and Freedman, *Hosea*, 547-552, regarding the translation of this verse.

[91]Cf. Andersen and Freedman, *Hosea*, 558, regarding *mĕ'ăṣātô*.

[92]Supra, 293.

[93]Supra, 261.

[94]1 Kgs 15:26, 33; 16:2, 7, 19, 26, 31; 2 Kgs 13:2, 11; 14:24; 15:9, 18, 24, 28.

[95]Harper, Nowack, Robinson, Nötscher, Lippl, Sellin, Nyberg, Wolfe, Peiser, Mays, Mauchline, Buss, Rudolph, Willi-Plein, and others.

[96]Supra, 276-278.

[97]With Andersen and Freedman, *Hosea*, 640-41, we read *yapri'* from the root *pr'*, "to be wild," an elative *hiphil* denominative of *pere'*, "ass."

[98]Supra, 124-125, 265-267.

[99]Gen 29:15-20.

[100]Cf. 5:11-14; 7:8, 11, 9; 9:11-13, 16; 10:11. Ephraim//Israel = 5:3 and 6:10.

[101]Cf. D. J. McCarthy, "Hosea XII 2: Covenant by Oil," *VT* 14 (1964) 216, and Dahood, "Minor Prophets," 50, regarding the significance of oil in treaty dealings.

[102]Marti, Wolfe, G. A. Smith, Nötscher, Sellin, Nowack, Lippl, Day, Wolff, Good, Mays, Jacob, Scharbert, Holladay, Willi-Plein, and others regard "Judah" as a Judean replacement for an original "Israel" in the *rib* of 12:3. The strongest argument in their favor seems to be the wordplay on the proper names in 12:4 and the reference to Jacob/Israel in 12:13. Yet, Hosea seems to include Judah in his accusation in 5:10-13a, 14. We would thus allow the text to stand, albeit conditionally.

[103]Wellhausen, *Die kleinen Propheten*, 129; Nowack, *Die kleinen Propheten*, 74-76; Willi-Plein, *Vorformen*, 211.

[104]Cf. supra, 239, fn. 325, regarding the *antanaclasis* on *mṣ'*.

[105]Cf. Kaatz, "Wortspiel," 436; Gertner, "Masorah and the Levites," 276; and McKeating, *The Books of Amos, Hosea and Micah*, 144, regarding the paronomasia between *'wn/'wn*.

BIBLIOGRAPHY

Achtemeier, Elizabeth. "The Theological Message of Hosea: Its Preaching Value," *RevExp* 4 (1975) 473-485.

Ackland, Donald. "Preaching from Hosea to a Nation in Crisis," *SWJT* 18 (1975) 43-55.

Ackroyd, Peter R. *Exile and Restoration. A Study of Hebrew Thought of the Sixth Century B.C.* Philadelphia: Westminster, 1968.

Ackroyd, Peter R. "Hosea and Jacob," *VT* 13 (1963) 245-259.

Allegro, J. M. "A Recently Discovered Fragment of a Commentary on Hosea from Qumran's Fourth Cave," *JBL* 78 (1959) 142-47.

Alt, Albrecht. "Die Heimat des Deuteronomiums," *Kleine Schriften zur Geschichte des Volkes Israel*. München: C. H. Beck, 1959, 2 Aufl. Band II, 250-275.

Alt, Albrecht. "Hosea 5:8--6:6. Ein Krieg und seine Folgen in prophetischer Beleuchtung," *Kleine Schriften zur Geschichte des Volkes Israel, II*. München: Beck, 1953, 163-87.

Amsler, Samuel. "Les prophètes et la communication par les actes." *Werden und Wirken des Alten Testaments*. R. Albertz et. al. (hrsg.) Göttingen: Vandenhoeck & Ruprecht, 1980, 194-201.

Andersen, F. I. "Note on Gen 30:8," *JBL* 88 (1969) 200.

Andersen, Francis I. and Freedman, David Noel. *Hosea: A New Translation with Introduction and Commentary.* Anchor Bible 24; Garden City: Doubleday & Co., 1980.

Andersen, Francis I. and Forbes, A. D. *A Synoptic Concordance to Hosea, Amos, Micah.* The Computer Bible 6; Wooster, Ohio: Biblical Research Asso., 1972.

Anderson, B. W. "The Book of Hosea," *Int* 8 (1954) 290-303.

Anderson, B. W. *The Eighth Century Prophets: Amos, Hosea, Isaiah, Micah.* Philadelphia: Fortress, 1978.

Anderson, B. W. "From Analysis to Synthesis: The Interpretation of Genesis 1-11," *JBL* 97 (1978) 23-29.

Anderson, B. W. "Tradition and Scripture in the Community of Faith," *JBL* 100 (1981) 5-21

Anderson, G. W. "Hosea and Yahweh: God's Love Story (Hos 1-3)," *RevExp* 4 (1975) 425-436.

André, Gunnel. *Determining the Destiny. PQD in the Old Testament.* Lund: Gleerup, 1980.

Baltzer, Klaus. "Considerations Regarding the Office and Calling of the Prophet," *HTR* 61 (1968) 567-581.

Balz-Cochois, H. *Das Ehegleichnis Hosea. Form, Kontext und Theologie.* Diss. München Fachbereich evangelische Theologie, 1980.

Balz-Cochois, H. "Gomer oder die Macht der Astarte. Versuch einer feministischen Interpretation von Hos 1-4," *EvT* 42 (1982) 37-65.

Barré, M. L. "Bullutsa-Rabi's Hymn to Gula and Hosea 6:1-2," *Or* 50 (1981) 241-245.

Barré, M. L. "New Light on the Interpretation of Hosea vi 2," *VT* 28 (1978) 129-41.

Barth, C. "Theophanie, Bundschliessung und neuer Anfang am dritten Tag," *EvT* 28 (1968) 521-533.

Barth, Hermann & Steck, Odil H. *Exegese des Alten Testaments*. Neukirchen-Vluyn: Neukirchener, 1971.

Bartlett, J. B. "The Use of the Word *r'š* as a Title in the Old Testament," *VT* 19 (1969) 1-10.

Batten, L. W. "Hosea's Message and Marriage," *JBL* 48 (1929) 257-73.

Bauer, J. B. "Drei Tage," *Bib* 39 (1958) 354-58.

Baumann, E. "'Wissen um Gott' bei Hosea als Urform von Theologie," *EvT* 15 (1955) 416-25.

Baumgärtel, F. "Die Formel *ně'ūm-jahwe*," *ZAW* 73 (1961) 277-290.

Beitzel, Barry J. "Exodus 3:14 and the Divine Name: A Case of Biblical Paronomasia," *Trinity Journal* 1 (1980) 5-20.

Bellefontaine, Elizabeth, "Deuteronomy 21:18-21 - Reviewing the Case of the Rebellious Son," *JSOT* 13 (1979) 13-31.

Bentzen, A. "The Weeping of Jacob, Hos 12:5a," *VT* 1 (1951) 58-59.

Bergant, Dianne, "Symbolic Names in Hosea," *TBT* 20 (1980) 159-160.

Berger, Peter L. "Charisma and Religious Innovation: The Social Location of Israelite Prophecy," *American Sociological Review* 28 (1963) 940-50.

Bewer, J. A. "The Story of Hosea's Marriage," *AJSL* 22 (1905-6) 120-30.

Birkeland, H. *Zum hebräischen traditionswesen: Die Komposition der prophetischen Bücher des Alten Testaments.* Oslo: Jacob Dybwad, 1938.

Bitter, Stephan. *Die Ehe des Propheten Hosea: Eine auslegungsgeschichtliche Untersuchung.* Göttingen Theologische Arbeiten 3; Göttingen: Vandenhoeck & Ruprecht, 1975.

Blankenbaker, George Vernon. *The Language of Hosea 1-3.* Diss. Claremont Graduate School, 1976.

Blankenbacker, George Vernon. "Tradition and Creativity: Hermeneutical Use of Language in Hosea 1-3," *SBLSP* 21 (1982) 15-29.

Böhl, Franz. "Wortspiele im Alten Testament," *JPOS* 6 (1926) 196-212.

Boling, R. G. *Judges. Introduction, Translation and Commentary.* AB 6A; Garden City: Doubleday, 1975.

Boling, R. G. "Prodigal Sons on Trial: A Study in the Prophecy of Hosea," *McCQ* 19 (1965) 13-27, 38.

Borbone, P. G. "Il capitolo terzo di Osea," *Henoch* 2 (1980) 257-266.

Brillet, G. *Amos et Osée.* Paris: Éditions du Cerf, 1944.

Brown, S. L. *The Book of Hosea.* London: Methuen, 1932.

Brueggemann, W. "Amos 4:4-13 and Israel's Covenant Worship," *VT* 15 (1965) 1-15.

Brueggemann, W. *Tradition for Crisis: A Study in Hosea.* Richmond: John Knox, 1968.

Buck, F. *Die Liebe Gottes beim Propheten Osée.* Rome: Pontifical Biblical Institute, 1973.

Budde, Karl. "Der Abschnitt Hosea 1-3," *TSK* 96/97 (1925) 1-89.

Budde, Karl. "Eine folgenschwere Redaktion des Zwölfprophetenbuchs," *ZAW* 39 (1922) 218-229.

Budde, Karl. "Hosea 1 und 3," *TBl* 13 (1934) 337-42.

Budde, Karl. "Zu Text und Auslegung des Buches Hosea (Hos 4:1-19)," *JBL* 45 (1926) 280-97.

Bühlmann, Walter & Scherer, K. *Stilfiguren der Bible. Ein kleines Nachschlagewerk.* BibB 10; Schweizerisches Katholisches Bibelwerk, 1973.

Buss, Martin J. "An Anthropological Perspective upon Prophetic Call Narratives," *Semeia* 21 (1982) 9-30.

Buss, Martin J. "Mari Prophecy and Hosea," *JBL* 88 (1969) 338.

Buss, Martin J. *The Prophetic Word of Hosea: A Morphological Study.* BZAW 111; Berlin: Alfred Töpelmann, 1969.

Buss, Martin J. "The Psalms of Asaph and Korah," *JBL* 82 (1963) 382-92.

Buzy, Denis. "Les Symboles d'Osée," *RB* 14 (1917) 376-423.

Cardellini, I. "Hosea 4, 1-3. Eine Strukturanalyse," *Bausteine Biblischer Theologie.* H.-J. Fabry, hrsg. Köln-Bonn: Peter Hanstein, 1977, 259-270.

Carlson, R. A. *David, the Chosen King. A Traditio-Historical Approach to the Second Book of Samuel.* E. J. Sharpe & Stanley Rudman, trans. Uppsala: Almqvist & Wiksells, 1964.

Carroll, Robert P. *When Prophecy Failed: Reactions and Response to Failure in the Old Testament Prophetic Traditions.* London: SCM, 1979.

Casanowitz, I. M. *Paronomasia in the Old Testament.* Boston: Norwood, 1894.

Casanowitz, I. M. "Paronomasia in the Old Testament," *JBL* 12 (1893) 105-67.

Caspari, W. "Die Nachrichten über Heimat und Hausstand des Propheten Hosea und ihre Verfasser," *NKZ* 26 (1915) 143-168.

Cassuto, U. "The Prophet Hosea and the Books of the Pentateuch," *Biblical and Oriental Studies, I: Bible.* I. Abrahams, trans. Jerusalem: Magnes, 1973, 79-100.

Cassuto, U. "The Second Chapter of the Book of Hosea," *Biblical and Oriental Studies, I: Bible.* I. Abrahams, trans. Jerusalem: Magnes, 1973, 101-140.

Cazelles, H. "The Problem of the Kings in Osée 8:4," *CBQ* 11 (1949) 14-25.

Ceresko, A. "The Function of *Antanaclasis* (*mṣ'* "to find" //mṣ' "to reach, overtake, grasp") in Hebrew Poetry, especially in the Book of Qoheleth," *CBQ* 44 (1982) 551-569.

Ceresko A.. "A Note on Psalm 63: A Psalm of Vigil," *ZAW* 92 (1980) 435-436.

Charlesworth, J.H. "Paronomasia and Assonance in the Syriac Text of the Odes of Solomon," *Semitics* 1 (1970) 12-26.

Cheyne, T. K. *Hosea, with Notes and Introduction.* Cambridge: University Press, 1892.

Childs, Brevard S. "The Canonical Shape of Prophetic Literature," *Int* 32 (1978) 46-55.

Childs, Brevard S. *Introduction to the Old Testament as Scripture*. Philadelphia: Fortress, 1979.

Chomsky, William. "Some Traditional Principles in Biblical Exegesis," *Essays on the Occasion of the Seventieth Anniversary of the Dropsie University*. Philadelphia: Dropsie Univ., 1979, 33-37.

Clements, R. E. "The Deuteronomistic Interpretation of the Founding of the Monarchy in I Sam VIII," *VT* 24 (1974) 398-410.

Clements, R. E. "Patterns in the Prophetic Canon," *Canon and Authority. Essays in Old Testament Religion and Theology*. G. W. Coats and B. O. Long, eds. Philadelphia: Fortress, 1977, 42-55.

Clements, R. E. *Prophecy and Tradition*. Oxford: Basil Blackwell, 1975.

Clements, R. E. "Understanding the Book of Hosea," *RevEx* 72 (1975) 405-23.

Clines, David J. A. "Hosea 2: Structure and Interpretation," *Studia Biblica 1978, I: Papers on Old Testament and Related Themes*. JSOTSup 11; Sheffield: JSOT, 1979, 83-103.

Cogan, Morton. *Imperialism and Religion: Assyria, Judah and Israel in the Eighth and Seventh Centuries, BCE*. SBLMS 19; Missoula: Scholars Press, 1974.

Coggins, Richard. "Changing Patterns of Old Testament Study," *JTSoA* 34 (1981) 17-24.

Condamin, Albert. "Interpolations ou Transpositions Accidentelles?" *RB* 11 (1902) 379-97.

Coote, Robert B. *Amos Among the Prophets: Composition and
Theology.* Philadelphia: Fortress, 1981.

Coote, Robert B. "The Application of Oral Theory to Biblical
Hebrew Literature," *Semeia* 5 (1976) 51-64.

Coote, Robert B. "Hosea XII," *VT* 21 (1971) 389-402.

Coote, Robert B. "Hos 14:8: 'They who are filled with grain
shall live,'" *JBL* 93 (1974) 161-173.

Coppens, J. "L'Histoire matrimoniale d'Osée. Un nouvel essai
d'interprétation," *Alttestamentliche Studien Friedrich
Nötscher zum 60. Geburtstag 10. Juli 1950.* H. Junker & G.
J. Botterweck, hrsg. BBB 1;Bonn: Hanstein, 1950, 38-45.

Cornill, Carl Heinrich. *The Prophets of Israel.* S. F. Corkran,
trans. Chicago: The Open Court , 1895.

Craghan, J. F. "The Book of Hosea: A Survey of Recent
Literature on the First of the Minor Prophets," *BTB* 1
(1971) 81-100; 145-170.

Craghan, J. F. "An Interpretation of Hosea," *BTB* 5 (1975)
201-207.

Cross, Frank Moore. *Canaanite Myth and Hebrew Epic.*
Cambridge: Harvard University, 1973.

Cross, Jr., Frank Moore and Freedman, David Noel. *Studies
in Ancient Yahwistic Poetry.* SBLDS 21; Missoula:
Scholars Press, 1975.

Crotty, R. "Hosea and the Knowledge of God," *AusBR* 19
(1971) 1-16.

Cruveilheir, P. "De l'interprétation historique des événements de la vie familiale du prophète Osée (1-3)," *RB* 13 (1916) 342-362.

Culley, R. C. "An Approach to the Problem of Oral Tradition," *VT* 13 (1963) 113-125.

Culley, R. C. "Oral Tradition and Historicity," *Studies on the Ancient Palestinian World*, J. W. Wevers and D. B. Redford, ed. Toronto: Univ. of Toronto, 1972, 102-116.

Culley, R. C. "Oral Tradition and the OT: Some Recent Discussion," *Semeia* 5 (1976) 1-33.

Dahood, M. "The Conjunction *pa* in Hosea 7,1," *Bib* 57 (1976) 247-48.

Dahood, M. "Hebrew Lexicography: A Review of W. Baumgartner's *Lexikon*," *Or* 45 (1976) 327-365.

Dahood, M. "The Minor Prophets and Ebla." *The Word of the Lord Shall Go forth. Essays in Honor of David Noel Freedman in Celebration of His Sixtieth Birthday*. Carol L. Meyers and M. O'Connor, eds. Winona Lake, IN: Eisenbrauns, 1983, 47-67.

Dahood, M. "New Readings in Lamentations," *Bib* 59 (1978) 174-97.

Davidson, R. "Orthodoxy and the Prophetic Word. A Study in the Relationship between Jeremiah and Deuteronomy," *VT* 14 (1964) 407-416.

Day, Edward. "Is the Book of Hosea Exilic?" *AJSL* 26 (1909/10) 105-32.

Day, J. "A Case of Inner Biblical Scriptural Interpretation. The Dependence of Isaiah 26:13--27:11 on Hosea 13:4--14:10

382   Bibliography

and Its Relevance to Some Theories of the Redaction of the
'Isaiah Apocalypse,'" *JTS* 31 (1980) 309-19.

Deem, A. "The Goddess Anath and Some Biblical Cruces,"
JSS 23 (1978) 25-30.

Deissler, A. "Das 'Echo' der Hosea-Verkündigung im
Jeremiabuch," in *Künder des Wortes. Beiträge zur Theologie der Propheten.* Josef Schreiner zum 60. Geburtstag.
Hrsg. L. Ruppert, P. Weimar, E. Zener. Würzburg: Echter,
1982, 61-75.

Deissler, A. *Zwölf Propheten. Hosea, Joel, Amos.* Die Neue
Echter Bibel; Würzburg: Echter, 1982.

Deller, K. "*šmn bll* (Hosea 12, 2). Additional Evidence," *Bib* 46
(1965) 349-52.

DeRoche, M. "Contra Creation, Covenant and Conquest (Jer
8:13)," *VT* 30 (1980) 280-290.

DeRoche, M. "The Reversal of Creation in Hosea," *VT* 31
(1981) 400-409.

DeRoche, M. "Structure, Rhetoric and Meaning in Hosea 4:
4-10," *VT* 33 (1983) 185-198.

DeRoche, M. "Zephaniah 1:2-3: The 'sweeping' of creation,"
VT 30 (1980) 104-109.

Devescovi, U. "La nuova alleanza in Osea (2, 16-25)," *BiOr* 1
(1959) 172-178.

Dietrich, F. *Die Anspielungen auf die Jakob-Tradition in
Hosea 12:1--13:3. Ein literaturwissenschaftlicher Beitrag
zur Exegese früher Prophetentexte.* Würzburg: Echter, 1977.

Dobbie, R. "The Text of Hosea 9:8," *VT* 5 (1955) 199-203.

Donner, H. *Israel unter den Völkern. Die Stellung der klassischen Propheten des 8. Jahrhunderts v.Chr. zur Aussenpolitik der Könige von Israel und Juda.* SVT, 11; Leiden: Brill, 1964.

Dreyfus, F. "'L'Araméen voulait tuer mon père': L'actualisation de Dt 26, 5 dans la tradition juive et la tradition chrétienne," *De la Tôrah au Messie.* M. Carrez, J. Doré, P. Grelot, eds. Paris: Desclée, 1981, 147-161.

Driver, G. R. "Hosea 6:5," *VT* 1 (1951) 246.

Driver, G. R. "Linguistic and Textual Problems: Minor Prophets, I." *JTS* 39 (1938) 154-66.

Driver, G. R." Problems and Solutions," *VT* 4 (1954) 240-245.

Driver, G. R. "Problems of the Hebrew Text and Language," *BBB* 1 (1950) 46-61.

Driver, G. R. "Studies in the Vocabulary of the Old Testament VI," *JTS* 34 (1933) 375-385.

Driver, S. R. *An Introduction to the Literature of the Old Testament.* Edinburgh: T&T Clark, 1913, 9th ed.

Duhm, B. "Anmerkungen zu den zwölf Propheten II. Buch Hosea," *ZAW* 31 (1911) 18-43.

Ehrlich, Arnold B. *Randglossen zur hebräischen Bibel. V: Ezechiel und die kleinen Propheten.* Leipzig: Hinrichs, 1912, 163-212.

Eichrodt, W. "'The Holy One in Your Midst.' The Theology of Hosea," *Int* 15 (1961) 259-73.

Eissfeldt, O. "Das Berufungsbewusstsein der Propheten als theologisches Gegenwartsproblem," *Kleine Schriften, II.* Tübingen: 1963, 4-28.

Eissfeldt, O. *The Old Testament: An Introduction.* P. R. Ackroyd, trans. New York: Harper and Row, 1865.

Eissfeldt, O. "The Prophetic Literature," *The Old Testament and Modern Study: A Generation of Discovery and Research.* H. H. Rowley, ed. Oxford: Clarendon, 1951, 115-161.

Elliger, Karl. "Eine verkannte Kunstform bei Hosea (Zur Einheit von Hos 5, 1f.)," *ZAW* 69 (1957) 151-160.

Ellison, H. L. "The Message of Hosea in the Light of his Marriage," *EvQ* 41 (1969) 3-9.

Ellison, H. L. *The Prophets of Israel from Ahijah to Hosea.* Grand Rapids: Eerdmans, 1969.

Emmerson, G. I. "Fertility Goddess in Hos 4:17-19?" *VT* 24 (1974) 492-7.

Emmerson, G. I. "The Structure and Meaning of Hosea VIII 1-3," *VT* 25 (1975) 700-710.

Engnell, I. "Methodological Aspects of Old Testament Study," *VTSup* 7 (1960) 13-30.

Engnell, I. "The Pentateuch," *A Rigid Scrutiny. Critical Essays on the Old Testament.* J. T. Willis, trans. Nashville: Vanderbilt Univ, 1969, 50-67.

Engnell, I. "Prophets and Prophetism in the Old Testament," *A Rigid Scrutiny. Critical Essays on the Old Testament.* J. T. Willis, trans. Nashville: Vanderbilt Univ., 1969, 123-79.

Engnell, I. "The Traditio-Historical Method in Old Testament Research," *A Rigid Scrutiny. Critical Essays on the Old Testament.* J. T. Willis, trans. Nashville: Vanderbilt Univ., 1969, 3-11.

Erlandsson, Seth, "*'acher*," *TDOT*, Vol. 1, 201-203.

Erlandsson, Seth. "*zānaḥ*," *TDOT*, Vol. 4, 99-104.

Eslinger, Lyle M. "Hosea 12:5a and Genesis 32:29: A Study in Inner Biblical Exegesis," *JSOT* 18 (1980) 91-99.

Ewald, Georg Heinrich. *Commentary on the Prophets of the Old Testament. Vol. 1: Joel, Amos, Hosea and Zechariah.* J. F. Smith, trans. London: Williams & Norgate, 1875.

Eybers, I. H. "The Use of Proper Names as a Stylistic Device," *Semitics* 2 (1971-72) 82-92.

Farr, G. "The Concept of Grace in the Book of Hosea," *ZAW* 70 (1958) 98-107.

Fensham, F. C. "Father and Son as Terminology for Treaty and Covenant," *Near Eastern Studies in Honor of W. F. Albright.* H. Goedicke, ed. Baltimore: Johns Hopkins University, 1971, 121-135.

Feuillet, A. "'S'asseoir à l'ombre de l'époux': Os 14:8a et Cant 2:3," *RB* 78 (1971) 391-405.

Fishbane, M. "Accusations of Adultery: A Study of Law and Scribal Practice in Numbers 5:11-31," *HUCA* 45 (1974) 25-45.

Fishbane, M. "The Qumran Pesher and Traits of Ancient Hermeneutics," *Proceedings of the VIth World Congress of Jewish Studies.* Jerusalem: World Union of Jewish Studies, 1977, 97-114.

Fitzmyer, Joseph A. *The Aramaic Inscriptions of Sefire.* Rome: Pontifical Biblical Institute, 1967.

Fitzmyer, Joseph A. *A Manual of Palestinian Aramaic Texts.* BibOr 34; Rome: Biblical Institute, 1978.

Fitzmyer, Joseph A. "A Re-Study of an Elephantine Marriage Contract (AP, 15)," *Near Eastern Studies in Honor of W. F. Albright.* H. Goedicke, ed. Baltimore: Johns Hopkins University, 1971, 137-168.

Fohrer, G. "Die Gattung der Bericht über symbolische Handlungen der Propheten," *BZAW* 99 (1967) 92-112.

Fohrer, G. "Die Glossen im Buche Ezechiel," *ZAW* 63 (1951) 33-53.

Fohrer, G. *Introduction to the Old Testament.* David E. Green, trans. Nashville: Abingdon, 1968.

Fohrer, G. *Die Propheten des Alten Testaments, I: Die Propheten des 8. Jahrhunderts.* Gütersloh: Gerd Mohn, 1974, 56-95.

Fohrer, G. "Remarks on Modern Interpretation of the Prophets," *JBL* 80 (1961) 309-319.

Fohrer, G. *Die symbolischen Handlungen der Propheten.* ATANT 54; Zurich: Zwingli, 1953.

Foresti, F. "Hos 12: A Prophetical Polemic against the Proto-Elohistic Patriarchal Tradition," *EphemCarm* 30 (1979) 179-200.

Freedman, D. N. "The Law and the Prophets," *VTSup* 9 (1963) 250-65.

Freedman, D. N. "*Pšty* in Hos 2:7," *JBL* 74 (1955) 275.

Frey, H. "Der Aufbau der Gedichte Hoseas," *Wort und Dienst* (NF) 5 (1957) 9-103.

Friedman, Mordechai. "Israel's Response in Hosea 2:17b: 'You are my Husband,'" *JBL* 99 (1980) 199-204.

Friedman, Richard Elliott. *The Exile and Biblical Narrative. The Formation of the Deuteronomistic and Priestly Works.* HSM 22; Chico, CA: Scholars Press, 1981.

Fück, J. "Hosea Kapitel 3," *ZAW* 39 (1921) 283-90.

Gabor, Ignaz. *Der Hebräische Urrhythmus.* BZAW 52; Giessen: A. Töpelmann, 1929.

Galbiati, E. "La struttura sintetica di Osea 2," *Mélanges Rinaldi. Studi sull' Oriente e la Bibbia.* Genova, 1967, 317-328.

Gallopin, Marc. "Le Désert. Sa signification chez les prophètes Osée, Jérémie et Ezéchiel," *Hokhma* 13 (1980) 2-19.

Gaster, Theodor H. "On Hosea 7:3-6, 8-9," *VT* 4 (1954) 78-79.

Geller, Markham J. "The Elephantine Papyri and Hosea 2, 3. Evidence for the Form of the Early Jewish Divorce Writ," *JSJ* 8 (1977) 139-48.

Gelston, A. "Kingship in the Book of Hosea," *OTS* 19 (1974) 71-85.

Gemser, B. "The *Rîb* or Controversy-Pattern in Hebrew Mentality," *VTSup* 3 (1960) 120-137.

Gertner, M. "The Masorah and the Levites. Appendix on Hos XII," *VT* 10 (1960) 241-284.

Gevaryahu, H. M. I. "Biblical Colophons: A Source for the 'Biography' of Authors, Texts and Books," *VTSup* 28 (1975) 42-59.

Gevirtz, Stanley, "Of Patriarchs and Puns: Joseph at the Fountain, Jacob at the Ford," *HUCA* 46 (1975) 33-54.

Ginsberg, H. L. "Hosea's Ephraim, More Fool than Knave. A New Interpretation of Hosea 12:1-14," *JBL* 80 (1961) 339-47.

Ginsberg, H. L. "Lexicographical Notes," *VTSup* 16 (1967) 71-82.

Glanzman, G. S. "Two Notes: Am 3, 15 and Os 11, 8-9," *CBQ* 23 (1961) 227-233.

Glück, J. J. "Paronomasia in Biblical Literature," *Semitics* 1 (1970) 50-78.

Glueck, N. *Ḥesed in the Bible*. Alfred Gottschalls, trans. Cincinatti: Hebrew Union College, 1967.

Gnuse, R. "Calf, Cult, and King: The Unity of Hosea 8:1-13," *BZ* 26 (1982) 83-92.

Good, E. M. "The Composition of Hosea," *SEÅ* 31 (1966) 21-63.

Good, E. M. "Hosea 5:8--6:6: An Alternative to Alt," *JBL* 85 (1966) 273-86.

Good, E. M. "Hosea and the Jacob Tradition," *VT* 16 (1966) 137-151.

Gordis, R. "Hosea's Marriage and Message: A New Approach," *Poets, Prophets, and Sages: Essays in Biblical Interpretation*. Bloomington: Indiana University, 1971, 230-254.

Gordis, R. "Midrash in the Prophets," *The Word and the Book: Studies in Biblical Language and Literature*. New York: KTAV, 1976, 108-113.

Gordis, R. "Studies in Hebrew Roots of Contrasted Meanings," *JQR* 27 (1936) [= *The Word and the Book: Studies in Biblical Language and Literature.* New York: KTAV, 1976, 185-210].

Gordis, R. "The Text and Meaning of Hosea 14:3," *VT* 5 (1955) 88-90.

Gordon, C. H. "Hos 2:4-5 in the Light of New Semitic Inscriptions," *ZAW* 54 (1936) 277-80.

Goshen-Gottstein, M. H. "'Ephraim is a well-Trained Heifer' and Ugaritic *mdl*," *Bib* 41 (1960) 64-66.

Gray, G. B. *Studies in Hebrew Proper Names.* London: Black, 1896.

Gray, John. *I & II Kings. A Commentary* London: SCM, 1964.

Greengus, Samuel. "A Textbook Case of Adultery in Ancient Mesopotamia," *HUCA* 40-41 (1969-70) 33-44.

Greenspahn, F. E. "The Number and Distribution of Hapax Legomena in Biblical Hebrew," *VT* 30 (1980) 8-19.

Greenwood, David C. "On the Hope for a Restored Northern Kingdom," *ZAW* 88 (1976) 376-85.

Gressman, Hugo. *Der Messias.* Göttingen: Vandenhoeck, 1929.

Grimm, E. "Erwägungen zu Hosea 12, 12 'in Gilgal opfern sie Stiere,'" *ZAW* 85 (1973) 339-347.

Gross, K. "Hoseas Einfluss auf Jeremias Anschauungen," *NKZ* 42 (1931) 241-256; 327-343.

Gross, K. *Die literarische Verwandschaft Jeremias mit Hosea.* Borne and Leipzig, 1930.

Groves, Joseph White. *Actualization and Interpretation in the Old Testament.* Diss. Yale University, 1979.

Guillaume, A. "Note on Hosea 2:23, 24 (21, 22)," *JTS* 15 (1964) 57-58.

Guillaume, D. F. "Paronomasia in the Old Testament," *JSS* 9 (1964) 282-290.

Gunkel, Hermann. "IIB. The Israelite Prophecy from the Time of Amos," *Twentieth Century Theology in the Making.* J. Pelikan, ed. R. A. Wilson, trans. New York: Harper and Row, 1969, 48-75.

Gunkel, Hermann. *Legends of Genesis.* New York: Schocken, 1964.

Gunneweg, A. H. J. *Mündliche und schriftliche Tradition der vorexilischen Prophetenbücher als Problem der neueren Prophetenforschung.* Göttingen: Vandenhoeck & Ruprecht, 1959.

Güttgemanns, Erhardt. *Candid Questions Concerning Gospel Form Criticism: A Methodological Sketch of the Fundamental Problems of Form and Redaction Criticism.* W. G. Doty, trans. Pittsburgh Theological Monographs 26; Pittsburgh: Pickwick, 1979.

Güttgemanns, Erhardt. "Linguistic-Literary Critical Foundation of a New Testament Theology," *Semeia* 6 (1976) 181-220.

Halévy, J. "Le Livre d'Osée." *RevSem* 10 (1902) 1-2; 97-33.

Halpern, Baruch. "Levitic Participation in the Reform Cult of Jeroboam I," *JBL* 95 (1976) 31-42.

Haran, Menachem. "From Early to Classical Prophecy: Continuity and Change," *VT* 27 (1977) 385-97.

Harper, William Rainey. *A Critical Exegetical Commentary on Amos and Hosea*. ICC 18; Edinburgh: T&T Clark, 1936.

Harvey, J. *Le Plaidoyer prophétique contre Israël après la Rupture de l'alliance*. Bruges: Desclée de Brouwer, 1967.

Harvey, J. "Le 'rîb-Pattern,' réquisitoire prophétique sur la Rupture de l'alliance," *Bib* 43 (1962) 172-196.

Hauret, C. *Amos et Osée*. Paris: Beauchesne, 1970.

Hayes, J. H. "The History of the Form-Critical Study of Prophecy," *SBLSP* 1 (1973) 60-79.

Hertzberg, H. W. "Die Nachgeschichte alttestamentlicher Texte innerhalb des Alten Testaments," *BZAW* 66 (1936) 110-121.

Heschel, A. J. *The Prophets*. New York: Harper & Row, 1962, 39-60.

Hillers, D. *Treaty-Curses and the Old Testament Prophets*. BibOr 16; Rome: Pontifical Biblical Institute, 1964.

Holladay, W. L. "Chiasmus, the Key to Hosea xii 3-6," *VT* 16 (1966) 53-64.

Holladay, W. L. "'On Every High Hill and Under Every Green Tree,'" *VT* 11 (1961) 170-76.

Holladay, W. L. *The Root Šûbh in the Old Testament*. Leiden: Brill, 1958.

Holland, M. *Der Prophet Hosea*. Wuppertaler Studienbibel; Wuppertal: R. Brockhaus, 1980.

Hölscher, G. *Die Profeten*. Leipzig: J. C. Hinrichs, *1914*.

Horton, R. F. *The Minor Prophets*. *Vol. 1*. London: Caxton.

Huffmon, Herbert B. "The Covenant Lawsuit in the Prophets," *JBL* 78 (1959) 285-295.

Huffmon, Herbert B. "Prophecy in the Mari Letters," *BA* 31 (1968) 101-124.

Humbert, P. "Osée le prophète bédouin," *RHPhR* 1 (1921) 97-118.

Hunter, A. Vanlier. *Seek the Lord: A Study of the Meaning and Function of the Exhortations in Amos, Hosea, Isaiah, Micah and Zephaniah*. Baltimore: St. Mary's Seminary & University, 1982.

Jacob, E. "La Femme et le Prophète. À propos d'Osée 12: 13-14," *Hommage à Wilhelm Vischer*. J. Cadier, ed. Montpellier: Cause Graille Castelnau, 1960, 83-87.

Jacob, E. *Osée*. Neuchâtel: Delachaux & Niestlé, 1965; CAT XIa, 1982, 2 ed.

Jacob, E. "Der Prophet Hosea und die Geschichte," *EvT* 24 (1964) 281-290.

Jacob, E. "Prophètes et Intercesseurs," *De la Tôrah au Messie*. M. Carrez, J. Doré, P. Grelot, eds. Paris: Descleé, 1981, 205-217.

Jeremias, Jörg. *Der Prophet Hosea*. ATD 24/1; Göttingen: Vandenhoeck & Ruprecht, 1983.

Jeremias, Jorg. "Hosea 4-7. Beobachtungen zur Komposition des Buches Hosea," *Textgemäss*. A. H. J. Gunneweg & O. Kaiser, hrsg. Göttingen: Vandenhoeck & Ruprecht, 1979, 47-58.

Jeremias, Jörg. "Zur Eschatologie des Hoseabuches." *Die Botschaft und die Boten. Fs. für Hans Walter Wolff zum 70. Geburtstag.* Jörg Jeremias & Lothar Perlitt, hrsg. Neukirchen-Vluyn: Neukirchener, 1981, 217-234.

Jüngling, Hans-Winfried. "Aspekte des Redens von Gott bei Hosea," *Theologie und Philosophie* 54 (1979) 335-359.

Junker, Hubert. "Textkritische, formkritische und traditionsgeschichtliche Untersuchung zu Os 4, 1-10," *BZ* 4 (1960) 165-73.

Kaatz, S. "Wortspiel, Assonanz und Notarikon bei Hosea," *Jeschurun* 11 (1924) 434-437.

Kaiser, Otto, *et. al. Exegetical Method: A Student's Handbook.* E. V. N. Goetchius, trans. and intro. New York: Seabury, 1963.

Kaufmann, Y. *The Religion of Israel. From Its Beginning to the Babylonian Exile.* Trans. and abridged by M. Greenberg. Chicago: Univ. of Chicago, 1960.

Kedar-Kopfstein, B. "Textual Gleanings from the Vulgate to Hosea," *JQR* 65 (1974-75) 73-97.

Keil, Friedrich. *The Twelve Minor Prophets. Vol. 1.* J. Martin, trans. Edinburgh: T&T Clark, 1878.

Kelber, Werner H. *The Oral and the Written Gospel. The Hermeneutics of Speaking and Writing in the Synoptic Tradition, Mark, Paul and Q.* Philadelphia: Fortress, 1983.

Kidner, Derek. *Love to the Loveless.* Leicester: Inter-Varsity, 1981.

Kinet, Dirk. *Ba'al und Jahweh. Ein Beitrag zur Theologie des Hoseabuches.* Frankfurt: Peter Lang, 1977.

King, Philip J. "Hosea's Message of Hope," *BTB* 12 (1982) 91-95.

Klein, Ralph. *Israel In Exile: A Theological Interpretation.* Philadelphia: Fortress, 1979.

Knauf, Ernst, "Beth Aven," *Bib* 65 (1984) 251-253.

Knierim, R. "Old Testament Form Criticism Reconsidered," *Int* 27 (1973) 435-68.

Knight, D. A. "Introduction: Tradition and Theology," *Tradition and Theology in the Old Testament.* Philadelphia: Fortress, 1977.

Knight, D. A. *Rediscovering the Traditions of Israel.* SBLDS 9; Missoula: Scholars Press, 1973, 1975 rev. ed.

Knight, G. A. F. *Hosea. God's Love.* London: SCM Press, 1960.

Koch, Klaus. *The Growth of the Biblical Tradition. The Form-Critical Method.* S. M. Cupitt, trans. London: Adam & Charles Black, 1969.

Koch, Klaus. "'ōhel," *TDOT*, Vol. 1, 118-130.

Koch, Klaus. *The Prophets. Vol. 1: The Assyrian Period.* Philadelphia: Fortress, 1983.

König, F. "Die Auferstehungshoffnung bei Osée 6:1-3," *ZTK* 70 (1948) 94-100.

Kraeling, Emil G. *The Prophets.* New York: Rand McNally, 1969.

Kraft, Charles F. "The Book of Hosea," *The Interpreter's One Volume Commentary on the Bible.* Charles M. Laymon, ed. Nashville: Abingdon, 1971, 451-460.

Kreutz, Edgar. *The Historical-Critical Method.* Philadelphia: Fortress, 1975.

Krszyna, H. "Literarische Struktur von Os 2, 4-17" *BZ* 13 (1969) 41-59.

Kselmann, J.S. "Design and Structure in Hebrew Poetry," *SBLSP* 116 (1980) 1-16.

Kugel, James L. *The Idea of Biblical Poetry. Parallelism and Its History.* New Haven: Yale University, 1981.

Kuhl, C. "Neve Dokumente zum Verständnis von Hosea 2: 4-15," *ZAW* 52 (1934) 102-109.

Kuhnigk, W. *Nordwestsemitischen Studien zum Hoseabuch.* BibOr 27; Rome: Biblical Institute Press, 1974.

Kümpel, R. *Die Berufung Israels. Ein Beitrag zur Theologie des Hosea.* Diss. Bonn, 1973.

Lagrange, A. "La nouvelle histoire d'Israel et le prophète Osée," *RB* 1 (1892) 203-238.

Lapointe, Roger. "Tradition and Language: The Import of Oral Expression," *Tradition and Theology in the Old Testament.* D. A. Knight, ed. Philadelphia: Fortress, 1977, 125-142.

Lescow, T. "Redaktionsgeschictliche Analyse von Micha 1-5," *ZAW* 84 (1972) 46-185.

Limburg, James, "The Prophets in Recent Study: 1967-1977," *Int* 32 (1978) 56-68.

Limburg, James. "The Root *ryb* and the Prophetic Lawsuit Speeches," *JBL* 88 (1969) 291-304.

Lindars, B. "'Rachel Weeping for her Children' - Jeremiah 31:15-22," *JSOT* 11 (1979) 47-62.

Lindbom, J. *Prophecy in Ancient Israel.* Oxford: Blackwell, 1962.

Lippl, Joseph & Theis, Johannes. *Die zwölf kleinen Propheten. I Hälfte: Osée, Joel, Amos, Abdias, Jonas, Michäas.* Bonn: Peter Hanstein, 1937.

Lohfink, N. "Hate and Love in Osée 9, 15,' *CBQ* 25 (1963) 417.

Lohfink, N. "Hos xi 5 als Bezugstext von Dtn xvii 16,' *VT* 31 (1981) 226-28.

Lohfink, N. "Zu Text und Form von Os 4, 4-6," *Bib* 42 (1961) 303-332.

Long, Burke O. *The Problem of Etiological Narrative in the Old Testament.* BZAW 108; Berlin: A. Topelmann, 1968.

Long, Burke O. "Prophetic Authority as Social Reality," *Canon and Authority.* G. W. Coats & B. O. Long, eds. Philadelphia: Fortress, 1977, 3-20.

Long, Burke O. "Recent Field Studies In Oral Literature and their Bearing on OT Criticism," *VT* 26 (1976) 187-98.

Long, Burke O. "Recent Field Studies in Oral Literature and the Question of Sitz-im-Leben," *Semeia* 5 (1976) 35-49.

Long, Burke O. "Social Dimensions of Prophetic Conflict," *Semeia* 21 (1982) 31-53.

Long, Burke O. "The Social Setting for Prophetic Miracle Stories," *Semeia* 3 (1975) 46-63.

Lord, A. B. *The Singer of Tales.* Cambridge, MA: Harvard Univ., 1964.

Loretz, O. "Tod und Leben nach altorientalischer und kanaan-äischbiblischer Anschauung in Hos 6, 1-3," *BN* 17 (1982) 37-42.

Lundbom, J. R. "Double-duty Subject in Hosea VIII 5," *VT* 25 (1975) 228-230.

Lundbom, J. R. "Poetic Structure and Prophetic Rhetoric in Hosea," *VT* 29 (1979) 300-308.

Lust, J. "Remarks on the Redaction of Amos 5:4-6, 14-15," *OTS* 21 (1981) 129-154.

Lys, Daniel. "J'ai deux amours ou l'amant jugé, Exercice sur Osée 2, 4-25," *ETR* 51 (1976) 59-77.

March, W. Eugene. "Redaction Criticism and the Formation of Prophetic Books," *SBLSP* 11 (1977) 87-101.

Martl, K. *Das Dodekapropheton: Hosea.* KHAT 13; Tübingen: JCBMohr, 1904, 1-108.

Martin-Achard, R. *From Death to Life. A Study of the Development of the Doctrine of the Resurrection in the Old Testament.* J. P. Smith, trans. Edinburgh & London: Oliver and Boyd, 1960.

Mauchline, John. "The Book of Hosea," *IB* 6 (1956) 552-725.

May, H. G. "The Fertility Cult In Hosea," *AJSL* 48 (1931-32) 73-98.

May, H. G. "An Interpretation of the Names of Hosea's Children," *JBL* 55 (1936) 285-91.

Mayes, A. D. H. *The Story of Israel Between Settlement and Exile. A Redactional Study of the Deuteronomistic History.* London: SCM, 1983.

Mays, James Luther. *Exegesis as a Theological Discipline.*
Inaugural Address Delivered April 20, 1960, Schauffler
Hall, Union Theological Seminary, Richmond, Virginia.

Mays, James Luther. *Hosea: A Commentary.* Philadelphia:
Westminster, 1969.

McCarter, P. K. *I Samuel.* AB 8; Garden City: Doubleday,
1980.

McCarthy, Dennis J. *"Běrît* in Old Testament History and
Theology," *Bib* 53 (1972) 110-121.

McCarthy, Dennis J. "Exod 3:14: History, Philology and
Theology," *CBQ* 40 (1978) 311-322.

McCarthy, Dennis J. "God as Prisoner of Our Own Choosing:
Critical-Historical Study of the Bible. Why and Whither,"
Historicism and Faith. Paul L. Williams, ed.   Scranton:
Northeast Books, 1980, 17-47.

McCarthy, Dennis J. "Hosea," *JBC* 2 (1968) 253-64.

McCarthy, Dennis J. "Hosea XII 2: Covenant by Oil," *VT* 14
(1964) 215-221.

McCarthy, Dennis J. "Notes on the Love of God in
Deuteronomy and the Father-Son Relationship between
Israel and Yahweh," *CBQ* 27 (1965) 144-147.

McCarthy, Dennis J. *Old Testament Covenant. A Survey of
Current Opinions.* Atlanta: John Knox, 1972.

McCartney, E. S. "Puns and Plays on Proper Names,"
Classical Journal 14 (1919) 343-358.

McDonald, J. R. B. "The Marriage of Hosea," *Theology* 67
(1964) 149-56.

McKane, W. "Prophecy and Prophetic Literature," *Tradition and Interpretation*. G. W. Anderson, ed. Oxford: Clarendon, 1979, 163-188.

McKane, W. "Prophet and Institution," *ZAW* 94 (1982) 251-66.

McKeating, Henry. *The Books of Amos, Hosea and Micah*. Cambridge: University Press, 1971.

McKeating, Henry. "Sanctions Against Adultery in Ancient Israelite Society, With Some Reflections on Methodology in the Study of Old Testament Ethics," *JSOT* 11 (1979) 57-72.

McKenzie, J. L. "Divine Passion in Osée," *CBQ* 17 (1955) 167-179.

McKenzie, J. L. "Knowledge of God in Hosea," *JBL* 74 (1955) 22-27.

McKenzie, Steve. "Exodus Typology in Hosea," *Restoration Quarterly* 22 (1979) 100-108.

Melugin, Roy F. "'Form' versus 'Formation' of Prophetic Books," *SBLSP* 22 (1983) 13-29.

Millard, Alan R. "In Praise of Ancient Scribes," *BA* 45 (1982) 143-153.

Miller, J. M. "The Fall of the House of Ahab," *VT* 17 (1967) 307-24.

Miller, Jr., Patrick D. *Sin and Judgment in the Prophets: A Stylistic and Theological Analysis*. SBLMS 27; Chico, CA: Scholars Press, 1982.

Misener, Austin P. *The Place of Hos 1-3 in Hebrew Literature*. Ph.D. Diss. University of Toronto, 1909.

400   Bibliography

Moor, J. C. de. *"ba'al,"* *TDOT* Vol. 2, 181-200.

Moran, William L. "The Ancient Near Eastern Background of the Love of God in Deuteronomy," *CBQ* 25 (1963) 77-87.

Mowinckel, Sigmund. *Prophecy and Tradition. The Prophetic Books in the Light of the Study of the Growth and History of the Tradition.* ANVAO, II; Oslo: J. Dybwad, 1946.

Mowvley, Harry. *Guide to Old Testament Prophecy.* Guildford/London: Lutterworth, 1979.

Muilenburg, J. "The 'Office' of the Prophet in Ancient Israel," in *The Bible in Modern Scholarship.* J. Philip Hyatt, ed. New York: Abingdon, 1965, 74-97.

Muntingh, L. M. "Married Life in Israel according to the Book of Hosea," *OTWSA* 7/8 (1964-65) 77-84.

Myers, Jacob Martin. *Hosea, Joel, Amos, Obadiah, Jonah.* London: SCM, 1959.

Napier, B. D. "The Omrides of Jezreel,' *VT* 9 (1959) 366-78.

Nations, A. L. "Historical Criticism and the Current Methodological Crisis," *SJT* 36 (1983) 59-71.

Nebe, G. W. "Eine neue Hosea-Handschrift aus Höhle 4 von Qumran," *ZAW* 91 (1979) 292-94.

Neher, A. "Le symbolisme conjugal: Expression de l'histoire de l'Ancien Testament,' *RHPR* 34 (1954) 30-49.

Nelson, Richard D. *The Double Redaction of the Deuteronomistic History.* JSOTSup 18: Sheffield: JSOT, 1981.

Neusner, Jacob. "I. Introduction: Metaphor and Exegesis," *Semeia* 27 (1983) 39-44.

Neusner, Jacob. *The Rabbinic Traditions About the Pharisees Before 70.* Leiden: Brill, 1971, Vol 3, 143-179.

Neusner, Jacob. "Redaction, Formation, and Form: The Case of Mishnah," *JQR* 70 (1979/80)) 131-147.

Newcome, William. *Twelve Minor Prophets.* London: Thomas Tegg & Son, 1836.

Nicholson, E. W. *Deuteronomy and Tradition.* Philadelphia: Fortress, 1967.

Nicholson, E. W. *Preaching to the Exiles. A Study of the Prose Tradition in the Book of Jeremiah.* Oxford: Blackwell, 1970.

Nicholson, E. W. "Problems in Hos 8:13," *VT* 16 (1966) 355-358.

Nielsen, Eduard. *Oral Tradition. A Modern Problem in Old Testament Introduction.* SBT 11; London: SCM, 1954.

Nielsen, Kirsten. *Yahweh as Prosecutor and Judge. An Investigation of the Prophetic Lawsuit.* Frederick Cryer, trans. JSOTSup 9; Sheffield: JSOT, 1978.

North, F. S. "Hosea's Introduction to His Book," *VT* 8 (1958) 429-32.

North, F. S. "A Solution to Hosea's Marital Problems by Critical Analysis," *JNES* 16 (1957) 128-30.

North, R. "Angel-Prophet or Satan-Prophet," *ZAW* 82 (1970) 31-67.

Noth, Martin. *The Deuteronomistic History.* JSOTSup 15; Sheffield: JSOT, 1981.

Nötscher, F. "Zur Auferstehung nach drei Tagen," *Bib* 35 (1954) 313-319.

Nötscher, F. *Zwölfprophetenbuch oder kleine Propheten.* Würzburg: Echter, 1948.

Nowack, W. *Die kleinen Propheten.* HAT III/4; Göttingen: Vandenhoeck und Ruprecht, 1903.

Nunnally-Cox, Janice. *Foremothers: Women of the Bible.* New York: Seabury, 1981.

Nyberg, H. S. *Studien zum Hoseabuch. Zugleich ein Beitrag zur Klärung des Problems der alttestamentlichen Textkritik.* Uppsala: A. B. Lundequistska, 1935.

Nyberg, H. S. "Das textkritische Problem des Alten Testaments am Hoseabuch demonstriert," *ZAW* 52 (1934) 241-54.

O'Connor, Michael P. "The Deceptions of Hosea," *TBT* 20 (1982) 152-158.

O'Connor, Michael P. *Hebrew Verse Structure.* Winona Lake, IN: Eisenbrauns, 1980.

Oded, B. "The Historical Background of the Syro-Ephraimite War Reconsidered," *CBQ* 34 (1972) 153-165.

Ostborn, G. *Yahweh and Baal. Studies in the Book of Hosea and Related Documents.* Lund: Gleerup, 1956.

Ottosson, Magnus. *Gilead: Tradition and History.* Lund: Gleerup, 1969.

Overholt, Thomas W. "Prophecy: The Problem of Cross-Cultural Comparison," *Semeia* 21 (1982) 55-78.

Overholt, Thomas W. "Seeing is Believing: The Social Setting of Prophetic Acts of Power," *JSOT* 23 (1982) 3-31.

Owens, J. J. "Exegetical Study of Hosea," *RevExp* 54 (1957) 522-43.

Paton, L. B. "Notes on Hosea's Marriage," *JBL* 15 (1896) 9-17.

Paul, S. M. "The Image of the Oven and the Cake in Hosea 7: 4-10," *VT* 18 (1968) 114-20.

Payne, D. F. "Characteristic Word-Play in 'Second Isaiah.' A Reappraisal," *JSS* 12 (1967) 207-229.

Payne, D. F. "Old Testament Exegesis and the Problem of Ambiguity," *Annual of the Swedish Theological Institute* 5 (1967) 48-68.

Peckham, Brian. "The Composition of Deuteronomy 5-11," in *The Word of the Lord Shall Go Forth*. Carol L. Meyers and M. O'Connor, eds. Winona Lake, IN: Eisenbrauns, 1983, 217-240.

Peeters, L. "Pour une Interprétation du jue de mots," *Semitics* 2 (1971/72) 127-142.

Peifer, Claude J. "The Marriage Theme in Hosea," *TBT* 20 (1982) 139-44.

Peiser, Felix E. *Hosea. Philologische Studien zum Alten Testament*. Leipzig: J. C. Hinrichs, 1914.

Perlitt, L. *Bundestheologie im Alten Testament*. Neukirchen-Vluyn: Neukirchner, 1969.

Perrin, Norman. *What is Redaction Criticism?* Philadelphia: Fortress, 1969.

Petersen, David L. *Late Israelite Prophecy: Studies in Deutero-Prophetic Literature and in Chronicles*. SBLMS 23; Missoula: Scholars Press, 1977.

Petersen, David L. *The Roles of Israel's Prophets*. Sheffield: JSOT, *1981*.

Pfeiffer, Robert H. *Introduction to the Old Testament*. New York: Harper and Bros., 1948, rev. ed.

Pfeiffer, Robert H. "The Polemic Against idolatry in the Old Testament," *JBL* 43 (1924) 229-240.

Phillips, Anthony, "Another Look at Adultery," *JSOT* 20 (1981) 3-25.

Plank, Karl A. "The Scarred Countenance: Inconstancy in the Book of Hosea," *Jud* 32 (1983) 343-354.

Plautz, W. "Die Form der Eheschliessung im Alten Testament," *ZAW* 76 (1964) 298-318.

Porter, J. "Samson's Riddle: Judges 14:18," *JTS* 13 (1962) 106-109.

Praetorius, Franz. *Die Gedichte des Hosea. Metrische und textkritische Bermerkungen*. Halle: Max Niemeyer, 1926.

Rad, G. von. *Das Gottesvolk in Deuteronomium*. BWANT III/11; Stuttgart: Kohlhammer, 1929, pp. 78-83 re: Dt and Hos.

Rad, G. von. *The Message of the Prophets*. London: SCM, 1968, pp. 110-117.

Rankin, O. S. "Alliteration in Hebrew Poetry," *JTS* 31 (1930) 285-291.

Rast, W. *Tradition History and the Old Testament*. Philadelphia: Fortress, 1972.

Reines, Ch. W. "Hosea XII, 1," *JJS* 2 (1951) 156-157.

Renaud, B. *La Formation du livre de Michée. Tradition et Actualisation.* Paris, 1977.

Renaud, B. "Genèse et unité rédactionnelle de Os 2," *RevScRel* 54 (1980) 1-20.

Renaud, B. "Le Livret d'Osée 1-3. Un travail complexe d'édition," *RevScRel* 56 (1982) 159-78.

Renaud, B. "Osée 1-3: analyse diachronique et lecture synchronique, problèmes de méthode," *RevScRel* 57 (1983) 249-260.

Renaud, B. "Osée 2,2: *'lh mn h'rṣ*: Essai d'interprétation," *VT* 33 (1983) 495-500.

Rendsburg, Gary. "Hebrew *rḥm* = 'rain,'" *VT* 33 (1983) 357-361.

Rendtorff, R. "Zum Gebrauch der Formel *nĕ'ūm jahwe* im Jeremiabuch," *ZAW* 66 (1954) 27-37.

Richardson, H. Niel, "Some Notes on *lyṣ* and Its Derivatives," *VT* 5 (1955) 163-179.

Richter, Wolfgang. *Exegese als Literaturwissenschaft Entwurf einer alttestamentlichen Literaturtheorie und Methodologie.* Göttingen: Vandenhoeck & Ruprecht, 1971.

Ricoeur, P. *Interpretation Theory: Discourse and the Surplus of Meaning.* Fort Worth: Texas Christian Univ., 1976.

Rieger, J. *Die Bedeutung der Geschichte für die Verkündigung des Amos und Hosea.* Giessen: Alfred Töpelmann, 1929.

Ringgren, H. "Oral and Written Transmission in the Old Testament," *ST* 3 (1950) 34-59.

Ritschl, D. "God's Conversion. An Exposition of Hosea 11," *Int* 15 (1961) 286-303.

Roberts, J. J. M. "Hosea and the Sacrificial Cultus," *Restoration Quarterly* 15 (1972) 16-26.

Robinson, George L. *The Twelve Minor Prophets*. Grand Rapids: Baker Book House, 1974.

Robinson, H. W. *The Cross of Hosea*. Philadelphia: Westminster, 1949.

Robinson, Theodore Henry. "Die Ehe des Hosea," *TSK* 106 (1935) 301-311.

Robinson, Theodore Henry. *Prophecy and the Prophets in Ancient Israel*. London: Gerald Duckworth, 1923.

Robinson, Theodore H. & F. Horst. *Die zwölf kleinen Propheten*. HAT 14; Tübingen, 1938.

Rohde, Joachim. *Rediscovering the Teaching of the Evangelists*. D. M. Barton, trans. London: SCM, 1968.

Rowley, H. H. "The Marriage of Hosea," *Men of God: Studies in Old Testament History and Prophecy*. London: Nelson, 1963, 66-97.

Rowley, H. H. "The Nature of Old Testament Prophecy in the Light of Recent Study," in *The Servant of the Lord and Other Essays on the Old Testament*. London: Lutterworth, 1952, 89-128.

Rowley, H. H. "The Prophet Jeremiah and the Book of Deuteronomy," *From Moses to Qumran. Studies in the Old Testament*. London: Lutterworth, 1963, 187-208.

Rudolph, Wilhelm. "Eigentümlichkeit der Sprache Hoseas," *Studia Biblica et Semitica Th. C. Vriezen dedicata*. W. C.

van Unnik & A. S. van der Woude, hrsg. Wageningen: H. Veenman & Zonen, 1966, 313-317.

Rudolph, Wilhelm. *Hosea*. KAT 13/1; Gütersloh: Gerd Mohn, 1966.

Rudolph, Wilhelm. "Präparierte Jungfrauen? (zu Hosea 1)," *ZAW* 75 (1963) 65-73.

Ruppert, L. "Beobachtungen zur Literar-und Kompositions-kritik von Hos 1-3," *Künder des Wortes. Beiträge zur Theologie der Propheten*. Josef Schreiner zum 60. Geburts-tag. L. Ruppert, P. Weimar, E. Zenger, hrsg. Würzburg: Echter, 1982, 163-82.

Ruppert, L. "Erwägungen zur Kompositions- und Redaktions-geschichte von Hos 1-3," *BZ* 26 (1982) 208-223.

Ruppert, L. "Herkunft und Bedeutung der Jakob-Tradition bei Hosea," *Bib* 52 (1971) 488-504.

Rupprecht, K. " 'lh mn h'rṣ (Ex 1:10; Hos 2:2): 'sich des Landes bemächtigen'?" *ZAW* 82 (1970) 442-447.

Rust, E. C. "The Theology of Hosea," *RevExp* 54 (1957) 510-21.

Sakenfeld, K. D. *The Meaning of Hesed in the Hebrew Bible*. Missoula: Scholars Press, 1978.

Sanders, J. A. "Text and Canon: Concepts and Method," *JBL* 98 (1979) 5-29.

Sandlin, Bryce. "A Teaching Outline of Hosea," *Southwestern Journal of Theology* 18 (1975) 61-68.

Sasson. J. M. "Word-Play in Gen 6:8-9," *CBQ* 37 (1975) 165-66.

Sasson, J. M. "Wordplay in the OT," *IDBSup*, 968-970.

Sawyer, John F. A. "A Change of Emphasis in the Study of the Prophets," in *Israel's Prophetic Tradition. Essays in Honour of Peter R. Ackroyd.* R. Coggins, A. Phillips and M. Knibb, eds. Cambridge: Cambridge University, 1982, 233-249.

Saydon, P. "Assonance in Hebrew as a Means of Expressing Emphasis," *Bib* 36 (1955) 36-50; 287-304.

Scanlin, Harold P. "The Emergence of the Writing Prophets in the Mid-Eight Century," *JETS* 21 (1978) 305-313.

Scharbert, Josef. *Die Propheten Israels bis 700 vor.Chr.* Köln: J. P. Bachem, 1965.

Schmidt, H. "Die Ehe des Hosea," *ZAW* 42 (1924) 245-72.

Schmidt, Kenneth W. "Prophetic Delegation: A Form-Critical Inquiry," *Bib* 63 (1982) 206-218.

Schmuttermayr, G. "*Rḥm* - Eine lexikalische Studie," *Bib* 51 (1970) 499-532.

Schneider, D. *The Unity of the Book of the Twelve.* Diss. Yale University, 1979.

Schottroff, W. "Jeremia 2, 1-3: Erwägungen zur Methode der Prophetenexegese," *ZTK* 67 (1970) 263-94.

Schreiner, Josef. "Hoseas Ehe, ein Zeichen des Gerichts (zu Hos 1, 2-2, 3; 3, 1-5)," *BZ* NF 21 (1977) 163-83.

Schwarz, V. "Das Gottesbild des Propheten Oseas," *Bibel und Liturgie* 35 (1961-62) 274-279.

Seeligmann, I. L. "Die Auffassung von der Prophetie in der deuteronomistischen und chronistischen Geschichtsschreibung (mit einem Exkurs über das Buch Jeremia)." *VTSup* 29 (1978) 254-284.

Seeters, John van. "Oral Patterns or Literary Conventions in Biblical Narrative," *Semeia* 5 (1976) 139-154.

Sellers, O. "Hosea's Motives," *AJSL* 41 (1924-25) 243-47.

Sellin, E. "Die geschichtliche Orientierung der Prophetie des Hosea," *NKZ* 36 (1925) 607-58, 807.

Sellin, E. "Hosea und das Martyrium des Mose," *ZAW* 46 (1928) 26-33.

Sellin, E. *Introduction to the Old Testament.* W. Montgomery, trans. London: Hodder & Stoughton, Ltd., 1923.

Sellin, E. *Das Zwölfprophetenbuch. Erste Hälfte: Hosea-Micha.* KAT 12; Leipzig: A. Deichertsche, 1929, 3 Aufl.

Selms, A. van. "Hosea and Canticles," *OTWSA* 7/8 (1964-65) 85-89.

Seow, C. L. "Hosea 14:10 and the Foolish People Motif," *CBQ* 44 (1982) 212-224.

Sheppard, G. T. *Wisdom as a Hermeneutical Construct.* BZAW 151; Berlin: W. de Gruyter, 1980.

Sherman, C. E. "The Relevance of Hosea," *SWJT*, 18 (1975) 33-42.

Sinclair, L. A. "A Qumran Biblical Fragment. Hos 4QXIIa," *BASOR* 239 (1980) 61-65.

Skipwith, G. H. "Note on the Order of the Text in Hosea i-iii," *JQR* 7 (1894-95) 480.

Smalley, S. S. "Redaction Criticism," *New Testament, Interpretation. Essays on Principles and Methods.* I. H. Marshall, ed. Exeter: Paternoster, 1977, 181-95.

Smith, George Adam. *The Book of the Twelve Prophets, I: Amos, Hosea, Micah.* London: Hodder and Stoughton, 1905, 211-354.

Smith, John M. P. *A Commentary on the Books of Amos, Hosea, and Micah.* New York: Macmillan, 1914.

Smith, Morton. "Pseudepigraphy in the Israelite Literary Tradition," *Pseudepigrapha I.* Entretiens sur l'antiquité classique, Tome 18; Vandoeuvres-Geneve: Fondation Hardt, 1972, 191-227.

Smith, Ralph L. "Major Motifs of Hosea," *SWJT* 18 (1975) 22-32.

Smith, W. Robertson. *The Prophets of Israel and Their Place in History, Introduction and Additional Notes by T. K. Cheyne.* London: Adam and Charles Black, 1895.

Snaith, Norman. *Mercy and Sacrifice. A Study of the Book of Hosea.* London: SCM, 1953.

Soggin, J. A. "Osea 11:5 (cfr. 10, 9b?): *lamed* enfatico?" *Bibbia e Oriente* 9 (1967) 42.

Speiser, E. A. "Word Plays on the Creation Epic's Version of the Founding of Babylon," *Or* 25 (1956) 317-23.

Sperber, Alexander. *The Bible in Aramaic.* Leiden: Brill, 1962, Vol. 1-3.

Spiegel, Shalom. "A Prophetic Attestation of the Decalogue: Hos 6:5 with Some Observations on Psalms 15 and 24," *HTR* 27 (1934) 105-145.

Stamm, J. J. "Eine Erwägung zu Hosea 6:1-2," *ZAW* 57 (1939) 266-268.

Stinespring, W. F. "Hosea, The Prophet of Doom," *Crozer Quarterly* 27 (1950) 200-207.

Stinespring, W. F. "Humor," *The Interpreter's Dictionary of the Bible.* Vol E-J. New York, 1962, 660-62.

Stinespring, W. F. "A Problem of Theological Ethics in Hosea," *Essays in Old Testament Ethics. J. P. Hyatt in Memoriam.* J. L. Crenshaw and J. T. Willis, eds. New York: KTAV, 1974, 133-144.

Stuart, Douglas. *Old Testament Exegesis: A Primer for Students and Pastors.* Philadelphia: Westminster, 1980.

Stuhlmueller, C. "The Influence of Oral Tradition upon Exegesis and the Senses of Scripture," *CBQ* 20 (1958) 299-326.

Swaim, G. G. "Hosea the Statesman," *Biblical and Near Eastern Studies. Essays in Honor of William Sanford LaSor.* G. A. Tuttle, ed. Grand Rapids: Eerdmans, 1978.

Szabó, A. "Textual Problems in Amos and Hosea," *VT* 25 (1975) 500-525.

Talmon, S. "The 'Desert Motif' in the Bible and in Qumran Literture," *Biblical Motifs.* A. Altmann, ed. Cambridge: Harvard University, 1966, 31-63.

Tångberg, K. A. "An Note on *pištî* in Hosea 2:7, 11," *VT* 27 (1977) 222-224.

Teeple, H. M. "The Oral Tradition that Never Existed," *JBL* 89 (1970) 56-68.

Thomas, D. W. "A Note on the Meaning of *yd'* in Hosea 9:7 and Isaiah 9:8," *JTS* 41 (1940) 43-44.

412   Bibliography

Thomas, W. "The Root *'aheb* 'love' in Hebrew," *ZAW* 57 (1939)
    57-64.

Thompson, M. E. W. *Situation and Theology: Old Testament
    Interpretations of the Syro-Ephraimite War.* Sheffield:
    Almond, 1982.

Toombs, L. E. "Love and Justice in Deuteronomy," *Int* 19
    (1965) 389-411.

Torczyner, Harry. "Dunkle Bibelstellen," *Marti Festschrift.*
    BZAW 41; Giessen: Alfred Töpelmann, 1925, 274-280.

Toy, C. H. "Note on Hosea 1-3," *JBL* 32 (1913) 75-79.

Tucker, Gene M. "Commentaries on Hosea: A Review,"
    Religious Studies Review 7 (1981) 132-136.

Tucker, Gene M. *Form Criticism of the Old Testament.*
    Philadelphia: Fortress, 1971.

Tucker, Gene M. "Form Criticism, OT," *IDBSup*, 342-345.

Tucker, Gene M. "Prophetic Speech," *Int* 32 (1978) 31-45.

Tucker, Gene M. "Prophetic Superscriptions and the Growth
    of a Canon," *Canon and Authority.* G. W. Coats and B. O.
    Long, eds. Philadelphia: Fortress, 1977, 56-70.

Tushingham, A. D. "A Reconsideration of Hosea Chapters
    1-3," *JNES* 12 (1953) 150-59.

Unterman, Jeremiah. "Repentance and Redemption in
    Hosea," *SBLSP* 21 (1982) 541-550.

Utzschneider, Helmut. *Hosea Prophet vor dem Ende.* Orbis
    biblicus et orientalis 31; Fribourg: Universitätsverlag;
    Göttingen: Vandenhoeck & Ruprecht, 1980.

Vansina, Jan. *Oral Tradition. A Study in Historical Methodology.* H. M. Wright, trans. Chicago: Aldine, 1965.

Vaux, Roland de. *Ancient Israel: Its Life and Institutions.* John McHugh, trans. New York: McGraw-Hill, 1961.

Vawter, Bruce. *The Conscience of Israel: Pre-exilic Prophets and Prophecy.* New York: Sheed & Ward, 1961.

Vermeylen, J. *Du prophète Isäie à l'apocalyptique. Isäie, I-XXXV, miroir d'un demi-millenaire d'experience religieuse en Israel.* Paris: Gabalda, 1977-78, 2 Vols.

Vetter, P. "Zeugnisse der vorexilischen Propheten über den Pentateuch. II Hoseas," *TQ* (1901) 94-112.

Vogels, W. "'Osée-Gomer' car et comme 'Yahweh-Isräel' Os 1-3," *NRT* 103 (1981) 711-27.

Vogels, W. "Les récits de vocations des prophètes," *NRT* 95 (1973) 3-24.

Vogels, W. "Studies of Hos 1-3," *BZ* 28 (1984) 94-98.

Vollmer, J. *Geschichtliche Rückblicke und Motive in der Prophetie des Amos, Hosea und Jesaia.* BZAW 119; Berlin: de Gruyter & Col., 1971.

Vriezen, T. C. "Hosea 12," *Nieuwe Theologische Studien,* 24 (1941) 144-149.

Vriezen, T. C. "La tradition de Jacob dans Osée 12," *OTS* 1 (1942) 64-78.

Vuilleumier, R. "Les traditions d'Isräel et la liberté du prophète: Osée," *RHPR* 59 (1979) 491-498.

Waldman, Nahum M. "The Breaking of the Bow," *JQR* 79 (1978) 82-88.

Wallis, G. "'ahabh, TDOT, Vol. 1, 99-118.

Ward, J. M. "Hosea," IDBSup. Nashville: Abingdon, 1976, 421-23.

Ward, J. M. Hosea: A Theological Commentary. New York: Harper & Row, 1966.

Ward, J. M. "The Message of the Prophet Hosea," Int 23 (1969) 387-407.

Warmuth, G. Das Mahnwort. Seine Bedeutung für die Verkündigung der vorexilischen Propheten Amos, Hosea, Micha, Jesaja und Jeremia. Frankfurt: Lang, 1976.

Waterman, L. "Hosea, Chapters 1-3, in Retrospect and Prospect," JNES 14 (1955) 100-109.

Waterman, L. "The Marriage of Hosea," JBL 37 (1918) 193-208.

Watson, W. G. E. "Reflexes of Akkadian incantations in Hosea," VT (1984) 242-247.

Weill, Julien, "Hosée 12:13--13:1 et le Prétendu martyre de Möise," REJ 87 (1929) 89-93.

Weinberg, Werner, "Language Consciousness in the OT," ZAW 92 (1980) 185-204.

Weinfeld, Moshe. "Ancient Near Eastern Patterns in Prophetic Literature," VT 27 (1977) 178-95.

Weinfeld, Moshe. "bĕrîth," TDOT 2 (1975) 253-279.

Weinfeld, Moshe. Deuteronomy and the Deuteronomic School. Oxford: Clarendon, 1972.

Weiser, A. *Das Buch der zwölf kleinen Propheten, I.* ATD xxiv/1; Göttingen: Vandenhoeck & Ruprecht, 1949, 1-88.

Wellhausen, Julius. *Die kleinen Propheten, übersetzt und erklärt.* Berlin: Reimer, 1898, 3 Aufl.

Wenham, G. "The Restoration of Marriage Reconsidered," *JJS* 30 (1979) 36-40.

Westermann, Claus. *Basic Forms of Prophetic Speech.* H. C. White, trans. Philadelphia: Westerminster, 1967.

Westhuizen, J. P. van der. "Assonance in Biblical and Babylonian Hymns of Praise," *Semitics* 7 (1980) 81-101.

Wharton, James A. "Hosea 4:1-3," *Int* 32 (1978) 78-83.

Wharton, James A. "Redaction Criticism, OT," *IDBSup* Nashville: Abingdon, 1976, 729-32.

Whitley, C. F. "The Semantic Range of *Ḥesed*," *Bib* 62 (1981) 519-526.

Widengren, G. "Oral Tradition and Written Literature among the Hebrews in the Light of Arabic Evidence, with Special Regard to Prose Narratives," *Acta Orientalia* 23 (1959) 201-62.

Wijngaards, J. "Death and Resurrection in Covenantal Context (Hos VI 2)," *VT* 17 (1967) 226-239.

Willi-Plein, Ina. *Vorformen der Schriftexegese innerhalb des Alten Testaments: Üntersuchungen zum literarischen Werden der auf Amos, Hosea und Micha zurückgehenden Bücher im hebräischen Zwölfprophetenbuch.* BZAW 123; Berlin: De Gruyter, 1971.

Williams, Donald L. "Annotated Bibliography on Hosea," *RevExp* 72 (1975) 495-501.

Williams, James. "The Social Location of Israelite Prophecy,"
    JAAR (1969) 153-165.

Willis, J. T. "Redaction Criticism and Historical
    Reconstruction." *Encounter with the Text. Form and History
    in the Hebrew Bible.* M. J. Buss, ed. Philadelphia: Fortress,
    1979, 83-89.

Wilson, Robert R. "Early Israelite Prophecy," *Int* 32 (1978)
    3-16.

Wilson, Robert R. "Form-Critical Investigation of the
    Prophetic Literature: The Present Situation," *SBLSP* 1
    (1973) 100-127.

Wilson, Robert T. "Prophecy and Ecstacy: A Reexamination,"
    JBL 98 (1979) 321-337.

Wilson, Robert T. *Prophecy and Society in Ancient Israel.*
    Philadelphia: Fortress, 1980.

Wilson, Robert T. "Prophecy in Crisis: The Call of Ezekiel," *Int*
    38 (1984) 117-130.

Wittstruck, T. "The Influence of Treaty Curse Imagery on the
    Beast Imagery of Daniel 7," *JBL* 97 (1978) 100-102.

Wolfe, R. E. "The Editing of the Book of the Twelve," *ZAW* 12
    (1935) 90-129.

Wolfe, R. E. *Meet Amos and Hosea.* New York: Harper & Row,
    1945.

Wolff, Hans Walter. *Dodekapropheton I: Hosea.* BKAT 14/1;
    Neukirchen-Vluyn: Neukircher, 1961, 1965 [= *A Commen-
    tary on the Book of the Prophet Hosea.* Philadelphia:
    Fortress, 1974].

Wolff, Hans Walter. "Der Grosse Jesreeltag (Hosea 2, 1-3). Methodologische Erwägungen zur Auslegung einer alttestamentlichen Perikope," *Gesammelte Studien zum Alten Testament.* München: Kaiser, 1964, 151-181.

Wolff, Hans Walter. "Guilt and Salvation. A Study of the Prophecy of Hosea," *Int* 15 (1961) 274-85.

Wolff, Hans Walter. *Die Hochzeit der Hüre. Hosea heute.* München: Kaiser, 1979.

Wolff, Hans Walter. "Hoseas geistige Heimat," *TLZ* 81 (1956) 83-94.

Wolff, Hans Walter. "Jahwe als Bundesvermittler," *VT* 6 (1956) 316-20.

Wolff, Hans Walter. "Prophecy from the Eighth through the Fifth Century," *Int* 32 (1978) 17-30.

Wolff, Hans Walter. "'Wissen um Gott' bei Hosea als Urform von Theologie," *Gesammelte Studien zum Alten Testament.* München: Kaiser, 1964, 182-205.

Wolff, Hans Walter. "Das Zitat im Prophetenspruch. Eine Studie zur prophetischen Verkündigungsweise," *Gesammelte Studien zum Alten Testament.* München: Kaiser, 1964, 36-129.

Worden, T. "The Literary Influence of the Ugaritic Fertility Myth on the Old Testament," *VT* 3 (1953) 273-297.

Yaron, Reuven. "Aramaic Marriage Contracts from Elephantine," *JSS* 3 (1958) 1-39.

Yaron, Reuven. "Matrimonial Mishaps at Eshnunna," *JSS* 8 (1963) 1-16.

Zakovitch, Yair. "The Woman's Rights in the Biblical Law of Divorce," *The Jewish Law Annual* 4 (1981) 28-46.

Zillessen, A. "Eine Frage zu Hos 12:1," *ZAW* 49 (1931) 150.

Zimmerli, W. "Form- und Traditionsgeschichte der prophetischen Berufungserzählungen, in Ezechiel," *BK* 8 (1955) 16-21.

Zimmerli, W. "Das Gottesrecht bei den Propheten Amos, Hosea und Jesaja," *Werden und Wirken des Alten Testaments*. Göttingen: Vandenhoeck und Ruprecht, 1980, 216-235.

Zimmerli, W. "Prophetic Proclamation and Reinterpretation," in *Tradition and Theology in the Old Testament*. D. A. Knight, ed. Philadelphia: Fortress, 1977, 69-100.

Zolli, J. "Hosea 4:17-18," 15 *ZAW* (1938) 175.

INDEX OF AUTHORS

Alt, A., 276-277
Andersen, F.I. and
Freedman, D.N., 15, 21-25,
31-32, 44, 67, 88, 167, 186,
234, 255, 265

Barré, M., 151
Bewer, J.A., 108-109
Birkeland, H., 8-10, 38
Budde, K., 4-5, 47, 54, 160,
265
Buss, M., 16-17, 47, 57, 83

Cardellini, I., 268
Casanowitz, I.M., 59
Cheyne, T.K., 2, 28
Clements, R.E., 178, 256
Coote, R., 245, 270

Dahood, M., 67
Day, E., 4, 270
DeRoche, M., 163
Dietrich, F., 232
Duhm, B., 67, 187, 205

Eybers, I.H., 241
Engnell, I., 35, 38
Eslinger, L., 234
Ewald, G.H., 2-3, 51

Feuillet, A., 138
Fohrer, G., 270
Frey, H., 13-15, 23, 24

Good, E., 277
Graetz, H., 2
Guillaume, A., 89
Güttgemanns, E., 42-44

Harper, W.R., 3-4, 28, 47,
115

Jacob, E., 210
Junker, H., 265

Kaatz, S., 74, 231
Kaufmann, Y., 52
Kelber, W., 39
Knight, D.A., 34, 38
Koch, K., 36
Kraeling, E., 52
Kuhnigk, W., 67

Lapointe, R., 39
Lohfink, N., 160, 222
Long, B.O., 114
Lord, A.B., 37, 39-41
Lundbom, J.R., 164
Lust, J., 270

Marti, K., 3, 28, 47, 83, 115,
161, 176
Mays, J.L., 28-29, 74, 88, 164

Noth, M., 121
Nowack, W., 161, 208
Nyberg, H.S., 5, 7-8, 38, 50

Peiser, F.E., 4, 13, 28, 47, 57,
161

Renaud, B., 111
Robinson, G.L., 52
Robinson, T.H., 54, 176
Rudolph, W. 167
Ruppert, L., 111, 117

Spiegel, S., 175
Szabó, A., 73, 217
Schottroff, W., 49
Schreiner, J., 57
Sellin, E., 109
Stinespring, W.F., 57

Vogels, W., 54

Wellhausen, J., 161, 208
Wijngaards, J., 151
Willi-Plein, I., 18-21, 30-31,
    44, 47, 111, 168, 173, 182,
    210, 245
Wolfe, R.E., 5-6, 18, 28, 47,
    67
Wolff, H.W., 10-13, 28,
    29-30, 47, 51, 67, 88, 103,
    142, 167

INDEX OF BIBLICAL REFERENCES

Genesis
15:5, 69
24:24, 233
24:28, 233
25:36, 232
27:28, 137
27:35, 303
27:36, 303
28:15, 236, 244
30:31, 244
32:13, 69
32:24-32, 232
32:29, 124, 233-234
33:4, 233
41:52, 134

Exodus
1:13-14, 243
3:14-15, 69
3:15, 236, 238
19:5-6, 81
19:8, 81
19:11, 151-152
19:15-17, 151-152
20:2, 238
33:7, 239
33:9-11, 239
34:15, 217

Leviticus
20:10, 124
26:23, 171

Numbers
25:1-2, 217, 293

Deuteronomy
1:13, 141
1:15, 141
1:30-31, 216
4:1, 206
4:3, 119, 293
4:6, 141
4:29-30, 147
4:29, 276
4:30, 206
4:36, 171, 206
5:1, 206
5:6-7, 252
5:6, 238
5:15, 243
6:12, 83
7:5, 297
8:2, 171
8:5, 171, 216
8:11, 83
8:13-14, 253
8:14, 83
8:15-16, 253
8:19, 83
9:9--10:11, 233
11:2, 171
12:1-14, 270
12:3, 297
12:10, 169
14:1, 216
17:16, 202, 222
17:18, 269
18:15-19, 177, 240
18:15, 177-178
21:18-21, 226-227
21:18, 171

22:22, 124
23:18-19, 119
26:5, 124, 303-304
26:14, 202
28:53-57, 213
28:68, 202
29:22, 225
29:24-25, 225
31:9-13, 268-269
31:16, 163-164
32:5-6, 216
32:6, 141
32:10-14, 253
32:10-11, 216
32:10, 220
32:17, 186, 252
32:18-20, 216
32:18, 83, 253
32:21, 186
32:23-24, 254
33:10, 269

Joshua
7:24-26, 90
24:17, 244

Judges
2:11, 119
2:13, 119
3:7, 119
8:33, 119
19:30, 208
20:11, 209
20:14, 209
20:20, 209
20:23, 209

Ruth
4:1, 124

1 Samuel
8:6-8, 256-257
8:8, 256

2 Samuel
7:14-16, 289
14:20, 141

1 Kings
8:33-34, 234-235
8:46-50, 147
12:25--13:34, 192
12:25-33, 121
12:28, 121-122
12:32-33, 118, 122
13:1-2, 120, 122
13:25-33, 297
22:54, 119

2 Kings
3:2, 119
15:8-31, 285
15:19-20, 276
15:30, 285
17:1, 250
17:13-14, 177-178, 240-241
17:13, 250
17:14-23, 192
17:14-15, 250
17:15-16, 250
17:16, 119, 250
17:18, 241, 251
17:19-20, 206
22:1, 122
23:5, 120, 122
23:14-15, 297

Job
5:17-18, 148-149

Psalms
7:11, 186
18:142, 186
23:1-3, 169

Canticles
2:1-3, 138-139
4:5, 138
4:11, 138
5:13, 138
5:15, 138

Isaiah
2:13-14, 118
13:4, 209-210
24:4-6, 143
28:7, 269
33:9, 143
49:9, 210
61:1, 210

Jeremiah
2:8, 186, 269
2:13, 210
3:19, 216
4:3, 153
5:31, 269
6:13, 269
6:27, 204
7:9-10, 267-268
8:10, 269
9:11, 141
12:4, 143
14:18, 269
15:17-18, 214
16:7, 202
16:17-18, 210-211
17:21-27, 118

18:18, 269
23:10, 143
23:11, 269
31:9, 216
31:15, 125, 304
31:18-20, 218-219
31:18, 211
31:27, 75
31:31-33, 86
35:15, 177, 241
42:11-16, 201
42:14, 188
42:15, 188
42:16, 188
42:17, 188
42:18, 188
42:22, 188
43:2, 188
44:1, 202
44:8, 188
44:12, 187-188
44:14, 188
44:27, 188

Ezekiel
4:13, 200
16:59-62, 86
20:12-13, 118
20:16, 118
20:21, 118
20:24, 118
20:33-34, 256-257
22:26, 118
34:13-15, 168-169
37:15-19, 73
37:21-22, 73

Hosea
1-3, 51-55, 71, 90-95, 97-125,
   127-130, 228-229, 131,
   247, 261
1:1, 1, 55-57, 63, 71, 91, 129,
   141-142
1:2-9, 79
1:2-4, 97, 112-115
1:2, 56, 58-61, 103, 107-111,
   113, 128
1:3, 58, 101, 104, 110
1:4, 64-65. 109, 111
1:5, 59, 64-66, 68-69, 83, 87,
   129, 213
1:6-7, 66-69, 73, 129, 134
1:6, 66-68, 97, 101, 104,
   109-115
1:7, 16, 59, 66, 86, 134, 213
1:8-9, 97, 112-115
1:8, 104, 110
1:9, 68-71, 103, 107, 109,
   111, 113, 138, 225-226
2:1-3, 11, 14, 16, 53-54, 59,
   68, 109
2:1-2, 155
2:1, 68-71, 129, 225-226
2:2-24, 76-77
2:2-3, 69, 71-72, 75, 77, 90,
   130
2:2, 68, 72-76, 80, 90
2:3, 71, 74-76, 155, 225, 267
2:4-24, 129
2:4-7, 97
2:4-5, 108, 117
2:4, 68, 74-75, 101, 103-115,
   118, 121-124, 127, 142,
   228, 265-67, 272, 302-304
2:5, 81, 103, 106, 118-124,
   266

2:6-7, 108-110, 112-115
2:6, 101, 128
2:7, 77-78, 110, 117-123, 266-
   267, 286
2:8-9, 59, 76-79, 82-83, 130,
   141
2:8, 77-78, 86
2:9, 77-78, 84, 133, 229
2:10-15, 106
2:10-11, 117-118, 157
2:10, 77-79, 84-86, 97, 115,
   118-120, 135, 190
2:11-15, 77-79, 82-83, 97,
   130
2:11, 78, 81, 115, 118,
   120-121
2:12, 108, 117-118, 120-124,
   128, 266-267
2:13-15, 115, 117-118, 122,
   292
2:14, 86, 118-121, 269
2:15, 82-84, 88, 119-122,
   144, 196, 253
2:16-17, 78-84, 90, 130, 239
2:16, 78-80, 215-216
2:17, 74, 79-81, 216
2:18, 82, 84-88, 97, 101, 106,
   112-115, 128, 144
2:19-20, 79
2:19, 84-86
2:20-24, 229
2:20, 65, 82, 86-87, 137, 143,
   151-152, 213, 254
2:21-22, 97, 101, 111-115,
   128, 262
2:21, 87
2:22, 87-88, 149
2:23-24, 81, 88-90, 133, 137,
   150-152, 157

2:23, 82, 89, 137, 144, 225
2:24-25, 64, 75, 90
2:25, 71-72, 75-78, 90, 130,
    135
3:1-5, 11, 14, 54, 57-65, 71,
    76, 85, 91-92, 129, 131-133,
    141-142
3:1, 58, 60-61, 86, 89,
    216-217
3:2, 58
3:3-5, 246
3:3, 59, 61
3:4-5, 57, 61-62, 78, 90, 147,
    199
3:4, 256
3:5, 57, 65-66, 68, 73, 133,
    153, 155
4--11, 51-52, 228-229, 247,
    261
4:1-19, 158-170, 262-272
4:1-3, 67, 142-143
4:1-2, 143, 280
4:1, 142-144, 157, 228, 254
4:2, 143, 267-268
4:3, 142-144, 157, 228-229,
    248, 254
4:4, 143, 265-269, 302
4:5, 160-161, 203, 265-269,
    293
4:6, 160-162, 288
4:7-10, 162-164
4:9, 161, 165
4:11-14, 181
4:11-12, 164-167
4:11, 161
4:12-13, 138
4:12, 166, 265, 269-270
4:13, 164-167, 289
4:14, 161, 164-167

4:15, 269-271, 293
4:16-17, 168-170
4:16, 199, 253, 271-272
4:18-19, 265-266, 271-272
5:1-15, 170-174, 272-278
5:1-7, 276-277
5:1-2, 170-171, 204
5:2, 170-171, 174, 184
5:3, 171-172, 278, 281
5:4, 171-172, 183
5:5-7, 275-276, 278
5:5, 182-183, 275-276, 281
5:6, 276
5:7, 280
5:8-14, 277-278
5:8-13, 279-280
5:10-14, 298
5:11-14, 298
5:13-14, 276
5:13, 172-173
5:14, 146, 148, 253, 279-280
5:15--6:3, 144-152, 157,
    228-229, 276
5:15, 146-147, 149, 151, 153,
    173-174
6:1-11, 174-179, 278-282
6:1-3, 147, 150-152, 174-175,
    178
6:1, 146-148, 173-174
6:2, 148
6:3, 149-150, 153, 176
6:4, 146, 175-176, 251,
    279-280
6:5, 175-178, 203, 240-241,
    269
6:6, 280
6:7-11, 277
6:7, 280, 288
6:8-10, 282

6:8-9, 281, 285
6:10, 278, 281-282
6:11, 7, 280-281
6:11--7:1, 178-179
7:1-16, 179-189, 282-286
7:1, 278, 281-282, 298
7:2, 285
7:3, 285
7:4, 180-181, 188
7:5, 285
7:6-7, 285
7:6, 180-181
7:7, 180, 285
7:8-11, 286
7:8, 298
7:9, 182-183, 189
7:10, 181-183, 185, 188, 204
7:11-13, 288
7:11-12, 156, 293, 298
7:11, 184, 286, 298
7:12, 184-185, 188
7:13-16, 197
7:14-16, 201
7:14, 185-188, 286
7:15, 185-188
7:16, 185-189, 192, 196, 213, 222
8:1-14, 189-197, 286-289
8:1-3, 197
8:1-2, 288
8:1, 288-289, 293
8:3, 288
8:4-5, 288
8:4, 189-192, 194, 250
8:5, 189-192
8:6, 189-193, 250
8:7, 193-197, 211
8:8-10, 289
8:8, 193-194

8:10, 196, 301
8:11, 196, 289
8:12, 299
8:13-14, 195-197
8:13, 189, 204
8:14, 190-191, 213, 222
9:1-17, 198-207, 289-293
9:1, 199, 206-207, 292
9:2-4, 198-200
9:2, 199
9:3, 189, 199
9:4, 199-202, 204
9:5, 292
9:6, 199, 200-202, 222
9:7, 202-204, 269, 292-293
9:8-9, 202-204
9:8, 203-205, 207, 269
9:9, 204, 208
9:10-17, 205
9:10, 292-293, 297
9:11-13, 298
9:11, 163, 293, 298
9:12-13, 293
9:13, 205, 293
9:14, 205-207
9:15, 293
9:16, 293, 297-298
9:17, 205-206
10:1-15, 207-214, 294-298
10:1, 297
10:2, 297
10:4, 297
10:7-8, 298
10:8, 207-208, 297
10:9-10, 207-211, 218
10:9, 204, 208-210
10:10, 209-211
10:11, 152, 199, 211, 218, 296, 298

10:12, 144-145, 150,
  152-153, 157-158, 191,
  193-194, 211-212,
  228-229
10:13-14, 212-213
10:13, 152-153, 298
10:15, 213, 298
11:1-11, 142, 214-229, 247,
  258
11:1-6, 226-227
11:1-4, 214-221
11:1-2, 224
11:1, 155, 217, 222, 227
11:2, 155, 217-218
11:3, 218-220
11:4, 216, 218, 220, 223
11:5-7, 221-223, 227
11:5-6, 224
11:5, 221-222
11:6, 222
11:7, 220-223
11:8-11, 142
11:8-9, 223-226
11:8, 224-225
11:9, 221, 225-226, 230-231,
  234
11:10-11, 144-145, 153-158,
  226-228
11:10, 154-156, 217-218
11:11, 82, 144, 156
12--14, 51-52, 228-229, 247,
  261
12:1-15, 229-248, 298-304
12:1, 230-231, 234, 302
12:2, 231, 302
12:3, 142, 228, 298, 302
12:4, 232-234, 302
12:5-7, 231-237, 302
12:5, 232-236, 244

12:6, 238
12:7, 236-237, 244
12:8-9, 238-239, 302
12:8, 302-303
12:9, 241-242, 303
12:10-12, 237-244
12:10-11, 243-244
12:10, 188, 236, 238-239,
  252
12:11, 176-177, 241, 250
12:12, 241-242
12:13, 124, 242-243, 245,
  303
12:14, 176-177, 188,
  237-244, 240, 243-246
12:15, 249-250
13:1-15, 248-259, 298-304
13:1-3, 248-251
13:1, 250
13:2, 250
13:3, 251
13:4-8, 251-254
13:4-6, 252
13:4-5, 188
13:4, 252-253, 256
13:5-6, 253
13:6, 253
13:7-8, 253-254
13:7, 255
13:9-11, 255-257
13:10-11, 257
13:10, 255, 257-258
13:12, 303
13:13, 302, 304
13:14, 255, 257-258
13:15, 302, 304
14:1, 304
14:2-10, 14, 131-142

14:2-9, 9, 142, 147, 150, 152,
    157-158, 221
14:2-8, 146
14:2-4, 132-135
14:2, 133, 141, 147
14:3, 133-134
14:4, 134-135, 187, 213, 225,
    253
14:5, 133, 135-136, 173, 225
14:6-9, 136-140
14:6, 137-138, 150, 153
14:7, 138
14:8-9, 166
14:8, 133, 138, 156, 199
14:9, 134, 138-140
14:10, 140-141, 166, 217,
    268

Joel
1:1, 56
1:8-10, 199

Amos
1:4, 196
2:5, 196
5:4-5, 270
7:17, 200
8:8, 143

Micah
1:1, 56
3:11, 269
4:11, 210
5:9-12, 191

Nahum
1:14, 191

Zephaniah
1:1, 56
1:11, 191

Zechariah
9:10, 191
9:11, 210
12:3, 210
13:2, 85
13:2, 191

Malachi
2:7-9, 269